APPLIED COMMUNICATION THEORY AND RESEARCH

COMMUNICATION
TEXTBOOK SERIES
Jennings Bryant—Editor

Applied Communication
Teresa Thompson—Advisor

NUSSBAUM • Life-Span Communication:
Normative Processes

RAY/DONOHEW • Communication and Health:
Systems and Applications

O'HAIR/KREPS • Applied Communication
Theory and Research

APPLIED COMMUNICATION THEORY AND RESEARCH

Edited by

DAN O'HAIR
Texas Tech University

GARY L. KREPS
Northern Illinois University

IEA LAWRENCE ERLBAUM ASSOCIATES, PUBLISHERS
1990   Hillsdale, New Jersey   Hove and London

20753842

Lawrence Erlbaum Associates, Inc., Publishers
365 Broadway
Hillsdale, New Jersey 07642

Library of Congress Cataloging-in-Publication Data

Applied communication theory and research / edited by Dan O'Hair, GaryKreps.
        p.   cm.—(Communication textbook series. Applied
communication)
    ISBN 0-8058-0400-5 (c) / ISBN 0-8058-0915-5 (p)
      1. Communication—Research—Methodology.   I. O'Hair, Dan.
    II. Kreps, Gary L.   III. Series.
    P91.A66   1990
    302.2'072—dc20   89-48835
                                                                   CIP

Printed in the United States of America
10 9 8 7 6 5 4 3 2 1

CONTENTS

v

HEALTH CONTEXTS

PREFACE

As the field of communication continues to gain respect and credibility among members of related social science disciplines, it becomes important that the assembly of new communication knowledge reflects the confluent treatment of both current research practices and theoretical foundations. It is only through the advancement of theory that a discipline can maintain vigor, sustenance, and vitality. The communication discipline has made great strides in the last few years in producing new and exciting theories on which to base new communication research efforts. Although applied research is often accused of atheoretical approaches to the discovery of knowledge, we contend that there is nothing inherently atheoretical about applied communication research. In fact, we are convinced that effective applied communication research can be approached only from a solid grounding in communication theory. Thus, we chose to title this book *Applied Communication Theory and Research,* suggesting an inextricable link between research processes that are pursued in search of answers and the theoretical rationale from which ideas and explanations are drawn. Basic (pure) research has much to offer applied researchers who are in need of generalized tenets of communication that guide the formulation of questions, facilitate data selection and collection, enhance analysis procedures, and inspire implications. On the other hand, applied researchers provide opportunities for the testing of basic theories in applied contexts, enhancing the generalizability and applicability of communication theory. Applied and basic researchers must rely on one another in promoting the development of heuristic communication theory that is relevant in a wide range of social contexts. It is hoped that this book will act as a catalyst for such conjoint activities.

As editors of this book, we have been involved in various forms of applied communication research for several years. Although we had not collaborated on anything of import prior to this project, our shared interests in applied communication theory and research was keen and we recognized the need for a book on this topic. The original impetus for the project came when Dan O'Hair received a call from Dale Leathers, then editor of *Southern Speech Communication Journal* (SSCJ), asking him to become guest editor for a special issue of the journal on the topic of "Relational Communication in Applied Contexts." Gary Kreps, one of the contributors to the SSCJ special issue, and Dan O'Hair agreed that the next logical step after the SSCJ issue was a book enlarging the topic to all applied communication contexts. Through the brilliant assistance of Teri Thompson, Jennings Bryant, and Jack Burton, Lawrence Erlbaum Associates sponsored the work that appears in this book. The book has a number of strengths that are directly attributable to the contributing authors, each being experts in the applied communication areas that they write about. The greatest shortcoming of this book is its comprehensiveness. We were not able to include a number of applied communication areas that are notable and exciting due to space limitations. More than anything else, this book provides a sampling of topics for applied communication inquiry and serves as a "teaser" for others who view applied communication theory and research as integral components of the communication discipline. Certainly we have not done justice to the extant area of applied communication theory and research nor was that the goal. The field of communication was in need of a primary source that promoted the cause of applied work in communication. We hope that applied communication researchers, as well as basic researchers with occasional applied interests, will benefit from the thoughts contained in this volume. It is those individuals to whom this book is dedicated, as well as to our respective families, who patiently supported our work on this project.

Dan O'Hair
Gary Kreps

PART I

FUNDAMENTAL VIEWPOINTS

CONCEPTUAL ISSUES

1

DAN O'HAIR
Texas Tech University

GARY L. KREPS
Northern Illinois University

LAWRENCE R. FREY
Loyola University of Chicago

How can theories of communication competence be transferred to organizational settings? What are the communication needs of the elderly or the handicapped and are these needs being met? Must women adopt traditional male communication patterns to succeed in business? Do training programs really make managers more effective in communicating with their subordinates? Which communication strategies should doctors use to get patients to comply with prescribed treatment regimen? Should parents let their children watch violent cartoon programs if these programs lead to aggressive communication behaviors? What role does interpersonal communication play in assimilating foreigners into a new culture?

Each of these questions addresses an important problem, or potential problem, in the real world. Furthermore, each question asks how communication principles or theories can be applied to solve a potential problem. This book is about how researchers conduct applied communication research. Applied communication research is the use of theory and method to solve practical communication problems. Applied communication research focuses on the identification and solution of communication problems that are salient to interested parties.

Applied communication research thus serves the needs of those who use communication in practical ways. Although applied research may well advance questions about theory and methodology posed by communication scholars from within the discipline, the primary purpose of applied communication research is to use theory and methodology in order to understand how communication works within particular settings to solve specific problems.

In this chapter, we examine the conceptual issues that serve as the foundation for applied communication research. We start by exploring in some detail the differences between basic and applied research. We then give an overview of the development of applied communication research. Next, we explore some of the requirements for conducting good applied research, with a primary focus on the importance of using theory to guide research. We conclude this chapter by providing an overview of how the remaining chapters address important theoretical and methodological issues facing applied communication researchers and practitioners within a variety of settings.

BASIC VERSUS APPLIED RESEARCH

Scholars in numerous disciplines recognize that there are two types of research. The first is *basic* or *pure* research, which tests theory, and the second is *applied,* which solves practical problems. Basic research in communication, and other social sciences, conforms to the model proposed by Parsons (1959) in which the goal of social science is to discover the laws that aid in explaining and predicting human behavior. Basic communication researchers, therefore, use research methods to test hypotheses, or predictions, derived from theories. They view their role in the inquiry process as discovering "laws of communication." Berger and Calabrese (1975), for example, maintained that one law of communication is that "all communication reduces uncertainty." They developed a research program to show that whenever we communicate, we reduce uncertainty about ourselves, others, and/or the situation.

Not all scholars use the terms *basic* and *applied,* but the terms that are used differentiate between these two types of research based on their purposes and goals. Coleman (cited in Lazarsfeld & Reitz, 1975), for example, used the terms *discipline* and *policy* to distinguish between these two forms of research. Discipline research advances knowledge of a scientific discipline, whereas policy research suggests guidelines and courses of practical action for actors or agents. Tukey (1960), on the other hand, viewed the differences between basic and applied research from a very pragmatic perspective by using the terms *conclusion-oriented* and *decision-oriented.* Conclusion-oriented research describes efforts that contribute to the knowledge of the discipline, whereas decision-oriented research refers to efforts that attempt to solve practical problems.

Regardless of which terms are used, there are some important differences between basic and applied research (see Table 1.1). For example, applied research typically is conducted under the sponsorship of a client, whereas basic research usually is not. Lévy-Leboyer (1988) as well as DeMartini (1982) referred to applied research as "client-centered" efforts. In applied research, clients or sponsors usually have very specific goals in mind for the research project and applied researchers are at the whim of those who pay their salary (or consultant fees). On the other hand, basic researchers typically have sole control over the purpose and design of the research.

Dubin (1976) maintained that because applied research typically is sponsored by clients, their concerns subsequently guide applied researchers. Preeminent among these concerns is the issue of change brought about by the research. Will change produce better results? Is there a strong rationale for suggesting change as a result of this research? In what direction should change go? These concerns function as contingencies that influence how applied researchers frame their research, conduct it, and report the findings to their clients, contingencies that are not the stuff that basic research is made of.

Dubin also argued that these concerns, in turn, impose a number of requirements on applied researchers. These requirements include the goals of research (i.e., clients focus on solving problems), validity issues (i.e., the validity of research for clients is related only to how useful the solution is), methodology and procedure (i.e., clients can dictate whether variables, such as salary increases, can be manipulated), and the implications for future research (i.e., clients often want follow-up research to

TABLE 1.1
Variations of Basic and Applied Communication Research (adapted from Duncan, 1980)

Issues	Basic Research	Applied Research
• Impetus for Research	Curiosity, tenure, merit raises, theory building, satisfaction.	Client, sponsor, imminent problem.
• Goals	Empirical explanation and/or validation of communication phenomenon.	Solving practical problems, designed for end users.
• Criteria upon which issues are selected for examination	Relevance to previous knowledge, theory building, personal interest.	Short-term, pragmatic solutions, improvement in real-world communication.
• Basis for accepting the validity of knowledge	Scientific rigor and sophistication.	Pragmatic utility of solution. Ease of implementation.
• Methodology, design, and procedure	Unrestricted, preference for labs.	Unrestricted, preference for fieldwork
• Oversight	Review committees, journal reviewers and editors.	Clients, sponsors, government agencies.

assess changes). For example, this difference in sponsorship certainly affects what variables applied researchers study. Champanis (1976) argued that basic experimental researchers choose independent and dependent variables for their "ease of control and manipulation in the laboratory, not for any practical goals" (p. 730). In contrast, applied researchers enjoy no such luxury because the variables are selected based on the requirements of the problem and the needs of the clients. Champanis contended that, "the value of a piece of applied research is determined not by its adherence to the formal rules of the game of science, but by the stern criteria of: 'Does it really work?' 'Does it make any practical difference?' " (p. 739).

Basic and applied communication research also differ according to consumption rates of information generated by respective fields. Although it is difficult to predict the consumption rate of these two bodies of knowledge, the majority of communication research outlets cater to basic research. For example, there are relatively few equivalent trade, popular, and applied outlets for communication research as there are in disciplines such as management, marketing, psychology, home economics, and electronics. Perhaps the lack of publications outlets for communication practitioners and the general public account for the often misunderstood and erroneous assumptions made about the field of communication. There is little doubt that the general public or practitioners would be less enthused with reading communication research published in such journals as *Communication Monographs, Human Communication Research,* or *Journal of Communication.* Articles in the scholarly journals in the communication field appeal almost exclusively to an academic audience. Additional applied communication publication outlets surely would allow practitioners and the general public to take advantage of the research findings generated by both basic and applied researchers.

A more subtle, but important distinction between basic and applied researchers involves the career paths taken by each group. We are not arguing that all academic researchers conduct basic work and practitioners and applied researchers myopically study practical problems, but the predominant tendencies of these researchers do conform to certain behavior. It is often argued that academic researchers pursue basic research because publishing articles in a relatively small number of journals is a primary index of their professional success. The number of articles on academicians' vitae is positively related to being perceived as successful. The rewards of such success are worthwhile: promotion, tenure, merit raises, sabbaticals, favorable teaching loads, and professional respectability. However, the knowledge that is accumulated in journals is frequently bland. In order that unique, exciting, important, and ground-breaking studies be published, a great deal of risk must be assumed by researchers, risks that may entail noteworthy results or those that are null. Because journals are not in the habit of publishing null results, academic researchers may have a tendency to be cautious, publishing studies with a high likelihood of significant results.

Applied researchers, on the other hand, view their success in terms of the number of clients served and problems solved. These problems are often very different from one project to the next and thus they are not as able to draw upon previous work as are basic researchers. Furthermore, applied researchers are held responsible for producing practical solutions and often must take enormous risks. If the risks taken are productive, a certain amount of gratitude is bestowed; however, if the risks taken prove disastrous, the livelihood of the risk-taker could be in jeopardy. Applied researchers are often asked to play the research game with a greater ante, more risk, and bigger stakes than basic researchers.

In spite of the apparent differences between basic and applied research, a number of similarities are obvious as well. Eddy and Partridge (1978), for example, contended that there is no real distinction between basic and applied research. They stated that:

> There is no genuine theoretical or methodological distinction between "pure" and "applied" science. In popular thought, scientists engaged in pure research have little concern with potential uses of the results of their labor, and applied scientists are not concerned with making theoretical contributions. Yet, as any physician or biologist will testify, this neat distinction does not exist in actual scientific work. Physicians use theory daily in order to diagnose and treat clinical cases, and the results they obtain alter both theory and clinical practice. If this were not the case, they would still be using unicorn horn, leeches, and extract of human skull. Similarly, biologists utilize theory to develop pesticides permitting the control of fruit flies, and modify theory when fruit flies multiply in the laboratory. (p. 4)

In actual practice pure research and theory guide informed decision making in many different fields of endeavor.

Another similarity between basic and applied research is that both promote shared knowledge. Many times applied researchers are regarded as "social engineers," researchers who only solve practical problems but do not really advance general knowledge. Janowitz (1971), however, contended that both basic and applied researchers extend our cultural understanding, and believed that a better model for applied research is that of "social enlightenment." Applied research not only provides practical advice for members of a practical social system, but also helps achieve societal goals. Helping foreigners adjust to a new culture, for example, promotes the societal goals of closer international ties and less ethnocentrism, whereas analyzing presidential debates helps the electorate understand better the issues involved in a campaign as well as to judge the critical thinking skills of candidates.

To summarize, there are some important differences between basic and applied research with respect to goals, sponsorship, variable selection, knowledge transfer, and other issues (see Table 1.1). In the final analysis, there are, however, important similarities that also should be recognized. Basic and applied research are interdependent in the sense that neither type of research can be as strong without the influence of the other. Miller and Sunnafrank (1984) argued that, "theoretically-oriented pure research and socially directed, applied research, divergent images notwithstanding, are, at best, inseparable and, at worst, complementary rather than antagonistic" (p. 212). Perhaps by combining the relative advantages of basic and applied research several general shortcomings can be overcome and the overall quality of communication research can be enhanced. Basic research can benefit from the practical accountability that drives applied researchers to take risks with their work, generating research data with high payoff. Applied researchers can benefit from the high levels of scientific rigor evident in most basic research, necessitated by the blind review system inherent in most traditional publication outlets. By increasing the richness of pure research and the rigor of applied research, communication inquiry can be enriched.

THE GROWTH OF APPLIED COMMUNICATION RESEARCH

The development of applied communication research as a field generally parallels the development of the communication discipline itself. Early communication research was limited by a lack of theoretical foundation and lead consequently to a limited range of communication studies (Cohen, 1985). Unable to draw upon theories endemic to the field itself, early communication researchers consistently and generously borrowed theories and methodologies from related disciplines such as psychology and sociology to study human communication (Cohen, 1985; Pearce, 1985). Of course, these disciplines had become established by relying on theories and methods used within the physical sciences, such as biology and chemistry.

This reliance on other disciplines for theory and methodology in early communication research tended to create some "interdisciplinary conceptual addiction." This addiction began with the assumption that the purpose of all research is to test predictions derived from theory. This was followed by a reliance on methodological procedures that were popular in the more well-established disciplines. Lewin (1943) labeled this methodological addiction "the law of the hammer." Just as a child pounds everything in sight once he or she discovers a hammer, so too did researchers study everything in sight using their favorite methodological procedure. This tendency, however, ignored how appropriate the methodology was for studying the particular social phenomena of interest (Pearce, 1985). For example, this methodological addiction led researchers to rely extensively on experimental procedures whereby variables are manipulated in order to observe their effects on other variables. Although there certainly has been an attempt to break away from such methodological addictions, they still exist today. Hewes (1978), for example, has been particularly critical of researchers' use of ANOVA procedures as a hammer to drive many an ill-advised nail.

These traditional methodological procedures, however, certainly helped legitimize the communication discipline as an academic field of study that had something to say about how people communicate. In particular, they were useful for advancing the cause of theory building in communication research. Carl Hoveland, for example, successfully employed experimental procedures to develop theories about how persuasion worked, theories that still guide research today.

Other social scientific disciplines, however, started recognizing the value of applying theories to solve important real world problems, and this orientation soon found its way into the study of communication, primarily because of the growth of the mass media and the desire to know how it affected people. Lazarsfeld is credited by Delia (1987) as the first bona fide applied communication researcher. Lazarsfeld was a sociologist who was interested in how audiences respond to radio broadcasts, and this research attracted the attention of both communication scholars and media policymakers. Delia (1987) claimed that, "More so than any other individual or group, Lazarsfeld cemented the emerging bridge between academic and commercial interests in communication research and established the theoretical relevance of communication research based on applied problems" (p. 51).

Since that time, efforts have been made to extend the range of applied work in communication research. Miller and his colleagues (Miller et al., 1975; Miller & Fontes, 1979), for example, have enjoyed a great deal of success examining the role of communication within courtroom proceedings. Cragan and Shields (1981) employed research methods to study communication within such applied settings as political campaigns, firefighting organizations, and the farming industry. Donohue and his colleagues (Donohue, 1978, 1981; Donohue, Allen, & Burrell, 1985; Donohue, Diez, & Hamilton, 1984) have studied the process of negotiations in applied settings such as organizations and the family. Dan Nimmo and Kathleen Jamieson have made careers out of applying theories to the

study of political contexts. A number of researchers have conducted theoretically based applied research in health care settings (Friemuth, Greenberg, DeWitt, & Romano, 1984; Kreps, 1986; Nussbaum, 1983; O'Hair,
1989, 1986; Thompson, 1984).

Such efforts truly have helped legitimize the role of applied methods in
communication research. The number of communication journal outlets
and association divisions devoted to applied theory and research are growing. For example, the Speech Communication Association recently began
sponsoring the *Journal of Applied Communication Research*. As the discipline of human communication matures as a field of human inquiry and
recognizes the important relationship between theory and application,
we foresee the use of applied research methods continuing to grow and
flourish.

There are several reasons for our optimism: (a) the need to apply communication in the real world in order to make a difference in the way
people actually communicate; (b) dissatisfaction with the exclusive reliance on basic research methods; (c) the opportunity to link together the five
important members of applied research culture (theorists, researchers,
practitioners, clients, and the general public); and (d) the opportunity to
secure funding opportunities.

The Need for Application.   As the body of research in the field of communication grows and theoretical and conceptual issues continue to be refined
it is increasingly important to test the pragmatic value of communication
theories. How well do our theories help us accurately describe and predict
actual communication events? Applied research can help test the validity
of communication theory by demonstrating the practicality of theoretical
concepts. Theory validated through applied research has demonstrated
value to the communication discipline and to the public.

It is also necessary to share this information with those who can best
make use of it on a regular basis. As we discussed earlier, basic research
can take a considerable amount of time getting to those who might be
able to apply it directly. Nevertheless, as practitioners and the general
public continue to see the value of communication research in their own
professional and personal lives, the demand for additional informed insight will burgeon. Applied researchers will respond to such a need by
asking questions and conducting studies that will provide solutions that
practitioners and layperson can make direct use of. Not only will the field
of communication at large prosper from this new found image building,
but applied research will gain increased credibility from basic researchers
as well as practitioners. Providing practitioners and the general public
with worthwhile and practical communication knowledge may become
especially critical given the general public's and legislature's dissatisfac-

tion with the operations of colleges and universities and the increased call for accountability among faculty (Tucker, 1981).

Dissatisfaction With Basic Research Methods.   Criticisms of basic research abound. Bannister (1966), for example, claimed that, "in order to behave like scientists we must construct situations in which our subjects . . . can behave as little like human beings as possible and we do this in order to allow ourselves to make statements about the nature of their humanity" (p. 24). Smith (1972) and Scriven (1964) argued that the results from basic research have offered nothing of value to the field of science. Ruback and Innes (1988) are especially concerned with the limited pragmatic value of basic research. They believe that interested consumers of basic research, such as policymakers, often are turned off by basic research because it holds little relevance and practical utility for making important decisions in the real world. Because a large portion of pure research is conducted in labs using university students it frequently is under attack for its lack of generalizability to the real world.

In essence, these criticisms boil down to a concern with the generalizability of basic research findings to the real world; that is, a concern with the *external validity* of basic research. However, we suggest that laboratory studies in the social sciences have been most criticized for failing to provide readers with an appropriate level of external validity.

Linking Together the Five Members of the Applied Research Culture.
Theorists, researchers, practitioners, clients, and the general public each have stakes in applied research. Although one individual may perform the functions and activities of several of these roles, it is important to view these membership roles as unique. Applied researchers often are in an enviable position because they are able to transcend a number of different levels of responsibility in their quest to obtain solutions to practical problems. Applied research requires that researchers be familiar with communication theory in order to develop sound explanations that solve problems. Theorists, therefore, provide valuable assistance to those conducting applied research. Clients, on the other hand, are linked inextricably to applied researchers, in that they provide problems as well as support, which guide researchers toward an eventual solution. Practitioners are members of this culture by virtue of their participation in the day-to-day activities that applied research addresses. Practitioners can serve as valuable tools in conducting needs analysis, formulating goals and objectives, as well as facilitating data collection. Furthermore, practitioners are "in the trenches" and their evaluation of proposed solutions can serve as a valuable feedback mechanism regarding the utility of research recommendations. Finally, the general public fulfills a signifi-

cant role in the process of applied research by implementing and responding to the advances made in communication phenomenon as it affects their daily lives. The general public is the final and ultimate source of feedback regarding research recommendations and, as a culture, can perform a valuable service by providing support (both financial and moral) for research efforts.

Funding Opportunities. A substantial portion of applied research is sponsored by external agencies, clients, or other interested parties and organizations. Applied research frequently is more costly than basic research and as a result requires outside financial support. When applied communication research must be conducted in the field due to the nature of the problem under investigation, costs will be incurred to remunerate subjects, data collectors and/or coders, and even lease equipment or facilities. Sponsoring agencies often assume the costs of research efforts and researchers are able to enjoy the amenities associated with funded work that would otherwise be unavailable (e.g., salaries, equipment, clerical support, etc.). In fact, some researchers may be unable to conduct basic research without the aid of sponsored projects. For that reason, individuals who might prefer to conduct basic research will don the hat of applied communication research in order to pursue their research agenda. For example, based on previous theory and research generated by Lazarsfeld and colleagues (Lazarsfeld, Berelson, & Gaudet, 1944; Lazarsfeld & Stanton, 1941, 1944), O'Hair and Hardman (1987) were interested in determining contemporary audience reactions to televised newscasts employing a computerized audience feedback system. To do so, they entered into a contract with a national affiliate, locally owned television station to conduct viewership surveys in order to obtain funds necessary to develop, construct, and prototype a costly computerized audience response analysis system. Without the financial support from the television station for the applied project, eventual basic research would have been economically infeasible. Therefore, applied research can provide the necessary financial support necessary to carry out a basic research program.

EFFECTIVE APPLIED COMMUNICATION RESEARCH

There are two basic factors that constitute effective applied research: (a) constructing predictions (hypothesizing) about solutions to communication problems, and (b) verifying or disconfirming solutions to communication problems (explanations). The first factor concerns the nature of theory and how theoretical concepts can be applied to practical problems, whereas the second factor focuses on the best available and most appropriate design, methodological, and analytical approaches to the study of practical communication concerns. In this section, we discuss the application of theory in applied communication research. The second stage of applied research, selection of methodology, design, and analysis, is treated specifically in chapter 2.

Constructing Predictions

The Role of Theory in Applied Research.   One of the criticisms often leveled against applied research is its atheoretical nature. Such negative judgments probably are not without foundation. There is, however, nothing intrinsically atheoretical about applied research, just as there is nothing intrinsically nonpragmatic about basic research. The important point is that there are competent and incompetent researchers operating in both domains. Applied research, therefore, does not have to be conducted within an atheoretical framework. In fact, many scholars argue that the best applied research is conceived and conducted with theory firmly in mind (Bernstein & Freeman, 1975; Miller & Sunnafrank, 1984). Therefore, we now turn our attention to the relationship between theory and method within applied research.

The Nature of Theoretical Explanations.   We do not intend to provide a comprehensive discussion of the philosophy of science in this section. Instead, we argue that applied researchers need to be guided by theory. Underlying all good research is a theoretical position.

The importance of establishing a link between theory, an explanation, and research, collecting evidence, has been supported from a number of standpoints. One obvious argument contends that the explanatory power of research findings are enhanced when discussed from a theoretical perspective. Just as behavior is deemed appropriate within a particular context, research findings can be explained effectively by the use of a theory. Theories of persuasion, for example, can help an applied researcher explain why a client's television advertisements that used a fear appeal worked in some instances but not in others.

Dubin (1976) also argued that neither concept in the theory–research linkage can stand alone adequately. Theories represent leaps of the imagination, but they do not qualify as scientific until research has verified the "reality" of such a model (Dubin, 1976). Theory requires research for verification and research requires theoretical infusion for explaining and predicting observed phenomena accurately.

Scholars often argue that one index of a theory's value is its ability to predict future events (Campbell, 1920; Russell, 1913). Popper (1959), for example, suggested that a theory is useful if universal generalizations can be made about the effects of variables and the relationships among the variables. More recently, Dubin (1976) suggested that a "theory is the attempt of man [sic] to model some aspect of the empirical world" (p. 26).

Thus, models are useful for explaining the complexity of the real world as well as for uncovering relationships among variables that do not appear at the surface level.

Theories, therefore, are valuable when they reveal, explain, predict, and generalize about observed phenomena. If so, theories certainly can enlighten applied communication researchers. However, what are the specific phases associated with the development and use of a good theory?

The process of advancing a theory begins by constructing a conceptual model that is composed of various elements. This conceptual model first identifies variables that are of interest to the theorist–researcher (Dubin, 1976). Variables studied in both basic and applied research can be generated intuitively from observed phenomena or result from previous work in the area determined by a review of the literature. In the case of the applied researcher, however, these variables more often are determined by a client's problem.

After identifying the relevant variables, the next phase of theory building is to demonstrate how these variables are related to one another. There are two issues that must be addressed in this phase. First, the relationships among variables must be specified in detail. The process of conceptualizing and operationalizing variables in communication research certainly is difficult due to the complexity and ambiguity of human communication behavior. Specifying relationships among these variables is an even more difficult task. Nevertheless, specific relationships among variables must be advanced during this phase of the theory building process. Second, tests of parsimony must be made to ensure that only those variables and accompanying relationships central to the proposed theory are included. Such "boundary" conditions (Dubin, 1976) are necessary so that a theory pertains only to those phenomena and conditions that are A theory often attempts to include too many variables that relevantsults in a lack of parsimony and subsequently limits its ability to explain.

Finally, a theory must specify the "system states" in which the variables and relationships operate (Dubin, 1976). All theories have limitations and these conditions need to be specified. For example, the system state that often is specified when discussing boiling water is that water at sea level boils at 100°C. Conditions related to elevation, therefore, must be specified or the theory of boiling water cannot be verified. However, the systems in which variables operate in the study of human behavior are especially dynamic and elusive. Indeed, this last requirement generally has inhibited generating extant theories of human communication.

Applied Theory. Snizek and Fuhrman (1980) distinguished between theories that are practically relevant (and thus useful to applied researchers) and those that are academically elegant (and thus useful to basic researchers). Accordingly, theories employed by applied social researchers are practically relevant in that they "should be simple, causal, and subject to manipulation" (p. 98). In applied research it is not always possible to control for many of the effects that impinge on the internal validity of a study and, therefore, researchers focus only on a few variables and their relationships in order to ensure that the results obtained are, in effect, true results. The theories used by applied researchers should be able, as much as possible, to suggest cause–effect relationships. Because the goal of applied research is to solve a problem by specifying what behavior produces the intended effects, measures of association rarely are useful in applied research (Snizek & Fuhrman, 1980). Additionally, because applied research is constrained by real-world contingencies, theories that include variables that can be manipulated easily should be used. Applied researchers often work with sponsors or clients who may restrict which theories can be selected because of cost, effectiveness, and the potential effects they may have (Snizek & Fuhrman, 1980). Academicians, on the other hand, do not experience the same demands as applied researchers and, therefore, can choose to select theories that only describe the association between variables (Snizek & Fuhrman, 1980).

Effects Versus Theory Application. Before leaving the area of theory or theory construction, it is useful to distinguish between effects application and theory application. In both instances, the goal is to generalize from specific events and phenomena to more general events and phenomenon. However, specific objectives, methods, and procedures vary for these application strategies.

Effects application is concerned primarily with generalizing findings that apply directly to real-world situations, and thus are the type most often employed by applied researchers. The procedures that are used allow an exact match between the research context and the real-world situation (Calder, Philip, & Tybout, 1981). For example, organizational communication researchers who have been given a specific charge by an organization to determine the causes of poor morale must employ instruments and procedures that emulate conditions and circumstances found in the workplace under study.

Theory application, on the other hand, embraces a specific theory and generalizes to other situations from the implications and explanations provided by the theory, not the specific effects that are found in support of the theory (Calder et al., 1981). Effects application requires research procedures that mirror the situation of interest, which Calder et al. (1981) have termed *correspondence procedures*. Four components are necessary for implementing correspondence procedures: (a) a representative sample of the real-world situation must be employed, (b) variables must be operationalized to approximate the real world, (c) a research setting that emulates real world conditions must be selected, and (d) designs that correspond to the situation of interest must be employed (Calder et al., 1981). Thus, with effects application any procedural deviation in the research methodology detracts from the generalizability of the results to real-world settings. In contrast, the primary concern with theoretical application is selecting samples, variables, research settings, and designs that control for extraneous effects that may confound the results and subsequently compromise the generalizability of the theory.

Summary. It should be obvious that applied research, like its counterpart of basic research, is conducted best within a theoretical framework. Although not all existing communication theory is appropriate for applied work, there potentially are a number of communication theories that have applied utility. Triandis (1980) argued that the goal of applied theory is to maximize pragmatic predictability. Thus, it is incumbent on applied researchers to select those theories that conform to the situational constraints of the particular settings studied, and put into place a working framework that maximizes pragmatic predictability.

The relative merits of any theory–research effort, therefore, should be based on the initial choice of theory, how well the methodology is performed, and how well this theory–research link achieves the goals (Snizek, 1982). Theory and research, therefore, are impossible to separate due to their interdependent relationship (Dubin, 1976). This interplay between theory and research is best summarized by Snizek and Fuhrman (1980) who stated that, "Theory guides research, and in turn is refined and reformulated by the findings of that research" (p. 94). We agree with both premises that although "there is nothing so practical as a good theory" (Lewin, 1951, p. 169), "there is nothing so theoretical as a good application" (Lévy-Leboyer, 1988, p. 785).

CONCLUSION

In this chapter we have briefly examined the fundamental issues that underlie applied communication research. These issues were addressed at the generic or conceptual level of analysis to provide an understanding of those matters most salient to the study and conduct of applied research. Applied communication research is the use of theory and method to solve practical communication problems. Although basic and applied research are designed and conducted to meet different goals, both demand a link between theory and method. Applied research must be conceived, developed, and conducted from sound theoretical positions if it is to result in stronger and more practically relevant solutions for clients or sponsors.

The contribution of applied research to theory building will benefit all members of the research community, including theorists and clients alike.

OVERVIEW OF THE BOOK

This section previews the remaining chapters of the book. In chapter 2, Frey, O'Hair, and Kreps examine how applied research is conducted. They first propose and explain a six-stage model of the applied communication research process: problem identification, conceptualization, operationalization, measurement, data analysis, and recommendations. They also explore in some depth four research methodologies that have been used to conduct applied communication research: experimental, survey, ethnography, and textual analysis. The chapter continues with a detailed examination of field research, including some of the most common designs that are used by applied communication researchers. They conclude by arguing that the best research, both applied and basic, is the result of triangulation, the process of answering the same research question using multiple research methodologies.

The remaining chapters of the book address a number of applied communication contexts where research has been conducted, or should be pursued. In each case the authors have intimate knowledge of the context and subject matter as a result of their work in the area. In the first section entitled "Organizational Contexts," three chapters are devoted to different examinations of applied communication in organizational settings. Carl Botan's chapter on industrial relations (chapter 3) provides comparisons between the disciplinary fields of industrial relations and communication. He assumes a rules perspective as an organizing framework for melding the two disciplines together in order that a more coherent approach to applied research in industrial relations can be made. The following chapter by Deanna Womack (chapter 4) involves a synthesis and critique of the relevant literature in the area of communication and negotiation. Womack laments the lack of applied work in negotiation, arguing that most research in negotiation conforms to a basic research mode. She contends that negotiation research could benefit from additional applied work in both lab and field settings. Her call for greater input from practicing negotiators is both timely and relevant. Gary Kreps' chapter on organizational development (chapter 5) describes a model of therapeutic consultation where interpretive organizational research is used to diagnose organizational problems and to develop interventions to help solve these problems. He contends that organizational communication researchers have the potential to solve many serious organizational problems by applying research to organizational development.

Two chapters representing the "Educational Context" are presented next, beginning with Gus Friedrich and Arthur Van Gundy's chapter on training and development (chapter 6). Friedrich and Van Gundy argue that communication training and development consultants will be in greater demand in the future as the work force continues to grow and require employee development in basic competencies areas. They contend that communication training and development is best approached from a competency perspective and present very specific recommendations for researchers and practitioners in this area. In the following chapter (chapter 7), Mary O'Hair and Bob Wright develop compelling arguments for the application of communication strategies in alleviating teacher stress. After reviewing the major causes of stress in public school systems, most of which are communication based, they make specific recommendations for the application of communication theory and research as methods of addressing the causes and symptoms of teacher stress.

Three chapters compose the "Sales and Marketing Context." All of the contributing authors in this section either have conducted actual applied research in their respective areas or have served as consultants on projects that produced theoretical explanations or research findings. Dale Leathers' chapter on impression management in the sales interview (chapter 8) provides an in-depth examination of the verbal, but primarily nonverbal behaviors that create impressions during sales interviews. His integration of communication theory and research on credibility, nonverbal behavior, and communication competence into the applied setting of sales is articulate and fascinating. Leathers views a sales interview as a communication act and makes specific recommendations regarding nonverbal behavior appropriate for creating the most desirable impression. In chapter 9, Connie Staley discusses the advantages and shortcomings of focus group research as a marketing strategy. Her chapter is written with the practitioner in mind and concentrates on the effective cooperation required between researcher and sponsor. Staley reports findings from a focus group in which she was involved and provides guidelines and recommendations for those interested in pursuing this type of applied research methodology. In chapter 10, Ralph Behnke and Dan O'Hair develop a rationale for utilizing computerized audience response analysis systems in various types of advertising, public relations, and marketing campaigns. They report findings from two studies in which both authors independently employed different types of response systems in order to collect data that would have been elusive in other methodologies. Their argument for on-line, real-time data is directed to those who want to avoid the pitfalls and limitations of retrospective data collection.

"Legal and Political Contexts" are represented by a chapter in each area. In chapter 11, Kathy Kendall examines numerous political contexts where applications of communication theory are made. Her extensive review of research in the political communication arena leads to some specific suggestions for future research. For example, Kendall identifies interpersonal relations and state government as contexts that are ripe for study. She recommends an increased use of participant observation research in political contexts. The chapter on legal communication written by Steven Goldswig and Mike Cody (chapter 12) is a comprehensive review of legal communication representing research from both rhetorical and communication traditions. Although the authors modestly claim that their treatment of the topic is limited, a vast number of legal communication topics and contexts are comprehensively reviewed and integrated into a coherent paradigm. Among the topics that they discuss are dramatistic perspectives to courtroom behavior, legal interviewing, detecting deception, and the communication implications of opening and closing arguments.

The final section in the book represents a burgeoning area of applied communication research, health communication. Five chapters are included in the "Health Communication Context" section beginning with one by Gary Kreps that provides an overview and synthesis of applied health communication research. Kreps reviews health communication inquiry by describing health communication research at the interpersonal, group, organizational, and mediated levels of analysis. He also identifies directions for future application of health communication research. In the next chapter, Mary Ann Fitzpatrick provides a framework for studying health communication according to family paradigms (chapter 14). She argues that one cannot study health or aging without relying on the family context. A number of family paradigms are presented that allow greater facilitation in explaining and coping with health issues. In the following chapter Sandy Ragan and Lynda Glenn advance compelling arguments for the use of discourse analysis in the area of gynecological communication. Because gender issues are involved in such a health-care context, it is useful to analyze data from gynecological exam settings to determine the implications of same sex and opposite sex provider–patient relationships. Ragan and Glenn's call for a greater use of phenomenological approaches to health care is persuasive. In chapter 16, Rick Street provides an often overlooked examination of the dentist–patient relationship. Through an extensive review of the literature, Street concludes that the most effective manner of examining dentist–patient communication is a functional approach. He argues that functions emerge from goals and motivations during interaction, from behaviors to accomplished goals, and from interpretations of the pattern of communication exchange. He recommends that future work include the communication dimensions, affiliation, dominance, and information. In the final chapter of the book,

Jon Nussbaum and James Robinson discuss a number of research issues associated with communication within nursing homes. They advance a number of recommendations for practitioners and researchers in the area of aging and the care of the elderly. For example, it is suggested that working with the nursing home staff to help nurses experience aging would not only improve job satisfaction, but would also serve to improve the care delivery in these institutions. Their call for new research in this area includes an increase in the "rich" descriptions of nursing home life, determining the friendship function of staff members to residents, and employing survey and ethnomethodological approaches to the study of applied communication in this setting.

Obviously, it is not possible to include every possible context where applied communication research is conducted. Rather, we have identified areas that represent a sampling of the applied research domain. The chapters that are included share an interest in identifying communication situations that require practical, but theoretically generated solutions. It is hoped that the reader will benefit from the diversity of the areas covered in this book.

REFERENCES

Bannister, D. (1966). Psychology as an exercise in paradox. *Bulletin of the British Psychological Society, 19*, 21–26.

Berger, C., & Calabrese, R. (1975). Some explorations in initial interaction and beyond: Toward a developmental theory of interpersonal communication. *Human Communication Research, 1*, 98–112.

Bernstein, I. N., & Freeman, H. E. (1975). *Academic and entrepreneurial research: The consequences of diversity in federal evaluation studies.* New York: Russell Sage.

Calder, B. J., Phillips, L. W., & Tybout, A. M. (1983). Beyond external validity. *Journal of Consumer Research, 10*, 112–114.

Campbell, N. R. (1920). *Physics: The elements.* Cambridge: Cambridge University Press.

Champanis, A. (1976). Engineering psychology. In M. D. Dunnette (Ed.), *Handbook of industrial and organizational psychology* (pp. 697–744). Chicago: Rand McNally.

Cohen, H. (1985). The development of research in speech communication: A historical perspective. In T. W. Benson (Ed.), *Speech communication in the 20th century* (pp. 282–298). Carbondale & Edwardsville, IL: Southern Illinois University Press.

Cragan, J. F., & Shields, D. C. (1981). *Applied communication research: A dramatistic approach.* Prospect Heights, IL: Waveland Press.

Delia, J. G. (1987). Communication research: A history. In C. R. Berger & S. H.

Chaffee (Eds.), *Handbook of communication science* (pp. 20–98). Newbury Park, CA: Sage.

DeMartini, J. R. (1982). Basic and applied sociological work: Divergence, convergence, or peaceful co-existence? *Journal of Applied Behavioral Science, 18,* 204–215.

Donohue, W. A. (1978). An empirical framework for examining negotiation processes and outcomes. *Communication Monographs, 45,* 247–257.

Donohue, W. A. (1981). Analyzing negotiation tactics: Development of a negotiation interact system. *Human Communication Research, 7,* 273–287.

Donohue, W. A., Allen, M., & Burrell, N. (1985). Communication strategies in mediation. *Mediation Quarterly, 10,* 75–90.

Donohue, W. A., Dietz, M. E., & Hamilton, M. (1984). Coding naturalistic negotiation interaction. *Human Communication Research, 10,* 403–425.

Dubin, R. (1976). Theory building in applied areas. In M. D. Dunnette (Ed.), *Handbook of industrial and organizational psychology* (pp. 17–39). Chicago: Rand McNally.

Eddy, E. M., & Partridge, W. L. (1978). Development of applied anthropology in America. In E. M. Eddy & W. L. Partridge (Eds.), *Applied anthropology in America* (pp. 3–45). New York: Columbia University Press.

Friemuth, V. S., Greenberg, R. H., DeWitt, J., & Romano, R. M. (1984). Covering cancer: Newspapers and the public interest. *Journal of Communication, 34,* 62–73.

Hewes, D. E. (1978). Interpersonal communication theory and research: A methodological overview. In B. D. Ruben (Ed.), *Communication yearbook 2* (pp. 155–169). New Brunswick, NJ: Transaction.

Janowitz, M. (1971). *Sociological models and social policy.* Morristown, NJ: General Learning Press.

Kreps, G. L. (1986). Description and evaluation of a nurse retention organizational development program. In H. Gueutal & M. Kavanagh (Eds.), *Proceedings of the Eastern Academy of Management* (pp. 18–22). New York: Eastern Academy of Management.

Lazarsfeld, P. F., Berelson, B., & Gaudet, H. (1944). *The people's choice.* New York: Duell, Sloan, & Pearce.

Lazarsfeld, P. F., & Reitz, J. G. (1975). *An introduction to applied sociological.* New York: Elsevier.

Lazarsfeld, P. F., & Stanton, F. N. (1941). *Radio research, 1941.* New York: Duell, Sloan, & Pearce.

Lazarsfeld, P. F., & Stanton, F. N. (1944). *Radio research, 1942–43.* New York: Duell, Sloan, & Pearce.

Lévy-Leboyer, C. (1988). Success and failure in applying psychology. *American Psychologist, 43,* 779–785.

Lewin, K. (1951). *Field theory in social science.* Chicago: University of Chicago Press.

Lewin, K. (1943). Problems of research in social psychology. In K. Lewin (Ed.), *Field theory in social science: Selected theoretical papers.* New York: Harper & Row.

Miller, G. R., & Fontes, N. E. (1979). *Videotape on trial: A view from the jury box.* Beverly Hills, CA: Sage.

Miller, G. R., Bender, D. C., Boster, F. J., Florence, B. T., Fontes, N. E., Hocking, J. E., & Nicholson, H. E. (1975). The effects of videotaped testimony in jury trials. *Brigham Young Law Review,* 331–373.

Miller, G. R., & Sunnafrank, M. J. (1984). Theoretical dimensions of applied communication research. *The Quarterly Journal of Speech, 70,* 255–263.

Nussbaum, J. (1983). Relational closeness of elderly interaction: Implication for life satisfaction. *The Western Journal of Speech Communication, 47,* 229–243.

O'Hair, D. (1986). Patient preferences for physician persuasion strategies. *Theoretical Medicine, 7,* 147–164.

O'Hair, D. (1989). Dimensions of relational communication and control during physician-patient interactions. *Health Communication, 1,* 97–116.

O'Hair, D., & Hardman, A. (1987). *Viewership survey for local 6:00 p.m. newscast utilizing the Computerize Audience Response Analysis System.* Unpublished report, Communication Resources Center, Las Cruces, NM.

Parsons, T. (1959). Some problems confronting sociology as a profession. *American Sociological Review, 24,* 547–559.

Pearce, W. B. (1985). Scientific research methods in communication studies and their implications for theory and research. In T. W. Benson (Ed.), *Speech communication in the 20th century* (pp. 255–281). Carbondale & Edwardsville, IL: Southern Illinois University Press.

Popper, K. R. (1959). *The logic of scientific discovery.* New York: Basic Books.

Ruback, R. B., & Innes, C. A. (1988). The relevance and irrelevance of psychological research: The example of prison crowding. *American Psychologist, 43,* 683–693.

Russell, B. (1913). On the notion of cause. *Proceedings of the Aristotelian Society, 13,* 1–26.

Scriven, M. (1964). Comments of Professor Scriven. In T. W. Wann (Ed.), *Behaviorism and Phenomenology* (pp. 163–183). Chicago: University of Chicago Press.

Smith, M. B. (1972). Is experimental social psychology advancing? *Journal of Experimental Social Psychology, 8,* 86–96.

Snizek, W. E., & Fuhrman, E. R. (1980). The role of theory in applied behavioral science research. *Journal of Applied Behavioral Science, 16,* 93–103.

Thompson, T. (1984). The invisible helping hand: The role of communication in health and human services professions. *Communication Quarterly, 32,* 148–163.

Triandis, H. C. (1980). Theoretical reflections on applied behavioral science. *Journal of Applied Behavioral Science, 16,* 229–230.

Tucker, A. (1981). *Chairing the academic department: Leadership among peers.* Washington, DC: American Council on Education.

Tukey, J. W. (1960). Conclusions vs. decisions. *Technometrics, 2,* 423–433.

APPLIED COMMUNICATION METHODOLOGY

2

LAWRENCE C. FREY
Loyola University of Chicago

DAN O'HAIR
Texas Tech University

GARY L. KREPS
Northern Illinois University

Selecting an appropriate methodology for applied communication research differs only slightly from basic communication research. Availability of resources, constraints on research participants, and ethical considerations, to name a few, influence how all communication research is
designed and conducted. The primary requisite for all research, however,
involves matching methodological procedures with the purpose of the
research and the research questions posed. Researchers must always fit
the method to the problem, not the other way around.

Effective communication research is a process where investigators fit
the method to the problem by combining two activities: ideation and
empiricism. *Ideation* is the conceptual activity whereby researchers examine the theoretical base that frames the research topic, review previous
research, design research, and interpret research findings. *Empiricism* is
the operational activity whereby researchers gather and analyze data.
Ideation leads researchers to construct explanations for observed communication phenomena, whereas empiricism enables researchers to collect
evidence to support explanations. By coordinating ideational and empirical research activities, communication researchers use past theory and
research to design and conduct research, and to interpret and apply the
research findings.

In this chapter we describe some research methodologies and strategies
that applied communication researchers use to gather and analyze the
most meaningful data. To guide the description of the applied communica-

tion research process, we first develop a six-stage model of inquiry that identifies the major ideational and empirical activities in which researchers engage. In explaining this model, we focus on two major measurement strategies used to collect evidence: self-reports and behavioral observations. We also explore four major methodologies that guide how applied researchers measure communication phenomena: experimental, survey, ethnography, and textual analysis. Because most applied communication research takes place in the field, we then examine field research methods in some depth. We conclude this chapter by recommending that applied communication research is best conceived and operationalized from a triangulated approach, in which multiple methods are used to analyze the same communication phenomenon.

THE RESEARCH PROCESS CYCLE

The applied communication research process can be viewed as an ongoing cycle of six interrelated sets of research activities: Stage 1—Problem identification; Stage 2—Conceptualization; Stage 3—Operationalization; Stage 4—Measurement; Stage 5—Data Analysis; and Stage 6—Recommendation (adapted from Frey, Botan, Friedman, & Kreps, in press) (see Fig. 2.1).

Problem Identification

Applied communication researchers begin the research process by determining potential problem areas associated with some communication phenomenon that occurs in naturalistic environments. Cissna (1982), as editor of the *Journal of Applied Communication Research,* explained that:

> *Applied* research sets out to contribute to knowledge by answering a real, pragmatic, social question or by solving a real, pragmatic, social problem. Applied *communication* research involves such a question or problem of human communication or examines human communication in order to provide an answer or solution to the question or problem. The intent or goal of the inquiry (as manifest in the research report itself) is the hallmark of applied communication research. Applied communication research involves the development of knowledge regarding a real human communication problem or question. (Editor's note)

The remaining chapters in this book identify many real problems of human communication within a variety of naturalistic contexts that have received or deserve attention from communication researchers.

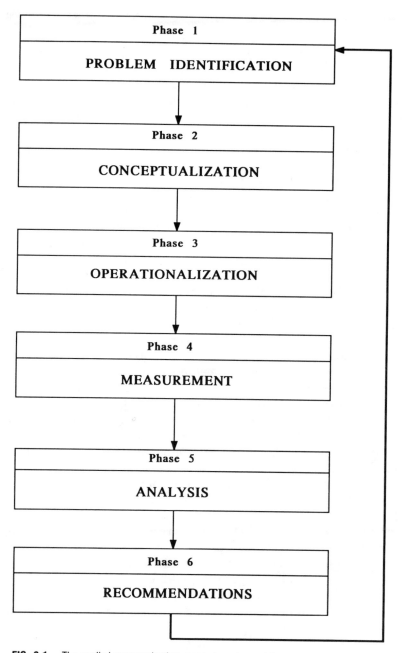

FIG. 2.1. The applied communication research cycle model.

Although applied communication research is not necessarily sponsored, most applied research, especially nonacademic applied research, requires that researchers consult with external agents in order to formulate problem statements. Researchers interested in applied communication phenomena may seek or even be contacted by sponsors or clients who are interested in solving practical communication problems that exist within their environments. An organization, for example, may hire a communication consultant to conduct an audit of the communication needs and flow within the organization.

Once work has been contracted, sponsors expect to participate in how communication problems are addressed by researchers. Discussions with sponsors are critical for assessing how to implement the remaining steps in the research process cycle. Practitioners refer to this process of consultation as *needs analysis*. Sponsors or practitioners, however, often view communication problems differently than academic researchers because their focus is more practical. Applied communication researchers can save themselves a great deal of time and effort by identifying problems carefully in concert with the sponsoring agent or agency.

Even without sponsoring agencies or clients as partners, communication researchers are guests within natural settings and must seek permission to observe communication behavior. Applied research often takes place within privately owned organizations or state-run agencies. Studying communication behavior within these settings is possible only if researchers are granted permission. Organizations granting permission may do so only if researchers refocus their problem statements to study communication phenomena that are of particular interest to them.

Identifying problems worth studying in applied research thus often demands extensive interaction between communication researchers and sponsors or hosts, interaction that often leads researchers to modify their original proposal. Sponsors or clients want pragmatic solutions to practical problems, whereas applied researchers are guided by theory and previous research. The negotiation process between applied researchers and sponsors is not problematic if two guidelines are kept in mind. First, researchers must educate sponsors and hosts about the value of theory-based research for solving problems. Second, researchers must demonstrate to sponsors and hosts that they understand the nature and scope of the practical problem at hand.

Conceptualization

Conceptualization, often considered the first step in designing basic research, involves reviewing previous theory and research for the purpose of defining relevant communication concepts that are worth studying in relation to the problem that has been identified. Unlike basic researchers who conceptualize research primarily from a theory or variable analytic perspective, applied researchers adhere to a conceptualization process that targets concepts that are directly relevant to problem-solving processes. After consulting with interested parties about the nature of the research problem, applied communication researchers must identify and use previous theory and research to formulate optimal approaches to studying the communication behavior of interest. As discussed in the first chapter, applied research is best conceived and conducted with communication theory firmly in mind.

Reviewing relevant theory and research during the conceptualization stage in the context of applied research is not fundamentally different from basic research. Library searches, examining archival data, government statistical and databases, and discussions with colleagues and clients provide initial data for conceptualizing the communication variables that are most important to study. These initial data allow researchers to do two things: (a) develop conceptual definitions for the communication phenomena being studied; and (b) pose formal research questions and/or hypotheses.

A conceptual definition describes a concept by relating it to other similar concepts. Suppose a researcher is interested in how doctors communicate social support to patients during medical examinations. A review of the literature would reveal the following conceptual definition for the term *social support:* "Verbal and nonverbal communication between recipients and providers which reduces uncertainty about the situation, the self, the other, or the relationship, and functions to enhance a perception of control in one's life" (Albrecht & Adelman, 1987, p. 19).

Once all the relevant concepts have been defined, researchers pose formal research questions and/or hypotheses regarding communication phenomena. Research questions and hypotheses seek primarily either to describe communication phenomena or explain relationships between variables. For example, an applied researcher might pose a formal research question about what are the communication needs of the elderly in nursing homes and whether these needs are being met. An applied researcher also might pose a hypothesis about the relationship between meeting the communication needs of the elderly and their satisfaction with nursing homes, such that the more their needs are met the more they are satisfied. A research question typically is asked in exploratory research when little is known about the communication phenomenon of interest, whereas a hypothesis is posed when researchers are in a position to make an educated guess, or prediction, about the outcome of the research.

Identifying and using relevant communication theory and research to develop conceptual definitions and pose research questions and/or hypotheses about the particular problem that has been identified allows applied

researchers to frame practical research within the context of a solid theoretical rationale. As a prerequisite for subsequent stages of the research
process cycle, conceptualization provides a framework that enables researchers to conduct applied research that is both theoretically and practically relevant.

Operationalization

Researchers never measure abstract concepts directly; instead, they measure observable characteristics of these abstract concepts. For example,
researchers cannot measure directly how variables such as communication competence, communication apprehension, communicator style, or
communication satisfaction operate in natural settings. Instead, researchers must specify what behaviors count as indicators of these abstract
concepts. Operationalization is the "process of transforming abstract constructs into a set of concrete indicators that can be observed and measured"
(Smith, 1988, p. 39).

Operationalization demands that researchers identify observable attributes of research concepts and develop specific strategies for observing and
measuring these attributes systematically. During this phase, researchers
use conceptual definitions to develop operational definitions that describe
a concept in terms of its observable characteristics. An operational definition for a cake, for example, is the recipe that specifies the steps a person
must take to bake it. Of course, a good conceptual definition allows researchers to develop a good operational definition. Operationalization,
therefore, involves identifying the appropriate criteria for observing the
primary variables that interest applied communication researchers.

In addition to concepts, variables also must be operationalized in order
that the relationship between conceptual ideas and measurement techniques is made more obvious. Smith (1988) referred to this process as
identifying empirical indicators, although a more common description is
specifying variables that are measurable and at the same time represent
the constructs being studied.

Variable specification in applied research may involve modifying existing variables that are used frequently in basic research. The specific
practical problem being investigated may require that a known variable
that typically is measured using a continuous scale (such as trust, satisfaction, competence, etc.) may best be measured using a discrete scale. The
most important requirement for operationalization procedures is that
abstract concepts must be made observable and measurable in a way that
is most conducive to the goal of applied research.

Measurement

Just as problem identification promotes conceptualization that leads to operationalization, careful operationalization prepares researchers for measuring the primary variables being studied. Measurement activities involve ascertaining the existence and/or size of a variable that has been defined operationally. Two primary measurement techniques and four primary research methods are used by applied communication researchers.

Measurement Techniques

Communication researchers rely on particular techniques to measure communication phenomena. Two general techniques for measuring communication phenomena are: self-reports and behavioral observations.

Self-Reports. Self-reports as a measurement technique rely on research participants' oral and/or written responses to statements or questions posed in a study. Questionnaires and interviews are the two techniques commonly used to gather self-report data.

Self-reports are extremely effective for measuring respondents' beliefs, attitudes, and values, because these exist inside of people's heads. They also may be accurate indicators of people's behavior. Self-reports may be problematic, however, because participants do not always provide accurate information about their beliefs, attitudes, values, and behaviors, especially when asked about controversial topics or ones with important ramifications. Organizational members, for example, may be hesitant to report accurately their attitudes toward their supervisor's communication behavior. Self-reports also may be problematic because of a low correlation between what people say they do and what they actually do, as evidenced by the saying, "Do as I say, not what I do."

Behavioral Observations. Behavioral observations are a second measurement technique available to applied communication researchers. Behavioral observations involve the direct, systematic inspection and interpretation of communication phenomena. Two common behavioral observation techniques that are available to applied communication researchers are physiological measures and observers' ratings.

Physiological measures are used to determine the physical behavior involved before, during, and/or after communication events occur. Physiological measurement is an exacting technique that usually requires instrumentation of some type, and consequently is most often employed in laboratory settings. For example, researchers can measure how excited research subjects become when watching an erotic film by using an electro-cardiogram (EKG) machine that measures rate of heartbeat.

Observers' ratings rely on direct observation of behavior by researchers and/or others involved in the research project. Observers, for example, could be asked to watch a videotape of a marriage counseling interaction and rate the amount of social support that was evidenced by the marriage partners. Researchers also use direct observations of behavior to measure variables. Miller and Boster (1989), for example, pointed out that the amount of money people contribute to a proabortion (or antiabortion) appeal is a good measurement of their attitude toward abortion.

Behavioral observations are effective because they measure people's actual behavior as opposed to what they say they do. Physiological measurements of people's behavior also are quite accurate and reliable. Observers also may be able to judge a person's behavior more objectively than the person may. Of course, behavioral observations only measure people's beliefs, attitudes, and values indirectly. We know from persuasion research that people often behave because of pressures to conform rather than because they have internalized the values associated with the behavior. Observers also are not necessarily more objective than participants themselves. Supervisors may well be biased or have vested interest, for example, when they rate their subordinates' communication behaviors.

Self-reports and behavioral observations thus have relative advantages and disadvantages. For that reason, it often is wise for applied researchers to measure variables using both self-reports and behavioral observations whenever possible. When the data obtained from self-reports are corroborated by the data obtained from behavioral observations, or vice versa, applied researchers have more confidence in the validity and reliability of their measurements.

Methods

Self-report and behavioral observation measurement techniques are employed within the guidelines and goals of four specific research methodologies: experimental, survey, ethnography, and textual analysis.

Experimental Methods.   Experimental methods are used to identify the causal influence of independent variables on dependent variables. Lazarsfeld (1959) identified three requirements necessary for inferring causality. First, the independent variable must precede the dependent variable. One event cannot cause another event to occur unless it comes before it in time. Running through a red light, for example, precedes an accident. Second, the independent and dependent variable must be related in a meaningful way. Heavy rain and flooding are related in a meaningful, and disastrous, way. Variables that may be correlated statistically but are not related meaningfully are referred to as *spurious relationships*. Third, changes in the dependent variable must be the result of changes in the independent variable and not some other, unknown variable. An experimental researcher "tries systematically to rule out variables that are possible 'causes' of the effects [s/]he is studying other than the variable that [s/]he has hypothesized to be the 'causes' " (Kerlinger, 1973, p. 4).

Frey et al. (in press) explained that experimental researchers exercise control in three ways. First, experimental researchers manipulate subjects' exposure to an independent variable. Some subjects may be exposed to a treatment whereas others do not receive it, or different groups of subjects may be exposed to different amounts or types of an independent variable. Second, researchers must make sure that these different experimental groups initially are equivalent. The most effective procedure for establishing equivalent experimental groups is random assignment of subjects to conditions. If random assignment is not possible, experimental researchers use pretests (measurements prior to the manipulation of an independent variable) to see whether subjects in the experimental groups generally are equivalent on a dependent variable or important, potentially confounding variables. Finally, experimental researchers must control for three general internal validity threats: (a) threats due to researchers, such as the researcher personal attribute effect (where researchers' characteristics influence subjects' responses) and the researcher unintentional expectancy effect (where researchers inadvertently let subjects know what responses are desired); (b) threats due to the way research is conducted, such as measurement and procedure validity and reliability, history (changes in the external environment that influence subjects' responses), sensitization (the tendency for an initial measurement or treatment to influence subjects' responses to a subsequent measurement or treatment), and using appropriate data analysis procedures; and (c) threats due to subjects, such as the Hawthorne effect (subjects behaving differently because they know they are being observed), subject selection, statistical regression (the tendency for subjects selected on the basis of extreme scores to regress toward the mean on a subsequent measurement), mortality differential loss of subjects from experimental conditions), maturation (internal changes in subjects that affect their responses, such as growing tired), and intersubject bias (subjects influencing each other).

Control usually is best accomplished in laboratories, settings created by researchers, although we show in the next section how applied researchers also conduct field experiments within natural settings. Laboratory experiments, however, can yield important insights about applied communication. Infante (1985), for example, used the experimental method to investigate whether women are perceived as more credible communication sources when they are induced to be more argumentative. Subjects first were classified as high or low in argumentativeness (the willingness to argue for one's positions). Twenty women who were high and 20 women who were low in argumentativeness were selected randomly, assigned the role of superior in a five-person group, and told to argue for adopting a proposal with two subordinates in separate sessions. One male and one female from each group (each of whom was moderately argumentative) were assigned randomly to the role of subordinate and one female and one male subject were assigned randomly to the role of observer. The subordinates received a sheet containing 10 lines of argument for opposing the superior's proposal. Half of the high and half of the low argumentative women were assigned randomly to a cued arguments condition, in which they were given a sheet with 10 lines of argument corresponding to the lines of argument given to the subordinates, whereas the other half were assigned to an uncued arguments condition, in which they simply were told to convince the subordinates. The two observers rated the credibility of the superior's communicative behavior during the arguments. The results showed that inducing women to be more argumentative had a favorable effect on their perceived credibility.

Survey Methods.   Survey methods are used to gather information about the attitudes and behaviors of a defined population from questions posed to samples selected from that population. Descriptive surveys ask people to report what, when, and how they communicate in order to understand better the nature of particular communication processes. Explanatory surveys ask people why they communicate as they do, and thus "build on descriptive data and explore the underlying theoretical reasons for descriptions" (Smith, 1988, p. 219).

Social scientific surveys involve three general processes: sampling, designing questions, and administering surveys. Sampling requires that researchers obtain a sample of respondents who are representative of the population being studied. Representative samples are best acquired through random selection techniques, where each person in a defined population has an equal chance of being selected. In cases where random sampling is not possible, researchers rely on nonrandom samples, such as convenience, volunteer, or purposive samples. Applied researchers often must rely on nonrandom samples simply because they must work within the constraints imposed by studying a particular problem within a specific setting.

Designing questions for survey research means making sure that they are valid, or accurate, and reliable, or consistent. How questions are worded certainly affects the responses researchers receive. Questions must be constructed so they produce the type of data that are necessary for answering the research questions. Valid questions are those that are understood, comprehended, and lead respondents to give accurate responses, whereas reliable questions are those that can be asked in the same manner to different respondents. Questions that are ill-conceived are unlikely to generate responses that reflect the true nature of respondents' knowledge, perceptions, attitudes, or behavior.

Administering surveys means choosing an appropriate procedure for conducting the research. Self-report, in-person, and telephone questionnaires and interviews are the most common methods for soliciting responses. Self-report questionnaires ask respondents to complete questions by themselves. Researchers conduct in-person interviews by approaching potential respondents, posing questions, and recording responses. Telephone interviews, like in-person interviews, involve direct questioning procedures, but remove interviewers and respondents from face-to-face interaction. Training and monitoring interviewers is, of course, a central concern for survey researchers.

Survey methods are quite prevalent in applied communication research. Johnson and Kusmierek (1987), for example, used the survey method to assess the status of evaluation research in communication training programs. They randomly sampled 169 in-house human resource (HR) trainers concerning evaluation practices used in planning, implementing, and assessing communication training programs. The results from the questionnaire showed that most HR trainers do not conduct a needs analysis while planning communication training programs, do not measure changes in cognitive, affective, and psychomotor behaviors or job performance that may occur as a result of participation in communication training programs, and are not likely to use experimental designs to evaluate such programs. Johnson and Kusmierek concluded from their survey that, "Although communication training programs have significantly increased in the past decade, the use of systematic and controlled evaluation research is presently not being undertaken to plan, implement, and assess communication training programs" (p. 144).

Ethnographic Methods.   Ethnographic methods are used to observe and describe the communication behavior of individuals within a particular natural setting. Ethnography is derived from the Greek word elements *ethno-* ("a tribe") and *-graphos* ("something written down"), and thus refers to a written report about a group of people (Philipsen, 1989).

Ethnography is used to examine the significant symbols that are used within a culture and how these symbols lead to patterned interactions. Van Maanan (1982) claimed that the goal of ethnography is to "discover and disclose the socially acquired and shared understandings necessary to be a member of a specified social unit" (p. 103). Ethnographers thus seek to:

> Show how social action in one world makes sense from the point of view of another. Such work requires an intensive personal involvement, an abandonment of traditional scientific control, an improvisational style to meet situations not of the researchers' making, and an ability to learn from a long series of mistakes. (Agar, 1986, p. 12)

Ethnographic methods have proven very useful in applied communication research. Kelly (1985), for example, used ethnographic methods to examine how organizational stories collected from companies could be used to understand the culture of high technology. She collected 58 stories from various organizational members of 33 different high tech organizations in Northern California's Silicon Valley. The results showed that a majority of the stories addressed three issues common to modern organizing—equality, security, and control. Sigman (1986) used ethnography to understand the variety of individual/psychological and institutional variables that influence patients' adjustments to life in nursing homes. Ethnographic observation and interviewing were conducted in one American nursing home over a 15-month period. The observations and interviews showed that both staff and residents placed demands and expectations on newcomers' behavior, and that patients were constrained in the range of socially acceptable behavior they were permitted to display by staff members' definitions of "successful" and "unsuccessful" adjustment.

Textual Analysis Methods.   Textual analysis is used to classify and evaluate the characteristics of written, electronic, and visual transcripts or texts. Textual analysis includes four general methods: rhetorical criticism, content analysis, conversation analysis, and unobtrusive measures.

Rhetorical criticism involves the "description, analysis, interpretation, and evaluation of persuasive uses" of human communication (Campbell, 1972, p. 12). Classical rhetorical criticism emphasized the central role of public communication in developing and maintaining society, whereas contemporary rhetorical criticism examines a broad spectrum of persuasive messages. Bormann (1972), for example, used fantasy theme analysis (analyzing how rhetoric creates a shared reality for a group of people) to show how fantasy themes (mythic stories present in communication involving characters with which people identify) "chain out" in a group when people jump on the bandwagon, and how this process creates a common, often faulty, rhetorical vision. Koch and Deetz (1981) used a method of metaphor analysis to show how metaphors displayed in organizational talk create organizational social reality.

Content analysis is "a research technique for making inferences by systematically and objectively identifying specified characteristics within a text" (Stone, Dunphy, Smith, & Ogilvie, 1966, p. 5). Content analysis was developed primarily for describing the characteristics of messages embedded within public and mass mediated texts, and often is combined with other methodologies in applied communication research. Willer, Bell, and Andersen (1987), for example, used content analysis and survey methods to evaluate whether what is taught in organizational communication classes is what is valued and effective in the workplace. The researchers first content analyzed 12 recent textbooks from organizational and business communication perspectives, identifying nine common communication themes that indicated important communication functions or results of good communication within an organization. One hundred and seventy subjects from a cross section of organizations and organizational positions then completed a mail questionnaire concerning the importance of these themes and whether the function was evaluated as part of the performance appraisal process. The results showed that there were significant differences between a judgment of the importance of a communication function and whether that function was a part of the performance appraisal process.

Conversation analysis is used by researchers to examine the messages exchanged during dyadic and group interactions in order to discover the "systematic and orderly properties which are meaningful to conversants [and researchers]" (Heritage, 1989, p. 23). Conversation analysts focus on describing and understanding the content, function, structure, and effects of conversation. Krueger (1985), for example, studied the relationships among communication strategies and patterns, egalitarian decision making, and marital satisfaction in dual-career couples. She asked nine dual-career couples to engage in a decision-making role play, and tape-recorded the conversations. She also had the couples complete a marital satisfaction questionnaire. The findings showed that the couples generally had high marital satisfaction and her analysis of the conversation demonstrated many of the communication strategies and patterns found previously in normal, highly satisfied couples, such as fairly equal turn lengths.

Finally, *unobtrusive measures* examine physical traces or artifacts to describe people and their communication behavior (Webb, Campbell, Schwartz, & Sechrest, 1973). Three primary techniques are used to gather data unobtrusively: archival research, bibliometrics, and trace measures. Archival research examines existing records of human behavior, such as public records (i.e., political and judicial records and transcripts of court trials) and private records (i.e., sales reports and personal, written documents). Parker (1963), for example, found that the withdrawal of nonfiction books from a public library increased after television was introduced into a town. Bibliometrics use clustering techniques, techniques that group things together, to study scholarly literature. Rice, Borgman, and Reeves (1988), for example, used bibliometrics to show that journals in the communication field fall into two primary cliques, interpersonal and mass communication journals. Trace measures examine people's behavior from physical traces left behind. Researchers study how physical objects are worn down by use (called measures of erosion) and how physical traces build up over time (called measures of accretion). Kinsey, Pomeroy, Martin, and Gebhard (1953), for example, studied the sexual behavior of men and women from inscriptions written in public toilets. Unobtrusive measures thus represent a creative way applied researchers gather data without subjects' awareness and direct participation in the research process.

Data Analysis

Stage 5 activities involve analyzing the data that have been collected and determining the results of the study. *Data analysis* are the methods researchers use to determine what conclusions are justified from the research observations. Data analysis transforms raw data into information, usable knowledge that can be shared with others.

There are two primary types of data analysis. *Quantitative data analysis* uses statistical techniques to interpret observations that are in numerical form. Two general purposes are associated with statistical analyses. Descriptive statistics are used to organize, tabulate, and graph data, a process referred to as "data reduction" because it reduces the complexity of data. Inferential statistics are used to generalize from a sample to a population and to test for significant differences between groups or significant relationships between variables.

Qualitative data analysis uses descriptive and critical techniques to interpret observations that have been preserved, as much as possible, as they were observed, in symbolic form. Qualitative data are analyzed and reported in the form of case studies, critiques, and other forms of verbal reports.

Quantitative and qualitative data analyses provide applied communication researchers with different, yet complementary ways of making sense of data. Quantitative data provide a high level of precision and statistical power for describing and inferring from research observations, whereas qualitative data provide researchers with great depth of information and richness for understanding research observations.

Recommendations

Once the data have been analyzed and the results have been determined, applied communication researchers forward their recommendations. In many ways, this stage is considered the focal point of applied research. Sponsors or clients are interested in recommendations that help solve their practical problems. In applied research, this "bottom line" permeates the conclusion of the research cycle.

Applied communication researchers also examine during this phase how the results change what is known about the communication concepts being studied. They discuss whether the results support previous theory and research, and whether the results suggest new ways of conceptualizing the research problem. Additionally, researchers identify implications for future research in the area. Because effective applied communication research is based on, and guided by, theoretical underpinnings, research results allow for building upon existing knowledge in the area. By doing so, the existing body of knowledge enlarges, allowing for greater explanatory power in scholars' theoretical understanding. Recommendation activities thus bring the applied communication research process to full circle by suggesting new directions for future research.

APPLIED COMMUNICATION FIELD RESEARCH

Field research means that research observations and data collection occur in naturalistic settings. Although applied research and field research often are equated, this is not necessarily the case. Applied communication research is conducted both in the laboratory or in the field. However, most applied research occurs in the field because researchers study how a specific problem within a particular setting can be solved. In this section, we examine the differences between field studies and field experiments, discuss the relative strengths and potential problems with field research, and explain some of the particular approaches to conducting field research.

Field Studies and Experiments

Field research involves both field studies and field experiments. *Field studies* involve behavioral observation in natural settings without any type of intervention or manipulation of an independent variable. Field researchers observe naturalistic behavior unobtrusively or seek information directly from research participants. In both cases, the researcher's intent is, "to disturb the behavioral system [s/]he is studying as little as possible so that the behavior observed is 'true' or 'natural' and is not behavior influenced by the research procedures themselves" (Runkel & McGrath, 1972, p. 90).

Street (1989), for example, conducted a field study to determine how dentists' communicative styles affect patients' satisfaction. Immediately after a dentist visit, 572 patients of 17 dentists answered a mailed questionnaire assessing perceptions of the dentists' communicative style and satisfaction with the dentist. The findings revealed that there was a strong, positive relationship between dentists' communicative involvement and patients' satisfaction. There also was a negative relationship between dentists' communicative dominance and patients' satisfaction. Street concluded by offering the following advice for practitioners: "When interacting with patients, display behaviors related to involvement and be cautious when exercising dominance" (p. 151).

Field experiments, on the other hand, also are used to observe behavior in naturally occurring contexts, but manipulate one or more independent variables. Unlike field studies, which examine naturally occurring variables, field experiments modify conditions in the natural environment in order to determine the causal relationships between independent and dependent variables (Bickman & Henchy, 1972).

Miller and Monge (1985), for example, conducted a field experiment to determine the effects of information on employee anxiety about organizational change. A company that was planning a move to a new building in 6 weeks was chosen. Information was manipulated by sending some employees positive information about the move, others negative information, and some received no information at all (a control group). One important finding from this field experiment was that positive or negative information reduced anxiety more than no information at all.

Strengths and Weaknesses of Field Research

A number of potential strengths and problems have been associated with conducting applied communication research in the field. We first review some of the more obvious reasons why applied communication research typically is conducted in the field, and then review some of the potential problems that confront applied communication researchers.

Strengths of Field Research

Field research offers a number of potential opportunities for applied communication researchers. These include opportunities to build theory and to conduct research that is ecologically valid.

Theory Building.   Although not known as a theory building technique, field research provides researchers with opportunities to generate questions and test hypotheses that lead to theory development. Babbie (1975) maintained that field researchers often approach the study of naturally occurring behavior without posing a priori hypotheses. Their goal is to make sense out of ongoing behavior that often is unpredictable prior to actual observation.

After making initial observations and developing some preliminary conclusions, however, field researchers often pose some tentative relationship between what is observed and what is already known (theory). Bickman and Henchy (1972), in fact, claimed that some hypotheses or model building may result accidentally during the observation of different and unrelated phenomena in field research.

External Validity.   External validity concerns researchers' ability to generalize findings from one study to different persons, settings, and times. Lynch (1982) identified three issues that permeate arguments made about external validity. The first issue is *statistical generalizability,* which requires that researchers use probability sampling procedures for generalizing to a larger population. The second issue involves *replicability* or robustness, which requires that researchers triangulate findings. Replicability increases researchers' confidence that the results obtained from a single study that uses a particular methodology, subjects, and setting can be found using different methods, subjects, and settings. The third issue is *ecological validity,* which means that the procedures and settings used in a study should be realistic. The more the procedures reflect what actually occurs in "real life," the more the results are generalizable.

Laboratory research often is criticized for its lack of external validity. One of the more common criticisms has focused on sampling procedures. First, the extensive use of convenience samples of college students in laboratory research has led to what McNemar (1946) first called a "science of sophomores." The problem is that college students are not necessarily representative of the population at large and, therefore, the results that are obtained cannot necessarily be generalized (Bickman & Henchy, 1972; Lynch, 1982; McNemar, 1946; Rosenthal & Rosnow, 1969). Furthermore, those "sophomores" sampled are not necessarily even representative of the general college population. Bickman and Henchy (1972) reported that 80% of all psychological research employs only 3% of the college population. Second, laboratory researchers often rely on volunteer subjects. Rosenthal and Rosnow (1969) argued that laboratory research has results in, "a science of just those sophomores who volunteer to participate in research and who also keep their appointment with the investigator" (p. 110). More importantly, volunteers have been shown to possess different attitudes and personalities than nonvolunteers, which limits the generalizability of the findings (Bickman & Henchy, 1972). Third, laboratory researchers often use students who are required to participate. Forced participation in research studies may produce negative perceptions and attitudes that limit the generalizability of the findings (Argyris, 1968). Finally, Fillenbaum and Frey (1970) argued that experimental subjects are too trusting and cooperative and, therefore, do not approximate everyday people.

Laboratory research also has been criticized for failing to facsimilate naturalistic conditions because of the inappropriate use of settings and variable manipulations (Dipboye & Flanagan, 1979; Mook, 1983). Representativeness usually is neglected in favor of strict control over conditions and variables.

In contrast, Bouchard (1976) identified several reasons why applied research conducted in the field tends to be more generalizable than research conducted in the laboratory. First, behavior differs depending upon the setting and field settings may be the best or the only option for studying certain, targeted behavior. Second, behavior in the field demonstrates a wider range of variation than is possible in the laboratory. Third, unanticipated events and behaviors often are present in the field that impact upon the problem being studied. Field researchers can observe these natural events and incorporate them into the study. Fourth, field research allows researchers to investigate the natural time span of phenomena (such as conference meetings, dentist–patient encounters), whereas laboratory research must estimate and approximate the time span involved in naturalistic interactional sequences.

Field research also tends to be more generalizable than laboratory research for a number of additional reasons. Risk, goal achievement, interpersonal relationships, uncertainty, and problem saliency are but some of the factors that are difficult to create in the laboratory, but that exist and can be observed easily in natural field settings. Field settings thus usually maximize researchers' ability to generalize obtained results to other settings that are similar in nature. Laboratory research, although useful for conducting internally valid research, does not enjoy the same degree of credibility regarding generalizability claims.

Problems With Field Research

Field research is not without its problems, however. The following shortcomings represent potential problems that affect the conduct of field research.

Subject Selection. Although laboratory research often is criticized for relying on convenience samples, such as college sophomores, field research also often demonstrates problems with sample selection. Dipboye and Flanagan (1979) argued that a large portion of field research relies extensively on a particular, convenient sample, middle-class males employed as professionals in for-profit organizations. Although professional males constitute a large portion of relevant sampling frames, the point is well taken that an overreliance on one type of subject limits the generalizability of results. Field researchers, therefore, must be cautious in selecting subjects to ensure that representative samples are maintained when the purpose is to generalize from a sample to a population.

Cost. Field research usually costs more than laboratory research. The cost of field research comes in many forms, including human resources, time, instrumentation, access, and even opportunity costs. The cost of fieldwork is even more expensive when one considers the "high-dross rate" (Bouchard, 1976) involved in observation, that a great deal of irrelevant behavior can be observed in the field before anything of significance is recorded. This wasted time and effort are considered costs that are not associated with efficient laboratory research.

Ethics. Although a number of ethical criticisms have been leveled against laboratory research (such as Milgram's infamous studies on conformity behavior), field research also involves difficult ethical choices. Subjects often are observed in the field without their awareness, and unobtrusive observation may infringe on their right to privacy. Subjects in laboratories know that their behavior is being observed and recorded. In the field, however, if subjects are aware of being observed, they may change their natural behavior. Ethical applied communication researchers, therefore, must strike a balance between considering subjects' privacy and their own need to observe behavior as it occurs naturally.

Disturbing the Environment. Field researchers frequently manipulate variables in the natural environment that may alter conditions to such an extent that behavior may not be represented naturally. Runkel and McGrath (1972) labeled this phenomenon the "principle of uncertainty."

Subjects in the field also may well be aware of being observed and change their behavior. It simply may not be possible to obtain the type of data desired using unobtrusive observation because such covert research may not allow researchers to observe certain types of behaviors (such as confidential meetings, etc.). Once the naturalness of the environment has been disturbed, researchers must decide if a contamination effect compromises the study.

Methodological Limitations. Manning (1987), a frequent field re-searcher, pointed out three common methodological limitations of field research. The first limitation concerns the use of *ad hoc problem selection.* There is a tendency in field studies to discover problem areas after researchers have started observing behavior. Although some field researchers see nothing wrong in such a research strategy (and, in fact, many encourage it), it also is argued that this limits, if not stifles, the "systematic pursuit of intellectually or theoretically formulated questions and problems" (Manning, 1987, p. 22). Formulating research questions and hypotheses prior to conducting research builds on existing theory and research. Ad hoc problem selection, however, is less likely to encourage theory building because it constitutes data-driven rather than theory-driven research.

The second methodological limitation of field research concerns the *limited domain of analysis.* Manning (1987) took issue with the microscopic range of behavior that generally is studied in field research, particularly that which relies on ethnographic methods. Because ethnographers study particular contexts, they may be unable to generalize beyond that context. Small samples or even single case studies often are studied in the field; therefore it is even more difficult for many field researchers to generalize beyond the sample being studied.

The third methodological limitation of field research is that *role relationships are not consistent.* Manning (1987) argued that often there are inconsistencies in how data are collected in various field studies. He claimed that:

> Field studies, as the above review illustrates, are not based upon consistent definitions of the role of the fieldworker: some overt, some covert; some are based on intense participation, some on very limited participation; some studies are systematically reflective and self-reflective, others are not; some rely importantly on key informants, while others are surveys. . . . Regardless of one's model of truth or knowledge, it is very difficult to compare these studies. Because self and role of the observer mediate the data gathered, information on the role of the observer is essential to questions of reliability and validity, or even of coherence of an explanatory framework. (p. 23)

Approaches to Field Research

Field research has matured into a complex and sophisticated system of behavioral observation, and much has been written about how to conduct it properly. Here we discuss some of the specific strategies that are available to applied communication researchers working in the field.

Experimental Field Research Designs

Taylor and Adams (1982) proposed a typology of experimental field research designs that focuses primarily on observing how naturalistic behavior is affected by researchers' intervention strategies. Taylor and Adams categorized design types according to the needs of the sponsoring organization, as some designs simply are more suited to some organizational types than are other designs.

Reversal Design. When determining causality is important to field researchers, moving beyond a before–after experimental design may be needed. With a before–after design, an intervention is introduced between pretests (to collect baseline data) and posttests, and any change between these two measurements is attributed to the intervention.

Because cause–effect relationships are difficult to determine, however, further evidence often is required to test the effects of the intervention. Taylor and Adams (1982) suggested that a reversal experimental design helps determine the effects of the intervention by reintroducing the baseline condition, and if the behavior "returns to the original baseline rate, this would suggest that the behavior was under the control of the intervention. If no change occurs . . . then other variables probably caused the improvement" (p. 96).

For example, suppose that a communication consulting group wanted to study the effects of a formal group facilitator on focus group discussions regarding political campaigns. Baseline data would be collected on networking patterns, rates of participation, and attitudes toward group function without a formal group facilitator. A formal group facilitator (expert) then is introduced to the group and allowed to work with the group for a predetermined period of time. Posttests then are used to determine differences from baseline data. If differences are observed, the group would be returned to the baseline condition to determine if formal group facilitation is responsible for the change in scores. If the group reverts back to baseline behavior, researchers are more confident that the intervention was successful.

Multiple Baselines. A second type of experimental design used in field research is called multiple baselines, which consists of three types: multiple baseline across behaviors, across individuals, and across situations. The primary consideration of each of these designs is ensuring that only the manipulation causes changes from baseline behavior.

A *multiple baseline across behaviors design* collects baseline data on two or more behaviors of research subjects. An intervention or experimental manipulation then is introduced for one of the behaviors while maintaining the baseline condition for the remaining behaviors. Subsequently, each behavior is introduced independently to the experimental condition and observed for change. Any change in baseline behavior then is attributed to the experimental condition, because the likelihood of extraneous variables having an impact for all affected behaviors is minimized.

A *multiple baseline across individuals design* collects baseline measurements on several subjects and then introduces the intervention (manipulation) to each subject individually and sequentially. As behavior changes for each subject as a result of the intervention, claims about change scores attributed to the experimental condition can be made. Taylor and Adams (1982) pointed out that this design is particularly "useful for those who work with clients, students, or subjects in more than one setting" (p. 99).

A *multiple baseline across situations design* can be employed when subjects exhibit similar behaviors in a number of different situations and researchers want to determine the cross-situational effects of interventions. After baseline data are collected on each subject, an intervention is introduced in one of the situations where behavior is apparent. Introducing the intervention in each subsequent situation is recorded to assess the situational effect.

Changing Criterion Design.   This design is used to observe behavioral change as a result of gradually changing the criteria by which one is judged for reward. For example, selected employees in an organization may be identified as chronic procrastinators and, after a baseline is established for each, individuals are rewarded by how often their behavior changes according to predetermined criteria. As behavioral goals are reached and rewarded, the criteria are changed to more rigorous and desirable levels.

Multiple-Element Design.   With the previous designs, a sequential or linear process was used to observe the effects of an experimental manipulation. The multiple-element design, in contrast, "intersperses baseline and interventions throughout the study" (Taylor & Adams, 1982, p. 101). Subjects are exposed to multiple experimental conditions and their behavior within each condition is observed. Employees might be told, for instance, that verbal instructions, written instructions, and a combination of both types will be communicated during a specified time period with observers watching for behavioral change or desired behavior in each condition. Improved behavior in one condition relative to another indicates a preferred choice of instructional type. Sulzer-Azaroff and Mayer (1977) pointed out that some of the advantages to this design include the ability to examine more than one independent variable and that it is likely to receive approval from sponsors and clients.

Approaches to Observational Field Studies

Field studies are not concerned with controlling extraneous variables as are field experimental designs. Instead, field studies are conducted to examine phenomena that occur naturally.

Field studies usually involve some type of observational research. Adler and Adler (1987) claimed that observational field studies, by their nature, are a subjective form of research. Analyzing subjective human behavior, therefore, often is best approached by field research techniques that possess built-in subjective elements. Manning (1987) pointed out that these techniques for obtaining knowledge about human behavior as it occurs naturally in the field include, "diaries, interviews, field notes, and level of participation" (p. 20). Here we review two general approaches to observational field studies: ethnomethodology and a clinical approach.

Ethnomethodology. Although much field research relies on quantitative approaches to data collection and analysis, field research also often is associated with qualitative methodologies, such as the Chicago School or, more generally speaking, ethnomethodology. Harold Garfinkel (1967), considered to be the founding figure in the development of ethnomethodology, saw this methodology as a technique for explaining how people make sense of their lives, other people, meanings, and even social order.

Adler and Adler (1987) explained that there are two general types of ethnomethodological approaches. The first type of ethnomethodology is *discourse analysis,* which is concerned with "formal descriptions of interactional structures" (p. 25). The second type of ethnomethodology is *situational analysis,* which is concerned with the "nature of practical reasoning in everyday situations" (p. 25). For both types, the research demands observing and collecting data about behavior that occurs naturally.

The discourse analytic approach is a more microscopic form of ethnomethodology than the situational analysis approach. For example, an applied communication researcher might use a discourse analytic approach to ethnomethodology to examine the specific conversational patterns generated by customer service representatives and their clients in a department store to identify effective and ineffective linguistic strategies for responding to customer problems. In contrast, an applied communication researcher might use a situational analytic ethnomethodological approach to examine more general contextual aspects of the customer service department, such as how the physical design and arrangement of furniture in the department enhance or impede service representative/ client interaction and problem solving.

Clinical Perspective.   Edgar Schein (1987), a noted management science expert, advanced a clinical approach to field research. Schein proposed than an in-depth inquiry into a client's organizational problems is similar to a counselor's or clinician's role in helping an individual deal with his or her problems.

Schein (1987) claimed that a clinical perspective has the following characteristics:

The process is client initiated.

The inquiry is client and problem centered.

The process involves exchange of services for fees.

Data come from client needs and perspectives.

Scientific results are secondary to helping.

Data are validated through predicting responses to interventions.

Data are analyzed in case conferences through sharing with colleagues. (p. 68)

Identifying problems and generating solutions thus are the primary foci for the clinical perspective. Schein claimed that such an approach is more humane and client-centered than other approaches to field research. Rather than force fitting an applied research program on a client, an applied researcher adopting the clinical perspective custom designs a research program to examine the specific problems described by a host. In a chapter later in this book, Kreps describes an adaptation of the clinical perspective to field research in his therapeutic model of the role of applied research in organizational development. In this model researchers are encouraged to collaborate with representatives of host organizations in diagnosing organizational problems, designing organizational interventions, conducting field research, and implementing organizational development strategies. By using this approach, the applied communication researcher can gather relevant data that are easily accepted and used by organizational members because those members who know the most about the organization and have the greatest influence on it have participated fully in the design and execution of the study.

The Role of the Observer

Field researchers using observational techniques must decide on the role they will assume vis-à-vis the people they study. Gold (1958) identified four observational roles researchers can assume: the complete observer, the observer-as-participant, the participant-as-observer, and the complete participant. These roles differ in terms of how much the observer participates in the activities being observed and whether people are aware of being observed (see Fig. 2.2).

The Complete Observer Role. A researcher assumes a complete observer role when he or she observes people without their awareness and does not participate in the activities being studied. A complete observer tries to examine people's behavior within a natural setting without actually becoming a part of that setting. Deakins, Ostering, and Hoey (1987), for example, eavesdropped on dyadic conversations in public to study what topics were discussed in same-gender and mixed-gender dyads. The conversants were unaware that they were being observed.

Assuming a complete observer role, in many ways, affords researchers the most amount of objectivity in recording data because they are not biased by participating with research subjects. This role may limit the breadth and depth of observations, however, because participants are not asked about what their behavior means to them. Complete observers also may become known to the subjects they study, which may cause them to change their natural behavior.

The Observer-as-Participant Role. A researcher assumes an observer-as-participant role when he or she participates partially with the people being observed and informs them that they are being observed. Researchers assuming this role try to fit into the natural environment but do not participate fully in the activities. For example, a newspaper reporter

OBSERVER PARTICIPATION

		High	Low
S U B J E C T	High	Participant as Observer	Observer as Participant
A W A R E N E S S	Low	Complete Participant	Complete Observer

FIG. 2.2. Two-dimensional structure of field observation.

who attempts to learn about social movement processes among migrant workers might ask the workers for permission to study them, follow them around for a specific period of time, and interview them. The researcher does not, however, participate actively in the activities of the movement, such as passing out leaflets.

Assuming an observer-as-participant role, in comparison to the complete observer role, increases researchers' ability to understand more fully the beliefs, attitudes, and motives that guide behavior because participants' views are solicited directly. The data, however, may be less objective than that acquired by the complete observer role, because researchers are involved more intimately with the people they study.

The Participant-as-Observer Role.   A researcher assumes a participant-as-observer role when he or she becomes immersed fully in the social setting being studied and the people know they are being observed. Researchers who assume this role try to understand a particular culture by living the life its members lead. Crawford (1986), for example, wrote to a commune seeking permission to join and then lived in it for a number of months. Van Maanan (1982) requested and received extensive police training to learn how the culture of law enforcement is transmitted to new recruits.

Assuming a participant-as-observer role enables researchers to learn about particular cultures firsthand. Such intimate association with members of a culture allows researchers to understand more fully the tacit processes that guide behavior. Researchers who assume this role, however, may compromise their objectivity if they become too intimate with members of a culture, which is known as "going native."

The Complete Participant Role.   A researcher assumes a complete participant role when he or she becomes immersed fully in a social setting but does not inform people that they are being observed. The researcher tries to fit into the social setting without being detected as an observer. Gold (1958) gave the example of a researcher who became a taxi driver to understand taxi drivers' social behaviors. Throughout the observational period, fellow taxi drivers were unaware that they actually were interacting with a researcher.

The complete participant role has many of the strengths and weaknesses of the participant-as-observer role. Researchers learn firsthand about the culture being studied, but they may become so involved that they lose their ability to report objectively. Additionally, researchers who adopt this role must deceive the people they interact with, and this raises difficult ethical questions.

Summary and Recommendations

Field research allows for the systematic observation of communication behavior within natural environments. Bouchard (1976) extolled a number of advantages associated with observing naturally occurring behavior in the field. First, field researchers focus their attention on the entire communication behavior of individuals instead of relying on microscopic analyses of behavior. Second, field research provides opportunities to discover additional, unanticipated behavior that may provide the impetus for additional studies or theory building, often termed the "serendipity effect" (Merton, 1949). Finally, field research allows for the confirmation (or disconformation) of behavior observed in laboratories.

One of the limitations often cited about field research, however, is the inability to guarantee observer objectivity. Although similar claims can be made about laboratory studies, there is a greater tendency in field research to perceive events and acts as subjects desire. A halo effect, therefore, is more likely to occur in field than laboratory research. Objectivity of field observations can be increased if the following guidelines proposed by Bouchard (1976) are kept in mind:

> Supplement observation data with other sources such as interviews, archival data, or comparison with other observers (intercoder reliability).
>
> Strive to maintain awareness of personal biases, prejudices, or predilections.
>
> Maintain awareness of subjects' biases, motivations, or stereotypes.
>
> Observe subjects in several different contexts.
>
> Maintain adequate relational distance from subjects. (p. 391)

TRIANGULATION IN APPLIED COMMUNICATION RESEARCH

It often is easy to criticize research we are not comfortable with or find inappropriate. Quantitative methodologists complain that qualitative researchers attempt to substantiate ideas using limited data, whereas the latter criticize the former for engaging in "blatant and meaningless empiricism" ("figures don't lie, but liars can"). Laboratory researchers argue that field studies do not control adequately for extraneous variables, whereas researchers who conduct field studies view laboratory research as being unrealistic. There is, of course, a ring of truth to all these criticisms.

Applied communication research, however, presents opportunities to avoid many of the criticisms leveled at any one approach or methodology by employing triangulation. *Triangulation* is a term borrowed from surveying that refers to locating a point in terms of two other fixed positions. Triangulation with respect to research is the process of combining several different methodologies, measurement techniques, and data analysis procedures to confirm and enhance confidence in the results obtained from individual studies. Campbell and Fiske (1959) explained that triangulation is a process whereby hypotheses or research questions can withstand the injection of several methodological techniques.

Researchers who employ triangulation assume that no *one* method can account adequately for human communication behavior and, therefore, a combination of approaches that link strategies is the preferred option (Snizek & Fuhrman, 1980). Hammersley and Atkinson (1983) claimed that, "What is involved in triangulation is not the combination of different kinds of data per se, but rather an attempt to relate different sorts of data in such a way as to counteract various threats to the validity of our analysis" (p. 199).

McGrath, Martin, and Kulka (1982) argued that the selection of comparative approaches to research problems should be complementary and distinct. They claimed that:

> Knowledge accrual requires convergence of findings derived from divergent methods. . . . We hypothesize that the next step in the knowledge accrual process should be as methodologically distant as possible from methods used in prior research on that same problem. *Effective triangulation,* we suggest, *requires distance between the observation posts.* So the best choice for a next step in the knowledge accrual process is a method that has as its strength(s) what the dominant methods used to gather the body of knowledge up to that time have as their major weakness(es). (p. 109)

Types of Triangulation

There are numerous ways in which applied communication research findings can be triangulated. Denzin's (1970) typology of triangulation methods identified four types: data, investigator, theory, and methodological triangulation.

Data Triangulation

Data triangulation is used by researchers to examine data from different perspectives. Data can be triangulated along temporal elements, perhaps by collecting similar data at different points in time. Data also can be triangulated spatially, by observing individuals as they interact in different structural environments (e.g., work, home, social settings, laboratories, etc.). Finally, data can be triangulated by studying the interactive composition of targeted subjects (e.g., dyads, organizations, etc.).

For example, in an organizational survey investigating sources of employee job dissatisfaction, the responses given by members of specific departments can be grouped and compared to identify relevant similarities and differences among these departments. Similarities in identified sources of dissatisfaction among departments can help identify widespread issues of concern within the organization, whereas sources of dissatisfaction identified only by one department can identify problems confronting a particular department.

Investigator Triangulation

Investigator triangulation involves the systematic study of data by more than one investigator. Triangulation in this sense is similar to establishing intercoder reliability, because it reduces interpretation bias that can accompany the analysis of data by only one source. Additional interpretations offer greater confidence in the validity and reliability of data.

Replication of research studies is the clearest example of investigator triangulation. Lykken (1968) and Kelly, Chase, and Tucker (1979) identified four types of replication: (a) *literal replication,* where the entire procedures are duplicated as closely as possible; (b) *operational replication,* where the sampling and experimental procedures are duplicated but different measurement and data analysis techniques are employed; (c) *instrumental replication,* where the measurement of the independent variable is used; and (d) *constructive replication,* where entirely different procedures are used to see whether the results themselves can be replicated.

By replicating the results of a particular study, the veracity of the conclusions drawn from the study is strengthened. Unfortunately, exact replications in the social sciences are rare (Denzin, 1970; Sterling, 1959). This may be due, in part, to journal editors' reluctance to publish replication (Kelly, Chase, & Tucker, 1979). However, the more the results of a study are replicated by future research, the more confident we are in the accuracy of the findings.

Theory Triangulation

Theory triangulation is used by researchers to examine the same data from different theoretical perspectives. Situational data often can be explained from several different standpoints depending on the level of interpretation involved. Comparing different theoretical concepts to the same data provides a greater understanding of the observations made while at the same time allows for further refinement in both data analysis techniques and theory generation.

For example, applied communication researchers might profitable analyze data on the decision-making patterns of chief executive officers from different theoretical perspectives, thereby enriching their understanding of the data. From an organizational cultural perspective, the decision-making patterns might be explained in terms of widely accepted organizational logics and members' expectations and images of their chief executive officers. From a systems perspective, the decision-making patterns might be examined in terms of the organizational levels at which the decisions were implemented, the internal and external organizational influence on particular decisions, and the long- and short-term functional implications of the decisions on organizational activities. Finally, from a Weickian perspective, the decision-making patterns might be analyzed in terms of the equivocality of the different problems addressed by the decisions made, the organizational rules that were used to guide decision making, and the specific interactional patterns that were used in addressing problems and reaching decisions.

Methodological Triangulation

Methodological triangulation is the type most often referred to and involves the application of different methodological approaches to answer the same research question. Denzin (1970) identified two types of methodological triangulation. The first type is considered to be a "within-method" approach, where the same methodology is applied on different occasions. The second type is referred to as a "between-method" approach, where researchers use different methods to study the same subjects. Earley (1984), for example, used observational and questionnaire data in a cross-cultural study of social interaction in workplaces in the United States, England, and Ghana.

Summary

Linking macro and microlevels of analysis is growing in popularity. Fielding and Fielding (1986) suggested that a combination of these analyses offers a "greater empirical and conceptual accountability on the part of the researcher" (p. 90). Results obtained from macrolevel research, such as surveys of large samples, can be linked with results obtained from microlevel research, such as case studies. Results obtained from microlevel studies conducted in laboratories can be used to corroborate findings obtained from macrolevel field research. Triangulation thus allows researchers a more full and accurate understanding about the applied communication phenomena being studied.

CONCLUSION

In this chapter we have provided an overview of various methodologies that applied communication researchers have at their disposal. As with all good research efforts, examining applied research problems requires a systematic process that begins with careful identification of the problem. Applied research differs from basic research, however, in that sponsors, clients, or host organizations usually must be consulted before full and proper identification of the problem is possible. Applied research, therefore, necessitates consultation between researchers and clients or sponsors.

Once the problem has been identified, applied researchers engage in conceptualization and operationalization activities by using previous theory and research to identify the specific variables appropriate for study and how these will be observed in actual practice. Measurement and data analysis stages follow, which involve selecting appropriate methods and measurement techniques and using proper procedures to analyze data. Once results have been obtained, applied researchers provide recommendations that meet the needs of clients and further the process of building theory.

This applied research process cycle usually takes place in the field. Although there are a number of advantages associated with field research, there also are some potential problems facing applied communication researchers. Finally, we argue that applied communication research is approached best using triangulation. Similar findings using different perspectives and procedures increases researchers' confidence in the validity and reliability of the results.

The following chapters examine a variety of methodological assumptions and procedures as they relate to specific areas of applied communication research, such as physician/dentist–patient encounters, political contexts, industrial relations, focus group interviews, legal interviewing, and many more. Of course, applied communication research within all of these contexts is only as good as the thinking and planning that goes into a project. Careful consideration of methodological approaches that are most appropriate for answering the research questions posed is a prerequisite for all good applied communication research.

REFERENCES

Adler, P. A., & Adler, P. (1987). *Membership roles in field research: Qualitative research methods* (Vol. 6). Beverly Hills: Sage.

Agar, M. H. (1986). *Speaking of ethnography: Qualitative research methods* (Vol. 2). Beverly Hills: Sage.

Albrecht, T. L., & Adelman, M. B. (1987). *Communicating social support.* Newbury Park, CA: Sage.

Argyris, C. (1968). Some unintended consequences of rigorous research. *Psychological Bulletin, 70,* 185–197.

Babbie, E. (1975). *The practice of social research.* Belmont, CA: Wadsworth.

Bickman, L., & Henchy, T. (1972). *Beyond the laboratory: Field research in social psychology.* New York: McGraw-Hill.

Bormann, E. H. (1972). Fantasy and rhetorical vision: The rhetorical criticism of reality. *Quarterly Journal of Speech, 58,* 396–407.

Bouchard, T. J. (1976). Field research methods: Interviewing, questionnaires, participant observation, systematic observation, unobtrusive measures. In M. D. Dunnette (Ed.), *Handbook of industrial and organizational psychology* (pp. 363–413). Chicago: Rand McNally.

Campbell, D. T., & Fiske, D. W. (1959). Convergent and discriminant validity by the multi-trait, multi-method matrix. *Psychological Bulletin, 56,* 81–105.

Campbell, K. K. (1972). *Critiques of contemporary rhetoric.* Belmont, CA: Wadsworth.

Cissna, K. N. (1982). Editor's note: What is applied communication research? *Journal of Applied Communication Research, 10,* iii–v.

Crawford, L. (1986). Reluctant communitarians: Personal stories and commune behavior. *Communication Quarterly, 34,* 286–305.

Deakins, A. H., Osterink, C., & Hoey, T. (1987). Topics in same sex and mixed sex conversations. In L. B. Nadler, M. J. Nadler, & W. R. Todd-Mancillas (Eds.), *Advances in gender and communication research* (pp. 89–108). Lanham, MD: University Press of America.

Denzin, N. K. (1970). *The research act: A theoretical introduction to sociological methods.* Chicago: Aldine.

Dipboye, R. L., & Flanagan, M. F. (1979). Research settings in industrial and organizational psychology: Are findings in the field more generalizable than in the laboratory. *American Psychologist, 34,* 141–150.

Earley, P. C. (1984). Social intervention: The frequency of use and valuation in the United States, England, and Ghana. *Journal of Cross-Cultural Psychology, 15,* 477–485.

Fielding, N. G., & Fielding, J. L. (1986). *Linking data: Qualitative research methods* (Vol. 4). Beverly Hills: Sage.

Fillenbaum, S., & Frey, R. (1970). More on the "faithful" behavior of suspicious subjects. *Journal of Personality, 38,* 43–51.

Frey, L. R., Botan, C. H., Friedman, P. G., & Kreps, G. L. (in press). *Investigating communication: An introduction to research methods.* Englewood Cliffs, NJ: Prentice-Hall.

Garfinkel, H. (1967). *Studies in ethnomethodology.* Englewood Cliffs, NJ: Prentice-Hall.

Gold, R. L. (1958). Roles in sociological field observations. *Social Forces, 36,* 217–223.

Hammersley, M., & Atkinson, P. (1983). *Ethnography: Principles in practices.* London: Tavistock.

Heritage, J. (1989). Current developments in conversation analysis. In D. Roger & P. Bull (Eds.), *Conversation: An interdisciplinary perspective* (pp. 21–47). Clevedon, England: Multilingual Matters Ltd.

Infante, D. A. (1985). Inducing women to be more argumentative: Source credibility effects. *Journal of Applied Communication Research, 13,* 33–44.

Johnson, J. R., & Kusmierek, L. A. (1987). The status of evaluation research in communication training programs. *Journal of Applied Communication Research, 15,* 144–159.

Kelly, C. W., Chase, L. J., & Tucker, R. K. (1979). Replication in experimental communication research: An analysis. *Human Communication Research, 5,* 338–342.

Kelly, J. W. (1985). Storytelling in high tech organizations: A medium for sharing culture. *Journal of Applied Communication Research, 13,* 45–58.

Kerlinger, F. N. (1973). *Foundations of behavioral research* (2nd ed.). New York: Holt, Rinehart & Winston.

Kinsey, A. C., Pomeroy, W. B., Martin, C. E., & Gebhard, P. H. (1953). *Sexual behavior in the human female.* Philadelphia: Saunders.

Koch, S., & Deetz, S. (1981). Metaphor analysis of social reality in organizations. *Journal of Applied Communication Research, 9,* 1–15.

Krueger, D. L. (1985). Communication patterns and egalitarian decision making in dual-career couples. *Western Journal of Speech Communication, 49,* 126–145.

Lazarsfeld, P. (1959). Problems in methodology. In R. K. Merton (Ed.), *Sociology today* (pp. 39–78). New York: Basic Books.

Lykken, D. T. (1968). Statistical significance in psychological research. *Psychological Bulletin, 21,* 151–159.

Lynch, J. G. (1982). On the external validity of experiments in consumer research. *Journal of Consumer Research, 9,* 225–239.

Manning, P. K. (1987). *Semiotics and fieldwork: Qualitative research methods* (Vol. 7). Beverly Hills: Sage.

McGrath, J. E., Martin, J., & Kulka, R. A. (1982). Some quasi-rules for making judgment calls in research. In J. E. McGrath, J. Martin, & R. A. Kulka (Eds.), *Judgment calls in research* (pp. 103–118). Beverly Hills: Sage.

McNemar, Q. (1946). Opinion–attitude methodology. *Psychological Bulletin, 43,* 289–374.

Merton, R. K. (1949). *Social theory and social structure.* Glencoe, IL: Free Press.

Miller, G. R., & Boster, F. J. (1989). Data analysis in communication research. In P. Emmert & L. L. Barker (Eds.), *Measurement of communication behavior* (pp. 18–39). New York: Longman.

Miller, K. I., & Monge, P. R. (1985). Social information and employee anxiety about organizational change. *Human Communication Research, 11,* 365–386.

Mook, D. G. (1983). In defense of external invalidity. *American Psychologist, 38,* 379–387.

Parker, E. B. (1963). The effects of television on public library circulation. *Public Opinion Quarterly, 27,* 578–589.

Philipsen, G. (1989). An ethnographic approach to communication studies. In B. Dervin, L. Grossberg, B. J. O'Keefe, & E. Wartella (Eds.), *Rethinking communication. Vol. 2. Paradigm exemplars* (pp. 258–268). Newbury Park, CA: Sage.

Rice, R. E., Borgman, C. L., & Reeves, B. (1988). Citation networks of communication journals, 1977–1985: Cliques and positions, citations made and citations received. *Human Communication Research, 15,* 256–283.

Rosenthal, R., & Rosnow, R. L. (1969). The volunteer subject. In R. Rosenthal & R. L. Rosnow (Eds.), *Artifacts in behavioral research* (pp. 59–118). New York: Academic Press.

Runkel, P. J., & McGrath, J. E. (1972). *Research on human behavior.* New York: Holt, Rinehart & Winston.

Schein, E. H. (1987). *The clinical perspective in fieldwork: Qualitative research methods (Vol. 7).* Beverly Hills: Sage.

Sigman, S. J. (1986). Adjustment to the nursing home as a social interactional accomplishment. *Journal of Applied Communication Research, 14,* 37–58.

Smith, M. J. (1988). *Contemporary communication research methods.* Belmont, CA: Wadsworth.

Snizek, W. E., & Fuhrman, E. R. (1980). The role of theory in applied behavioral science research. *Journal of Applied Behavioral Science, 16,* 93–103.

Sterling, T. D. (1959). Publication decisions and their possible effects on inferences drawn from tests of significance—or vice versa. *Journal of the American Statistical Association, 54,* 30–34.

Stone, P. J., Dunphy, D. C., Smith, M. S., & Ogilvie, D. M. (1966). *The general inquirer: A computer approach to content analysis.* Cambridge, MA: MIT Press.

Street, R. L., Jr. (1989). Patients' satisfaction with dentists' communicative style. *Health Communication, 1,* 137–154.

Sulzer-Azaroff, B., & Mayer, G. (1977). *Applying behavior-analysis procedures with children and youth.* New York: Holt, Rinehart & Winston.

Taylor, R. L., & Adams, G. L. (1982). A review of single-subject methodologies in applied settings. *Journal of Applied Behavioral Science, 18,* 95–103.

Van Maanen, J. (1982). Fieldwork on the beat. In J. Van Maanen, J. M. Dabbs, Jr., & R. R. Faulkner (Eds.), *Varieties of qualitative research* (pp. 103–151). Beverly Hills: Sage.

Webb, E. J., Campbell, D. T., Schwartz, R. D., & Sechrest, L. (1973). *Unobtrusive measures: Nonreactive research in the social sciences.* Chicago: Rand McNally.

Willer, L. R., Bell, K. D., & Andersen, P. A. (1987). Is what we teach about organizational communication what they practice in organizations? *Journal of Applied Communication Research, 15,* 95–112.

PART II

CONTEXTS

ORGANIZATIONAL CONTEXTS

INDUSTRIAL RELATIONS COMMUNICATION

3

CARL BOTAN
Rutgers University

Industrial relations includes "all phases of relations between employer and employee, including collective bargaining, safety, employee benefits, etc." (Black, 1979, p. 698). The relationship of employers and organized employees is one main area of focus, but industrial relations also addresses nonunionized employer–employee relations.

Communication between employers and their more than 111.5 million employees (U.S. Bureau of the Census, 1987) is what drives our $4.235 trillion a year economy. Employee–employer communication is, therefore, a large and important example of applied communication. Much of this communication is about the specifics of the task, organizational structure, or social relationships in the workplace, and has been extensively studied by organizational communication scholars. But another large part of this communication is specifically about the industrial relations relationship—Industrial Relations Communication—and has not received much attention as an instance of applied communication (cf. Botan & Frey, 1983).

Importance

Although industrial relations communication is always important, it is of particular importance today. Our economy is experiencing a wrenching reorientation that may make questions of employer–employee communication ever more salient as new relationships are worked out. For example,

61

the increased frequency of concession contracts, the fact that unions started losing a majority of both certification and decertification elections as long ago as 1980, and the fact that unions today represent only about 17.5% of all employees[1] all suggest that the stakes in industrial relations communication are as high as ever, maybe higher. In addition, factors such as this country's expanding trade deficit and the transformation from a manufacturing to a service-based economy suggest that new questions about industrial relations communication will be confronting us in the coming years.

The current body of communication literature on industrial relations communication suffers from one obvious and one potential weakness. First, it is not nearly as large as might be expected given the immense size and economic importance of the relationship addressed. Second, we have tended to address industrial relations communication within specific contexts or levels, such as interpersonal superior–subordinate communication, small group communication, organizational communication, networks, and as negotiation and bargaining. Although these are appropriate approaches, keeping analyses within particular levels or contexts might have had the effect of obscuring patterns or issues that may cut across the various levels and contexts.

This chapter compares the largely unfamiliar field of industrial relations and the more familiar field of communication. The purpose is to demonstrate how we might use the lessons learned in this applied communication arena to help address some of the theoretic issues confronting communication. Industrial relations and communication are such large fields that one chapter cannot make all the possible comparisons so, wherever possible, the discussion focuses on union certification and decertification elections as one exemplar of industrial relations communication.

Certification, or unionization, campaigns are efforts by labor organizations to become certified as sole collective bargaining agents for employees. Decertification, or deunionization, campaigns are attempts by management to have the certification of a labor organization revoked. Both kinds of campaigns are conducted under the auspices of the appropriate

---

[1]Since 1980 American workers have been voting against union representation in record numbers. In the 12-month period that ended September 30, 1980, unions won only 45% of the 8,043 representation elections held, the smallest percentage since the National Labor Relations Board (NLRB) was created, according to Urban C. Lehner of the *Wall Street Journal* (July 28, 1980, Sec. 2, p. 1.). In addition, since 1980 workers have been voting to decertify (deunionize) unions as their bargaining agents in 7 out of every 10 decertification elections according to a *Detroit Free Press* article of May 13, 1980 (Sec. B, p. 4). That this trend is continuing is shown by the 2.6% drop in the percent of the civilian workforce that is in unions (20.1% to 17.5%) from 1983 to 1986 (U.S. Bureau of the Census, *Statistical Abstract 1988*).

government body (usually the National Labor Relations Board or NLRB), which places a set of restrictions on the communicative behavior of both sides. With my colleagues, I have argued elsewhere that these campaigns meet the definition of persuasive campaigns as the term is used in communication, and have a number of characteristics in common with political, advertising, and public relations campaigns (Brock, Botan, & Frey, 1985).

Industrial Relations Communication

Industrial relations law is the body of law based on the National Labor Relations Act (NLRA) and its amendments, the Taft–Hartley and Landrum–Griffin Acts. This body of law regulates the relationship between employers and employees and is based specifically on the premise that good industrial relations, based on effective communication, is in the best interest of the nation and its people. This is an instance in which the national government has declared that effective applied communication is a goal.

National laws, state laws, and administrative bodies have been evolved to assure that communication occurs between employer and employee and to provide rules governing that communication. The greatest emphasis in these laws is placed on the right of employees to form unions and bargain collectively, so there is much detail about what messages, message contexts, and communication mediums labor and management may employ during election campaigns. The subject matter that may and may not be bargained as a result of these elections is also spelled out, as is the obligation to "bargain in good faith"—a requirement that the two parties exchange verbal messages whether or not they can agree on the content of those messages.

Overview

The first part of this chapter looks for similarities between the industrial relations and communication fields, in terms of domains of inquiry, age, and structure. The second part, the principal task of this chapter, looks at similarities between industrial relations and communication with respect to theoretic approaches and common variables employed. Finally, the last section employs one specific example, that of the rules perspective, to illustrate how the two fields can employ the same theoretic perspective in similar and dissimilar ways.

INDUSTRIAL RELATIONS
AND COMMUNICATION AS FIELDS

Domains of Inquiry

At first glance the industrial relations and communication fields appear
to address different domains, the former concerned with rules, methods,
and laws pertaining to the employer–employee relationship and the latter
concerned with how human beings employ symbols to share meaning. But
the rules, methods, and laws studied in industrial relations are worked
out communicatively, so the domains may be expected to overlap.

Industrial Relations.   Industrial relations often treats communication
concepts as independent variables that can facilitate or inhibit certain
goals such as productivity or an effective industrial relations atmosphere.
Communication is seldom treated as a dependent variable. For example,
Getman, Goldberg, and Herman (1976) sought to discover what independent variables, including discussions with peers or superiors and printed
communications, influenced voting for unions in certification elections.

Communication.   On the other hand, communication treats industrial
relations concepts as both independent and dependent variables. Using an
industrial relations concept as an independent variable, communication
scholars might ask, "How does the presence of a union organizing drive
improve communication climate?" Using an industrial relations concept
as a dependent variable, communication scholars might ask, "How does
a good communication climate affect the outcome of a union organizing
drive?"
    Industrial relations and communication do seem to address some of the
same domains. But they also may have other pronounced similarities with
respect to both age and structure.

Age of Fields

Industrial Relations.   There have been industrial relationships since
there have been employees, but the identifiable field known as industrial
relations can trace its lineage back 40 to 60 years to the "Wisconsin
School" of economics. John R. Commons and, to a lesser extent, Selig
Perlman were the first identifiable names in industrial relations.
    Shalev (1985) specifically identified two of Commons' books, *Legal
Foundations of Capitalism* in 1924 and *The Economics of Collective Action*
in 1950, as books to which the field of industrial relations owes a debt.
Similarly, Sayles (1969) made reference to "the field of human relations

in industry, which had its meteoric rise in the United States during the 1940's and 1950's" (p. 125). It was during this period that the principal scholarly body in the field, the Industrial Relations Research Association (IRRA), was founded in 1947.

Communication. Communication may be approached from two perspectives, as classical rhetoric and as social scientific communication theory. How similar communication and industrial relations are in terms of age depends on which communication perspective is adopted.

From a rhetorical perspective the communication field stretches back more than 2,400 years to the study of rhetoric and the sophists. From this perspective industrial relations campaigns could be approached through a rhetorical study of how management and labor seek to apply "all the available means of persuasion." New insights into how and why decertification campaigns succeed or fail might well be gained by employing the teachings of Aristotle or Cicero. Modern day rhetorical-critical methodology has also been used to study union certification and decertification campaigns (Brock et al., 1985). From this perspective communication is far older than the relatively modern field of industrial relations.

Littlejohn (1983) suggested that the social science perspective on communication can trace its roots to the era around 1950, or the founding of the National Society for the Study of Communication (the precursor of ICA) in 1949. In the same vein, Daly and Korinek (1982) said that the study of organizational communication, the subarea of communication that would most likely address industrial relations communication, "is historically a relatively young field of inquiry" (p. 11).

Industrial relations and the social science perspective on communication are very similar with respect to age. Both are children of the postwar era and are relative infants as fields of inquiry.

Structure of the Fields

Industrial Relations. Industrial relations describes itself as a multidisciplinary field that faces the same kinds of internal questions as other multidisciplinary fields. In a self-assessment, which might make communication scholars feel right at home, Cooke (1985) said:

> Although most scholars agree that industrial relations can best be understood from a multidisciplinary perspective, our theoretical understanding of the subject remains sketchy at best and at worst is a hodge-podge of hypotheses without a coherent framework. (p. 223)

With respect to the disciplines that contribute, industrial relations, it is said, "attracts scholars from nearly every social science discipline" (Cooke, 1985, p. 223). Lewin and Feuille (1983) noted that "other than economics, the social science disciplines most frequently applied to the study of unions and industrial relations are psychology, social psychology, and sociology" (p. 345).

Communication.   Littlejohn (1983) identified communication as a similarly multidisciplinary field when he said, "the body of theories related to communication has been produced by a variety of disciplines" (p. 300). The two fields even have much in common with respect to the disciplines that have contributed to them. Littlejohn (1983) identified some of the same ones as Lewin and Feuille:

> Over the years four primary fields have been responsible for most of the work on communication: psychology, sociology, anthropology, and philosophy. . . . Of course, many other disciplines have contributed to our understanding of communication, including management, journalism, speech sciences, political science, mathematics, engineering, and others. (p. 300)

This section has briefly examined how industrial relations and communication are similar with respect to domains of inquiry, age, and structure. The next section provides a summary of similarities between the fields in theoretic approaches and the kinds of variables that each employs.

THEORETIC APPROACHES AND VARIABLES

Lawler (1987) suggested that industrial relations has a tendency to eschew rigorous theory building. Such a tendency makes the identification of similar theoretic perspectives a difficult task. This section addresses the task two ways. First, the general theoretic perspectives that can be identified in industrial relations, and the similarity to communication, are examined. Second, because a theory is "a set of statements asserting relationships among classes of variables" (Bowers & Courtright, 1984, p. 13), a brief examination of the variables the two fields use to study certification and decertification campaigns is offered in the hope of adding detail to the comparison.

Theories Employed

Early theory development in industrial relations was described by Somers in 1969:

> Older theories of unionism and labor–management relations have stemmed from the Commons–Perlman tradition in emphasizing the historical development of union structure and union ideology. In a somewhat later tradition theories have grown from analysis of union–management peace and conflict. More recently still, John Dunlop [1958] has presented a model emphasizing the patterns of labor–management rules which develop under the impact of changing technology, market, and sociological environmental factors. (p. ix)

The Dunlop model was based on a systems theoretic perspective.

Systems Theory. Although communication scholars accept systems theory as one of three major perspectives (Cushman, 1977), it plays an even more important role in industrial relations theory. The Dunlop work, which Somers referred to earlier, was one of the watershed pieces in industrial relations theory. In the book entitled *Industrial Relations Systems* (1958) Dunlop established the systems perspective as probably the leading paradigm in industrial relations. Dunlop suggested that an industrial relations system is "not a subsidiary part of an economic system but is rather a separate and distinctive subsystem of the society" (p. 5).

In what communication scholars might see as a systems-based rules perspective, Dunlop (1958) said "an industrial relations system at any one time in its development is regarded as comprised of . . . a body of rules" (p. 7). He also said that:

> The actors in given contexts establish rules for the work place and the work community, including those governing the contacts among the actors in an industrial-relations system. This network or web of rules consists of procedures for establishing rules, the substantive rules, and the procedures for deciding their application to particular situations. The establishment of these procedures and rules—procedures are themselves rules—is the center of attention in an industrial relations system. (p. 13)

Certification and decertification campaigns address existing networks of rules and decide who will have how big a voice in determining what shape future sets of rules will take. A rules perspective is also implicit in most certification and decertification campaign studies, including Getman et al. (1976) and Cooke (1983).

Dunlop's (1958) perspective on industrial relations systems as webs of rules certainly does no violence to modern day rules-oriented communication theorists such as Shimanoff (1980) who defined a rule as "[a] follow-able prescription that indicates what behavior is obligated, preferred, or prohibited in certain contexts" (p. 57). A further analysis of the relation-ship of the rules perspective in industrial relations and communication follows in the final section of this chapter.

Structural Functionalism. That Dunlop's (1958) systems approach is based on a structural functional perspective is shown in his five-page application of structural functionalism to his own analysis (pp. 28–32). In addition, Cooke (1985) identified structure as "a salient feature of all organizations" (p. 235), and went on to analyze how structure affects both formalized documentation and the web of rules, and vice versa.

Cooke (1985) could have been doing a structural functional analysis of current organizational communication research on quality circles when he said that "organizations with worker participation schemes that allow for greater autonomy are likely to enhance worker control over work rules" (p. 236). Cooke could have added that worker participation schemes are formal (and informal) communication networks that are part of the organizational structure, and that such worker participation plans pro-duce recommendations for changes intended to enhance the functioning of the organization that in turn is intended to facilitate achievement of organizational goals.

Other Theoretical Approaches. Beyond a generalized systems theory approach the industrial relations literature shows little consensus on theoretic approaches. Investigations are often undertaken from an eco-nomic "institutionalist" perspective and employ theories that industrial relations has not yet fully tested. Lewin and Feuille (1983) summarized the situation as:

> The absence of a general theory to integrate research efforts in the field is well recognized . . . some of the leading theories of union formations, collec-tive bargaining, and the union impact on management remain those con-structed by institutionalists decades ago. These theories are subject to major criticisms and have not been rigorously tested, but they remain dominant. (p. 358)

Lewin and Feuille's remarks may explain one communication scholar's observation that:

> Much of the current research in industrial relations centers on the growth and development of unions, union mergers, the structure of union bureaucra-cies, and the effect of strike activities of union members. The bulk of these

studies adopt econometric techniques or historical methods that contribute very little to our understanding of communication. (Putnam, 1985, p. 24)

Putnam correctly assessed the contribution to date of industrial relations research to our understanding of communication. The following analysis of how variables familiar to organizational communication scholars have been employed in existing industrial relations research may, however, contribute to overcoming this limitation.

Overlapping Variables

Variables are operationalized constructs that have been made measurable for the purpose of formal study. Because communication and industrial relations draw from the same contributing disciplines, they employ many of the same constructs and therefore operate with many of the same variables. A summary of some of the attitude and communication variables used in industrial relations follows.

Attitude Variables. Unlike communication, industrial relations employs attitude variables most frequently as independent variables. Examples include attitude toward other people and sensitivity (Sayles, 1969), loyalty (Sayles, 1969), predispositions to vote a particular way in certification elections (Getman et al., 1976), determinants of other predispositions (Getman et al., 1976), effect of attitudes on productivity (Norsworthy & Zabala, 1985), and relationship of attitudes to vote outcomes or union activity (Gordon & Long, 1981; Hamner & Smith, 1978; Kochan, 1979; Lewin & Feuille, 1983; Schriesheim, 1978) among others. Also addressed are the effects of attitudes toward particular referents including unions (Smith & Hopkins, 1979), absenteeism and unrest (Thompson & Borglum, 1973), and union leadership role (Miles & Ritchie, 1968).

Written and Spoken Communication. Written and spoken communication often have been the focus of industrial relations research. One example is the famous Getman et al. study of 1976, which includes letters, written material, posters, leaflets, buttons, bulletin boards, personal conversations, private interviews, informal peer discussions, and superior–subordinate discussions as variables. Participation, mostly verbal, has also been studied as it relates to satisfaction with the union (Glick, Mirvis, & Harder, 1977).
   Several books written with the intent of helping to influence the outcome of certification or decertification elections also focus heavily on written and spoken communications including those by Demaria (1980) for

the management side and Gagala (1983) for the union side. Training manuals for the campaign staffs of both sides also emphasize written and spoken tactics as critically important to the outcome of elections, for example, Kistler's (no date) *The Organizer's Sourcebook* for the union side and Dougherty's (1972) *Union-Free Management: And How to Keep It Free* for the management side. Finally, the National Labor Relations Act and its amendments (Taft–Hartley and Landrum–Griffin) have given rise to an entire body of administrative law that has as one of its primary goals controlling the use of written and spoken communication during certification and decertification campaigns.

Other Variables. Some other familiar variables employed by industrial relations include: promises (Getman et al., 1976); group interaction and peer pressure (Cooke, 1983; Heneman & Sandver, 1983; Imundo, 1975); and deference, affiliation, and dominance (Cangeme, Lynn, & Harryman, 1976). Clearly, communication and industrial relations do use some similar theoretic perspectives and variables, although not always in the same way.

The preceding discussion has investigated areas of overlap between industrial relations and communication research and theory. The next section uses one of the areas of overlap identified earlier, the rules approach, to illustrate how the two fields apply the same theoretic approach in both complementary and noncomplementary ways.

APPLICATION OF RULES THEORY

As discussed earlier, an industrial relations system is partly composed of "a web of rules" (Dunlop, 1958, p. 26). Other industrial relations theorists, including some who do not necessarily describe themselves as systems theorists, have also seen rules as central to theory and research in industrial relations. Cooke (1985), in attempting to provide a foundation for a general theory of industrial relations, provided four axioms for such a theory, three of which specifically mention rules, and summarized his position on rules as follows:

> The common denominator of the employment relationship, therefore, is one where both workers and managers actively seek maximum control over the full set of formal and informal work rules that define and govern the employment relationship. (p. 226)

Rules also play a major role in communication theory. Littlejohn (1983) lauded Pearce and Cronen's (1980) coordinated management of meaning theory, in part because it "attempts to explain basic processes by which individuals mesh their rules for interaction" (p. 308). Cushman and Whiting (1972) took the analysis one step further when they said, "communication is an activity which gains meaning and significance from consensually shared rules" (p. 217).

But the fact that both fields use a rules perspective does not assure us of increased understanding of one based on our understanding of the other. For this we need to see how the two fields apply the rules perspective in similar and different ways.

Similarities in Approach

The notion of rules plays a very broad role in industrial relations and communication. In industrial relations rules include those that cover: (a) compensation in all its forms, (b) the duties and performance expected from workers including rules of discipline for failure to achieve these standards, and (c) rules defining the rights and duties of workers, including new or laid-off workers, to particular positions or jobs (Dunlop, 1958). These three kinds of substantive rules are in addition to the previously mentioned procedural rules for establishing rules and rules for deciding the application of rules in particular situations.

In communication the notion of rules is often applied to how people work out their communicative relationships. But communication scholars also acknowledge rules as a broad notion. In fact, Cushman (1977) talked about a continuum on which can be ordered seven classes of rule behavior. Cushman's notion of rules is probably as broad as that employed in industrial relations.

Some similarity in handling the notion of rules can also be found in the idea that they do not necessarily have to be followed. Shimanoff (1980) spoke of rules as "followable" (p. 39) and discussed negative rule-reflective behavior that occurs when "an actor concludes that a rule is not valuable and s/he chooses to reject and violate it" (p. 134). In industrial relations both employees and management make ongoing decisions about whether to obey this or that rule. Nowhere is the conscious decision to violate rules more obvious than in certification and decertification campaigns.

For example, Demaria (1980), speaking about certification campaigns, said that "history shows that employers often respond to the union's presence by using methods and means that overstep the law" (p. 26). This happens because employers often consciously decide that the economic sanctions for violating the law are so minor that they are an appropriate business expenditure if the cost of collective bargaining is rendered less likely as a result. Industrial relations scholars recognize that treating formal laws as mere rules (followable, or not) is so frequent that they sometimes include the frequency of violation as data in their studies. For example, Getman et al. (1976) reported that "of the thirty-one elections studied, the employer was found to have engaged in unlawful campaigning in twenty-two" (p. 111).

Differences in Approach

Merely sharing some theoretical perspectives and variables does not mean, however, that the two fields can contribute directly to each other in all cases. When one field borrows from another there can be both theoretic and methodological pitfalls. Jablin (1980) warned of precisely this problem:

> Given the complexities of human communication and man-made communication systems, an eclectic orientation to the study of organizational communication appears appropriate and equivalent to the nature of the phenomenon being investigated. However, when the field adopts concepts and approaches from other disciplines, it also needs to be cognizant of the theoretical and methodological issues associated with the appropriate application of these tools. (p. 327)

An example of a theoretic pitfall is that assumed theoretic relationships may differ across fields. In industrial relations, for instance, systems and rules are often treated as almost one and the same. A web of rules partially comprises an industrial relations system (Dunlop, 1958). Rules and systems are presented, and therefore presumably investigated, as complementary notions. In communication, however, rules and systems are typically presented as two entirely different perspectives. Cushman (1977) said, "three potentially fruitful perspectives for the scientific development of human communication theory are those of laws, systems, and rules" (p. 30), while Littlejohn (1983) called rules and systems different general theories and covered them in two separate chapters.

Clearly, the two fields deal with the same theoretic perspective, that of rules, very differently with respect to another major theoretic perspective, systems. This kind of difference is potentially harmful if communication scholars were to simply transpose insights that industrial relations might offer about rules into communication studies. On the other hand, such differences are potentially beneficial if, for example, communication scholars find a way to use the seeming synthesis of rules and systems in industrial relations to broaden our own understanding of the relationship between these two perspectives.

An example of a methodological pitfall is that even the same theoretical perspective interpreted or operationalized in different ways can produce significantly different results. So Littlejohn's (1983) warning that "a multitheoretical approach is necessarily a multimethods approach" is important in light of the discussion earlier which established that both industrial relations and communication are multitheoretical fields. There are therefore two sets of methodologies meeting when one attempts to borrow from the other.

CONCLUSION

This chapter sought to provide an introduction to the multidisciplinary field of industrial relations from a communication theory perspective and to help provide some anchor points with which to "fit" that field to communication. No attempt was made to be exhaustive but several common variables were identified and theoretical perspectives common to both fields were discussed.

Communication scholars may wish to apply their own methodological insights and theoretical orientations to industrial relations research. Or, they may wish to apply existing industrial relations research to ongoing communication research projects. In either case, communication scholars will find a great degree of overlap between the fields, but would be well advised to be careful because the two fields may apply the same concepts differently.

Within these limitations, however, lies a potential benefit for applied communication research. Both industrial relations and communication have developed strong bases of applied knowledge, and significant bodies of literature. Developing the requisite understanding of the industrial relations approach might allow communication scholars and practitioners to draw out both new application strategies and new understandings of relations between theoretic perspectives.

REFERENCES

Black, H. M. (1979). *Black's Law Dictionary*. St. Paul, MN: West.

Botan, C. H., & Frey, L. W. (1983). Do workers trust labor unions and their messages? *Communication Monographs, 50*, 233–245.

Bowers, J. W., & Courtright, J. A. (1984). *Communication research methods*. Glenview, IL: Scott, Foresman.

Brock, B. L., Botan, C. H., & Frey, L. W. (1985). The rhetoric of union busting: Analysis of a management manual for union decertification campaigns. *The Michigan Association of Speech Communication Journal, XX*, 51–63.

Cangeme, J. P., Lynn, C., & Harryman, M. E. (1976). Differences between prounion and procompany employees. *Personnel Journal, 55,* 451–53.

Cooke, W. N. (1983). Determinants of the outcomes of union certification elections. *Industrial and Labor Relations Review, 36,* 402–414.

Cooke, W. N. (1985). Toward a general theory of industrial relations. In D. B. Lipsky (Ed.), *Advances in industrial and labor relations: A research annual* (Vol. 2, pp. 223–252). Greenwich, CT: JAI Press.

Cushman, D. P. (1977). The rules perspective as a theoretical basis for the study of human communication. *Communication Quarterly, 25,* 30–45.

Cushman, D. P., & Whiting, G. C. (1972). An approach to communication theory: Toward a consensus on rules. *Journal of Communication, 22,* 217–238.

Daly, J. A., & Korinek, J. T. (1982). Organizational communication: A review via operationalization. In H. H. Greenbaum & R. L. Falcione (Eds.), *Organizational communication: Abstracts, analysis and overview* (Vol. 7, pp. 11–46). Beverly Hills: Sage.

Demaria, A. T. (1980). *How management wins union organizing campaigns.* Englewood Cliffs, NJ: Prentice-Hall.

Dougherty, J. L. (1972). *Union-free management: And how to keep it free.* Chicago: Dartnell.

Dunlop, J. T. (1958). *Industrial relations systems.* Carbondale, IL: Southern University Press.

Gagala, K. (1983). *Union organizing and staying organized.* Reston, VA: Reston Publishing.

Getman, J. G., Goldberg, S. B., & Herman, J. B. (1976). *Union representation elections: Law and reality.* New York: Russell Sage.

Glick, W., Mirvis, P, & Harder, D. (1977). Union satisfaction and participation. *Industrial Relations, 16,* 145–151.

Gordon, M. E., & Long, L. N. (1981). Demographic and attitudinal correlates of union joining. *Industrial Relations, 20,* 306–311.

Hamner, W. C., & Smith, F. J. (1978). Work attitudes as predictors of unionization activity. *Journal of Applied Psychology, 63,* 415–421.

Heneman, H. G., & Sandver, M. H. (1983). Predicting the outcome of union certification elections: A review of the literature. *Industrial and Labor Relations Review, 36,* 537–559.

Imundo, L. V. (1975). Why federal employees join unions. *Journal of Collective Negotiations, 4,* 319–328.

Jablin, F. N. (1980). Organizational communication theory and research: An overview of communication climate and network research. In D. Nimmo (Ed.), *Communication yearbook 4* (pp. 327–347). New Brunswick, NJ: Transaction.

Kistler, A. (no date). *Organizer's sourcebook.* Alan Kistler chairman of eleven-member committee. AFL–CIO national headquarters.

Kochan, T. A. (1979). How American workers view labor unions. *Monthly Labor Review, 102,* 15–22.

Lawler, J. J. (1987, May). *Theory and research in industrial relations: The analysis of union growth and decline.* Paper presented to the International Communication Association Convention, Montreal.

Lewin, D., & Feuille, P. (1983). Behavioral research in industrial relations. *Industrial and Labor Relations Review, 36,* 341–360.

Littlejohn, S. W. (1983). *Theories of human communication* (2nd ed.). Belmont, CA: Wadsworth.

Miles, R. E., & Ritchie, J. B. (1968). Leadership attitudes among union officials. *Industrial Relations, 8,* 108–117.

Norsworthy, J. R., & Zabala, C. A. (1985). Worker attitudes, worker behavior, and productivity in the U.S. automobile industry, 1959–1976. *Industrial and Labor Relations Review, 38,* 544–557.

Pearce, W. B., & Cronen, V. (1980). *Communication action and meaning.* New York: Praeger.

Putnam, L. L. (1985). Collective bargaining as organizational communication. In P. K. Tompkins & R. McPhee (Eds.), *Organizational communication: Traditional themes and new directions* (pp. 129–148). Beverly Hills: Sage.

Sayles, L. (1969). Industrial relations and organization behavior: Parent and child? In G. S. Somer (Ed.), *Essays in industrial relations theory* (pp. 123–136). Ames, IA: Iowa State University Press.

Schriesheim, C. A. (1978). Job satisfaction, attitude toward unions, and voting in a union representation election. *Journal of Applied Psychology, 63,* 548–52.

Shalev, M. (1985). Labor relations and class conflict: A critical survey of the contributions of John R. Commons. In D. B. Lipsky (Ed.), *Advances in industrial relations: A research annual* (Vol. 2, pp. 319–363). Greenwich, CT: JAI Press.

Shimanoff, S. B. (1980). *Communication rules: Theory and research.* Beverly Hills: Sage.

Smith, R. L., & Hopkins, A. H. (1979). Public employee attitudes toward unions. *Industrial and Labor Relations Review, 32,* 484–495.

Somers, G. G. (Ed.). (1969). *Essays in industrial relations theory.* Ames, IA: Iowa State University Press.

Thompson, D. E., & Borglum, R. P. (1973). A case study of employee attitudes and labor unrest. *Industrial and Labor Relations Review, 27,* 74–83.

U.S. Bureau of the Census, (1987). *Statistical abstract of the United States 1988.* Washington, DC: U.S. Government Printing Office.

COMMUNICATION AND NEGOTIATION

4

DEANNA F. WOMACK
Harvard University

Applied research on communication in the field of negotiation is in its infancy according to Smith's (1988) description: "[Applied research] explores theoretical relationships for the purpose of understanding and solving problems related to everyday communicative actions and interactions" (p. 182). Although communication researchers have frequently used instruments associated with such applied communication methods as survey research, their investigations have been conducted primarily in laboratory settings with student participants. As would be expected of research in a relatively new area, almost all the communication research in negotiation has been conducted with two-party negotiations rather than with larger formats that might lead to coalition formation and related complications. As with any basic research, investigators have attempted to describe communication patterns typical of various types of negotiations and to explore the relationships between key communication variables that affect negotiation. Because the study of communication in negotiation is relatively recent, such an emphasis seems appropriate. Few researchers have attempted to make practical generalizations or to find implications for communicating during the negotiation process. However, implications for negotiators may be drawn from some contemporary communication research that has no explicit applied focus, and three lines of applied communication research have been developed by scholars studying negotiation in professional contexts.

THE ROLE OF COMMUNICATION
IN NEGOTIATION

As a joint decision-making process (Pruitt, 1981), negotiation is governed by shared formal and informal rules negotiated by the bargainers. After the rules have been determined, the bargainers cooperate within those rules in order to achieve some goal, often to gain a competitive advantage over the other bargainer (Schelling, 1960). As a conflict management process, negotiation emphasizes the exchange of proposals by parties in order to reach a joint settlement (Putnam & Poole, 1987). Communication during negotiation may also involve tacit bargaining (Putnam & Poole, 1987; Schelling, 1960; Walton & McKersie, 1965). Verbal and nonverbal communication constitutes the fabric of negotiations. "More specifically, communication undergirds the setting and reframing of goals; the defining and narrowing of conflict issues; the developing of relationships between disputants and among constituents; the selecting and implementing of strategies and tactics; the generating, attacking, and defending of alternative solutions; and the reaching and confirming of agreements" (Putnam & Poole, 1987, p. 550). Communication, then, is central to the bargaining process, whether bargaining occurs as an institutionalized form of conflict resolution such as collective bargaining, or whether it involves negotiating marketing agreements, legal contracts and settlements, or managing inter and intragroup or interpersonal disputes. This chapter follows the common practice of treating *negotiation* and *bargaining* as equivalent terms (Putnam & Poole, 1987).

OVERVIEW OF RESEARCH
IN NEGOTIATION COMMUNICATION

Early Experimental Approaches

The motivation behind negotiation research has always been practical: to predict settlement points and to identify strategies and tactics that will allow parties to achieve their goals in negotiation. The mathematical theory of negotiated games (Luce & Raiffa, 1957) was designed to predict just such outcomes, but early game theory experiments usually precluded communication or investigated it as the absence or presence and use of communication channels (Deutsch & Krauss, 1960, 1962; Krauss & Deutsch, 1966; Siegel & Fouraker, 1960). In fact, the Deutsch and Krauss (1960, 1962; Krauss & Deutsch, 1966) trucking game studies demonstrated that "the mere availability of communication channels provides no guarantee that they will be used or used effectively" (Rubin & Brown, 1975, p. 92). Results indicated that even when the opportunity for communication was present, bargainers communicated infrequently and used communication to threaten or intimidate each other rather than to cooperate (Deutsch & Krauss, 1962).

Difficulties in Conducting Negotiation Communication Research

Several difficulties are inherent in drawing conclusions about negotiation effectiveness from the early research. First, messages serve multiple functions and are generated in response to a particular context (Putnam & Poole, 1987). Messages are simultaneous attempts to convey information and to influence the other party's interpretations and future actions (Donohue, Diez, & Stahle, 1983). Thus message strategies are interdependent and should be studied as such. However, messages have typically been treated as independent variables (Putnam & Jones, 1982b). In addition, some types of negotiation serve a ritual function (i.e., collective bargaining; Bullis & Putnam, 1985); bargainers may use the negotiation process merely to inform the other side about offers or to posture (Colosi, 1983). Another complication revealed by empirical research is that negotiators may base their responses more on directives from their constituents than on their counterparts' bargaining strategies (Roloff & Campion, 1987; Tjosvold, 1977). Particular negotiation outcomes such as impasse can become a bargaining strategy designed to influence future negotiations (Theye & Seiler, 1979). Perhaps the major difficulty in studying negotiation communication is that the same utterance may perform multiple functions and lead toward multiple goals simultaneously (Putnam & Poole, 1987).

Special Problems in Negotiation Communication

The rather discouraging results of Deutsch and Krauss (1962) and the recent focus of communication scholars on conflict and negotiation have led to attempts to overcome the dysfunctional aspects of negotiation communication identified by Deutsch (1969):

> Communication between the conflicting parties is unreliable and impoverished. The available communication channels and opportunities are not utilized or they are used in an attempt to mislead or intimidate the other. Little confidence is placed in information that is obtained directly from the other; espionage and other circuitous means of obtaining information are

relied upon. The poor communication enhances the possibility of error and misinformation of the sort which is likely to reinforce the preexisting orientations and expectations toward the other. (p. 12)

Deutsch noted that the competitive nature of many negotiation situations constrains open and effective communication. Although this chapter presents implications of current negotiation research related to three goals of bargainers—distributive goals (maximize individual gains and minimize losses), integrative goals (maximize joint gains), and settlement goals (to reach some settlement and avoid impasse) (Walton & McKersie, 1965)—it does not repeat other reviews of the basic research in negotiations (i.e., Rubin & Brown, 1975) or in negotiation communication (see Putnam, 1985; Putnam & Jones, 1982b; Putnam & Poole, 1987, for reviews of the negotiation communication findings). Instead, the focus is on implications that may be drawn from current basic research conducted with high external validity or from applied research.

EFFECTIVE NEGOTIATION COMMUNICATION

It seems evident that effective negotiation communication must be defined situationally. Negotiation effectiveness can only be determined contextually, with regard to a goal, and it differs with different perspectives. What one party deems effective, the other might not, because the payoff structure of many negotiations precludes both parties' completely accomplishing their goals. In some contexts (e.g., international relations) the goal might be merely to find some settlement acceptable to both sides. A goal often cited in environmental negotiations is the benefit of the public or community. Effectiveness might also imply finding a lasting settlement that will need to be renegotiated only infrequently or reaching a settlement without the need to involve a third party as mediator or arbitrator. Effectiveness might also be achieved if satisfactory interpersonal or business relationships between the negotiating parties are maintained, regardless of outcome. Effectiveness in achieving distributive goals involves maximizing profits or outcomes for one side. Maximizing the parties' joint payoff would reflect effective attainment of an integrative goal. From the radical humanist perspective, effectiveness consists of "the degree of freedom rather than constraint imposed on the actors by the reified structures which result from their own social construction of reality" (Bullis & Putnam, 1985, p. 19). Bullis and Putnam (1985) reported a negotiation between teachers and school board in which teachers were quite satisfied with the negotiation outcome, yet could have obtained higher payoffs. Thus, satisfaction may result from a situation in which negotiators underestimate their ability to achieve the majority of their goals. For this reason, Bullis and Putnam (1985) argued that multiple indications of effectiveness should be used.

Following Walton and McKersie (1965), the communication research on negotiation is presented as related to three types of goals: distributive (emphasizing outcomes for oneself), integrative (emphasizing outcomes for all parties), and settlement goals (leading to some settlement acceptable to all sides but not necessarily equally beneficial or acceptable). Greenhalgh, Gilkey, and Pufahl (1984) indicated that distributive goals are most appropriate for negotiations in which the parties are relatively independent of each other. There is little need to maintain an ongoing relationship and little cost in damaging interpersonal relations. Negotiations between parties who are relatively dependent on each other and who will continue to do business with each other in the future usually involve integrative goals. Putnam and Poole (1987) noted that most negotiations involve both distributive and integrative bargaining goals. Finally, a section summarizing effective communication characteristics across the various goals is presented.

COMMUNICATION DESIGNED TO ACHIEVE DISTRIBUTIVE GOALS

Effective Communication Behaviors

Putnam and Poole (1987) summarized the empirical research related to communication in distributive bargaining: Distributive negotiations are characterized by deceptive arguments, few concessions, and lengthy negotiations (Gruder, 1971). Negotiators mask their true intents and needs by using linguistic codes, exaggerating emotions and demands, and exhibiting conflicting verbal and nonverbal cues (Lewicki & Litterer, 1985). Threats, put-downs, irrelevant arguments, commitments, demands, blaming statements, and bluffs are common in distributive negotiation (Lewicki, 1983; Putnam & Jones, 1982b; Walton & McKersie, 1965). Inexperienced negotiators who used tactics with greater attacking power, who made high initial offers and refused to concede (Donohue, 1981a), and who used greater firmness more consistently had higher payoffs than their opponents who did not use such tactics (Donohue, 1981b). This finding is consistent with game theory research results on the effect of concession patterns on negotiator payoff (Pruitt, 1981; Rubin & Brown, 1975).

Distributive negotiators use threats, rejections, requests for information, and attacking arguments as offensive maneuvers; defensive maneuvers include demands, retractions, commitments, and self-bolstering arguments (Donohue 1981a, 1981b; Putnam & Jones, 1982a; Putnam & Poole, 1987). While attacking, negotiators use linguistic behaviors such as disclaimers, hedging, omissions, and vague language to project an image of strength. Negotiators defend against attacks by using language forms such as retractions, corrections, qualifiers, and warnings (Borah, 1963; Brown, 1968; Putnam & Poole, 1987). Negotiators can reduce the use of distributive tactics by increasing the parties' mutual dependence (Bacharach & Lawler, 1980) or by verbally emphasizing it in negotiations (Beisecker, 1970).

Bargainers develop distributive issues by adding facts and accentuating their positions (Putnam & Bullis, 1984; Putnam & Poole, 1987). Using questions to elicit information from the other party is more effective than demanding information because of the implied obligation to answer the question (Donohue & Diez, 1983; Putnam & Poole, 1987).

Problematic Communication Behaviors

Research indicates that bluffs are an effective but risky tactic (Putnam & Poole, 1987). Although bluffs may increase a negotiator's payoffs, they can also cause the opponent to "lose face." If bluffs embarrass the opponent, they can escalate the level of conflict and cause the opponent to be more unyielding, thus resulting in lower payoffs for the bluffer than might have been achieved without the bluff (Lewicki, 1983). Bluffs are especially likely to escalate conflicts concerned with value issues (Lewis & Pruitt, 1971; Pruitt & Lewis, 1975). Increasing face-to-face oral communication between negotiators reduces their tendencies to bluff (Crott, Kayser, & Lamm, 1980). Thus, negotiators who wish to bluff should limit face-to-face encounters; negotiators who wish to minimize bluffs should maximize the use of face-to-face negotiating sessions.

Some strategies and tactics have been identified as dysfunctional in distributive negotiations. These include making a high number of concessions (regardless of relative advantage) (Donohue, 1981a) and reciprocating aggressive strategies with aggressive strategies, which may provoke a conflict spiral leading to impasse (Donohue, Diez, & Hamilton, 1984; Putnam & Jones, 1982a; Putnam & Poole, 1987).

Applied Research in Legal Negotiations

Most of the applied research focusing on negotiation communication has been conducted by scholars in professional schools. Gerald Williams (Williams, 1983; Williams, England, Farmer, & Blumenthal, 1977) investigated effective communication in legal negotiations in order to draw implications for training attorneys. Using interviews, surveys, and video-taped simulated negotiations, Williams (1983) identified three clusters of traits related to effective negotiators. The negotiators were divided into those using cooperative (65%) and aggressive styles (24%); the 11% of attorneys who did not cluster into cooperative or aggressive styles exhibited no particular pattern of traits. Then negotiators exhibiting each of the two styles were subdivided into groups reflecting three levels of effectiveness, ineffective, average, and effective. Descriptions of goals for aggressive attorneys were consistent with those identified above for distributive negotiations.

Ineffective Aggressive Attorneys.   Williams (1983) found that, whereas both aggressive and cooperative attorneys were effective and shared some characteristics, they also differed. Ineffective aggressive negotiators were characterized as irritating and frequent complainers. They were unsure of the value of the case, used bluffs and threats, were unwilling to share information, refused to move from their positions, and exhibited socially undesirable behavior. These attorneys showed no concern about how the other negotiator might look to his or her client. They were rude, emotional, quarrelsome, hostile, obstructive, and disinterested in the needs of the opposing client and attorney. Their counterparts perceived their goals to be maximizing profit for themselves or outmaneuvering the other attorney. Ineffective and effective aggressive attorneys shared only one characteristic: egotism (Williams, 1983).

Effective Aggressive Attorneys.   Effective aggressive attorneys were described as dominating, forceful, attacking, rigid, and uncooperative. They used threats, took initial positions described as unrealistic by their counterparts, and were willing to stretch the facts. They also carefully observed their opponents, planned their timing and strategies, and revealed information gradually (Williams, 1983). Williams' research showed comparable effectiveness ratings for both aggressive and cooperative attorneys. However, Williams (1983) cautioned that cooperative strategies are more often effective than tough strategies because they produce more favorable outcomes and result in fewer impasses. In fact, Williams' survey revealed that cooperative effectives were unable to settle 16% of their cases before trial, whereas aggressive effectives went to trial twice as often, in 33% of the cases surveyed. Williams (1983) asserted that there are "a substantially greater number of effective attorneys of the cooperative type than of the competitive types" (p. 41).

Cultural Differences in Marketing Negotiations

An additional source of applied communication knowledge is the intercultural marketing research conducted by Graham (1983, 1985) with experienced business people enrolled in executive education programs. Although conducted in the laboratory, the experiment was designed for high external validity. The videotaped marketing negotiations involved Brazilian, Japanese, and U.S. business people bargaining with others of their nationality in their native language during a simulated buyer–seller negotiation; in the initial experiment, the negotiations consisted of 19 American/American, 22 Japanese/Japanese, and 25 Brazilian/Brazilian interactions (Graham, 1983). More recent research involved 18 negotiations, six each in the three conditions noted above; differences in verbal and nonverbal behavior patterns were observed through a process analysis of negotiation transcripts and videotapes (Graham, 1985). Graham's (1983) research is presented here even though he discussed some integrative bargaining goals because the dependent variable in his research was individual payoffs rather than joint outcomes (p. 48). Thus it was likely that individuals sought to maximize individual gains and the bargaining communication would follow a primarily distributive pattern.

American Negotiating Style. As expected, the experiments in the Graham study revealed differences in effective negotiating behaviors in the different cultures. Overall, individual personality and demographic variables had less impact than interpersonal measures such as interpersonal attractiveness, power, and credibility, the types of strategies used, and situational variables such as culture. Contrary to predictions from communication research, negotiators' credibility was not related to their own payoffs for any cultural group (Graham, 1983). Instead, for Americans, deceptive opponents decreased a negotiator's payoff, indicating that Americans could be taken advantage of (Graham, 1983). Americans whose opponents gave more information about themselves achieved higher payoffs than those with nondisclosive opponents. Graham (1983) suggested not that Americans should withhold information to lower the other's payoffs, but that both bargainers ought to reveal more information, resulting in greater payoffs for both.

Brazilian Negotiating Style. The Brazilian negotiating style differed most from the Japanese and American styles. Brazilian bargainers made more extreme opening offers and larger initial concessions. The Brazilian negotiations involved more touching and eye gazing and many more interruptions than American or Japanese negotiations. Brazilians also made fewer promises and commitments, gave more commands, and used the word "no" much more frequently than the other two groups (Graham, 1985). In addition, Brazilians interrupted more than twice as often as the other negotiators and tended to talk simultaneously for extended periods of time. Brazilians, like Americans, tended to give commands in the later negotiation stages (Graham, 1985). In the Brazilian negotiations higher payoffs were related to bargaining power and use of deceptive bargaining strategies (Graham, 1983).

Japanese and American Stylistic Differences. Graham (1985) found little support for propositions put forth by Van Zandt (1970) regarding differences between Japanese and American sales negotiation behaviors. Compared to Americans, Japanese did not ask more questions or make more concessions near the end of negotiations. Americans also did not use aggressive persuasive strategies (i.e., commands) more frequently than Japanese, although Americans did use commands at an earlier stage than Japanese. The use of aggressive persuasive strategies was reserved for Japanese buyers, who used them in later negotiation stages after other strategies had proven ineffective (Graham, 1985). Americans tended to make more moderate initial offers and larger concessions than Japanese. Periods of silence were more characteristic of Japanese than Brazilian or American negotiations (Graham, 1985). Both Japanese and Americans who felt their opponents were interpersonally attractive had lower profits (Graham, 1983). Despite the equal power structure of the game, the buyer or seller role was the strongest predictor of Japanese payoffs, with the buyer having the upper hand.

Recommendations for Bargaining with Americans, Brazilians, and Japanese

Graham (1983) gave advice to practitioners based on the results of his experiment. He suggested that, to maximize individual profits, Americans should encourage their opponents to reveal task-related information. Higher payoffs also result when Americans bargain against opponents who are younger, less experienced, and extroverted. Graham (1983) located the source of foreigners' complaints of "American naivete" in business negotiations in the finding that Americans "can be easily victimized by deceptive opponents" (p. 58). Americans should also be wary of finding the opponent interpersonally attractive.

Graham (1985) concluded that, "The Brazilian bargaining process observed appears to be different from both the Japanese and American style in almost every respect" (p. 92). Because of these differences, Americans might view Brazilians as "very aggressive, pushy, or even rude" (p. 93). In Brazilian negotiations, bargainers who exercise more negotiating power and "who are difficult to size up" receive higher payoffs (Graham, 1983, p. 58). Graham interpreted these results as favoring a hard-sell approach for use with Brazilian negotiators. He also recommended that representatives of firms negotiating in Brazil take special care to establish trusting relationships before negotiating so that deceptive strategies will be identified or inhibited. The research linked deceptive strategies to lower payoffs for Brazilian negotiators (Graham, 1983). Overall, Graham (1985) expected Americans and Japanese to have trouble negotiating with Brazilians because of the vast stylistic differences.

As indicated by much of the research on Japanese negotiations, Graham (1983) found that "the key factor in Japanese business negotiations is the interpersonal relationship determined *before the negotiations*" (p. 58). Role and status relationship rather than information exchange was the primary influence on payoffs in the Japanese negotiations. Graham's (1983) findings also indicate the importance of accurate impression formation and interpersonal communication skills such as putting the opponent at ease for Japanese negotiations.

Although Graham made specific suggestions for negotiating with persons from the different nationalities and he noted the difficulties involved for Americans and Japanese in negotiating with Brazilians, he did not make specific suggestions for overcoming the verbal and nonverbal communication difficulties. He also did not state that he expects Brazilians to have difficulty negotiating with Americans and Japanese (Graham, 1985). There is an additional assumption implicit in his work that the tactics effectively used by someone from one's native culture will be equally effective if used by someone from another culture (Graham, 1983); that is, Americans bargaining with Brazilians will be effective if they use the tactics recommended for use by another Brazilian bargainer. This assumption remains to be tested. Graham (1985) also noted the difficulty of predicting how representatives will adapt or should adapt when faced with someone from a culture with a very different bargaining style. He noted the potential for impasse and difficulties; future research is needed to make specific suggestions for intercultural effectiveness.

COMMUNICATION DESIGNED TO ACHIEVE INTEGRATIVE GOALS

Effective Communication Behaviors

Communication behaviors associated with achieving integrative goals generally appear in sharp contrast to those designed to lead to distributive settlements. Problem solving is generally the recommended approach for achieving an integrative settlement (e.g., Fisher & Ury, 1981). Multiple formal and informal communication channels are used (Lewicki & Litterer, 1985; Putnam & Poole, 1987; Walton & McKersie, 1965). Negotiators attempt to redefine problems, analyze the causes of settlement difficulties, and explore a wide range of mutually acceptable, alternative solutions through maximum sharing of information and disclosure of each party's needs and interests (Fisher & Ury, 1981; Lewicki & Litterer, 1985; Putnam & Poole, 1987). Negotiations using face-to-face, rather than audio or audio-video, channels provide the highest joint outcomes (Turnbull, Strickland, & Shaver, 1976).

It is important to note that Weingart, Thompson, Bazerman, and Carroll (1988), using Donohue's (1981a) coding scheme to analyze buyer–seller negotiation transcripts, found no tactics that were effective across different negotiations. Instead, they argued, "Negotiators' tactical behavior should be flexible and based upon the information obtained during the negotiation" (1988, p. 23). Weingart and her colleagues also found that negotiations with a high number of offers and counter-offers were less effective in achieving integrative outcomes; they believed the frequency of offers substitutes for perspective taking and exchanging information with the other negotiator. They concluded that revealing information about one's interests and engaging in longer question–response chains may lead to higher joint payoffs in integrative negotiations (Weingart et al., 1988).

Effective integrative negotiators listen for both cognitive and emotional content. They drop defensive barriers, which hinder effective listening (Lewicki & Litterer, 1985; Putnam & Poole, 1987). Verbal communication involves exploratory problem solving, arguments that support the other, and acceptances of the other's analysis and proposals (Putnam & Jones, 1982a). Integrative strategies result in negotiations characterized by more reactions from opponents, more offers near the time of settlement, generation of more alternative solutions, and more references to self and others than to the constituency they represent, compared to distributive negotiations (Putnam & Jones, 1982a).

One of the key components of integrative bargaining is generating alternative proposals. Creative proposals are developed when negotiators drop, simplify, and package issues (Gulliver, 1979; Putnam & Poole, 1987). Separating and prioritizing subissues allows negotiators to clarify and simplify points of dispute (Bullis & Putnam, 1985). Putnam and Geist (1985) found that changing the type of claim initially argued (i.e., fact, value, definition, policy) and adding qualifiers to proposals facilitated the formation of new proposals. Putnam, Wilson, Waltman, and Turner (1986) discovered that a longer search process eventually led to the development of creative solutions. In the teachers' collective bargaining negotiation they analyzed, disagreements over definitions and causes of an issue led to harm and disadvantage statements, which were associated with a longer search process than other types of statements (Putnam & Poole, 1987; Putnam, Wilson, Waltman, & Turner, 1986).

On the level of group-wide and organization-wide communication, Putnam and her colleagues examined the role of stories and rituals in integrative bargaining. Fantasy themes promoted the uniting of the teachers and school board against outsiders, whom both perceived as enemies and villains (Putnam & VanHoeven, 1986). Interpretive themes allowed both sides to use their perceptions to find a "scapegoat" to take blame for impasses. Blaming some consensually validated perception of the other party as the reason for negotiation difficulties allowed each side to be tolerant of the other's tactics and to maintain an integrative atmosphere, rather than becoming angry with the other's intransigence (Putnam & VanHoeven, 1986). Using external rather than internal attributions allowed both sides to excuse, forgive, and transcend the other's dysfunctional behavior instead of allowing it to bring negotiations to an impasse or to damage the relationship.

Problematic Communication Behaviors

Bullis and Putnam (1985) found that, although stories and rituals maintained integrative goals, the stories and rituals were also ineffective. They constrained the teachers' thinking about possibilities for behavior and led to the teachers' failure to win outcomes that management had been willing to concede. Thus, from the radical humanist perspective Bullis and Putnam (1985) adopted, the teachers' trust both in their chief negotiator and in their stories and rituals was dysfunctional because the stories and rituals severely curtailed the teachers' freedom to explore a wider range of negotiation tactics and strategies. The chief negotiator's interpretation of reality was enacted with few challenges (Bullis & Putnam, 1985). These findings underscore the role of conflict in generating alternative solutions and avoiding groupthink (Janis, 1972).

Effective and Ineffective Cooperative Attorneys

As with aggressive negotiators, Williams' (1983) research on effective cooperative negotiators revealed some differences between effective and ineffective cooperative negotiators. Descriptions of goals for cooperative attorneys were consistent with those identified previously for integrative negotiations (Williams, 1983). Although both effective and ineffective cooperative attorneys were described as experienced, fair, personable, trustworthy, and ethical, ineffective cooperative attorneys tended to be "milquetoasts" (Williams, 1983, p. 41). Ineffective cooperative attorneys apparently lacked confidence and vacillated between being patient and forgiving, and demanding and argumentative. They were described as idealistic, a characterization that Williams (1983) believed indicated their "lack of versatility, adaptability, creativity, and wisdom" (p. 35).

On the other hand, effective cooperative negotiators were described as courteous, tactful, sincere, and trustworthy. They were fair-minded, adopting "realistic" opening positions, were willing to share information, and probed the opponent's position. They avoided the use of threats. Williams (1983) believed that the majority of effective attorneys adopt a cooperative style. As noted earlier, the research revealed that effective *competitive* attorneys had twice the percentage of impasses of effective *cooperative* attorneys (Williams, 1983).

COMMUNICATION DESIGNED TO ACHIEVE SETTLEMENT GOALS

Effective Communication Behaviors

Lewis and Fry (1977) examined verbal and nonverbal behavior associated with negotiation settlements. They found that dyads who reached impasse engaged in nonverbal behaviors similar to those of dyads who achieved a settlement, but that those behaviors were perceived differently (Putnam & Jones, 1982a). "For the impasse groups, the type of negotiation influenced the display and meaning of cues in bargaining interaction" (Putnam & Jones, 1982a, p. 273). Dyads who reached agreement exhibited similarities regardless of whether the negotiation was designed to be integrative or distributive. Agreement dyads offered proposals even after one acceptable settlement had been discovered. They used strategies including avoiding disruptive negotiation tactics, initiated many proposals designed to provide the same payoff before lowering their aspirations, and elicited their counterparts' reactions to statements. Important nonverbal behavior differences consisted of nonthreatening behaviors such as avoiding direct eye gaze and maintaining physical distance (Lewis & Fry, 1977; Putnam & Jones, 1982a).

Donohue (1981a) concluded that settling a distributive negotiation requires a more complementary style of interaction in which one negotiator submits to the other's attacks. Thus, if any settlement at all is more valuable than reaching an impasse, a negotiator may need to concede when the balance of power favors the opponent or when the opponent does not need the settlement as much as the negotiator. This suggestion is consistent with several studies that indicate settlements are more likely when negotiators respond to offensive tactics by using defensive tactics or integrative behaviors (Donohue, 1981b; Donohue, Diez, & Hamilton, 1984; Putnam & Jones, 1982a).

Problematic Communication Behaviors

Several researchers have confirmed that matching tactics frequently results in an impasse. Countering defensive maneuvers with defensive tactics or offensive maneuvers with offensive tactics leads to escalation of the conflict, and frequently to impasse (Donohue, Diez, & Hamilton, 1984; Putnam & Jones, 1982a; Putnam & Poole, 1987). Williams' (1983) research reported earlier indicated that effective attorneys adopting an aggressive strategy had twice the percentage of cases going to trial as that of effective attorneys employing a cooperative strategy. Although aggressiveness does not constitute ineffectiveness (Williams, 1983), distributive bargaining tactics may lead to more impasses for reasons previously noted in the section on distributive goals.

Implications for Effective Communication Behaviors

The implication that should be drawn from the research presented earlier is that intense emotional tone affects the interpretation of verbal and nonverbal behaviors. Negotiators who wish to avoid impasse must make sure that their nonverbal behavior is interpreted by the opponent in ways that will facilitate agreement, especially if their behavior might be interpreted as aggressive. Putnam and Jones concluded from their research that "escalating conflicts appear to evolve from the *mismanagement of distributive communication* . . ." (1982a, p. 191). From the point of view of achieving a settlement and avoiding impasse, the most effective means of managing conversation patterns is to avoid reciprocal patterns of offensive tactics.

COMMUNICATION DESIGNED
TO MEDIATE DISPUTES

Like negotiators, mediators use a variety of communication strategies to accomplish their purpose, to help negotiators resolve an impasse, and to reach a solution acceptable to both. Because mediators are impartial (Douglas, 1962) and usually become involved only after the parties have experienced difficulty in forming their own solution, much of the mediator's task involves giving the parties a new perspective, repairing relationships, and generating new alternatives, behaviors similar to those involved in integrative negotiations.

Mediator Strategies and Tactics

Putnam and Poole (1987) identified four groups of mediator strategies and tactics: procedural, reflexive, directive, and nondirective. Reflexive tactics such as humor regulate the emotional tone of the negotiations. Directive strategies, such as proposing a particular settlement, involve more intervention into the negotiation content than nondirective strategies such as controlling information flow and clarifying misunderstandings (Putnam & Poole, 1987). Research indicates that reflexive tactics are most effective in facilitating collaboration (Carnevale & Pegnetter, 1985). Other investigators have found that directive tactics are related to achieving a settlement (Donohue, Allen, & Burrell, 1988; Kolb, 1983; Womack, 1985). Research suggests that this effectiveness is due to mediator interruptions used "to reframe arguments, to create alternatives, and to develop new interpretations of proposals" (Putnam & Poole, 1987, p. 572).

CHARACTERISTICS OF EFFECTIVE MEDIATORS

Donohue and his colleagues conducted a program of applied communication research designed to identify characteristics of effective mediators, those whose mediations end in agreement (Donohue, Allen, & Burrell, 1985, 1988). Previous research had revealed that disputants exercised more cooperative problem solving with mediators who exercised more control in structuring the process (McGillicuddy, Welton, & Pruitt, 1987). Donohue and his colleagues believed that without control over the process, divorce mediators involved in highly emotional disputes may be limited in their flexibility and so unable to use reframing strategies and requests effectively. Analysis of negotiation transcripts revealed that mediators in negotiations that reached agreement intervened more after integrations; mediators in negotiations in which there was no settlement intervened more after attacks. The authors indicated that controlling the process through structuring strategies created timing opportunities for the mediator (Donohue, Allen, & Burrell, 1985). The clear implication of this research is that controlling the mediation process is essential to help negotiators reach a settlement. It is unclear whether the timing of interventions has an effect separate from the effect of structuring strategies.

Karim and Pegnetter (1983) conducted field research at a more macro level by analyzing data from a questionnaire sent to participants in actual collective bargaining disputes involving mediators. They found that variables associated with settlement differed for management and union negotiators. Management negotiators in disputes that were settled reported that they were affected by discussing the cost of disagreement and by the mediator's expertise, trust, impartiality, and face-saving strategies. On the other hand, union negotiators were most responsive to the neutrality and confidentiality of the mediator and to the mediator's role in structuring negotiations and changing expectations (Karim & Pegnetter, 1983).

Taken together, the research on effective mediator communication indicates that structuring communication is a paramount mediation skill. Interventions that allow the mediator to build on integrating statements to move the negotiation forward are more effective than those that follow attacks. Directive tactics are more effective than nondirective ones in promoting settlements. Strategies designed to manage the affective tone of negotiations lead to greater cooperation between the parties. The aforementioned conclusions are supported by research from various trends in the literature; however, it is important to note differences between the types of negotiations investigated. Divorce mediation, with and without custody issues, and collective bargaining provide quite diverse contexts for mediation. Further research is needed to explore precisely what similarities and differences there are in effective mediation communication skills for different negotiating environments. Donohue, Allen, and Burrell (1988) noted the difficulty of drawing causal inferences from actual transcripts because of contaminating variables such as difficulty of the cases. Laboratory research similar to that of Williams (1983) and Graham (1983, 1985) would be useful for isolating settlement strategies leading to mediator effectiveness.

CHARACTERISTICS OF EFFECTIVE NEGOTIATORS

Implications of the early applied negotiation research have tended to be confirmed through applied investigations. For example, Reiches and Harral (1974) observed that, "Successful negotiators may exhibit an awareness of an interactive, rather than a linear, view of the communication process" (p. 43). The applied research of Williams (1983) in legal negotiations bears out this statement. He believed that one of the most important characteristics shared by effective negotiators of different styles is skill "in reading their opponent's cues. This refers not only to the ability to judge an opponent's reactions in negotiating situations, but to affirmatively learn from the opponent" (Williams, 1983, p. 29).

Williams (1983) discovered six characteristics common to effective ne-gotiators using either aggressive or cooperative strategies. Both types of negotiators were prepared on the facts and on the law, were effective trial attorneys (i.e., had a real threat potential if the case went to court), and took satisfaction in using their legal skills. In addition, both groups were self-controlled and observed legal etiquette and courtesies. Both groups were viewed as trustworthy, honest, and ethical, although these charac-teristics rank in the top 10 descriptors in terms of priority for cooperative negotiators but in the bottom 10 for competitive negotiators. In comparing the two groups, Williams commented on their experience and the limita-tions imposed by their realism, rationality, and analytical skills. "They mean more than the idea of 'thinking like a lawyer'; they impose limits on how far a negotiator may credibly go in such things as interpretation of facts, claims about damages and other economic demands, and levels of emotional involvement in the case" (Williams, 1983, p. 28). Williams (1983) identified perceptive reading of the opponent's cues as perhaps the most important common characteristics (see also Lewicki & Litterer, 1985).

It seems reasonable to conclude that sensitivity to the opponent's needs, the needs of the opponent's constituents, the power balances involved, and the parameters of the situation are related to effectiveness for all types of bargainers. This style seems similar to Rubin and Brown's (1985) descrip-tion of bargainers with a high interpersonal orientation. It is important to note that effective bargaining behaviors are culturally bounded. A more aggressive style may be most effective with Brazilians, for example (Graham, 1985). Research on both integrative and distributive negotia-tions with Americans indicates that revealing information results in higher joint payoffs (Graham, 1985; Weingart et al., 1988). Face-to-face channels are recommended. Stories and rituals surrounding negotiations have the potential both to facilitate negotiations and to constrain the parties' flexibility in viewing the situation from many perspectives.

The research on sequences of bargaining behavior is less conclusive. Results from case studies of bargaining patterns need to be replicated or investigated through laboratory experiments such as those suggested previously concerning mediation effectiveness. Apparently inconsistent results that related integrative effectiveness to packaging issues but sepa-rating subissues need further exploration (Putnam et al., 1986). Some conclusions can be drawn with a reasonable degree of confidence. Research reveals that both effective distributive and integrative negotiators create a pattern of questions followed by brief responses through which their opponents reveal information (Donohue & Diez, 1983; Putnam & Poole, 1987). Weingart et al. (1988) found a similar pattern for effective integra-tive negotiations. Longer question–response chains may be effective in achieving distributive goals because they provide information about the other's needs and constraints, and effective in achieving integrative goals when used to explore interests and develop a wide range of alternative solutions. Spiraling cycles of aggressive tactics countered with aggressive responses should be avoided because they tend to lead to impasse.

Although threats are effective in achieving distributive goals, negotiators who use them must have superior perspective-taking skills to determine when the threats might become counter-productive and lead to impasse. They must be sensitive to the needs of the other as well as to their own. Similarly, bluffs may be effective, but may also promote impasse. Patterns of communication interaction that are ineffective for achieving distributive goals are making multiple concessions, which result in lower payoffs, and countering aggressive strategies with aggressive responses, a pattern that may lead to impasse as noted earlier.

Integrative strategies are generally less risky than distributive ones because they lead to higher joint outcomes and to fewer impasses (Williams, 1983). Generating large numbers of creative alternative proposals is a key component of effectiveness in integrative bargaining. Taken as a whole, the research confirms Williams' (1983) suggestion that the effective characteristics of integrative bargainers are more generalizable than those of effective distributive bargainers. Williams' final recommendation was that attorneys analyze their own personalities and bargaining habits, then modify them to conform to the characteristics he discovered for effective negotiators exhibiting similar bargaining behavior. Until more research exploring negotiating communication from a process perspective has been conducted, Williams' advice appears reasonable.

NEW DIRECTIONS

Communication researchers are currently extending theory building in negotiation in several primary directions. Putnam and her colleagues (Putnam & Wilson, 1982; Wilson & Waltman, 1988; Yelsma, 1987), Ross and DeWine (1987, 1988), and Riggs (1983) have developed and tested conflict instruments or typologies for coding communication strategies, tactics, or intentions. These instruments appear to investigate communication behaviors similar to those identified by Williams (1983). Conrad (1985), Greenhalgh et al. (1984), Nadler and Nadler (1987), Shockley-Zalabak (1981) and Shockley-Zalabak and Morley (1984), and Womack (1987) have studied male–female differences in negotiations. Jones' work (1987) on nonverbal communication in negotiation has begun to fill a vital need for theory building (Knapp, Putnam, & Davis, 1988). Practitioners, such as Keltner (1987) writing in the area of mediation, can provide a more applied perspective in guiding future research. A relatively new but fast-growing body of communication literature has also been developing in the area of intercultural negotiations (see, for example, Nadler, Broomer, & Nadler, 1985; Ting-Toomey, 1985). Discourse analysis of negotiations and examination of stories and rituals involving bargaining are two areas of development in communication research reported earlier and designed to examine negotiation from more micro (Donohue and his colleagues) and more macro (Putnam and her colleagues) perspectives than have been used by previous researchers (see, for example, Donohue & Diez, 1983; Donohue, Diez, & Hamilton, 1984; Donohue, Diez, & Stahle, 1983; Putnam & VanHoeven, 1986; Putnam, Wilson, Waltman, & Turner, 1986).

It is surprising that Donohue and his colleagues are pursuing the only truly applied research conducted by scholars identified with the discipline of communication. Although basic research needs to be advanced in the areas noted previously and naturalistic investigations are an advance over the early negotiation experiments that exhibited little external validity, work similar to that of Graham (1983, 1985) and Williams (1983) is sorely needed to provide advice to practitioners and to test theoretical associations or predictions. Designs emphasizing the development of bargaining communication from a processual approach and allowing for causal associations between communication and bargaining outcomes are the primary needs for both basic and applied research in bargaining communication.

For quantitative researchers, a good starting point might be the literature on negotiation styles. Several different instruments have been used for a number of years to train business negotiators (Womack, 1988). Although many researchers believe that a negotiator's approach to conflict differs with the negotiation context, this remains a question that needs to be fully explored empirically. Researchers can at present identify a negotiator's style or predisposition to negotiate in a particular fashion through the self-report instruments available. The next step is to observe a negotiator's style empirically and to relate the observed style or styles both to the reported predispositions and to criteria of negotiation effectiveness. Time series analysis methods would allow researchers to examine how one's cluster of negotiating strategies and tactics changes over time or with different opponents. Methods such as round-robin analysis highlight the elements that are stable in an individual's behavior over time and those that change with different opponents or different types of negotiations. Statistical methods such as multiple regression, specifically two stage least squares, provide highly unbiased ways of relating first-round to second-round data, thus capturing changes in strategies and tactics, and of using these first- and second-round styles to predict negotiation effectiveness. Effectiveness might be measured as payoff to the individual, as joint payoff, as reported individual or joint satisfaction with the outcome, as length of time that an agreement remains in force, or as number of third-party interventions required to maintain the agreement, i.e., number of cases brought before an arbitrator during a labor contract. Each specific measure of effectiveness has strengths and weaknesses. Training practitioners to negotiate is valuable, but to date there have been no empirical explorations of the situations in which styles posited by the different instruments are most effective. In order for styles to be related to negotiation effectiveness, they must first be identified in actual use, not merely through self-reports.

The greatest overall need in the exploration of negotiation styles is to relate negotiation strategies and tactics to specific communication behaviors (Putnam, 1988). The field of nonverbal communication in negotiation is only beginning to be explored, yet nonverbal behavior provides an important set of negotiation cues (Knapp et al., 1988). Nonverbal communication differences may be absolutely critical to effectiveness in intercultural negotiations. Effective listening is another area that communication scholars have long recognized as important, but no one has yet conducted applied research regarding the impact of attending behaviors on negotiation effectiveness. Content analysis of transcripts and/or videotapes is one method that allows for thorough exploration of the very rich data provided in actual negotiations (Graham, 1985). If taping of actual negotiations is not possible, laboratory experiments involving naturalistic settings, ideally with experienced negotiators as participants, would be acceptable so long as care is taken to maximize external validity.

An additional need is the exploration of effectiveness in a wider variety of contexts of negotiation practice. The work by Graham (1983, 1985) in contract negotiations and by Williams (1983) in legal negotiations represents a first step in this direction. Communication researchers should follow their lead and that of Donohue and his colleagues in mediation. As traditional speech communication or communication studies departments encompass new areas such as advertising and public relations, so should communication research investigate negotiation in these areas. An important part of the job of the public relations or advertising account executive involves negotiating financial arrangements and strategic decisions about campaign design and development. No empirical research has yet been conducted in negotiation communication in these contexts. Traditional job areas for negotiators include real estate, insurance and right-of-way negotiations. Although practitioners in these fields have long been trained by communication scholars, no empirical research has been conducted to explore effective communication in these negotiation contexts. The variety of negotiation contexts that provide new and fertile ground for researchers is almost without limit.

The growth of studies of the narrative paradigm and the recent resurgence of interest in interpretive approaches to organizational communication has begun to produce studies of negotiation using these research perspectives. The work of Putnam and her colleagues mentioned earlier provides an example of how researchers might study stories, rituals, and argument in bargaining (Putnam & Bullis, 1984; Putnam & VanHoeven, 1986; Putnam et al., 1986). The need is for scholars to relate the current descriptive research to negotiation effectiveness. In this area also, transcripts and/or videotapes of negotiations as well as methods such as observation, participant observation, and interviews provide very rich data for analysis. One way to analyze such materials is to identify effective and ineffective negotiators independently, then explore differences and similarities in their communication. For example, one might look at the types of claims, warrants, and grounds used by effective and ineffective negotiators in different contexts. Analyzing transcripts or tapes allows researchers to compare issues that were settled with those that were not, in order to identify differences in argumentation in the two cases. The tradition of communication studies of argument should be pursued even more vigorously by communication researchers. The modern twist that applied research demands is the connection between theoretical studies of argument types and bargaining stories and rituals with negotiation outcomes, specifically effectiveness.

Applied study of negotiation is not only an exciting area of research, but one that contains some groundwork on which to build and little "hallowed ground" claimed by giants in the field to limit the possibilities for budding researchers. The area is fertile for researchers using quantitative, qualitative, and interpretive methodologies. It is full of possibilities, both for those who wish to continue ancient traditions such as the study of argumentation and for those who are interested in contemporary research contexts such as public relations, advertising, insurance, and legal communication. Areas long investigated through basic research in business, psychology, and political science have yet to be explored by communication scholars from an applied perspective. There are many interesting questions that need to be asked, much beneficial information to convey to practitioners, much work to be done, and unlimited opportunities for applied researchers to explore the field of negotiation communication.

REFERENCES

Bacharach, S. B., & Lawler, E. J. (1980). *Power and politics in organizations.* San Francisco: Jossey-Bass.

Beisecker, T. (1970). Verbal persuasive strategies in mixed-motive interactions. *Quarterly Journal of Speech, 56,* 149–160.

Borah, L. A. (1963). Effects of threat in bargaining: Critical and experimental analysis. *Journal of Abnormal and Social Psychology, 66,* 37–44.

Brown, B. R. (1968). Face-saving and face-restoration in negotiation. In D. Druckman (Ed.), *Negotiations* (pp. 275–299). Newbury Park, CA: Sage.

Bullis, C. A., & Putnam, L. L. (1985). *Bargaining as social construction of reality: The role of stories and rituals.* Unpublished manuscript, Purdue University, West Lafayette, IN.

Carnevale, P. J. D., & Pegnetter, R. (1985). The selection of mediation tactics in public sector disputes: A contingency analysis. *Journal of Social Issues, 41,* 65–81.

Colosi, T. (1983). Negotiation in the public and private sectors. *American Behavioral Scientist, 27,* 229–253.

Conrad, C. (1985, November). *Gender, interactional sensitivity and communication in conflict: Assumptions and interpretations.* Paper presented at the annual convention of the Speech Communication Association, Denver, CO.

Crott, H., Kayser, E., & Lamm, H. (1980). The effects of information exchange and communication in an asymmetrical negotiation situation. *European Journal of Social Psychology, 10,* 149–163.

Deutsch, M. (1969). Conflicts: Productive and destructive. *Journal of Social Issues, 25,* 7–41.

Deutsch, M., & Krauss, R. M. (1960). The effect of threat upon interpersonal bargaining. *Journal of Abnormal and Social Psychology, 61,* 181–189.

Deutsch, M., & Krauss, R. M. (1962). Studies of interpersonal bargaining. *Journal of Conflict Resolution, 6,* 52–76.

Donohue, W. A. (1981a). Analyzing negotiation tactics: Development of a negotiation interact system. *Human Communication Research, 7,* 273–287.

Donohue, W. A. (1981b). Development of a model of rule use in negotiation interaction. *Communication Monographs, 48,* 106–120.

Donohue, W. A., Allen, M., & Burrell, N. (1985). Communication strategies in mediation. *Mediation Quarterly, 10,* 75–90.

Donohue, W. A., Allen, M., & Burrell, N. (1988). Mediator communicative competence. *Communication Monographs, 55,* 104–119.

Donohue, W. A., & Diez, M. E. (1983, November). *Information management in negotiation.* Paper presented at the annual convention of the International Communication Association, Dallas, TX.

Donohue, W. A., Diez, M. E., & Hamilton, M. (1984). Coding naturalistic negotiation interaction. *Human Communication Research, 10,* 403–425.

Donohue, W. A., Diez, M. E., & Stahle, R. (1983). New directions in negotiation research. In R. W. Bostrom (Ed.), *Communication yearbook 7* (pp. 249–279). Newbury Park, CA: Sage.

Douglas, A. (1962). *Industrial peacemaking.* New York: Columbia University Press.

Fisher, R., & Ury, W. (1981). *Getting to yes.* New York: Penguin.

Graham, J. L. (1983). Brazilian, Japanese, and American business negotiations. *Journal of International Business Studies, 14,* 47–61.

Graham, J. L. (1985). The influence of culture on the process of negotiations: An exploratory study. *Journal of International Business Studies, 16,* 81–96.

Greenhalgh, L., Gilkey, R. W., & Pufahl, S. J. (1984, August). *Effects of sex-role differences on approach to business negotiations.* Paper presented at the annual convention of the Academy of Management, Boston, MA.

Gruder, L. (1971). Relationships with opponent and partner in mixed-motive bargaining. *Journal of Conflict Resolution, 15,* 403–416.

Gulliver, P. H. (1979). *Disputes and negotiations.* New York: Academic Press.

Janis, I. L. (1972). *Victims of groupthink.* Boston: Houghton-Mifflin.

Jones, T. S. (1987, March). *An analysis of gender differences in mediator–disputant interaction for successful and unsuccessful divorce mediation.* Paper presented at the annual Temple University Discourse Conference, Philadelphia, PA.

Karim, A., & Pegnetter, R. (1983). Mediator strategies and qualities and mediation effectiveness. *Industrial Relations, 22,* 105–114.

Keltner, J. W. (1987). *Mediation: Toward a civilized system of dispute resolution.* Annandale, VA: ERIC/SCA.

Knapp, M. L., Putnam, L. L., & Davis, L. J. (1988). Measuring interpersonal conflict in organizations: Where do we go from here? *Management Communication Quarterly, 1,* 414–429.

Kolb, D. M. (1983). Strategy and tactics of mediation. *Human Relations, 36,* 247–268.

Krauss, R. M., & Deutsch, M. (1966). Communication in interpersonal bargaining. *Journal of Personality and Social Psychology, 4,* 572–577.

Lewicki, R. J. (1983). Lying and deception: A behavioral model. In M. H. Bazerman & R. J. Lewicki (Eds.), *Negotiating in organizations* (pp. 68–90). Newbury Park, CA: Sage.

Lewicki, R. J., & Litterer, J. (1985). *Negotiation.* Homewood, IL: Irwin.

Lewis, S. A., & Fry, W. R. (1977). Effects of visual access and orientation on the discovery of integrative bargaining alternatives. *Organizational Behavior and Human Performance, 20,* 75–92.

Lewis, S. A., & Pruitt, D. G. (1971). Orientation, aspiration level, and communication freedom in integrative bargaining. *Proceedings of the 79th Annual Convention of the American Psychological Association, 6,* 221–222.

Luce, R. D., & Raiffa, H. M. (1957). *Games and decisions: Introduction and critical survey.* New York: Wiley.

McGillicuddy, N., Welton, G., & Pruitt, D. (1987). Third-party intervention: A field experiment comparing three different models. *Journal of Personality and Social Psychology, 53,* 104–112.

Nadler, L. B., Broome B. J., & Nadler, M. K. (1985). Culture and the management of conflict situations. In W. Gudykunst, L. Stewart, & S. Ting-Toomey (Eds.), *Communication, culture, and organizational processes* (pp. 87–113). Newbury Park, CA: Sage.

Nadler, M. K., & Nadler, L. B. (1987). The influence of gender on negotiation success in asymmetric power situations. In L. B. Nadler, M. K. Nadler, & W. R. Todd-Mancillas (Eds.). *Advances in gender and communication research* (pp. 189–218). Lanham, MD: University Press of America.

Pruitt, D. G. (1981). *Negotiation behavior.* New York: Academic Press.

Pruitt, D. G., & Lewis, S. A. (1975). Development of integrative solutions in bilateral negotiation. *Journal of Personality and Social Psychology, 31,* 621–633.

Putnam, L. L. (1985). Bargaining as organizational communication. In R. D.

McPhee & P. K. Thompkins (Eds.), *Organizational communication: Traditional themes and new directions* (pp. 129–148). Newbury Park, CA: Sage.

Putnam, L. L. (1988). Communication and interpersonal conflict in organizations. *Management Communication Quarterly, 1,* 293–301.

Putnam, L. L., & Bullis, C. (1984, May). *Intergroup relations and issue redefinition in teachers' bargaining.* Paper presented at the annual meeting of the International Communication Association, San Francisco, CA.

Putnam, L. L., & Geist, P. (1985). Argument in bargaining: An analysis of the reasoning process. *The Southern Speech Communication Journal, 50,* 225–245.

Putnam, L. L., & Jones, T. S. (1982a). Reciprocity in negotiations: An analysis of bargaining interaction. *Communication Monographs, 49,* 171–191.

Putnam, L. L., & Jones, T. S. (1982b). The role of communication in bargaining. *Human Communication Research, 8,* 262–280.

Putnam, L. L., & Poole, M. S. (1987). Conflict and negotiation. In F. M. Jablin, L. L. Putnam, K. H. Roberts, & L. W. Porter (Eds.), *Handbook of organizational communication: An interdisciplinary perspective* (pp. 549–599). Newbury Park, CA: Sage.

Putnam, L. L., & VanHoeven, S. A. (1986, April). *Teacher bargaining as a cultural rite of conflict resolution.* Paper presented at the annual convention of the Central States Speech Association, Cincinnati, OH.

Putnam, L. L., & Wilson, C. E. (1982). Communicative strategies in organizational conflicts. In M. Burgoon (Ed.), *Communication yearbook 6* (629–652). Newbury Park, CA: Sage.

Putnam, L. L., Wilson, S. R., & Waltman, M. S., & Turner, D. (1986, April). *The evolution of case arguments in teachers' bargaining.* Paper presented at the annual convention of the Central States Speech Association, Cincinnati, OH.

Reiches, N., & Harral, H. B. (1974). Argument in negotiation: A theoretical and empirical approach. *Communication Monographs, 41,* 36–48.

Riggs, C. J. (1983). Communication dimensions of conflict tactics in organizational settings: A functional analysis. In R. W. Bostrom (Ed.), *Communication yearbook 7* (pp. 516–531). Newbury Park, CA: Sage.

Roloff, M. E., & Campion, D. E. (1987). On alleviating the debilitating effects of accountability on bargaining: Authority and self-monitoring. *Communication Monographs, 54,* 145–164.

Ross, R. G., & DeWine, S. (1987, May). *Communication messages in interpersonal conflict: Reliability and validity of an assessment tool.* Paper presented at the annual meeting of the International Communication Association, Montreal, Canada.

Ross, R. G., & DeWine, S. (1988). Assessing the Ross-DeWine Organizational Conflict Management Message Style (CMMS). *Management Communication Quarterly, 1,* 389–413.

Rubin, J. Z., & Brown, B. R. (1975). *The social psychology of bargaining and negotiation.* New York: Academic Press.

Schelling, T. C. (1960). *The strategy of conflict.* Cambridge, MA: Harvard University Press.

Shockley-Zalabak, P. (1981). The effects of sex differences on the preference for utilization of conflict styles of managers in a work setting: An exploratory study. *Public Personnel Management, 10,* 289–295.

Shockley-Zalabak, P., & Morley, D. D. (1984). Sex differences in conflict style preferences. *Communication Research Reports, 1*, 28–31.

Siegel, S., & Fouraker, L. E. (1960). *Bargaining and group decision making: Experiments in bilateral monopoly*. New York: McGraw-Hill.

Smith, M. J. (1988). *Contemporary communication research methods*. Belmont, CA: Wadsworth.

Theye, L. D., & Seiler, W. J. (1979). Interaction analysis in collective bargaining: An alternative approach to the prediction of negotiated outcomes. In D. Nimmo (Ed.), *Communication yearbook 3* (pp. 375–394). Newbury Park, CA: Sage.

Ting-Toomey, S. (1985). Toward a theory of conflict and culture. In W. Gudykunst, L. Stewart, & S. Ting-Toomey (Eds.), *Communication, culture, and organizational processes* (pp. 71–86). Newbury Park, CA: Sage.

Tjosvold, D. (1977). Effects of constituent's affirmation and opposing negotiator's self-presentation in bargaining between unequal status groups. *Organizational Behavior and Human Performance, 18*, 146–157.

Turnbull, A. A., Strickland, L., & Shaver, K. G. (1976). Medium of communication, differential power, and phasing of concessions: Negotiating success and attributions to the opponent. *Human Communication Research, 2*, 262–270.

Van Zandt, H. F. (1970, November/December). How to negotiate in Japan. *Harvard Business Review*, pp. 45–56.

Walton, R. E., & McKersie, R. B. (1965). *A behavioral theory of labor negotiations: An analysis of a social interaction system*. New York: McGraw-Hill.

Weingart, L. R., Thompson, L. L., Bazerman, M. H., & Carroll, J. S. (1988). *Tactics in integrative negotiations* (Working Paper No. 22). Chicago: Northwestern University, Kellogg Graduate School of Management.

Williams, G. R. (1983). *Legal negotiation and settlement*. St. Paul, MN: West.

Williams, England, Farmer, & Blumenthal. (1977). Effectiveness in legal negotiation. In H. T. Edwards & J. J. White (Eds.), *The lawyer as a negotiator* (pp. 8–28). St. Paul, MN: West.

Wilson, S. R., & Waltman, M. S. (1988). Assessing the Putnam–Wilson Organizational Communication Conflict Instrument (OCCI). *Management Communication Quarterly, 1*, 367–388.

Womack, D. (1985). The role of argument in mediation styles. *Journal of the American Forensic Association, 21*, 215–225.

Womack, D. F. (1987). Cooperative behavior by female negotiators: Experts or masochists? In L. B. Nadler, M. K. Nadler, & W. R. Todd-Mancillas (Eds.), *Advances in gender and communication research* (pp. 219–233). Lanham, MD: University Press of America.

Womack, D. F. (1988). A review of conflict instruments in organizational settings. *Management Communication Quarterly, 1*, 437–445.

Yelsma, P. (1987, March). *Assessments of organizational conflict management: A comparison of self-reported and observed behaviors*. Paper presented at the annual Temple University Discourse Conference, Philadelphia, PA.

ORGANIZATIONAL COMMUNICATION RESEARCH AND ORGANIZATIONAL DEVELOPMENT

5

GARY L. KREPS
Northern Illinois University

Organizational communication is a relatively young, yet popular area of communication inquiry where scholars study the many ways human communication influences the development and maintenance of social organization. In the past three decades organizational communication has grown into a major interdisciplinary area of social scientific inquiry. Organizational communication has become a popular topic for research, with increasing numbers of theses, dissertations, books, and articles written concerning the subject (Redding, 1985). It has also become an area of curricular growth, with the introduction of undergraduate and graduate courses and programs focusing on organizational communication at most colleges and universities (Redding, 1985). There have also been corresponding development and growth of organizational communication divisions in major communication and management professional associations (Kreps, 1986c).

A major impetus underlying the dramatic growth of organizational communication inquiry is the pragmatic value and relevance of the subject. Organizational communication is an inherently applied area of communication inquiry, where the pragmatic influences of human communication on organizational activities and outcomes are examined. Clearly, organizational communication knowledge can be used to help people understand organizational life and direct organizational activities. This chapter describes one way that organizational communication research has been fruitfully used to help diagnose organizational difficulties and direct organizational innovation. A therapeutic model of organizational communication consultation is described to illustrate the ways interpretive organizational communication inquiry has been used to direct organizational development (Kreps, 1989c).

Organizational communication researchers can help increase organizational effectiveness by using their scholarship to direct organizational development efforts. Data gathered through interpretive organizational communication research can generate insightful information about important issues confronting organizations. By providing such salient information to key organizational representatives, communication researchers can increase these individuals' understanding of their organization, enhancing organizational reflexivity (Kreps, 1989c, 1990). By enhancing organizational reflexivity the communication researcher can help organization members identify relevant organizational constraints and opportunities, and facilitate their development of proactive organizational activities and problem-solving organizational interventions.

ORGANIZATIONAL COMMUNICATION AND ORGANIZATIONAL EFFECTIVENESS

A primary objective of organizational development is to enhance organizational effectiveness (Mitroff & Kilmann, 1975; Schein, 1969, 1985, 1987). Organizational communication researchers are particularly well situated to help promote this objective because the effectiveness of organizing activities is largely dependent on how well organization members are able to communicate and use relevant information (Axley, 1980; Kreps, 1985, 1989b, 1989c; Pace, 1983). By using organizational communication research to evaluate the effectiveness of internal and external communication activities, communication researchers can identify communication difficulties, develop intervention strategies to reduce these problems, and help direct organizational development to promote organizational effectiveness.

The ability to communicate effectively both internally and externally in organizational life enables organization members to create and maintain an ongoing state of organization, balancing interdependent, yet often contradictory, organizational needs for stability and innovation (Kreps, 1985, 1986, 1989b, 1989c). In effective organizations, members use internal channels of communication to elicit cooperation from other members to coordinate the daily accomplishment of organizational activities, promoting organizational stability. Members of effective organizations also use external communication to adapt to and influence their organization's relevant environment, promoting organizational innovation.

The organizational need for adaptation is in striking contrast to the related need for order in organizations. Although organizational change happens naturally, most naturally occurring change is probably not in the best interests of organization because it is usually haphazard and undirected (Cohen, March, & Olsen, 1972; Kreps, 1986c; Weick, 1979, 1987). Innovation is a special type of change that is planned and directed to address specific problems and improve organizations and organizational life. Because of emergent internal and external constraints on and challenges to the accomplishment of organizational goals, there is a constant need for innovative ideas to direct the responses of organization members in addressing these challenges (Berrien, 1976; Kreps, 1986c). Communication researchers can increase organizational effectiveness by using applied organizational communication research to examine internal and external organizational communication, identifying relevant issues, opportunities, and constraints on effective communication, and fueling organizational adaptation and development (Kreps, 1989c; Miller & Sunnafrank, 1984).

A large body of organizational communication research has demonstrated strong positive relationships between the effectiveness of human communication and the effectiveness of organizational outputs and processes (Clampitt & Downs, 1983; Downs & Hain, 1982; Kreps, 1986c). For example, O'Reilly and Roberts (1977) found that active participation in organizational communication networks and effective use of information were related to high work performance ratings. Similarly, Tubbs and Hain (1979) compared two production plants and found that the more productive of the two organizations had higher employee ratings of communication effectiveness. Along the same lines, Tavernier (1980) and Tubbs and Widgery (1978) reported productivity increases in organizations where communication training programs were implemented. Furthermore, evidence suggests that organizations with strong supportive cultures that nurture members and integrate them into the communication activities of organizational life are also likely to promote organizational effectiveness (Kreps, 1985; Peters & Waterman, 1982).

ORGANIZATIONAL DEVELOPMENT AND INTERPRETIVE ORGANIZATIONAL RESEARCH

Organization development (OD) is an applied area of study where data is gathered and theory is built about developing strategies for directing organizational change to increase organizational effectiveness. Beckhard (1969) defined OD as a renewal and change effort that is (a) planned, (b) organization-wide, and (c) managed from the top of the organization, to (d) increase organizational effectiveness through (e) planned interventions in organizational activities using behavioral science methods. An OD effort involves a systematic diagnosis of the problems and constraints facing an organization, the development of a strategic plan for helping the organization rectify the problems diagnosed, and the mobilization of resources to carry out the intervention strategy. The applied communication researcher/consultant can direct OD efforts by gathering the primary data from interpretive organizational communication research and then applying the data to the identification and resolution of organizational problems.

Organizational development specialists can help organization members resolve serious organizational problems by facilitating discovery of their problems and examining the underlying symbolic structures held by key organizational representatives to identify impending organizational constraints and opportunities (Kreps, 1989c; Schein, 1969, 1987). Interpretive research methods are particularly appropriate for identifying the major themes and issues of organizational life by gathering in-depth organizational information for systematically diagnosing organizational problems and identifying intervention strategies for organizational development (Kreps, 1983b, 1989c, 1990; Mitroff & Kilmann, 1975; Wilkins, 1983). Interpretive research can generate revealing data that can provide organization members with reflexive feedback about their organization to help these individuals identify serious organizational problems and facilitate development of problem-solving organizational interventions.

Interpretive methods are a significant departure from more traditional approaches to conducting organizational communication research (Deetz, 1982; Putnam, 1982). Interpretive research is descriptive and ethnographic, designed to fully describe the symbolic structures members create about their organization and the communication behaviors they perform to develop and maintain these collective symbolic structures. Interpretive research is phenomenologically based, in that it strives to gather in-depth descriptions of organizational life from the personal perspectives of organizational representatives. The qualitative, ethnographic nature of interpretive organizational communication research provides richly textured "thick descriptions" of organizational phenomena that enable the researcher to clearly explain in great depth many of the complexities of organizational life (Geertz, 1973; Pacanowsky, 1988; Weick & Browning, 1986; Wilkins, 1983, 1984). Furthermore, by gathering interpretive data representing individual members' perspectives on organizing, the organizational development specialist can attempt to represent the needs of all organization members in intervention efforts, rather than falling prey to the typical consultation ethical dilemma of serving only the needs of management, perpetuating a management bias (Deetz, 1979; Kreps, 1986b).

Interpretive research can be used to identify and examine revealing stories organization members and environmental representatives tell about organizations (Kreps, 1990). The stories recounted about organizational life usually contain important information about key organizational events, values, and logics (Martin & Powers, 1983; Mitroff & Kilmann, 1975; Weick & Browning, 1986). Stories serve as cultural storehouses for organizational intelligence, providing members with information about how they can react to the difficult situations they encounter (Kreps, 1990). Organizational intelligence develops from experience, through preservation of key information about how the organization has responded in the past (Kreps, 1986c; Weick, 1979). Every time organization members cope with a unique situation they learn something new about how to organize. Rather than responding to every situation as though it were totally unique, in effect "reinventing the wheel," members can utilize information gained from past organizational experiences that has been stored in organizational intelligence (Kreps, 1986c; Wilensky, 1977). Stories are a natural repository for such information (Kreps, 1990). Such embedded information is valuable for evaluating organizational performance, identifying unresolved organizational problems, and developing intervention strategies to accomplish system-wide organizational development (Kreps, 1990). Interpretive analysis of organizational stories can facilitate identification of key elements of organizational intelligence for directing organizational development.

THERAPEUTIC CONSULTATION
AND ORGANIZATIONAL DEVELOPMENT

Kreps (1989c) described a therapeutic model of organizational communication consultation that uses the data gathered through interpretive organizational communication research to direct organizational development efforts. According to this model, the therapeutic consultant conducts interpretive communication research to evaluate the current status and health of the organization from the perspective of organization members and key representatives of the organization's relevant environment. By adopting the therapeutic model of organizational consultation, communication researchers can help organization members recognize and utilize the significant issues, symbols, and communication rituals that comprise organizational life to enhance organizational effectiveness.

In this model, the therapeutic organizational consultant gathers data about members' and relevant environmental representatives' interpretations of organizational life by observing their communicative behaviors and rituals, conducting organizational surveys (usually open-ended, unstructured, in-depth interviews), and analyzing key communication texts and artifacts (stories, metaphors, symbols, documents) to identify relevant issues influencing the organization and its relevant internal and external audiences. By reviewing the data generated through interpretive organizational communication research with organizational representatives, the therapeutic consultant can facilitate these members' recognition of the underlying psycho-logics used to create organizational reality and direct organizational behaviors (Kreps, 1986c; Mitroff & Kilmann, 1975). The process of probing, analyzing, and reviewing underlying psycho-logics has potentially powerful therapeutic benefits for the organization and its members because it enables members to review and assess organizational activities and performance (Kreps, 1989c; Schein, 1987). The researcher, like the therapist, attempts to help members use the introspective data generated by organizational communication research to provide insight into organizational phenomena and redirect their activities to better accomplish individual and organizational goals.

Therapeutic communication has been defined in many different ways (Barnlund, 1968; Fuller & Quesada, 1973; Kreps, 1989a; Pettegrew, 1977; Rogers, 1957; Truax & Carkhuff, 1967), yet Barnlund's (1978) definition of therapeutic communication is most useful to the organizational communication researcher/consultant. Barnlund explained that communication is therapeutic when it helps facilitate communicators' development of personal insight or reorientation, and when it helps these individuals enhance their effectiveness and satisfaction with future communication. This approach to therapeutic communication implies that the potential for communicating therapeutically is based upon the person's ability to help others understand themselves more fully, thereby aiding their abilities to direct their communication behaviors to best achieve their needs and goals (Kreps, 1989a). Similarly, in therapeutic organizational communication consultation the communication researcher provides organizational representatives with key information about their organization, based upon data gathered through organizational communication research, increasing their understanding of the organization and its problems to help them develop strategies for improving the effectiveness of the organization.

According to Barnlund's (1978) perspective, feedback is a primary element of therapeutic communication. Feedback is also a key component in the therapeutic model of consultation. Interpretive organizational communication research can generate data that the researcher/consultant can provide to the organization as therapeutic feedback, informing organization members about how the organization is being perceived by relevant others (both internal and external to the organization), and offering a clear picture of the reactions key internal and external organizational audiences have to organizational communication (Kreps, 1989c). The ability to gather information about the critical reactions relevant others have about organizational behaviors enables members to evaluate the relative effectiveness of messages sent and to develop appropriate communication strategies for future interactions to best achieve individual and organizational goals.

Kreps (1989c) describes six successive cyclic phases of the therapeutic model of organizational communication consultation:

1. *Collaboration,* where the consultant and representatives of the organization develop a cooperative plan to examine and solve troublesome organizational problems. The therapeutic consultant must work cooperatively with organization leaders and other members in examining communication data to identify organizational problems and design strategies for intervention (Kreps, 1989c; Schein, 1969, 1985, 1987). By building a cooperative consulting relationship with organization members the consultant can limit resistance and gain support for OD efforts. The best interventions are ones that are jointly developed and implemented by the consultant and members of the organization because organization members will understand and identify with the interventions (Schein, 1969, 1987).

2. *Data gathering,* where interpretive organizational communication research is conducted to examine the problems confronting the organization. In therapeutic consultation traditional quantitative, close-ended, survey-based communication audit research tools should be supplemented with more ethnographic interpretive organizational communication data-gathering strategies. Nondirective, ethnographic forms of data gathering, where researchers are concerned about observing actual communication behaviors, examining communication texts and artifacts, and encouraging organizational representatives to provide full accounts of their perspectives on organizational performance, rather than constraining subjects' responses to limited-response, close-ended measurement scales (as do many typical communication audit instruments), can provide the therapeutic consultant with extremely relevant and revealing data (Deetz, 1982; Koch & Deetz, 1981; Manning, 1979; Martin & Powers, 1983; Pettigrew, 1979; Putnam & Pacanowsky, 1983).

3. *Feedback and diagnosis,* where research results are described to representatives of the organization and jointly interpreted by the consultant and organization members. Organization members need feedback about organizational activities to direct successful innovation within their organizations (Nadler, 1977; Rowe & Boise, 1973). Therapeutic consultation should provide organization members with salient information about

environmental changes and constraints, as well as information about internal organizational conditions to guide organizational innovation. These data are used to increase organizational reflexivity (the ability of organizational decision makers to see the organization as others do) (Kreps, 1986, 1989b, 1989c). Increased reflexivity enables organization members to recognize important performance gaps (Kreps, 1986c, 1989c). "Performance gaps are discrepancies between an organization's expectations and its actual performance" (Rogers & Agarwala-Rogers, 1976, p. 70). By identifying and examining performance gaps that emerge from the data gathered the consultant, in collaboration with organizational representatives, can diagnose the underlying issues that may be causing organizational difficulties.

4. *Intervention planning,* where the researcher and organizational representatives jointly plan strategies for resolving organizational problems by applying data generated through the research to the development of interventions. To direct organizational innovation the therapeutic consultant must first diagnose performance gaps that organizations are experiencing, and then identify slack resources available within organizations to use in implementing innovations. By cooperatively evaluating strategies to address the underlying issues causing organizational difficulties, the consultant and the client organization can develop realistic plans for organizational intervention. The organizational representatives know what has been used in the past, and what kinds of interventions are likely to work well in their particular organization.

5. *Intervention implementation,* where the intervention strategies that were planned are actually put into action within the organization. The therapeutic consultant works closely with the organization to bring intervention plans to life. The consultant helps direct implementation of the intervention strategies that have been jointly planned. Care must be taken to inform and involve all members of the organization in implementing any innovations thereby reducing the natural resistance many organization members may have to changing their job rituals. The more the consultant can prepare organization members for innovations the smoother the implementation of the intervention will be.

6. *Intervention evaluation,* where evaluation data is gathered about the impact of the intervention on the organization to identify the effectiveness of the innovations implemented. The therapeutic consultant wants to gather data about the short-term and long-term effectiveness of organizational interventions. The consultant seeks feedback from members about their reactions to the innovation strategies, evoking suggestions for fine-tuning the interventions. Because the intervention evaluation phase often facilitates recognition of new and potential performance gaps, it can bring the consultant and the organization back full cycle to the first of the

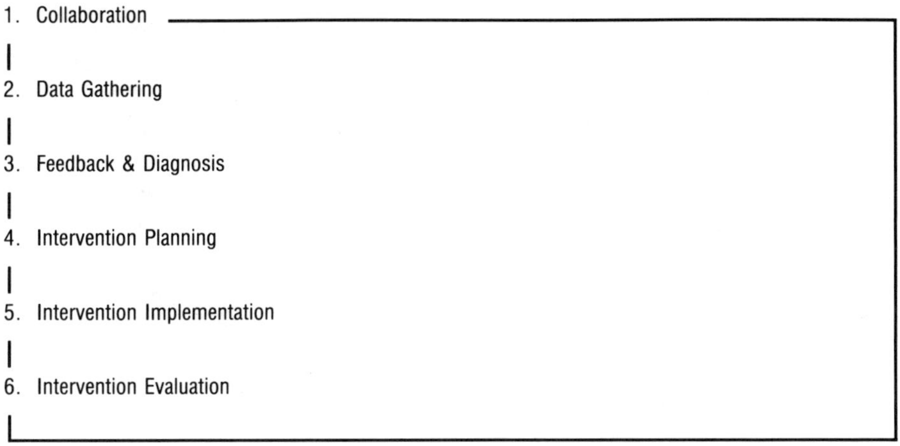

1. Collaboration
|
2. Data Gathering
|
3. Feedback & Diagnosis
|
4. Intervention Planning
|
5. Intervention Implementation
|
6. Intervention Evaluation

FIG. 5.1.   The therapeutic model of consultation.

therapeutic consultation phases, collaboration, by introducing new issues for examination. This is a very healthy outcome of consultation, because it helps the organization develop strategies for continually identifying and evaluating new and potential performance gaps, increasing the organization's ability to resist future performance gaps. The more effective organization members are at identifying and acting upon performance gaps the more proactive their organization will become.

The model should be interpreted as if it were a flow chart, with each phase leading successively to the next phase. The last of the six phases, intervention evaluation, eventually leads the consultant back to the first phase. In evaluating the intervention the consultant may identify new organizational issues and/or shortfalls in the intervention program that should be examined for future organizational development efforts, thus bringing the therapeutic consultation model full cycle in an ongoing process of examination and intervention. The cyclic nature of the therapeutic model of consultation illustrates the perpetual need for innovation in organizational life. (See Fig. 5.1 for a depiction of the Therapeutic Model of Consultation.)

EXAMPLES OF USING RESEARCH TO GUIDE ORGANIZATIONAL DEVELOPMENT

The therapeutic model of consultation is a research process model (describing research and development processes) rather than a content-specific form of intervention (describing specific intervention techniques and strategies). The model can be applied in a wide range of different kinds of organizations to address a virtually limitless array of organizational problems. Four representative organizational development research programs guided by the therapeutic consultation model are briefly described to illustrate the different applications of such research. These applied communication research projects include: (a) a hospital-based nurse retention organizational development research program (Kreps, 1983a, 1986a, 1989c), (b) a corporate organizational socialization research program (Kreps, 1983b, 1990), (c) a rehabilitation center market research program (Kreps, 1988, 1990), and (d) a federal health information dissemination evaluation research program (Kreps, Hubbard, & DeVita, 1988).

The Nurse Retention Program

This organizational development research program was designed to resolve the problem of high turnover of nursing staff at a large urban county hospital by using interpretive organizational communication research to identify the specific problems (performance gaps) nurses encountered in performing their jobs and then using the data gathered to develop strategies for addressing the problems identified. Nursing staff were identified as an important, yet underutilized, source of relevant information in the organization. Therefore, three different research phases were designed and conducted to gather interpretive information from nurses about the hospital: (a) questionnaires examining nurses' perceptions of organizational climate and job satisfaction, (b) in-depth interviews with nurses about their job concerns, and (c) focus group discussions to evaluate the issues identified in the previous two research phases and to develop intervention strategies. These three research phases combined quantitative and qualitative methods of analysis, providing a means of "method triangulation" to interpret organizational reality through the eyes of key organization members (Albrecht & Ropp, 1982; Faules, 1982; Jick, 1979). The questionnaires were used to identify general issues of concern to nursing staff members and provide a baseline for examining changes in nurses' interpretations about organizational life, whereas the interviews and focus groups were used to provide in-depth information about issues facing nurses and recommendations for relieving the problems identified.

The data gathered from nursing staff were used to enhance organizational reflexivity, develop and implement strategies for organizational intervention, and promote system-wide organizational development. Based on the data gathered, a system-wide nurse retention intervention program was developed involving implementation of formal feedback channels between nursing staff and hospital administration, and providing nurses with organizationally approved communication channels for expressing their concerns and resolving problems. A retention committee was formed (composed of representatives from different areas and levels within nursing service at the hospital) to examine specific problem areas, concerns, and organizational suggestions generated through the research, seek additional information about the issues identified, provide information to hospital decision makers to initiate informed change, and ultimately increase nurse retention at the hospital. The retention committee was designed as an ongoing structural change in the organization to provide a two-way information link between nursing staff and hospital administration, as well as to help the hospital administration make informed choices, based on the expertise of nursing staff, in directing the development and introduction of organizational innovations needed to improve retention of nursing staff. Evaluation of the retention program has shown that the intervention led to significant reductions in turnover of nurses in the hospital and facilitated implementation of a wide range of nurse-initiated problem-solving interventions (Kreps, 1986a, 1989c).

The Organizational Socialization Program

This applied communication research study was conducted with RCA VideoDisc Operations in Indianapolis (Kreps, 1983a). This division of RCA had experienced tremendous growth as they began gearing up for introducing the RCA VideoDisc system to the commercial electronics market. Enormous amounts of research, planning, product development, and technical staff additions had occurred during a short period of time. The division was faced with a unique personnel situation where the number of employees working at the center was expanded over a period of months from approximately 300 to more than 900. Traditional means of orienting new employees to the organization, its goals, operation, and organizational culture were found to be insufficient to handle the increased volume of new employees. As a result, many new employees were confused about their roles in the organization, the nature of the product they were working on, as well as the history and philosophy of the company.

A descriptive study of the significant symbols that made up the culture of the organization was conducted to identify organization members' perceptions of the situation confronting the organization. Interpretive data were gathered in three ways: (a) through in-depth interviews with organization members at all levels and areas of the organization (several of these interviews were videotaped and excerpts were used as part of an organizational intervention); (b) through content analyses of relevant organizational documents such as reports, speeches, advertisements, annual reports, and videotapes; and (c) through direct observations (participant observations) of organization members' behavior.

In the interviews organization members were asked to discuss their experiences with the organization. The stories the members told provided the research team with extremely revealing information about both the nature of the problems facing the organization and the strategies by which they had been able to overcome the problems. The stories not only provided rich data about the organization, but also were used as primary components of the organizational development intervention that was implemented. The data gathered from the interpretive research were translated into a meaningful script about RCA organizational culture, which was further developed into a videotape orientation tool designed to educate new members about the logics and legends of organizational culture at RCA. Several of the videotaped stories organization members told about their experiences with the organization were incorporated into the orientation program to help new members better understand the unique culture of the organization and learn about many of the organizational logics other employees used to overcome organizational constraints.

The videotape orientation tool was implemented as an important element of the employee orientation program at the company, and was also used in new-employee recruitment. The new orientation tool was developed to preserve and disseminate organizational intelligence, thereby increasing organizational reflexivity within the division. Evaluation data indicated the videotape orientation tool was effective at providing new organization members with relevant information and helped increase the effectiveness of the division (Kreps, 1983a).

The Market Research Program

A market research organizational development study was conducted to gather information about public perceptions and attitudes toward a residential adolescent substance abuse rehabilitation program in a large midwestern city, as well as to identify strategies for increasing public acceptance of and support for the program (Kreps, 1988). Three relevant groups of parents participated in this research program: (a) parents with children who had already *completed* treatment at the program, (b) parents with children who were *currently* in treatment at the program, and (c) representative parents with children who were within the *potential* age range and geographic region served by the program. Focus group discussions were held with each of these three groups of parents to gather interpretive data, identifying these parents' key experiences, ideas, and concerns about the specific programs and services offered by the program, as well as to describe the parents' more general beliefs and values about adolescent substance abuse, substance abuse treatment, and sources of information about treatment and support.

In the focus group discussions parents were encouraged to discuss as openly as possible their ideas and experiences concerning adolescent substance abuse and treatment. Each of the three focus group discussions was audiotaped to preserve group member comments for in-depth analysis. The audiotapes were transcribed and content analyzed. Through content analysis the data were arranged into primary content themes concerning parents' specific impressions of and experiences with the program, as well as their general experiences with and ideas about adolescent substance abuse and treatment. Parents often told stories about their experiences. The stories were used to identify specific strengths and weaknesses within the program, as well as to direct future marketing, education, and public relations efforts.

The data gathered in this research program increased organizational reflexivity by helping program administrators understand the experiences, ideas, and concerns of their customers. The parents were able to provide the program administrators with organizational intelligence about which elements of the program worked most effectively and which worked least effectively. These data led to the development of several strategic interventions and revisions within the organization, as well as to new marketing and public education strategies. Evaluation data indicate that the organizational interventions have helped the program address many of the concerns the parents expressed, provide parents with relevant information about substance abuse, and increase the effectiveness of public relations efforts (Kreps, 1988).

The Evaluation Research Program

This study was a large-scale formative evaluation of the Physician Data Query (PDQ) information system, an on-line computerized database developed and administered by the National Cancer Institute (NCI) to disseminate state-of-the-art clinical cancer research and practice information from the cancer clinical research community to the general cancer treatment community (Kreps, Hubbard, & DeVita, 1988; Kreps, Maibach, Naughton, Day, & Annet, 1986; Kreps & Naughton, 1986). The evaluation was conducted to provide key information about the uses of the system and to identify to what extent there had been diffusion of the information in the PDQ system to relevant public audiences. Such information is crucial for directing further development of PDQ as part of the NCI's cancer control efforts (Kreps, Hubbard, & DeVita, 1988).

There were four components (A, B, C, and D) to the PDQ evaluation plan (Kreps, Hubbard, & DeVita, 1988). Component A of the evaluation was a comprehensive review and assessment of the processes by which the information contained within the PDQ system was collected and is maintained based upon in-depth interviews with members of the PDQ administrative staff, analysis of PDQ documents and files, and telephone interviews with individuals listed in the PDQ system to test the accuracy of system files. Component B was an assessment of the technical characteristics and competence of the PDQ information system and the delivery systems it employs, as well as an examination of PDQ distribution and usage trends based on technical tests, analysis of billing and usage records, and interviews with system users. Component C of the evaluation was an assessment of system dissemination activities and user reactions to the PDQ system to identify areas for technical revisions, potential new users, and strategies for expanding system use based on interviews with system users and review of system dissemination procedures. Component D of the evaluation plan was to assess the impact of the PDQ system on the diffusion of state-of-the-art cancer treatment information in the medical community and the resultant impact on cancer treatment, morbidity, and mortality based upon interviews with system users and consumers of PDQ information, trial observations of practitioner uses of PDQ, as well as analyses of public health data patterns.

Each of the four components of the PDQ evaluation was designed to provide reflexive information to administrators of the PDQ system about current levels of performance, acceptance, and impact of PDQ. Information gathered through interviews with system users provided interpretive data about the experiences and concerns of these users, identifying and preserving relevant organizational intelligence that only these individuals possess. Such information was channeled back into the PDQ system to direct system enhancements and innovations in system implementation.

Ongoing formative evaluation of the PDQ information system has helped identify key issues, problems, and stumbling blocks in the implementation of the PDQ system and in effective dissemination of cancer information (Kreps & Naughton, 1986). For example, longitudinal evaluation data were gathered about changing patterns of use of the PDQ system, as well as about users' reactions to the the performance of the system (see the following for examples of PDQ evaluation data: Kreps, Hubbard, & DeVita, 1988; Kreps, Maibach et al., 1986; Kreps & Naughton, 1986). These data helped identify performance gaps between actual system use and optimal system use, helping to enhance organizational reflexivity by increasing PDQ administrators' understanding of the experiences of system users. Evaluation research data have provided PDQ administrators with information about potential new information sources, new audiences, new delivery media, and innovations for the PDQ system to enhance future health information dissemination efforts. Several revisions, improvements, and system interventions have been developed and implemented based on these data (Kreps, Hubbard, & DeVita, 1988). Continued rigorous database maintenance, formative evaluation, and refinements of the PDQ system will further enhance effective dissemination of relevant cancer treatment information to those individuals that need such information to increase the quality of cancer care.

SUMMARY AND DIRECTIONS
FOR FUTURE RESEARCH

Each of the four applied communication research projects described earlier used interpretive organizational data to identify key issues, constraints, and performance gaps facing the organization being studied. These data were fed back to the host organization to help increase organizational reflexivity and direct the development and implementation of relevant organizational interventions to increase organizational effectiveness. In this way, the data gathered helped the organization preserve and utilize organizational intelligence. The research programs described demonstrate the utility of the therapeutic model of organizational communication consultation for promoting organizational development by generating data that can inform organization members about salient organizational problems and providing insights about how to solve the problems identified.

Because the therapeutic model of consultation is an applied research process model, focusing on communication issues central to all organizations, future research, based on the model, can fruitfully examine a virtually limitless array of different organizations and organizational problems. It is important, however, that when conducting applied organizational communication research the therapeutic researcher/consultant facilitates change by fully involving organization members in all levels of the organizational development process. The therapeutic model is a collaborative model of organizational development, from designing the research plan, to interpreting research data, to identifying performance gaps and slack resources, to planning intervention strategies, to implementing interventions, to evaluating interventions, and to building long-term commitment to proactive organizational development efforts. By adopting a truly collaborative approach to applied organizational communication research, therapeutic consultation can help reorient organization members (and members of the organization's relevant environment) to new ways of seeing the organization, helping these individuals develop effective strategies for achieving personal and organizational goals.

REFERENCES

Albrecht, T. L., & Ropp, V. A. (1982). The study of network structuring in organizations through methods triangulation. *Western Journal of Speech Communication, 46,* 162–178.

Axley, S. R. (1980, May). *Communication's role in organizational change: A review of the literature.* Paper presented to the International Communication Association conference, Acapulco, Mexico.

Barnlund, D. C. (1978). Therapeutic communication. In D. C. Barnlund (Ed.), *Interpersonal communication: Survey and Studies* (pp. 613–645). Boston: Houghton-Mifflin.

Beckhard, R. (1969). *Organization development: Strategies and models.* Reading, MA: Addison-Wesley.

Berrien, F. K. (1976). A general systems approach to organizations. In M. Dunnette (Ed.), *Handbook of industrial and organizational psychology* (pp. 41–62). Chicago: Rand McNally.

Clampitt, P. G., & Downs, C. W. (1983, November). *Communication and productivity.* Paper presented to the Speech Communication Association conference, Washington, DC.

Cohen, M., March, J., & Olson, J. (1972). A garbage can model of organizational choice. *Administrative Science Quarterly, 17,* 1–25.

Deetz, S. (1979). Social well-being and the development of an appropriate organizational response to de-institutionalization and legitimation crises. *Journal of Applied Communication Research, 7,* 45–54.

Deetz, S. (1982). Critical interpretive research in organizational communication. *Western Journal of Speech Communication, 46,* 121–136.

Downs, C. W., & Hain, T. (1982). Productivity and communication. In M. Burgoon (Ed.), *Communication yearbook 5* (pp. 435–453). New Brunswick, NJ: Transaction.

Faules, D. (1982). The use of multi-methods in the organizational setting. *Western Journal of Speech Communication, 46,* 150–161.

Fuller, D., & Quesada, G. (1973). Communication in medical therapeutics. *Journal of Communication, 23,* 361–370.

Geertz, C. (1973). *The interpretation of cultures.* New York: Basic Books.

Jick, T. D. (1979). Mixing qualitative and quantitative methods: Triangulation in action. *Administrative Science Quarterly, 24,* 602–610.

Koch, S., & Deetz, S. (1981). Metaphor analysis of social reality in organization. *Journal of Applied Communication Research, 9,* 1–15.

Kreps, G. L. (1983a, August). *Nurse retention and organizational reflexivity.* Paper presented to the Academy of Management conference, Dallas.

Kreps, G. L. (1983b). The use of interpretive research to develop a socialization program at RCA. In L. Putnam & M. Pacanowsky (Eds.), *Communication and organization: The interpretive approach* (pp. 243–256). Beverly Hills: Sage.

Kreps, G. L. (1985). Organizational communication and organizational effectiveness. *World Communication, 15,* 55–70.

Kreps, G. L. (1986a). Description and evaluation of a nurse retention organizational development research program. In H. Guetal & M. Kavanagh (Eds.), *Fifty Years of Excellence in Management Research and Practice: Proceedings of the Third Annual Meeting of the Eastern Academy of Management* (pp. 18–22). Eastern Academy of Management.

Kreps, G. L. (1986b). Ethical dimensions of organizational communication. In W. E. Hamel (Ed.), *Human resources management and organizational behavior proceedings: Vol. 1* (pp. 285–289). Virginia Beach, VA: Maximillian Press.

Kreps, G. L. (1986c). *Organizational communication: Theory and practice.* White Plains, NY: Longman.

Kreps, G. L. (1988) *Rosecrance Center market research program executive summary.* Research report prepared for Rosecrance Center Adolescent Substance Abuse Rehabilitation Center, Rockford, IL.

Kreps, G. L. (1989a). The nature of therapeutic communication. In G. Gumpert & S. Fish (Eds.), *Mediated therapeutic communication.* Norwood, NJ: Ablex.

Kreps, G. L. (1989b). Reflexivity and internal public relations: The role of information in directing organizational development. In C. Botan & V. Hazleton (Eds.), *Public relations theory* (pp. 265–279). Hillsdale, NJ: Lawrence Erlbaum Associates.

Kreps, G. L. (1989c). A therapeutic model of organizational communication consultation: Application of interpretive field methods. *Southern Communication Journal, 55,* 1–21.

Kreps, G. L. (1990). Stories as repositories of organizational intelligence: Implications for organizational development. In J. Anderson (Ed.), *Communication yearbook 13* (pp. 19–202). Newbury Park, CA: Sage.

Kreps, G., Hubbard, S., & DeVita, V. T. (1988). The role of the Physician Data Query on-line cancer information system in health information dissemination. *Information and Behavior, 2,* 362–380.

Kreps, G. L., Maibach, E. W., Naughton, M. D., Day, S. H., & Annett, D. Q. (1986). PDQ usage trends: Implications for evaluation. In A. Levy & B. Williams (Eds.), *Proceedings of the American Association for Medical Systems and Informatics Congress 86* (pp. 71–75). Washington, DC: AAMSI.

Kreps, G. L., & Naughton, M. D. (1986). The role of PDQ in disseminating cancer information. In R. Saloman, B. Blum, & M. Jorgensen (Eds.), *MEDINFO 1986* (pp. 400–404). Amsterdam: North Holland Press/Elsevier.

Manning, P. K. (1979). Metaphors of the field: Varieties of organizational discourse. *Administrative Science Quarterly, 84,* 796–810.

Martin, J., & Powers, M. (1983). Organizational stories: More vivid and persuasive than quantitative data. In B. M. Staw (Ed.), *Psychological foundations of organizational behavior* (pp. 161–168). Glenview, IL: Scott, Foresman.

Miller, G. R., & Sunnafrank, M. J. (1984). Theoretical dimensions of applied communication research. *Quarterly Journal of Speech, 70,* 225–263.

Mitroff, I., & Kilmann, R. (1975). Stories managers tell: A new tool for organizational problems solving. *Management Review, 64,* 19–20.

Nadler, D. R. (1977). *Feedback and organization development: Using data based methods.* Reading, MA: Addison-Wesley.

O'Reilly, C. A., & Roberts, K. H. (1977, August). *Communication and performance in organizations.* Paper presented to the Academy of Management conference, Orlando, FL.

Pacanowsky, M. (1988). Slouching towards Chicago. *Quarterly Journal of Speech, 74,* 453–467.

Pace, R. W. (1983). *Organizational communication: Foundations for human resource development.* Englewood Cliffs, NJ: Prentice-Hall.

Peters, T., & Waterman, R. (1982). *In search of excellence.* New York: Harper & Row.

Pettegrew, L. (1977). An investigation of therapeutic communicator style. In B. D. Ruben (Ed.), *Communication yearbook 1* (pp. 593–604). New Brunswick, NJ: Transaction.

Pettigrew, A. M. (1979). On studying organizational cultures. *Administrative Science Quarterly, 24,* 570–581.

Putnam, L. (1982). Paradigms for organizational communication research: An overview and synthesis. *Western Journal of Speech Communication, 46,* 192–206.

Putnam, L., & Pacanowsky, M. (Eds.). (1983). *Communication and organizations: The interpretive approach.* Beverly Hills: Sage.

Redding, W. C. (1985). Stumbling towards identity. In R. McPhee & P. Tompkins (Eds.), *Organizational communication: Traditional themes and new directions* (pp. 15–54). Newbury Park, CA: Sage.

Rogers, C. (1957). The necessary and sufficient conditions of psychotherapeutic change. *Journal of Consulting Psychology, 21,* 95–103.

Rogers, E., & Agarwala-Rogers, R. (1976). *Communication in organizations.* New York: Free Press.

Rowe, L., & Boise, W. (Eds.). (1973). *Organizational and managerial innovation.* Pacific Palisades, CA: Goodyear.

Schein, E. H. (1969). *Process consultation: Its role in organization development.* Reading, MA: Addison-Wesley.

Schein, E. H. (1985). *Organizational culture and leadership.* San Francisco: Jossey-Bass.

Schein, E. H. (1987). *The clinical perspective in fieldwork.* Newbury Park, CA: Sage.

Tavernier, G. (1980). Using employee communication to support corporate objectives. *Management Review, 69,* 8–13.

Truax, C., and Carkhuff, R. (1967). *Toward effective counseling in psychotherapy: Training and practice.* Chicago: Aldine.

Tubbs, S., & Hain, T. (1979, August). *Management communication and its relationship to total organizational effectiveness.* Paper presented at the Academy of Management conference, Atlanta, GA.

Tubbs, S., & Widgery, R. N. (1978). When productivity lags are key managers really communicating? *Management Review, 67,* 20–25.

Weick, K. E. (1979). *The social psychology of organizing.* (2nd ed.). Reading, MA: Addison-Wesley.

Weick, K. E. (1987). Theorizing about organizational communication. In F. Jablin, L. Putnam, K. H. Roberts, & L. Porter (Eds.), *Handbook of organizational communication* (pp. 97–122). Newbury Park, CA: Sage.

Weick, K. E., & Browning, L. D. (1986). Argument and narration in organizational communication. *Journal of Management, 12,* 243–259.

Wilensky, H. (1977). *Organizational intelligence.* New York: Basic Books.

Wilkins, A. L. (1983). The cultures audit: A tool for understanding organizations. *Organizational Dynamics, 12,* 24–38.

Wilkins, A. L. (1984). The creation of cultures: The role of stories and human resource systems. *Human Resource Management, 23,* 41–60.

EDUCATIONAL CONTEXTS

TRAINING AND DEVELOPMENT FOR COMMUNICATION COMPETENCE

6

GUSTAV W. FRIEDRICH
ARTHUR VANGUNDY
University of Oklahoma

Our recent and ongoing transition from a postindustrial society to an information-based society has made skillful communication the fundamental resource of the age. Nowhere is this more noticeable than in the areas of employment and career success. John and Merna Galassi (1978), summarizing 60 years of research on the job interview, concluded: "researchers consider communication and interpersonal skills as the single most important set of factors in the interview" (p. 191). Not only are communication skills an important determinant in obtaining jobs, they are equally relevant to success and promotion in those positions. A recent study of the graduates of the 13 degree-granting institutions that compose the University of Wisconsin system concluded that the three factors given the greatest importance in the assessment of job candidates (interpersonal skills, attitude, and oral communication skills) correspond closely to the three highest ranked factors for successful employment (interpersonal skills, motivation, and written and oral communication skills). The importance that the responding organizations place on communication skills is further revealed by the fact that more than 90% of them provide additional training for their employees in both oral and written communication (Page & Perelman, 1980).

Employers of University of Wisconsin graduates are not unique. Over 10 years ago, William C. Norris ("Training talks," 1977), chair and chief executive officer of Control Data Corporation, estimated total expenditures for training in American industry at $100 billion annually—or about the same amount spent for education at the primary, secondary, and college levels; not only is this estimate dated, it does not include expenditures by agencies of the federal government, departments of state government, departments of local government, and professional and trade groups. Currently, it is likely that expenditures for formal learning by U.S. organizations exceed $300 billion annually (Carnevale, 1989).

The goal of this chapter is to explore communication training and development that occur in the workplace as a research and teaching focus for academics interested in applied communication. The first section describes the scope of this domain. The second section provides suggestions for individuals who are interested in serving as communication consultants and providing communication training and development.

TRAINING AND DEVELOPMENT

"Training and development" is the phrase most frequently used to designate a process by which an organization helps employees and managers improve job performance and increase job satisfaction. When the process is targeted toward improving specific, required job skills (e.g., learning how to conduct an appraisal interview), it is called training; when the target is broader than the performance of a specific task (e.g., a workshop on listening geared toward enhancing an individual's personal life as well as her or his work performance), the process is labeled development. Training and development can be focused either on individuals (human resource development) or on the structure of the organization (organizational development). In the latter case, a consultant helps the organization to study itself and create a planned approach to monitoring, modifying, and maintaining a maximally effective organization. This chapter focuses primarily on human resource development because it is at this level where organizations target most of their training and development resources and where communication academics have the greatest potential to contribute to the process.

Given expenditures in excess of $300 billion for job training and development, it is surprising how little information is available on the actual activities that are being funded. One noteworthy exception is an annual survey supported by and reported in *Training* magazine. Limiting its focus to U.S. business organizations with 100 or more employees, the most recent survey (the seventh) was reported in the October 1988 issue. Here is a sample of the findings:

Total dollars budgeted for formal training this year by U.S. organizations with 100 or more employees: $39.6 billion.

Total number of individuals who will receive formal, employer-sponsored training this year: 37.5 million.

Total hours of training those individuals will receive: 1.2 billion.

Total dollars budgeted by training departments for outside expenditures: $9 billion (this amount is divided among: seminars and conferences = $2.76 billion; hardware = $1.87 billion; outside services = $1.41 billion; custom materials = $1.71 billion; off-the-shelf materials = $1.23 billion).

Percentage providing general types of training: management skills/development = 81.3%; supervisory skills = 78.9%; technical skills/knowledge = 76.4%; communication skills = 72.1%; customer relations/services = 63.6%; clerical/secretarial skills = 59.7%; basic computer skills = 59.2%; new methods/procedures = 58.6%; personal growth = 56.0%; executive development = 58.6%; sales skills = 47.8%; wellness = 45.5%; employee/labor relations = 45.3%; customer education = 38.3%; remedial basic education = 24.3%.

Percentage providing specific types of communication-related training: performance appraisals = 66.2%; leadership = 62.0%; hiring/selection = 59.6%; train-the-trainer = 52.6%; listening skills = 52.4%; team building = 51.2%; motivation = 48.7%; problem solving = 48.0%; delegation skills = 46.8%; public speaking/presentation = 45.3%; interpersonal skills = 45.1%; goal setting = 44.9%; decision making = 43.2%; writing skills = 41.4%; conducting meetings = 38.4%; negotiating skills = 35.5%.

Percentage using particular instructional methods: videotapes = 87.1%; lectures = 83.1%; one-on-one instruction = 70.6%; role plays = 60.3%; slides = 49.7% games/simulations = 49.1%; case studies = 48.1%; self-assessment/self-testing instruments = 44.7%; films = 41.8%; noncomputerized self-study programs = 31.4%; teleconferencing = 9.5%; computer conferencing = 4.2%.

Large U.S. businesses, then, represent an area where communication consultants are needed and used—most frequently as providers of workshops, seminars, lectures, or training materials. Based on a survey of 17 experienced communication consultants, Pace (1983) identified the following five broad categories of organizations as even more likely to use the services of a communication consultant:

1. *Agencies of the federal government,* including the Civil Service Commission, military and veterans administration, Department of

Agriculture (such as the Forest Service), and Department of Interior (such as the National Park Service).

2. *Departments of state government,* including transportation and highway patrol, health and social services, water resources and environment, and engineering.

3. *Departments of local government,* including city police, fire and streets, and county agencies.

4. *Professional and trade groups,* such as dental associations (dentists, dental assistants, and dental technicians), medical associations (doctors, nurses and hospitals), legal associations (lawyers, public defenders), educational units (school districts, PTA), and labor unions (construction).

5. *Medium-size businesses and industries,* including district offices of large corporations, such as banks, retail and direct sales, utilities, restaurants, accounting, construction and manufacturing, and advertising and public relations firms.

The annual survey just described provides some information on the most common communication topics involving training and development efforts. A list of topics used for a survey by Putnam (1979) elaborates upon that information. It is slightly reorganized and expanded for this presentation:

Interpersonal Communication Skills
    Communicator Style
    Listening
    Coaching Skills
    Nonverbal Communication
    Giving and Receiving Compliments
    Giving and Receiving Feedback
    Humor
    Being Assertive
    Dating Behavior
    Intimate Communication
    Family and Marital Communication
    Intercultural Communication
    Impression Formation
    Telephone Skills
Interviewing
    Performance Appraisal Interviews
    Employment Interviews

Counseling Interviews
Exit Interviews
Journalistic Interviews
Persuasive Interviews
Teacher/Parent Interviews
Nursing Interviews

Leadership
Motivating People
Delegating Authority
Giving Criticism
Handling Grievances
Giving Directions
Managerial Communication
Power

Group Communication
Running Effective Meetings
Team Building
Conference Planning
Negotiation Sessions
T Groups, Encounter Groups
Creative Decision Making
Arbitration and Mediation Practices

Public Speaking
Use of Visual Materials
Sales Training
Presentation of Oral Reports
Persuasive Speaking
Informal Public Presentations

Message Flow in Organizations
Downward Communication
Upward Communication
Lateral Communication
Rumor Channels
Improving Organizational Public Image
Message Design

Communication Climate
Participative Decision Making
Superior/Subordinate Supportiveness
Openness Between Employees
Employee Trust and Credibility
Sufficiency of Information

Organizational Development
Human Relations

Written Communication
Memorandum and Letter Writing
Preparation of Technical Reports
Newsletters, Press Releases
Proposal Writing

In summary, job training and development is a large and expanding domain that requires the skills of individuals interested in applied communication. Although being a communication consultant is an attractive full-time occupation (the November issue of *Training* magazine reports annually on the salaries of various categories of human resource development practitioners), it can also be a worthwhile part-time activity for academics. The advantages of meeting this challenge were summarized by Rudolph and Johnson (1983). According to them, the academic can:

1. Find out whether the things they teach *in* the classroom work *outside* the classroom.
2. Make contacts that might result in student internships, summer jobs, and/or placement.
3. Conduct research that results in their being able to contribute to the state of the art of their discipline.
4. Supplement their academic income.

Training and Development
for Communication Competence

Assuming that one accepts the challenges of communication consulting, it is important to begin with a clear concept of what it means to be a competent communicator. Three emphases dominate current conceptualizations of communication competence: a focus on skills, a focus on knowledge, or a focus on goal attainment. The skills orientation is an attempt to identify those characteristics, traits, or behaviors deemed necessary for labeling someone as a competent communicator. Illustrative of these efforts is Bochner and Kelly's (1974) description of the competent communicator as someone who is characterized by (a) empathy, (b) descriptiveness, (c) owning feelings, (d) self-disclosure, and (e) behavioral flexibility. Although it is not a necessary concomitant of such approaches, most have assumed that skills appropriate for one situation are appropriate for all situations.

A second orientation to describing the competent communicator focuses on knowledge rather than behavior. Much like Chomsky, who argued that language competency is concerned with a mental capacity underlying actual behavior, individuals within this tradition have focused on how people think about the communication process. Thus, for example, Delia and his colleagues at Illinois (Delia, O'Keefe, & O'Keefe, 1982) developed constructivism as a way of exploring individuals' ability to interpret the requirements of a communication situation as a function of their cognitive complexity.

A third orientation, goal attainment, places the emphasis on an individual's ability to specify and obtain communication goals. This orientation has two thrusts: The first is concerned with an individual's ability to fulfill individual goals; the second suggests that goal attainment must be relational—that is, all parties in a communication encounter must have the opportunity to mutually satisfy goals. Illustrative of the first approach is Parks (1977) specification of a six-step effectuation process: (a) goal specification, (b) information acquisition, (c) prediction making, (d) strategy selection, (e) strategy implementation, and (f) environmental testing. Wiemann's (1977) approach is more consistent with a relational perspective: "Communication competence is the ability of an interactant to choose among available communication behaviors in order that he may successfully accomplish his own interpersonal goals during an encounter while maintaining the face and line of his fellow interactants within the constraints of the situation" (p. 197).

Although all three orientations possess utility, training and development activities that seek to improve communication are best viewed from the perspective of a definition that applies knowledge and behavior to the attainment of communication goals. The following definition is an attempt to provide this synthesis: Communication competency is a situational ability to set realistic and appropriate goals and to maximize their achievement by using knowledge of self, other, context, and communication theory to generate adaptive communication performances.

Given such a synthesis, the communication consultant is in a position to ask two questions: (a) Is there an area of communication competence that warrants an effort at improvement? (b) If so, what is/are the probable cause(s) of this need for improvement? Answers to the first question can be obtained either informally or formally, using such assessment devices as interviews, self-report inventories, behavioral observation, ratings by peers and significant others, and self-monitoring. Usually there is little difficulty in agreeing on an answer to this question.

The second question, however, is both more difficult to answer and more important. Answers to the second question have important implications for focusing training and development activities. To illustrate:

1. Is the probable cause inappropriate, unclear, and/or unachievable goals? If so, then the consultant will need to help trainees with goal analysis.

2. Is the probable cause a lack of skill (inappropriate frequency, duration, intensity, or form for verbal or nonverbal behaviors)? If so, then the focus should be skill training, perhaps using direct instruction and video playback.

3. Is the probable cause a lack of knowledge (knows how, but not when and where)? If so, then the focus should be on appropriate timing, perhaps using modeling and role playing.

4. Is the probable cause a lack of motivation (knows how, when, and where, but makes a choice not to perform). If so, then the focus should be on the necessity for and methods of motivation.

5. Is the probable cause performance anxiety (knows how, when, and where, but is afraid to perform)? If so, then the focus should be on techniques for reducing apprehension, perhaps using systematic desensitization and/or cognitive modification.

Few skills are more important to a consultant than an ability to use assessment instruments. Analyzing needs correctly is crucial to the successful delivery of training and development activities. A very useful resource for this area is *The University Associates Instrumentation Kit,* edited by J. William Pfeiffer (1987). The kit is a collection of 105 reproducible instruments, surveys, rating scales, and questionnaires, each categorized in terms of primary and secondary use. The kit also includes a User's Guide that provides helpful tips on selecting and administering instruments. The kit, of course, is not a substitute for knowledge of the basic principles of assessment (e.g., sampling, levels of measurement, reliability, validity). There are no instruments for many areas where assessment is required and the consultant will, therefore, need to create new instruments. Pfeiffer and Ballew (1988) described a 10-step sequence that is useful for the development and administration of a new instrument: definition, specification, scaling, keying, duplication, administration, scoring, interpretation, norming, and critiquing.

The Challenges of Communication Consulting

As a communication consultant, you will face a number of challenges. Among the most important of these are how to: (a) assess your resources, (b) broadcast your availability, (c) identify and clarify goals, and (d) create effective training designs that include feedback loops.

Assess Your Resources.   There are at least two categories of resources that affect the communication consultant: (a) personal and (b) situational. Personal resources are qualities consultants bring to a consulting relationship; situational resources are intrinsic or extrinsic characteristics of a situation.

A variety of consultant personal qualities have been prescribed in the literature: diagnostic ability, empathy, goal-setting ability, problem-solving ability, imagination, flexibility, honesty, consistency, and trust (e.g., Havelock, 1973; Lippitt, 1961). In addition to these prescriptive qualities, communication academics already possess considerable personal consulting resources. For instance, Rudolph and Johnson (1983) identified: availability and flexibility, state-of-the-art knowledge, excellent research skills, innovative applications of theoretical concepts, earned credibility, high ethical standards, and effective presentation skills honed by countless hours in the classroom.

To apply these resources, you should develop a consulting specialty. Such a specialty should be perceived as important by potential clients. In marketing terminology, you should target a market and position yourself so that you will be seen as "the" expert in your area (e.g., leadership, problem solving, public speaking, listening, conflict resolution). Some consultants also specialize according to type of organization (e.g., government agencies, service industries, health-care organizations). Such specialization forces you to remain current with new developments that might affect both communication content and its application to relevant organizations. It also permits you to enhance credibility by authoring articles, instruments, and instructional materials in a specialty area.

In addition to refining personal qualities and abilities, consultants also face the challenge of using and obtaining resources (e.g., time, people, money, equipment, information). Such resource use is situational and can be categorized generally as intrinsic or extrinsic. Intrinsic situational resources are those that are immediately apparent in the situation; extrinsic resources are those that you must assess and pursue outside of the immediate situation. For instance, if you are working with research and development problem-solving groups, most of the information you need will exist within the groups. However, you also may need to obtain additional information from external sources such as marketing personnel.

The challenge is to accurately evaluate existing resources so that you do not expend unnecessary effort obtaining extrinsic resources. Thus, the costs of obtaining additional resources must be weighed against your evaluation of existing resource adequacy.

Broadcast Your Availability.   Although there are a multitude of ways to locate clients, a few simple strategies will normally produce the majority of responses. First, establish your credibility as an expert in the area. In addition to lecturing and publishing on the topic, this requires that others know of these activities. Thus, for example, when you make a presentation at a convention or give a speech to a local service organization, use your college/university news service to create and disseminate descriptive stories for the newspaper. Second, solicit and agree to do "freebies" for campus, civic, religious, and other organizations. You might, for example, do a workshop on effective listening for employees on your campus or present a lecture to a local Lions, Rotary, or Kiwanis club on "Can Employees Be Taught to Communicate Better?" In either case, in addition to gaining valuable experience, you will have an opportunity to do a little soft selling by talking about the kinds of training you do. Often freebies produce contacts with business and civic leaders that result in paid contracts. Third, tell your colleagues and other consultants about your consulting interests. Although this can be done informally, it can also be done within the context of professional organizations. One especially useful professional network is the American Society for Training and Development (ASTD). ASTD links private, free-lance consultants with trainers who work full-time within organizations. This link can keep the communication consultant current with trends in human resource development. It can also provide contacts with in-house trainers who hire free-lance consultants for special projects.

Identify and Clarify Your Goals.   This is one of the most important challenges you will face as a consultant. It often has been said that if you do not know where you are going, then any road will get you there. Without clearly defined and understood goals, neither you nor the client can be assured that training will be effective.

There are several advantages to identifying and clarifying goals. First, goals define the parameters of a consulting relationship. When used to establish joint expectations, goals set and illuminate limits surrounding the consultant and client. In effect, understood goals provide a psychological cement to bind the consulting relationship (Schein, 1969). Therefore, the expected contributions of each are clearer. Second, goals also furnish direction for training and development efforts. The validity of training decisions can be tested by comparing probable outcomes with agreed upon goals. If a decision is not congruent with goals, the training process can be adjusted to achieve conformity. Finally, goals help create ownership of a training effort. If both parties perceive they have a stake in the process, they will be more committed to its success.

Identifying and clarifying goals is an interactive process. You should determine your client's goals and share yours. If there are no major discrepancies or conflicts, you can continue training; if there is goal incongruity, you will need to resolve the differences. The goals you both identify also should be consistent with the organization's broader goals. Jointly discussing this consistency can avoid working at cross-purposes with each other and the organization.

Create Effective Training Designs. Once an area for improvement and probable causes are identified, the two most salient features that affect training design are people and time. Trainees are adults who are taking time away from work and family. They expect training that is problem-centered and real-world focused, rather than theoretical and abstract (Sork, 1984). Time is an issue because most training is conducted in half-day or full-day blocks. Given these features, it is important to consider the following characteristics in creating an effective training design.

1. *Relevance.* Derive training objectives from a careful needs assessment, thus ensuring that learning goals are relevant to the organization and to the persons involved in training.

2. *Learner Comfort.* Because learning is inhibited if the environment is uncomfortable (e.g., crowded room, hard chairs, too hot or too cold temperature), the consultant needs to obtain/create the most comfortable environment possible. This includes the availability of snacks and drinks. Social and psychological comfort is also important. Consultants can reduce anxiety by using appropriate ice-breaking activities and by anticipating and coping with common fears (e.g., fear of being forced to participate, fear of being subjected to destructive criticism).

3. *Variety of Method.* For many reasons (e.g., to break up extended blocks of time, to accomplish different goals, to accommodate learner differences), it is important to use a variety of instructional strategies. Because active participation facilitates learning and provides valuable feedback on trainee progress, strategies that require active participation by trainees are preferred. When more passive strategies are used (e.g., lectures), an effort can and should be made to encourage trainees to ask questions and critically examine the ideas. A list of some instructional alternatives is provided here:

- Behavioral Rehearsal: or role playing, it involves the practice of target behaviors in simulated settings.
- Bibliotherapy: reading of articles or books concerned with personal improvement.
- Case Method: a written description of a real decision-making situation for which group members determine problems, analyze their significance, offer solutions, choose the best alternatives, and implement them.

- Cognitive Restructuring: teaching individuals to identify anxiety provoking self-statements and replace them with more adaptive, non-anxiety-provoking coping statements.

- Computer Assisted Instruction: any of a wide range of techniques that rely on a computer to assist in the presentation of learning materials.

- Contract Learning: written agreements between consultant and client concerning amount of client work and procedures to credit or reward this work.

- Covert Rehearsal or Visualization: imagined practice of the target behavior.

- Direct Instruction or Coaching: behavioral description, explanation, and feedback concerning the target performance.

- Feedback: procedures that are used to both motivate and inform learners concerning the correctness and/or appropriateness of their responses.

- Games: activities in which people agree to abide by a set of conditions in order to create a desired state or end.

- Goal Setting: changing general and idealistic goals into descriptions of specific and realistic actions to be performed.

- Instrumentation: used to provide instrumented feedback to group members, manipulate group composition, teach theory of interpersonal functioning, or study here-and-now process in groups.

- In Vivo Practice: also called Homework, it involves actual implementation of the target behavior in life situations.

- Modeling: observation of people who perform the target behavior effectively.

- Programmed Instruction: material is broken down into small steps, frequent student response is required, and there is immediate confirmation of right or wrong answers.

- Self-Control: a behavioral approach for proceeding from self-monitoring to self-evaluation to self-reinforcement.

- Self-Modeling: observing oneself on videotapes that have been edited to show only desired target behavior.

- Self-Monitoring: identification and recording of client's target behaviors by client.

- Simulations: activities that model reality to teach general knowledge, attitudes, and/or skills.

- Systematic Desensitization: treatment of anxiety via graduated pairing, through imagery, of anxiety-eliciting stimuli with the relaxed stage.

- Video Playback: use of video technology for social skills training.

Many useful applications of the above techniques are available through University Associates, Inc., 8517 Production Avenue, San Diego, CA 92121. Especially useful are: (a) the *HRD Annual Series* (starting in 1972), which annually provides approximately 300 pages of structured experiences, instrumentation, and professional development papers, and (b) Volumes I–X (1974–1985) of *A Handbook of Structured Experiences,* containing 240 activities that relate to such topics as self-disclosure, feedback, listening, interpersonal trust, leadership, and conflict resolution.

4. *Appropriate Sequencing and Pacing.* Once activities have been selected, they should be sequenced to build from basic and simple concepts and skills to more complex ones. In addition, the consultant needs to be alert for and sensitive to direct and indirect signs of boredom, overload, or exhaustion, and then pace breaks and activities accordingly. As a supplement to observation, helpful information about pacing issues can often be obtained by simply asking the group for their advice.

5. *Feedback Loops.* Consultants need to develop and use strategies for obtaining information at all stages in the process. Initially, this involves obtaining information about the trainees and their needs. As the workshop proceeds, it involves obtaining and sharing with trainees feedback on what they are learning and the effectiveness of the training design. End of session feedback on learning and on the design is important to guide future activities. Methods that can be used to gather relevant information include interviews, open discussion, questionnaires, tests, and playback of videotapes.

CONCLUSION

Most communication academics are asked to provide training and development activities, whether in the form of an occasional lecture or conducting workshops and seminars for on-campus groups. A goal of this chapter has been to encourage individuals to accept and meet the challenges of engaging in communication consulting. Should you do so, an abundant literature is available to assist you in developing the requisite skills. A recent addition to this literature is Arnold and McClure's (1989) *Communication Training & Development.* Arnold is an academic who serves as a consultant to many firms and organizations; McClure is president of a management consulting firm. The book they have written overviews the many decisions involved in preparing, running, and evaluating programs that apply a communication consultant's knowledge of communication theory to the task of human resource development. A book with a similar task and set of authors is Friedman and Yarbrough's (1985) *Training Strategies From Start to Finish*. Rudolph and Johnson (1983) have written a briefer overview of the area, *Communication Consulting: Another Teaching Option,* as part of the Theory & Research into Practice series of the ERIC/RCS Speech Communication Module. Two additional publications that warrant mention are edited collections of essays. Baird, Schneier, and Laird's (1983) contribution includes readings, checklists, questionnaires, models, and methods for analysis that are valuable for designing, implementing, and evaluating training and development activities. Buchholz's (1983) book, produced on behalf of the American Business Communication Association, contains essays that explore the present and future of communication consulting (both written and oral) and provide advice on topics ranging from "Obtaining, negotiating, and pricing your first consulting job" to "A model syllabus for in-house corporate speech training."

Increasing your competence as a communication consultant, of course, involves more than learning about resource materials. You must also cognitively integrate conceptual material in a manner consistent with a personal model of communication competency. For instance, you might determine the face validity of various communication skills, knowledge bases, and goal attainment components, and then selectively incorporate different aspects into your own operational model. In other words, decide what theoretical concepts are useful and integrate them with your "model-in-use."

When developing and elaborating your model of communication competency, you should consider societal influences upon the training field. For instance, traditional training philosophy is based upon societal values that reinforce hierarchical authority structures. Evolving societal changes, however, have made such a philosophy increasingly less relevant. A diminishing unskilled labor pool and a growing high tech, highly skilled labor pool have obscured the boundaries between management and labor. Other issues to be considered include the continued need for training, the value of a strategic emphasis, and the importance of evaluation.

In spite of all the resources invested in training and development, the need exists for more. The American Society for Training & Development estimates that only 55% of Americans receive preparation for their jobs; only 35% receive skill improvement training once they are on the job (Carnevale, 1989). As our society becomes less dependent on machine capital and relies more on human capital, the role of the training professional assumes expanding importance.

There is a great opportunity for today's communication consultant to prepare for tomorrow's training challenges. Such efforts, however, must be linked closely with organizational strategy. This will ensure that training is geared to an organization's needs and will maximize the training investment.

Although alignment of goal and strategy is necessary for training effectiveness, it will not guarantee it. More stringent evaluation methodologies also need to be implemented. In a domain where there is little validated research to support one training approach over another, managers are faced with a bewildering array of training programs and evaluation approaches. Communication consultants can help reduce the uncertainty involved in making choices.

Today's communication consultants can increase their competency by proper motivation and by awareness of the skills, knowledge, and goals required. The real challenge they face is that of developing responses that will allow them to adapt to an evolving information-based society.

REFERENCES

Arnold, W. E., & McClure, L. (1989). *Communication training & development.* New York: Harper & Row.

Baird, L. S., Schneier, C. R., & Laird, D. (Eds.). (1983). *The training and development sourcebook.* Amherst, MA: Human Resource Development Press.

Bochner, A., & Kelly, C. (1974). Interpersonal competence: Rationale, philosophy, and implementation of a conceptual framework. *Speech Teacher, 23,* 279–301.

Buchholz, W. J. (1983). *Communication training and consulting in business, industry, and government.* Urbana-Champaign, IL: University of Illinois at Urbana-Champaign, American Business Communication Association.

Carnevale, A. P. (1989, February). The learning enterprise. *Training and Development Journal,* 26–33.

Delia, J. G., O'Keefe, B. J., & O'Keefe, D. J. (1982). The constructivist approach to communication. In F. E. X. Dance (Ed.), *Human communication theory: Comparative essays* (pp. 147–191). New York: Harper & Row.

Friedman, P. G., & Yarbrough, E. A. (1985). *Training strategies from start to finish.* Englewood Cliffs, NJ: Prentice-Hall.

Galassi, J. P., & Galassi, M. (1978). Preparing individuals for job interviews: Suggestions from more than 60 years of research. *Personnel and Guidance Journal, 57,* 188–192.

Havelock, R. (1973). *The change agent's guide to innovation in education.* Englewood Cliffs, NJ: Educational Technology Publications.

Lippitt, R. (1961). Dimensions of the consultant's job. In W. Bennis, K. Benne, &

R. Chinn (Eds.), *The planning of change* (pp. 142–146). New York: Holt, Rinehart & Winston.

Pace, R. W. (1983). Consulting opportunities for speech communication faculty. In W. J. Buchholz (Ed.), *Communication training and consulting in business, industry, and government* (pp. 83–87). Urbana-Champaign, IL: University of Illinois at Urbana-Champaign, American Business Communication Association.

Page, P., & Perelman, S. (1980). *Basic skills and employment: An employer survey.* University of Wisconsin System: Interagency Basic Skills Project.

Parks, M. (1977, February). *Issues in the explication of communication competency.* Paper presented at the annual meeting of the Western Speech Communication Association, Phoenix, AZ.

Pfeiffer, J. W. (1987). *The University Associates instrumentation kit.* San Diego: University Associates.

Pfeiffer, J. W., & Ballew, A. C. (1988). *Using instruments in human resource development.* (UA Training Technologies: 2). San Diego: University Associates.

Putnam, L. L. (1979). Role functions and role conflicts of communication trainers. *The Journal of Business Communication, 17,* 37–52.

Redding, W. C. (1979). Graduate education and the communication consultant: Playing God for a fee. *Communication Education, 28,* 346–352.

Rudolph, E. E., & Johnson, B. R. (1983). *Communication consulting: Another teaching option.* Speech Communication Association: Speech Communication Module, ERIC/RCS. Library of Congress Catalog Card No. 83-061688.

Schein, E. (1969). *Process consultation: Its role in organization development.* Reading, MA: Addison-Wesley.

Sork, T. J. (Ed.) (1984). *Designing and implementing effective workshops.* New Directions for Continuing Education, no. 22. San Francisco: Jossey-Bass.

Training talks to the top. (1977, October). *Training, 14,* 31.

Wiemann, J. (1977). Explication and test of a model of communication competence. *Human Communication Research, 3,* 195–213.

APPLICATION OF COMMUNICATION STRATEGIES IN ALLEVIATING TEACHER STRESS

7

MARY JOHN O'HAIR
Texas Tech University

ROBERT WRIGHT
New Mexico State University

Teaching is rapidly becoming one of the most stressful occupations in the United States, rivaled only by air traffic controllers. Although the issue of teacher stress is not a new one, the severity and scope of the problem appear unprecedented (Halpin, Harris, & Halpin, 1985; Litt & Turk, 1985; O'Hair, 1987; O'Hair & Housner, 1989). Teacher stress may be defined as the experience of unpleasant, negative emotions and distress that exist when the problems confronting teachers threaten their well-being and surpass their ability to resolve these problems (Forman, 1982; Kyriacou & Sutcliffe, 1978; Litt & Turk, 1985). The widespread recognition of teacher stress among the majority of teachers in the United States today is well documented; however, frequently less is known about the specific stress producing environments. In particular, when examining stress producers among teachers the majority of teachers reported higher stress levels due to lack of administrative support concerning student discipline and ineffective administrator communication leading to interpersonal problems (Feitler & Tokar, 1982; Raschke, Dedrick, Strathe, & Hawes, 1985). It is the purpose of this chapter to explore from a social power and interpersonal communication perspective factors concerning teacher stress and burnout with particular attention focused on teacher communication with students, colleagues, and administrators.

This chapter is divided into three sections. First, we explore the results of unmitigated teacher stress. The second section focuses on stress producers in three interpersonal communication environments: teacher–student, teacher–teacher, and teacher–principal. Last, section three examines communication strategies that decrease teacher stress and promote student learning.

RESULTS OF TEACHER STRESS

High stress levels experienced by teachers have been linked to several dangerous and potentially lethal results. The four most documented results related to stress involve physical and mental problems, negative effects on students, teacher turnover, and teacher burnout. The literature reveals that, in almost every case examined, as levels of stress increase so do symptoms of physical illness. Bradfield and Fones (1985) reported that of the high stress teachers in their sample there were an average of 5.2 physical distress symptoms compared to an average of only 2.9 symptoms per teacher in the low stress population. Bloch (1978) found that many teachers were now having to be treated for the kindred disturbances that soldiers in combat are likely to experience. Research findings purport that increasingly teachers tend to be experiencing such stress-produced problems as hypertension, cardiovascular difficulties, shortness of breath, colitis, sleep disturbances, peptic ulcers, eating disturbances, displacement phobias, and family crises (Bloch, 1978; Eskridge & Coker, 1985). Stress appears to be one of the worst health problems teachers have yet had to face (Litt & Turk, 1985).

In addition to stress-related physical symptoms, many behavioral symptoms may be stress-induced. Cardinell (1980) reported abrupt mood swings, lowered tolerance for frustration, increased irritability, loss of caring for people, feelings of helplessness and/or lack of control, paranoia, suspiciousness, and greater professional risk-taking as common symptoms of stress-related behavior changes.

Often the stress experienced by the teacher will affect job performance. A decrease in the performance of a teacher will cause negative effects on students, resulting in a deterioration in learning and classroom climate. Teacher stress has been linked to low pupil–teacher rapport (Petrusich, 1966), pupil anxiety (Doyal & Forsyth, 1973), poor classroom management (Kaiser & Polczynski, 1982), and low pupil achievement (Forman, 1982; Kaiser & Polczynski, 1982). Job frustrations experienced by teachers are passed on to the students, and negative results are numerous. Physical and behavioral symptoms may lead to dysfunctional behaviors in the classroom.

The final results of stress-induced behaviors lead to, among other things, staff turnover, absenteeism, and chronic burnout. Stress has been cited as a major factor in teachers' decisions to leave teaching (Kyriacou

& Sutcliffe, 1978). Reduced efficiency, tardiness, and absenteeism are frequent indicators of teacher stress (Eskridge & Coker, 1985). Administrators are concerned particularly with teacher turnover due to the implications for future hiring practices and concern for the retention of good teachers. Teacher turnover is extremely costly for school districts and disrupts the continuity of educational programs and personnel.

The ultimate result of stress is burnout. Burnout reflects a failure to cope effectively with stress (Cherniss, 1981; Etzion & Pines, 1986). In addition, burnout may be characterized by any of the following: a state of fatigue or frustration; loss of concern of all emotional feelings; physical depletion; feelings of helplessness and hopelessness; emotional drain; and development of negative attitudes toward work, life, and people (Maslach & Jackson, 1981). Often burnout may be a greater problem than teacher turnover. A teacher suffering burnout may choose to remain in the profession and do a poor job of teaching rather than quit in order to allow a new, and possibly enthusiastic, teacher assume the job. Administrators rank teacher burnout as the most serious problem facing educators in the 1980s (Farber, 1984).

STRESS PRODUCERS

Organizational stressors responsible for producing teacher stress are discussed in the context of research on social power and interpersonal communication among teacher–student, teacher–teacher, and teacher–principal. The concept of social power has been defined in numerous ways by numerous theorists. Popular synonyms include social influence, persuasion, coercion, dominance, leadership, authority, control, and compliance-gaining (Berger, 1985). For the purposes of this chapter, we analyze social power relationships from an interactional approach (dyadic and groups). This is not to suggest that related approaches such as institutional and societal influences are not important. Rather than examining all documented global approaches, we elected to concentrate our study of social power and interpersonal communication on the teacher in the public school classroom, emphasizing social power interactions among students, fellow teachers, and administrators.

The Teacher

When examining the individual teacher from an intrapersonal perspective several approaches to understanding social power are apparent. Berger (1985) in his chapter on social power in the *Handbook of Interpersonal Communication* reported on Freudian and neo-Freudian approaches, motivational approaches, Machiavellianism, the authoritarian personality, and locus of control. For our purposes two constructs are discussed: authoritarian personality and locus of control.

Before describing the authoritarian teacher in relation to social power and interpersonal communication, the authoritarian personality must be defined. The authoritarian individual tends not only to show a great concern for personal power in interpersonal interactions with others (Adorno, Frenkel-Brunswick, Levinson, & Sanford; 1950) but also tends to admire uncritically persons who are in positions of power (Berger, 1985). High authoritarian teachers tended to report higher levels of stress in the classroom (Harris, Halpin, & Halpin, 1985), often as a result of expecting persons with lower power (students) to accept, without question, influence from the person with higher perceived power levels (teacher). Unfortunately, students fail to respond accordingly to the authoritarian teacher and, as a result, student discipline has been a constant source of stress for the authoritarian teacher.

In terms of demographic effects, several are noteworthy. Gender differences and school level (high school, junior/middle, elementary) are reported in the literature. Most male teachers tended to have a more authoritarian orientation in the classroom and in general than females (Sowa & Lustman, 1984). In addition, male teachers reported higher stress levels associated with teaching than females (Harris et al., 1985). The overall authoritarian philosophy or mind set is increasingly apparent in our secondary schools, particularly the high school. High schools are viewed as being male-dominated institutions that cater to male philosophies and needs. During teacher performance evaluations, male high school teachers seemed to prefer a more authoritarian principal, whereas females preferred a principal from a more humanistic model (O'Hair, 1987). This male-dominated secondary school environment appears to be a major source of stress and alienation to female teachers (Calabrese & Anderson, 1986).

Internal/External Locus of Control. Locus of control refers to cognitive processes and individual behaviors congruent with self-perceptions (Rotter, 1966). Individuals with an internal locus of control tend to view their world as being conditional on their own actions or skills rather than on the basis of chance or luck. Externals have no such belief. They feel that rewards are not contingent upon their actions and that luck, chance, or "powerful others" control what happens to them (Glogow, 1986; Rotter, 1971). Rotter (1966) clearly delineated the difference as follows:

> When a reinforcement is perceived by the subject as following some action of his own but not being entirely contingent upon his action, then, in our culture, it is typically perceived as the result of luck, chance, fate, as under

the control of powerful others, or as unpredictable because of the great complexity of forces surrounding him. When the event is interpreted in this way, we have labeled this a belief in external control. If the person perceives that the event is contingent upon his own behavior or his own relatively permanent characteristics, we have termed this a belief in internal control. (p. 1)

Externals attribute successes and failures to others and events rather than themselves, for example, teachers who view their discipline problems in the classroom as being a result of poor principal or parental support in lieu of self-developed skills in classroom management and instruction. Berger (1985) related locus of control to social power:

It is obvious that persons with high levels of internal locus of control or origins are those who believe that they are responsible for effecting change in their environments, whereas their externally controlled or pawn counterparts feel that they are controlled by their environments. Because several of the definitions of social power reviewed earlier emphasized the notion that persons with power are able to effect changes in the behavior or attitudes of others, then these locus of control measures may represent attitudes or beliefs that persons have about their abilities to exercise influence. (p. 447)

The attitude or belief of feeling in control (internal locus of control) is not a new concept; however, there is little empirical research testing this theoretical postulation in an educational setting regarding teacher stress (Halpin, Harris, & Halpin, 1985). O'Hair (1987) surveyed 161 teachers from two Southwest states and found that female elementary teachers reported a higher internal locus of control score on the *Teacher Locus of Control Scale* (Hall, Smitley, Villeme, & Schwartz, 1980) than male junior high or high school teachers who reported an external orientation. In addition, a significant SCHOOL AGE interaction effect found that young elementary teachers demonstrated a strong internal locus of control orientation, whereas young junior high school teachers and middle-age junior high school teachers reported an external locus of control. Farkas (1983) studied the locus of control orientations of school principals; specifically, the degree of situational anomie they felt with respect to their jobs. He found the degree of internality (perceived locus of control) to be inversely related to level of perceived occupational stress. The more the principals felt in control, the less they were adversely affected by job stress.

Teacher–Student Communication

In this section we examine interaction approaches to power. Berger (1985) delineated the difference between individual and interaction approaches to power; the interaction theorists "view power as the product of interactions between persons and not the result of individuals' desires to wield influence over others" (p. 449). We are concerned with teacher–student interaction in relation to communication competence as a control variable when examining classroom discipline. Although communication competence definitions inevitably vary widely, and the task of defining communication competence has been described as "trying to climb a greased pole" (Parks, 1985; Phillips, 1984), we define the construct in terms of control over the environment through effective interactions. In the late 1960s, de Charms (1968) argued that individuals need to feel a sense of security toward the environment and that a lack of control may lead to feelings of incompetence. Miller and Steinberg (1975) stated that the basic function of communication is control over the physical and social environment. Interpersonal behavior, by nature, is presumed to be essentially control-oriented and manipulative (Wood, Weinstein, & Parker, 1967). When teachers experience a lack of effectiveness in affecting their classroom environment, job-related stress and burnout occurs. Often documented as the biggest challenge for teachers in controlling their environments is student discipline.

Teachers with less than five years of experience reported that the most stressful aspect of teaching was handling student discipline or *lack* of student discipline (Eskridge & Coker, 1985). O'Hair, Wright, and Alley (1989) found a direct correlation between teacher reported stress levels and student discipline. The fewer discipline problems a teacher reported the less job-related stress.

Teachers are not the only ones concerned with student discipline. Sixteen of the last twenty polls developed by Gallup (1988), seeking to identify the public's perception of the most important problems facing local public schools, have identified "lack of discipline" as the greatest problem. In the other four years "lack of discipline" was listed as the second most important problem. Consistent with public opinion, teachers rate lack of discipline a major problem. Feitler and Tokar (1982) found in a study of 3,300 teachers in grades K–12 that the most universal reason teachers felt pressure was related to student misbehavior.

In addition to public opinion and lack of discipline in general, teachers surveyed felt that administrators fail to support them adequately in matters of student discipline and that teachers are often bypassed when it comes to major decisions in their area of expertise—the instructional program (Galen, 1987; Wright, O'Hair, & Alley, 1988). Teacher–principal communication research is needed.

Teacher–Principal Communication

Teachers with over five years teaching experience reported the greatest job-related stressor to be linked to interpersonal communication among principals, colleagues, and students (Eskridge & Coker, 1985). Teachers resent the one-up communication characterized during teacher–principal interaction in settings such as performance evaluation and career ladder advancements. Farber (1984) reported that teachers in both suburban and urban schools perceived administrators and parents as contributing more to the problems that teachers face than to the help teachers need. Conditions in the Gupta (1981) study that frustrated teachers the most and received the highest rankings for stress were the following: (a) Principals not defending or being supportive of teachers, (b) Principals being overly critical of teachers, (c) Principals delegating bureaucratic duties to teachers, (d) Principals caring only about the work of the teachers and not about their social-emotional needs.

Performance Evaluation. An excellent applied setting to examine when analyzing teacher–principal interaction is the performance evaluation conference. Before examining the stylistic preferences of teachers in actual performance evaluation pre and postobservational conferences, it is important to establish the national climate concerning teacher evaluation. In recent years, teacher evaluation has become a major concern of educators and the general public. This concern is not new to educators, but the public pressure on educators to do a better job is recent. The pressure is manifest in legislative mandates in many states, career ladders, and merit pay. The pressure reflects two beliefs: the conviction that teachers who lack minimum competence to teach are being licensed, hired, and awarded tenure (Medley, 1982), and that some of the best teachers are leaving the field (Vance & Schlechty, 1982) because they are not adequately rewarded (Coker, 1985). Educators must deal with both problems when devising teacher performance evaluation criteria and plans.

Teacher evaluation plans are viewed as vague, confusing, and chaotic by teachers. Current methods of teacher evaluation have frequently used one or more of the following measures: competency tests to measure teacher qualifications, achievement test scores of students in the teacher's classroom, or ratings of teacher performance in the classroom (Soar, Medley, & Coker, 1984). Evaluation plans have succeeded in increasing stress levels among teachers (Eskridge & Coker, 1985).

Teachers often report that the principal has not spent enough time on evaluation. A study by Webb (1985) concluded that teachers tend to take for granted the daily routine of the principal. Surveys show that a typical principal spends about 65% of the time in face-to-face dealings with individuals or groups, with an additional 10% spent on the telephone or intercommunication system. That leaves only 25% of the day for filling out forms, performing central office paperwork, handling disciplinary problems, *evaluating teachers,* supervising the curriculum, and motivating the staff, not to mention planning, organizing, directing, and controlling the operation of the school. The need for exemplary communication skills cannot be denied. Wise and Darling-Hammond (1984–1985) summarized teachers' anticipation of the evaluation: "Teachers anticipate that annual brief visit from the principal who, according to the stereotype, stands stone-faced at the back of the classroom filling out a form. Principals rush to squeeze in their visits to teachers admidst their myriad of other duties" (p. 29). In addition to the principal's lack of time for evaluation purposes, the lack of immediate feedback often increases stress among teachers.

A second factor responsible for producing teacher stress during the evaluation process is the lack of teacher input into the process. In the best-selling book *In Search of Excellence,* Peters and Waterman (1982) noted that those private sector enterprises that thrive find some means of making employee involvement meaningful and of providing employees with a sense of at least some control over the forces in the workplace (Richards & Johnson, 1984–1985). Very few researchers and/or public school administrators have asked teachers what they perceive to be their major difficulties. In addition, teachers are not asked routinely to participate in solving problems and/or in implementing innovations (Kelleher, 1985). This lack of control has been linked early to an increase in stress among teachers. Wise and Darling-Hammond (1985) summarized the situation:

> In many school districts, teacher evaluation is a perfunctory, routine, bureaucratic requirement that yields no help to teachers and no decision-oriented information to the school district. The process does nothing for teachers except contribute to their weariness and reinforce their skepticism of bureaucratic routine. Isolated from decision making and planning, it does little for administrators except add to their workload. It does not provide a mechanism for the school system to communicate its expectations concerning teaching, except that teaching is a fit subject for bureaucratization. (p. 29)

Teachers often complain of individuals in administrative and/or supervisory roles who do not have the experience or professional skills to adequately judge teaching performance. They also felt that most supervisors or principals could not cope with the classroom situations in which teachers operate on a daily basis (Eskridge & Coker, 1985). John Goodlad (1984), in his ever popular book titled *A Place Called School,* described the evaluation situation as being:

> naive and arrogant to assume that principals, who may or may not have been effective teachers, can acquire and maintain a higher level of teaching expertise than teachers engaged in teaching as a full-time occupation. This concept becomes particularly absurd at the secondary level, where presum-

ably the principal who has attended some special institutes on teaching, necessarily for short periods of time, will have acquired teaching competence beyond that of the teacher of each of the diverse subjects. (p. 302)

Principal awareness of communication strategies that reduce teacher stress is needed. O'Hair (1987) reported on the effects of principal message strategies on teacher stress levels during performance appraisal interviews and concluded that a principal should be aware of the different teacher preferences for message strategies during performance evaluation. Demographic variables linked to preferred principal message strategies were teacher age, gender, and school level. For example, of the 161 teachers from two Southwest states, high school teachers preferred a more authoritative communication style, whereas elementary teachers preferred a more democratic style. Principal awareness of preferred message strategies is an essential ingredient to reduced teacher stress.

Finally, it is becoming increasingly important to remember that teachers are not the only educators reporting high stress levels due to ineffective communication with principals. It is important to note how school principals perceive stressful school situations. Koff, Laffey, Olson and Cichon (1979–1980) surveyed 1,291 school principals and discovered that out of 48 events examined, the 5 most stressful were: (a) forcing the resignation or dismissal of a teacher, (b) dealing with unsatisfactory performance of professional staff, (c) involuntary transfer to another principalship, (d) preparing for a teachers' strike, and (e) refusal of a teacher to follow policies. Principals obviously feel stress when dealing with teachers.

Teacher–Teacher Communication

Art Costa (1989) characterized the "act of teaching" as being the "second most private act." Specifically, in this section we explore factors impacting peer communication: isolation and leadership. Teaching has always been characterized as a lonely profession in which teachers rarely have the opportunity to communicate with other teachers but rather discover their lives dictated by bells and intercom systems. Teachers seldom are afforded the opportunity to observe teaching by their peers or participate in team teaching. Isolation in the classroom has been the persistent reality of most teachers. The vast majority of schools are organized in a manner that makes it difficult for teachers to find time to work with one another and often makes teachers wary of their own colleagues (Lieberman, 1988). Merit pay plans and career ladders have resulted in a competitive rather than collaborative atmosphere among teachers.

There is an obvious need for communication research that is designed to study barriers that have kept teachers isolated from one another and the establishment of a more professional culture in the schools. Lieberman (1988, p. 650) presented several questions as to the development of collegiality in schools. First, should teachers spend half of their time in the classroom and the other half working with other teachers? Would a ratio of 60% to 40% be better? Should they instead spend one year in the classroom full-time and the next year working with other teachers full time?

Currently, research in the area of teacher–teacher communication has only scratched the surface of the problem. In the past, a particularly notable group of teachers who have reported high occupational stress levels attributable to low peer interaction are English-as-a-second language (ESL) teachers (O'Hair, 1987). A logical explanation might be that bilingual teachers teaching ESL students and/or special education students may feel isolated from mainstream teachers, and as a result, tend to form cliques with peers teaching similar students rather than join the majority of teachers. Also, these teachers may tend to share in the high frustrational levels experienced by their students, which may account for higher stress levels.

COMMUNICATION STRATEGIES THAT PROMOTE STUDENT LEARNING

Improved communication between teachers and students has become a goal of educators across the nation. The bottom line in measuring a school district's or state's success in educating children is student learning. Teacher communication skills are viewed as a must for improving student learning. Almost every state now requires formal assessment of teachers for initial or for continuing certification or licensure, and almost all tests claim to evaluate communication abilities (McCaleb, 1987). Two and a half decades ago Solomon, Bezdek, and Rosenberg (1963) suggested that the uncertainty about variables influencing effective teacher–student interactions is the result of a lack of ability to make sense of individual research findings within a common reference. Research on teacher–student interactions is available but what is lacking is a model interrelating individual findings of effective interactions (Gorham, 1988). Communication behaviors examined in this section attempt to formulate a working model of effective teacher communication in the classroom (Fig. 7.1). Specifically, verbal/nonverbal immediacy, time on task, responsibility training, and teaching styles are examined as communication strategies improving student–teacher communication while reducing teacher stress. Each are discussed in relation to an interactional model of teacher–student communication effectiveness.

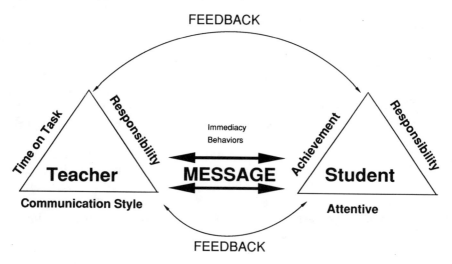

FIG. 7.1.   Teacher/student interaction model.

Verbal Immediacy

Verbal immediacy is defined by Mehrabian (1967, 1981) as stylistic differences in expression from which like–dislike is inferred. Teachers who
verbalize the positive results of on-task behavior are perceived as more
immediate than those who verbalize the negative consequences of failing
to comply and that a particular set of power messages is likely to be
related to increased learning (Gorham, 1988). The Gorham (1988) study
indicated that student perceptions of teacher immediacy are influenced
by verbal as well as nonverbal behaviors. Immediacy behaviors that were
documented to contribute significantly to learning were: (a) teacher's use
of humor in class; (b) praise of students' work, actions, or comments; (c)
frequency of initiating and/or willingness to become engaged in conversations with students before, after, or outside of class; (d) a teacher's self-
disclosure; (e) asking questions or encouraging students to talk; (f) asking
questions that solicit viewpoints or opinions; (g) following up on student-
initiated topics; (h) referring to class as "our" class and what "we" are
doing; (i) providing feedback on students' work; (j) asking how students
feel about assignments, due dates, or discussion topics; and (k) inviting
students to telephone or meet with the teacher outside of class if they
have questions or want to discuss something (Gorham, 1988, p. 47–48).

  The contribution of teachers' verbal behavior to learning has been
explored in terms of the use of prosocial messages (based on reward,
expert, and referent power) as opposed to antisocial messages (based on
coercive and legitimate power). Increased perceptions of teacher immedi-

acy leads to greater affective (Gorham, 1988; Plax, Kearney, McCroskey, & Richmond, 1986) and cognitive (Gorham, 1988; Richmond, McCroskey, Kearney, & Plax, 1985) learning.

A different research approach focusing on student–teacher immediacy behaviors in the public school classroom was recently reported at the Association of Teacher Educators Annual Conference. O'Hair et al. (1989) reported that traditional undergraduate student teachers exhibited a significantly greater number of verbal and nonverbal immediacy behaviors using the Gorham (1988) scale than did nontraditional graduate student teachers completing a fifth-year program. Undergraduate student teachers appeared more relaxed and confident in the classroom. This assessment was based on ratings of an independent observer viewing student teachers teaching in actual classrooms via videotapes. Significant implications of the O'Hair et al. (1989) study question the Holmes Group and Carnegie Foundation report, among other prominent professional groups, which supports the national movement to eliminate undergraduate teacher education programs and rely solely on fifth-year programs for teacher certification and perhaps even masters degrees.

Immediacy behaviors directly linked to student learning reflect the message in the *Teacher/Student Interaction (TSI) Model.* (See Fig. 7.1.) Variables influencing the message origin (the teacher) are time on task, responsibility training, and communicator style. The message receiver (the student) is influenced by achievement, responsibility for one's own learning, and attentiveness. In the following section, each variable in the TSI Model is explored in depth.

Time on Task Communication

The first notable teacher communication variable linked to student learning is time on task. Specific teacher communication behaviors that contribute to increased time on task correlate to classroom management and teacher stress in the classroom. Emmer and Evertson (1981) defined those teacher behaviors that produce good classroom management as those that "produce high levels of student involvement in classroom activities, minimal amounts of student behaviors that interfere with the teacher's or student's work, and efficient use of instructional time" (p. 342). Effective classroom managers have been differentiated from ineffective classroom managers on the basis of their familiarity with and practice of behaviors that increase students' time spent on task (Brophy & Evertson, 1976; Emmer, Evertson, Sanford, Clements, & Worsham, 1984; Jones, 1987). Time on task is the single best predictor of learning (Denham & Lieberman, 1980; McGarity & Butts, 1984). Teachers who actively keep their students involved in challenging academic tasks, no matter what instructional method is used, are more likely to be effective in helping students learn (Woolfol & McCune-Nicolich, 1984).

Responsibility Training. The pertinent question for communication and education scholars to ask is, "What specific teacher communication behaviors improve time on task?" Jones (1987) defined those teacher communication behaviors as behaviors that promote teaching students to be responsible for their own actions. A key element to improving time on task is teaching students to cooperate. The important teacher response in responsibility training is the answer to the student question, "Why should I cooperate with you?" or just, "Why should I?" Jones (1987) outlined the three management options for obtaining cooperation: (a) teach well and reward well; (b) nag, threaten, and punish; and (c) lower one's standards and make peace with the fact that cooperation will not be forthcoming. Without the systematic use of incentives teachers will get cooperation only from those students who feel like giving it, and teachers will get nothing from the rest. Without complete cooperation teachers will either become punitive or lower their standards (pp. 146–147). Further research is needed in the area of teacher communication behavior that promotes responsibility training in the classroom.

Contrasting Jones' student cooperation/learning model, Richmond and McCroskey (1984) reported "the communication of power in the classroom has a major association with student learning, both cognitive and affective" (p. 135). With teacher power as the center issue, research utilizing compliance-gaining and Behavior Alteration Techniques (BAT) provides insights into the classroom. After close to a decade of teacher communication research using the BAT, several findings are noteworthy. The results of the Allen and Edwards (1988) study revealed "perceptions of good, average, and poor teachers indicate that principals associated certain BATs with more effective teaching strategies. In general, principals equate reward-type messages with effective teaching and punishment-type messages with ineffective teaching" (p. 195). Eighty-two Louisiana principals perceive that ineffective teachers use communication strategies involving punishment from teacher, teacher authority, guilt, and debt more often than effective teachers (Allen & Edwards, 1988). In the strictest sense, the issue of power by the teacher over the student is not successful if students perceive messages to be negative in nature.

Communication Style

Effective teachers in the classroom are difficult to characterize in terms of communication style. One common denominator effective teachers tend to share is communicating a positive learning environment generally through a well-planned lesson and lively presentation. Javidi, Downs, and Nussbaum (1988) in a descriptive study of dramatic teaching styles concluded that college, high school, and middle school teachers who incorporate humor, self-disclosure, and narratives are perceived by students as more effective in the classroom. An effective teacher's classroom performance provided new teachers with a temporary pedagogical model, a temporary scaffolding from which novices may learn to be more expert (Berliner, 1986). On the other hand, an ineffective teacher is described by Norton and Holladay (1983) as a teacher who is "not very lively or animated, does not have a very precise style . . . is not very relaxed, and does not use a dramatic style" (p. 238). As the TSI Model demonstrates, a teacher who successfully communicates time on task and responsibility training through the use of a dramatic style and immediacy behaviors will discover increased student responsibility, achievement, and attentiveness.

IMPLICATIONS FOR FUTURE RESEARCH

With the research information available on "good" teaching practices as opposed to "bad" teaching practices, perhaps attention should now be focused on teacher–student interaction rather than practices. The following questions focus on the study of classroom interaction: How might communication researchers begin studying teacher–student interactions? What should school districts do to facilitate a research/training program to uncover stress and decrease it? What should an applied research agenda look like?

First, how might researchers begin? In the past the most successful applied researchers were individuals with recent public school teaching experience (substitute teaching is acceptable). Teachers respect teachers and are generally willing to actively participate in applied or action research programs when conducted by ex-teachers or current teachers. The ivory tower professor wishing to conduct research in the public schools will face not only district barriers but also lack of teacher cooperation. Unlike most training and development manuals for consultants, applied communication researchers should not begin at the top of the organization in education. Of course district approval is needed, but the key approval or acceptance is needed from the teachers and building principal. Team research projects involving the university and district personnel are often fruitful. The major obstacles frequently plaguing applied researchers are the lack of communication between groups and the slow process resulting from lengthy planning sessions. Working with professional teacher organizations or teacher unions is productive. If the union is convinced of the importance of the research project, the membership is cooperative and helpful. There are many avenues to pursue when beginning an applied communication research project but none can substitute for time spent in the public schools as a teacher, substitute, or teacher's assistant.

Teacher stress research requires a large commitment from school districts. Pinpointing stress sources is relatively simple. What becomes more complex is developing effective stress reduction programs designed to meet the specific needs of the district. Recently, a school district in the Southwest determined classroom management to be a major source of stress among teachers in the district. After the specific discipline program was determined, communication researchers studied intervention strategies that maintained lasting effects. One of the most neglected areas of research in teacher in-service training is long-term effects.

What should an applied research agenda look like in a public education setting? First, adopt a "real" issue (i.e., lack of public support for education, drugs, discipline, teacher stress, etc.). Avoid molding a communication concept based exclusively on college sophomore classrooms such as compliance gaining, Machiavellianism, power in the classroom, etcetera. Although these are excellent concepts by which to study specific educational contexts or problems, they should not be used as the focal point for the research design. Second, observe teachers in realistic situations. Relying on videotaped classrooms may not reflect a naturalistic setting. Capturing naturalistic interaction between students and teachers requires the researcher to become a part of the environment. If a researcher is studying play of children, the researcher must play with children for days until becoming a fixture on the playground just like the monkey bars or swings. At that date, realistic data is available. Last, conduct in-service workshops designed to present results of the study to school officials and teachers. In addition to presenting results, the researcher should develop and implement treatment programs. Not only is the researcher making a contribution by identifying the problem but also by providing problem resolution. Often, we as researchers stop one step short after the study has been accepted for publication and neglect the treatment stage. Remember, applied research unlike basic research addresses specific problems. In addition, applied communication research in the public education setting involves real people, children, teachers, principals, and parents, who deserve a complete applied research program.

REFERENCES

Adorno, T., Frenkel-Brunswick, E., Levinson, J., & Sanford, R. (1950). *The authoritarian personality*. New York: Harper & Row.

Allen, T., & Edwards, R. (1988). Evaluators' perceptions of teachers' use of behavior alteration techniques. *Communication Education, 37*(3), 188–197.

Berger, C. (1985). Social power and interpersonal communication. In M. L. Knapp & G. R. Miller (Eds.) *Handbook of interpersonal communication* (pp. 439–499). Beverly Hills: Sage.

Berliner, D. (1986). In pursuit of the expert pedagogue. *Educational Researcher, 15*, 5–13.

Bloch, A. (1978). Combat neurosis in inner-city schools. *The American Journal of Psychiatry, 135*, 1189–1192.

Bradfield, R., & Fones, D. (1985). Special teacher stress: Its product and prevention. *Academic Therapy, 21*, 91–97.

Brophy, J., & Evertson, C. (1976). *Learning from teaching: A developmental perspective*. Boston: Allyn & Bacon.

Cardinell, C. (1980). Teacher burnout: An analysis. *Action in Teacher Education, 2*, 9–10.

Cherniss, C. (1981). Preventing burnout: From theory to practice. In J. W. Jones (Ed.), *The burnout syndrome* (pp. 172–176). Park Ridge, IL: London House Management Press.

Coker, H. (1985). Consortium for the improvement of teacher evaluation. *Journal of Teacher Education, 36*, 12–17.

Costa, A. (1989, April). *What human beings do when they behave intelligently and how they can become more so*. Paper presented at New Mexico Association for Supervision and Curriculum Development, Albuquerque, NM.

de Charms, R. (1968). *Personal causation: The internal affective determinants of behavior*. New York: Academic Press.

Denham, C., & Lieberman, A. (1980). *Living to learn*. Washington, DC: National Institute of Education.

Doyal, G., & Forsyth, R. (1973). Relationship between teaching and student anxiety levels. *Psychology in the Schools, 10*, 231–233.

Emmer, E. T., & Evertson, C. (1981). Synthesis of research on classroom management. *Educational Leadership, 38*, 342–347.

Emmer, E., Evertson, C., Sanford, J., Clements, B., & Worsham, M. (1984). *Classroom management for secondary teachers*. Englewood Cliffs, NJ: Prentice-Hall.

Eskridge, D., & Coker, D. (1985). Teacher stress: Symptoms, causes, and management techniques. *The Clearing House, 59*, 387–390.

Etzion, D., & Pines, A. (1986). Sex and culture in burnout and coping among human service professionals. *Journal of Cross-Cultural Psychology, 17*(2), 191–209.

Farber, B. (1984). Teacher burnout: Assumptions, myths, and issues. *Teachers College Record, 86*, 321–338.

Farkas, W. (1983). Stress and the school principal: Old myth and new findings. *Administrator's Notebook, 30*(8), 1–4.

Feitler, F., & Tokar, E. (1982). Getting a handle on teacher stress: How bad is the problem. *Educational Leadership, 39*, 456–458.

Forman, S. (1982). Stress management for teachers: A cognitive-behavioral program. *Journal of School Psychology, 20*, 180–187.

Galen, H. (1987). Helping veteran teachers in our brave new world. *Principal, 66*(3), 33–35.

Gallup, A. (1988). The 20th annual Gallup poll of the public's attitude toward the public schools. *Phi Delta Kappan, 70*(1), 33–46.

Glogow, E. (1986). Research note: Burnout and locus of control. *Public Personnel Management, 15*(1), 79–83.

Goodlad, J. (1984). *A place called school*. McGraw-Hill.

Gorham, J. (1988). The relationship between verbal teacher immediacy behaviors and student learning. *Communication Education, 37*(1), 40–53.

Gupta, N. (1981). *Some sources and remedies of work stress among teachers*. Washington, DC: National Institute of Education. (ERIC Document Reproduction Service No. ED 21496)

Hall, B., Smitley, W., Villeme, G., & Schwartz, J. (1980). *Development and validation of teacher locus of control scale*. Paper presented at the meeting of the National Council on Measurement in Education, Boston.

Halpin, G., Harris, K., & Halpin, G. (1985). Teacher stress as related to locus of control, sex, and age. *Journal of Experimental Education, 53*, 136–140.

Harris, K., Halpin, G., & Halpin, G. (1985). Teacher characteristics and stress. *Journal of Educational Research, 78*, 346–350.

Javidi, M., Downs, V., & Nussbaum, J. (1988). A comparative analysis of teachers' use of dramatic style behaviors at higher and secondary educational levels. *Communication Education, 37*(4), 278–288.

Jones, F. (1987). *Positive classroom discipline*. New York: McGraw-Hill.

Kaiser, J., & Polczynski, J. (1982). Educational stress: Sources, reactions, preventions. *Peabody Journal of Education, 10*, 127–134.

Kelleher, P. (1985). Inducing incompetent teachers to resign. *Phi Delta Kappan, 66*, 362–364.

Koff, R., Laffey, J., Olson, G., & Cichon, D. (1979–1980). Stress and the school administrator. *Administrator's Notebook, 28*, 1–4.

Kyriacou, C., & Sutcliffe, J. (1978). Teacher stress: Prevalence, sources, symptoms. *British Journal of Educational Psychology, 48*, 159–167.

Lieberman, A. (1988). Teachers and principals: Surf, tension, and new tasks. *Phi Delta Kappan, 69*(9), 648–653.

Litt, M., & Turk, D. (1985). Sources of stress and dissatisfaction in experienced high school teachers. *Journal of Educational Research, 78*, 178–185.

Maslach, C., & Jackson, S. (1981). The measurement of experienced burnout. *Journal of Occupational Behavior, 2*, 1–15.

McCaleb, J. (Ed.). (1987). *How do teachers communicate? A review and critique of assessment practices* (Teacher Education Monograph No. 7). Washington, DC: ERIC Clearinghouse on Teacher Education.

McGarity, J., & Butts, D. (1984). The relationship among teacher classroom management behavior, student engagement, and student achievement of middle & high school science students of varying aptitude. *Journal of Research in Science Teaching, 21*, 55–61.

Medley, D. (1982). *Teacher competency testing and the teacher educator*. Charlottesville: University of Virginia, Association of Teacher Educators and the Bureau of Educational Research, School of Education.

Mehrabian, A. (1967). Attitudes inferred from nonimmediacy of verbal communication. *Journal of Verbal Learning and Verbal Behavior, 6*, 294–295.

Mehrabian, A. (1981). *Silent messages: Implicit communication of emotions and attitudes*. Belmont, CA: Wadsworth.

Miller, G., & Steinberg, M. (1975). *Between people: A new analysis of interpersonal communication.* Chicago: Science Research Associates.

Norton, R., & Holladay, S. (1983, May). *A structural normative analysis of behaviors of effective teachers.* Paper presented at the meeting of the International Communication Association, Dallas, TX.

O'Hair, M. (1987). The effects of principal message strategies on teacher stress levels during performance appraisal interviews. *Dissertation Abstracts International, 48,* 1371. (New Mexico State University, DA8719793).

O'Hair, M., & Housner, L. (1989, March). *Traditional versus nontraditional education student: Is one more effective in the classroom?* Paper presented at the American Educational Research Association, San Francisco.

O'Hair, M., Wright, R., & Alley, R. (1989). *Student teacher discipline problems: Is self-report data accurate?* Paper presented at the Association of Teacher Educators, St. Louis.

Parks, M. (1985). Interpersonal communication and the quest for personal competence. In M. Knapp & G. R. Miller (Eds.), *Handbook of interpersonal communication* (pp. 171–201). Beverly Hills: Sage.

Peters, T., & Waterman, R. (1982). *In search of excellence: Lessons from America's best-run companies.* New York: Harper & Row.

Petrusich, M. (1966). Separation anxiety as a factor in the student teaching experience. *Peabody Journal of Education, 14,* 353–356.

Phillips, G. (1984). A competent view of "competence." *Communication Education, 33,* 24–36.

Plax, T. G., Kearney, P., McCroskey, J., & Richmond, V. (1986). Power in the classroom VI: Verbal control strategies, nonverbal immediacy, and affective learning. *Communication Education, 35,* 43–55.

Raschke, D., Dedrick, C., Strathe, M., & Hawes, R. (1985). Teacher stress: The elementary teacher's perspective. *The Elementary School Journal, 85,* 559–564.

Richards, R., & Johnson, R. (1984–1985). The nominal group technique as a way for teachers to define stressors. *Educational Research Quarterly, 9,* 12–14.

Richmond, V., & McCroskey, J. (1984). Power in the classroom II: Power and learning. *Communication Education, 33,* 125–136.

Richmond, V. P., McCroskey, J., Kearney, P., & Plax, T. (1985). *Power in the classroom VII: Linking behavior alteration techniques to cognitive learning.* Paper presented at the annual meeting of the Speech Communication Association, Denver.

Rotter, J. (1966). Generalized expectancies for internal versus external control of reinforcement. *Psychological Monographs, 80,* 1–28.

Rotter, J. (1971). External control and internal control. *Psychology Today,* 37–53.

Soar, R., Medley, D., & Coker, H. (1984). Teacher evaluation: A teacher's fantasy. *Phi Delta Kappan, 50,* 44–47.

Solomon, D., Bezdek, W., & Rosenberg, L. (1963). *Teaching style and learning.* Chicago: Center for the Study of Liberal Education for Adults.

Sowa, C., & Lustman, P. (1984). Gender differences in rating stressful events, depression, and depressive cognition. *Journal of Clinical Psychology, 40,* 1334–1337.

Vance, V., & Schlechty, P. (1982). The distribution of academic ability in the teaching force: Policy implications. *Phi Delta Kappan, 64,* 22–27.

Webb, D. (1985). The perfect principal: A teacher's fantasy. *Phi Delta Kappan, 67,* 27.

Wise, A., & Darling-Hammond, L. (1984–1985). Teacher evaluation and teacher professionalism. *Educational Leadership, 42,* 28–33.

Wood, R., Weinstein, E., & Parker, T. (1967). Children's interpersonal tactics. *Sociological Inquiry, 37,* 129–138.

Woolfol, A., & McCune-Nicholich, L. (1984). *Educational psychology for teachers* (2nd ed.). Englewood Cliffs, NJ: Prentice-Hall.

Wright, R., O'Hair, M., & Alley, R. (1988). Student teachers examine and rate classroom discipline factors: Help for the supervisor. *Action in Teacher Education, 10*(2), 85–91.

SALES AND MARKETING CONTEXTS

THE DYNAMICS OF IMPRESSION MANAGEMENT IN THE SALES INTERVIEW

8

DALE G. LEATHERS
University of Georgia

The stereotype of the used-car salesperson has been a highly resilient one for decades. If you have seen the portrayal of the used-car salesperson in the movie *Used Cars* with Kurt Russell, then the image is probably indelibly imprinted on your mind. Russell and his cohorts at the used-car lot surreptitiously roll back odometer readings, literally reattach loose bumpers with chewing gum, and use "water-based" paint to restore the finish of the used cars. The movie parodies the stereotype of the hard-sell salesperson. This stereotypical salesperson is the aggressive, bombastic, insensitive, fast-talking, fender-thumping, tasteless slob who is decidedly short on both ethics and education.

The modern corporate sales representative bears little resemblance to the stereotypical figure in the used-car lot who is at the same time both legendary and unsavory. Today's salesperson is a sophisticated person with communication skills. Communication skills are necessary because the modern salesperson must match wits with and persuade professional purchasing agents who possess communication skills that are comparable if not superior. The professional purchasing agent will probably also have in-depth knowledge of a set of sales techniques so numerous that little the salesperson can offer will be truly new.

Tomorrow's corporate salesperson will be totally immersed in an information-intensive profession where the computer is at once both servant and master. In *Personal Selling* (1988), Marks wrote that:

The computer will free salespeople from many of the routine aspects of their jobs, but it will also add demands. With the development of small computer terminals, salespeople will be able to order direct from their customers' offices or from their cars without spending time on unproductive paperwork. They will also act as information brokers for their customers, dialing into their company's system and finding out about the status of previous orders. (pp. 21–22)

THE IMPORTANCE OF PERSONAL SELLING: THE SALES INTERVIEW

Personal selling has rapidly become a challenging and respected profession. In order to appreciate personal selling as a vitally important type of persuasive communication three factors need to be considered.

The Values of Personal Selling

Personal selling is much more than a meal ticket for salespeople. In fact, personal selling serves many values that are important to society even if they are not typically known to and appreciated by the average person.

Clearly salespeople fill an important role as agents for progress and change. Steven Jobs did not develop the Apple Computer, for example, but he sold it. Without the sales efforts of people such as Jobs new ideas, concepts, processes, and products would never be tried or accepted by the general public with the dramatic effects on the everyday lives of the buyers that result.

Second, salespeople not only promote economic activity in a general sense but stimulate the type of competition that results in more efficient methods of production and less expensive products. If you do not believe that personal selling produces the type of competition that results in higher quality products and lower prices, perhaps you would be interested in buying a Delorean sports car.

Third, personal selling creates customer satisfaction. As Wendel and Gorman (1988) wrote, a "well-informed salesperson can tell buyers things about a product that will help enhance buyer understanding of a product's value and increase its useful life. A better-informed and better-assured buyer is a more satisfied customer. Thus the value of that information and assurance approximates the value of what is given in exchange" (p. 11).

Personal Selling in the Marketing Mix

You may ask: Is personal selling really that important? After all, a decision to buy may be affected by other factors of equal or greater importance such as quality of the product, pricing, and distribution. These are all important factors in what is known as the *marketing mix*. The marketing mix is the way a company's product, pricing, distribution, and promotion strategies interrelate and interact to form the "total package" that is considered by the buyer (Wendel & Gorman, 1988).

A colleague, Dr. Clyde Harris, discusses the relative importance of these factors in the marketing mix in one component of a sales and communication training program he presents with me. For the decades of the 1960s, 1970s, and 1980s, Harris found that the relative importance of the factors in the marketing mix remain fixed: Promotion effort is ranked as most important and is followed in turn by product effect, distribution effort, and pricing effort.

When one looks at specific marketing activities, the importance of personal selling becomes even more apparent. Over the last three decades sales managers have rank-ordered marketing activities from most to least important in this order: personal selling, service, technical research and development, marketing research, and the print media.

Elements of the Selling Process

Personal selling is not, of course, defined solely by the critically important communicative interaction between seller and buyer that occurs during the sales interview. A *selling process* is involved, which consists of four interacting steps: prospecting, pre-approach, approach, and the sales interview (Marks, 1988).

Sales trainer Clyde Harris has developed a creative way of conceptualizing and illustrating the sales process. He conceives of the sales process as a baseball diamond with first base representing prospecting, second base as the pre-approach, third base as the approach, and the sales interview with a successful close as home plate. In our Sellcomm training program for General Electric Harris, stressed that "all bases must be touched. Otherwise an appeal is made by the customer (C) and the salesperson is subject to being put out. Calling on the wrong prospect and failing to do proper pre-call work are as harmful as an improper approach. Each base must be touched" (Sellcomm Training Manual, p. 51).

Although prospecting, pre-approach, and approach are all important elements in the sales process, the sales interview itself is of paramount importance. Traditionally, the sales interview has been thought of as accentuating the use of the salesperson's sales and communication skills. Certainly, many contemporary scholars see the sales interview as fundamentally a communicative phenomenon. The central thesis of this chapter is that impression management is the communication phenomenon of greatest significance in the sales interview.

THE IMPORTANCE OF IMPRESSION MANAGEMENT

In a general sense the importance of impression management should be apparent to almost anyone who has daily interaction with other human beings. No matter what the nature of our profession or vocation, all of us—except the masochists in our midst—must be concerned about the impressions we make on others. Most of us must be concerned with the formidable task of selling ourselves in the real world.

Selling ourselves in the real world is undeniably important. James Gray, Jr. (1982) wrote in *The Winning Image* that the image traits that others attribute to us are frequently major determinants of success or failure in a variety of communication situations. Said Gray (1982), "your image is a tool for communicating and for revealing your inherent qualities, your competence, abilities, and leadership. It is a reflection of qualities that others associate with you, a reflection that bears long-lasting influence in your bid for success" (p. 6).

Impression Management in the Real World

Impression management (IM) has become an important subject in recent years. This is so because members of many professional groups recognize that the impressions they make in public are central if not controlling determinants of their success. Attorneys, doctors, politicians, executives, and many other professionals know that they must make favorable impressions in order to be successful. Knowledge of impression management gives them the potential to do so.

The importance of impression management is hardly limited to a handful of communication contexts, however. In fact, the dividends to be derived from the use of impression management skills in the classroom (Gorham, 1988; Plax, Kearney, McCroskey, & Richmond, 1986), in medical communication (Harrigan & Rosenthal, 1983; Heath, 1984), in the family (Fry & Grover, 1983), in counselling (Friedlander & Schwartz, 1985), in the police interview (Leathers, 1986), in intercultural communication (Almaney & Alwan, 1982; LaFrance & Mayo, 1978), and in the job interview (Gifford, Ng, & Wilkinson, 1985) are becoming increasingly apparent.

Such staid institutions are banks are now hiring experts in impression management to determine not only how they are perceived by their customers but also what impression management activities they must undertake to be perceived as they wish to be perceived. Thus, City National Bank decided to explore the possibility of expanding its ATM network with the confident expectation that "increased accessibility to its ATM system should improve its image of both convenience and size" (Wofford, Preddy, & Gup, 1982, p. 73).

Impression Management in the Sales Interview

The importance of impression management in achieving success in a variety of *organizational contexts* is now receiving increasing attention (Caldwell & O'Reilly, 1982; Galinat & Muller, 1988; Onkvisit & Shaw, 1987). Thus, Gardner and Martinko (1988) emphasized in a recent article in *The Journal of Management* that impression management skills can be extremely valuable in organizations for a number of reasons. Impression management behaviors are potentially related to individual success and promotability within organizations, may be an important influence mechanism for leaders in generating support for their actions, and are necessary to gain some measure of control in an organizational environment where reality is socially constructed.

Although the value of impression management is rapidly becoming established in a variety of organizational contexts, its value in the sales interview is already recognized by many. Because impression management focuses upon the development and use of principles that can be used to sell ourselves, it is not surprising that impression management skills are particularly important in the sales interview. Indeed, King and Booze (1986) emphasized that leading salespeople must be skillful impression managers: "The ace salesperson knows how to make his body support and complement every word of the convincing sales presentation. . . . Thus, a salesperson needs to know how to read buyer behavior and how to manage his own signals to gain a positive attitude from the buyer" (p. 53).

If it is true that the exercise of impression management skills is a major determinant of success in the sales interview, it is also true that nonverbal cues typically exert a major—if not controlling—influence on impressions made in the sales interview.

Recently the central role of nonverbal cues in managing impressions in personal selling has been receiving increasing attention by marketing scholars. Thus, Stewart, Hecker, and Graham (1987) wrote that "the area of marketing activity that has already incorporated much of what is known about nonverbal communication is the personal selling and negotiation function. Sales training programs, particularly those of larger organizations, and organizations that sell across cultures often include a strong emphasis on recognizing and using nonverbal cues" (p. 317).

In fact, authors of personal selling books now often devote many chapters to the impression management functions of nonverbal cues in the sales interview. Credibility, for example, is generally recognized as the most important component of the impressions we make on others. In his insightful treatment of credibility in personal selling Marks (1988) made quite clear that nonverbal cues are vitally important:

> Nonverbal communication is especially important in establishing the credibility of the salesperson. Prospective buyers' response to communication is heavily influenced by their attitude toward the source of the communication. If the source is viewed as believable, the message is more likely to be influential. . . . The external characteristics of salespeople are of great importance in conveying an image of credibility. (p. 127)

THE SKILLED SALESPERSON

Traditionally, salespeople have been led to believe that they must develop two sets of interrelated skills if they are to be successful: sales and communication skills. Among scholars there is a rather high degree of agreement as to the nature of the most important sales skills. Salespeople must: (a) *determine* the precise nature of the *customer's needs,* (b) determine such needs in part by refining the *art of questioning,* (c) determine such needs also by developing their *listening skills* (both aural and visual listening skills, (d) relate their message(s) to the customers' needs and concerns via accurate *interpretation of* and sensitive response to the *customers' feedback,* and (e) employ FAB (Feature/Advantage/Benefit) *selling* in a way that relates directly the relevant features and benefits of their product to the customers' needs (Alessandra, Cathcart, & Wexler, 1988; Marks, 1988; Wendel & Gorman, 1988).

When the communication skills of the salesperson are considered, two things are apparent at minimum. Communication skills are now recognized by both scholars and trainers as central to the success, or lack of success, of the salesperson. Second, sales and communication skills interrelate and overlap to such a degree as to make them almost indistinguishable.

Alessandra et al. (1988) recognized the predominant importance of communication skills in personal selling:

> Selling is many things but first and foremost it is a process of communication. It is a people-business in which you establish relationships, give and receive information, solve problems and build mutually beneficial associations with many people. . . . Salespeople who truly want to excel will work on their communication skills as diligently as their product knowledge, prospecting, strategies, promotion, and so on. (p. 241)

Interestingly, Alessandra et al. (1988) identified the major communication skills of the salesperson as the fine art of questioning, the effective uses of feedback, and utilization of the full communicative potential of three types of nonverbal communication—body language, proxemics, and the voice.

In his book, *Nonverbal Selling Power,* Gschwandtner (1985) further blurred the distinction between sales and communication skills. Part I of this book is devoted entirely to the nature and importance of nonverbal communication whereas Part II focuses exclusively on how nonverbal communication can be used in different parts of the selling process. Rasicot (1986) went even further and devoted all of his book, *Silent Sales,* to a demonstration of the role of nonverbal cues in personal selling.

In this chapter the unclear and unenlightening distinction between sales and communication skills is abandoned. Conceptually, it makes more sense to subsume these two sets of skills under the more encompassing label of impression management. Increasingly, sales and communication skills are exercised in the sales interview to achieve an objective of overriding importance: the management of impressions by the salesperson. When these skills are exercised for this purpose, they are impression management skills. Impression management in turn is defined as an individual's conscious attempt(s) to exercise control over selected communicative behaviors and cues for purposes of making a desired impression.

SUCCESSFUL IMPRESSION MANAGEMENT IN THE SALES INTERVIEW

Although the importance of impression management in the sales interview is now recognized by scholars, sales trainers, and salespeople, our knowledge of the dynamics of impression management in this context remains limited. This is true because an explicit conceptualization of the impression management process that is based on and derived from existing theory and research has not been developed.

The conceptualization that follows represents a refinement of my recent description and discussion of the impression management process; the steps of the process are applied in this instance to the persuasive communication that occurs in the sales interview (Leathers, 1988).

In fact, my own training work has served as a major impetus for the attempt to develop a complete conceptualization of impression management. A colleague and I have presented a communication and sales training program, Sellcomm, for a number of years for General Electric as well as other corporations. As the benefits of the impression management component have become increasingly apparent to individuals enrolled in the Sellcomm program, I have been expanding the amount of time devoted to the subject.

Impression management may be viewed as a process consisting of four interrelated stages. When used in sales training or by salespeople in the actual sales interview, the four stages in the process may more appropriately be considered as steps. The "four-step" description has proven to be particularly helpful in spelling out the sequence of actions that are necessary if the salesperson is to be an effective impression manager. When implemented by the salesperson as impression manager in the sales interview/negotiation, these four interrelated and interacting steps provide an operational definition of the dynamics of impression management in personal selling.

The four steps in the impression management process are:

Stage I: Familiarization with the communication of successful impression managers

Stage II: Identification, selection, and application of principles of impression formation, and of impression management

Stage III: Measurement of impressions made

Stage IV: Modification of undesirable communicative behaviors/cues to control impressions made

Studies of individuals who become successful impression managers suggest that they typically begin by studying the efforts of notably successful impression managers. Whether a politician, auto executive, religious leader, or an attorney, for example, the successful impression manager usually is a voracious reader of autobiographies; autobiographies often reveal not only the major strategies used by the successful impression manager but such tactical factors as the gestural nuances and appearance cues that were crucial to success.

Our best model impression managers tend to be well-known public personalities; this is so because fairly detailed written, audiotaped, and videotaped records of their impression management activities are available for study. General George Patton, J. Edgar Hoover, and Prime Minister Margaret Thatcher are good examples of individuals who carefully contemplated their own impression management goals. They consciously controlled their own communication for purposes of accentuating certain "image dimensions" that defined the impressions they made on people who were important to them. Patton, for example, left little to chance.

In his insightful book, *Impression Management,* Schlenker (1980) wrote that "Patton recognized the importance of controlling nonverbal activities to create the impression he desired. . . . He developed hypotheses about what attributes soldiers would most respect in their commander and acted accordingly" (p. 235). Thus, Patton practiced his "war face" in front of a mirror so that he would look particularly determined, brave, and powerful. He also believed that a strong leader should be seen going to the front but not returning from it. As a result, Patton frequently went to the front by road during the day but returned at dusk or even after dark—sometimes in a small liaison plane. Similarly, the impression activities of J. Edgar Hoover and Prime Minister Thatcher have been chronicled in detail (Atkinson, 1984; Ehrlichman, 1982).

Ideally, of course, the persons used as "model impression managers" should have the same type of job and job responsibilities as the group of individuals who seek to develop their own impression management skills. Salespeople working for the Lighting Division of General Electric can unquestionably improve their impression management skills by studying model impressions managers such as Patton, Hoover, and Thatcher. For salespeople, studying the vocation-specific impression management efforts of master salesperson Lee Iacocca is even better. To study the subject, field, or industry-specific impression management activities of an award-winning salesperson who is employed by the GE Lighting Division would be best of all for sales trainees from the GE Lighting Division.

Stage II in the impression management process requires the ability to identify, select, and apply in the sales interview principles of impression formation, and principles of impression management. On a conceptual level, impression formation and impression management must be recognized as inseparably interrelated but nonetheless distinguishable phenomena.

Impression formation is defined by the set of interacting factors that affect the attributions of the person who is the target of impression management activities. As Harvey and Weary (1984) pointed out in their exhaustive review of attribution theory and research, attribution is a perceptual phenomenon that focuses upon our attempts to assign causes for the behaviors of people we observe and with whom we interact. In our attempts to explain the behaviors of those with whom we associate, we

typically attribute sets of "image traits" to these individuals. Such attributions are often grounded in cultural stereotypes. We know, for example,
that Americans are strongly predisposed to form the impression that
shifty-eyed persons are "deceptive."

In spite of the importance of Stage II in the impression management
process, no detailed set of principles of impression formation has previously been developed that might be used by salespeople, or other professionals, to become effective impression managers. I have developed a
rather detailed set of such principles for use in my sales training but cite
only a limited number of these principles in this chapter for purposes of
illustration.

Principles of Impression Formation

Salespeople frequently assume an active role as impression managers.
They must recognize, however, that their success as impression managers
is at least partially dependent on their understanding of principles of
impression formation. These principles help explain how and why prospects and customers react as they do to the salesperson's communication
(Baumeister, 1982; Harvey & Weary, 1984; Riggio & Friedman, 1986;
Schlenker, 1985; Tedeschi & Riess, 1981).

The following principles focus directly upon the personal selling that
occurs in the sales interview or sales negotiation:

1. The single most important judgment a sales prospect will make
about the image you project is how credible you are. Although you should
take pains to build your personal credibility in the eyes of the sales
prospect, salespeople should exert particular effort to try to enhance their
perceived competence; competence is the most important dimension of
credibility.

2. Business associates frequently examine the image a salesperson
projects very carefully to see whether the image is consistent or inconsistent with information believed by business associates to be true. In business situations we are expected to be what we present ourselves to be.
Salespeople should, therefore, make no claims with regard to individual
abilities or personal qualities that do not have substantial factual support.
If you doubt the validity of this principle, consider the case of Senator Joe
Biden, who for a time sought the Democratic nomination for President.
When his claims about his academic achievements in college and law
school proved to be not only grossly distorted but demonstrably false, his
credibility as a presidential contender was destroyed.

3. We tend to give more weight to negative information about others than to positive information. Salespeople should, therefore, carefully monitor their communication during a sales call with the objective of eliminating the most negative features of the communication.

Principles of Impression Management

As impression managers, salespeople must of course be concerned about the personality traits and personal qualities that they are presumed to have by others. Over the years, many attempts have been made to identify the *actual* personality traits that define the personality profile of the salesperson. Recently, for example, Plotkin (1987) attempted to define the personality profile of the salesperson by highlighting such "personality dimensions" as *sociability, cynicism, competitiveness,* and *dominance.* Alessandra et al. (1988) went a step further in trying to define the "Image of Excellence" of the top 5% of salespeople who are most successful. Among the characteristics of excellence allegedly exhibited by "the top 5 percenters" are depth of knowledge, flexibility, sensitivity, and enthusiasm. It is interesting to note that the personality profile of the average salesperson closely mirrors the "salesperson stereotype" whereas the personality profile of the most successful salesperson does not.

Such efforts to identify the *actual* personality traits of salespeople have been less than satisfying for a number of reasons. Methodological procedures used are often flawed or vague; the research is based on the assumption that salespeople exhibit the same, fixed traits in all sales situations, and a number of researchers assume that *actual* personality traits are more important than *perceived* personality traits.

In fact, the impressions that salespeople make in the sales interview on others are defined by the *perceptions* of business associates. These impressions are not unidimensial in nature. Indeed, a number of empirical studies suggest that the impressions we make are defined by a number of "image dimensions" that are essentially independent (Kern, 1982; Meuhlenhard & Scardino, 1985; O'Sullivan, Ekman, Friesen, & Scherer, 1985; Tedeschi & Riess, 1981). Although the image dimensions that emerge in a given study will depend in part on the nature of the communicative interaction and context being studied, the following image dimensions seem to be particularly important in the sales interview: *credibility, likeability, assertiveness, interpersonal attractiveness, truthfulness,* and *interestingness.*

The impression management principles identified here are used for purposes of illustration; the complete set of principles I have developed for use in training salespeople in impression management is available upon request.[1]

Image Dimension I: Credibility

1. Vocal cues—such as relatively fast rate, substantial volume, and short pauses—are related to perceptions of increased competence (Burgoon & Saine, 1978; Street & Brady, 1982).

2. Individuals who exhibit insincere smiles at inappropriate times will probably be viewed as less trustworthy than individuals who smile sincerely in context (Ekman & Friesen, 1982).

3. Individuals who exhibit bodily tension and rigidity are seen as less dynamic than individuals who are relaxed and those who use bodily movement to emphasize the points they are making (Richmond, McCroskey, & Payne, 1987).

Image Dimension II: Likeability

4. Communicators who exhibit open body positions, direct bodily orientations, smiling, affirmative head nodding, and direct and sustained eye contact will be better liked than communicators who do not exhibit these nonverbal cues (Kleinke, 1986; Richmond, Gorham, & McCroskey, 1987).

Image Dimension III: Assertiveness

5. Communicators who speak with a soft voice, smile out of context, laugh out of context, exhibit nervous gestures, such as hand-wringing and lip-licking, do not look directly at others, and whose bodies are rigid are apt to be seen as nonassertive (Lange & Jakubowski, 1976; Schlenker, 1980).

Image Dimension IV: Interpersonal Attractiveness

6. Tall communicators with large, endomorphic body builds should wear lighter colored suits and accent items to make them seem less intimidating and more approachable (Bixler, 1984; Rasicot, 1986).

Image Dimension V: Truthfulness

7. Communicators who exhibit an abnormal number of hand-to-body gestures, eye contact of short duration, and nonfluencies are more likely

---

[1]The full set of principles of impression formation and of impression management as well as a copy of the complete Impression Sensitivity Instrument (which are actually used in the Sellcomm training program) are available by writing to the author.

to be perceived as deceptive than those who do not (Cody & O'Hair, 1983; Ekman, 1985).

Image Dimension VI: Interestingness

8. Communicators who exhibit a narrow pitch and volume range are often perceived to be uninteresting (Leathers, 1986).

Impression managers who are equipped with a detailed set of principles of impression formation, and impression management, clearly have the potential to make the desired changes in the impressions they are making. Before they become actively engaged in trying to modify the impressions they make on others, however, they must obtain rather detailed and objective information from business associates or others with regard to how positive or negative are the impressions they are making.

The *Impression Sensitivity Instrument* (ISI) is a measurement tool I am developing that can be used by salespeople to have customers or other business associates assess the impressions they are making on them. The ISI consists of sets of semantic-differential-type scales that measure the degree of positiveness or negativeness of the impression a salesperson has made on each of the six "image dimensions" just discussed. Because the image dimension of credibility is defined by the separate factors of competence, trustworthiness, and dynamism, for example, the competent–incompetent, trustworthy–untrustworthy, and assertive–unassertive scales are used to measure these three factors. Similarly, the image dimension of truthfulness is measured with scales such as truthful–dishonest and straightforward–evasive.

In Stage IV of the impression management process, impression managers attempt to modify those communicative behaviors and cues that they conclude are primarily responsible for the negative impressions they have made in terms of specific image dimensions. Image information obtained from a measurement tool such as the ISI is used to determine on which image dimension(s) the impression manager is deficient.

IMPRESSION MANAGEMENT PROBLEMS IN THE SALES INTERVIEW

In order to master the dynamics of impression management in the sales interview, the salesperson must determine how positively or negatively he or she is viewed with regard to each of the six "image dimensions" that define the impressions made by that person: (a) credibility, (b) likeability,

(c) assertiveness, (d) interpersonal attractiveness, (e) truthfulness, and (f) interestingness.

An instrument such as the Impression Sensitivity Instrument will provide information that pinpoints on which image dimensions, if any, the salesperson is making an unacceptably negative impression. For example, a salesperson who is viewed as competent but not likeable or interesting has at least two impression management problems that require attention. Furthermore, solutions to such impression management problems are frequently not simple; they may involve tradeoffs. The changes in communicative behaviors and cues that may enhance liking, for example, may depress perceived competence. Thus, Rasicot (1986) wrote that the "higher on the power scale people dress, the lower on the friendliness scale they are perceived, and vice versa" (p. 41).

In the past 10 years I have had extensive opportunities to observe the types of impression management problems that occur most frequently in the sales interview. In fact, I have observed corporate sales representatives sell products ranging from light bulbs to wine to fertilizer to antiaircraft guns to sonar imaging equipment used in the most sophisticated medical centers. Although the products and processes that are sold tend to vary dramatically, salespeople seem to encounter certain basic types of impression management problems that are similar in nature.

Take the image dimension of credibility for example; competence and trustworthiness have repeatedly been found to be the two most important factors that define credibility. Although a number of communicative behaviors and cues may negatively affect the salesperson's perceived competence in the sales interview, two types of nonverbal behaviors have proven to be particularly pervasive and serious treats to *competence:* (a) salespeople looking down as they begin to answer a question and looking down as they begin to describe the most compelling benefits of their product; and (b) salespeople becoming dysfluent.

Trustworthiness tends to decline rapidly when the salesperson fails to sustain eye contact during the greeting, smiles and laughs out of context, and communicates via inconsistent messages. If you had seen a salesperson smile or laugh when informed by the customer that a sale worth over a quarter of a million dollars had just been lost (as I have on a number of occasions), then you would realize why such incongruous behavior depresses judgments of the salesperson's trustworthiness. You may have experienced this phenomenon firsthand if you saw the Reverend Jimmy Swaggart cry on command almost precisely 5 minutes before he made his appeal for money at the end of his television program.

Liking is the second important image dimension. Trite though it may sound we tend to like people who like us or at least appear to like us. In the sales interview the person who gets low ratings on liking is often physically unresponsive and emotionally uncommunicative. Salespeople who exhibit a lack of immediacy behaviors are typically seen as unlikeable; they remain relatively fixed, even rigid, in their chair, are visually inattentive listeners, rarely communicate interest and positive reinforcement via postural shifts, head nodding, and forward lean, and disclose little if anything about their feelings and emotions.

Salespeople should strive to be judged appropriately *assertive;* the extremes of unassertiveness and aggressiveness as they define this third image dimension are both undesirable. In the first instance the salesperson is branded as a status inferior whereas in the second instance the customer is treated as an inferior.

Visually unassertive salespeople are anxious and communicate their anxiety in many ways. Their anxiety may be reflected in such signs of submissiveness as the palms-up handshake, hand-wringing, briefcase guarding body, constant blinking, and frequent throat clearing (Gschwandtner, 1985). They may also communicate their unassertive communication style with a "soft" voice and a rigid body. Like their aggressive counterparts unassertive salespeople respond in inappropriate nonverbal ways when they encounter sales resistance or receive negative feedback from the customer.

The aggressive salesperson frequently fixes the prospect or customer with an unremitting stare, assumes a belligerent posture, and shakes a finger in the prospect's face in order to emphasize a selling point. Exaggerated gestures and posture are often combined with manipulative questions and judgmental statements such as "Don't you agree?" and "That's a false economy, son." Whereas unassertive salespeople become defensive when they encounter sales resistance, the aggressive salesperson often becomes condescending.

One of the most important components of the image dimension of *interpersonal attractiveness* is personal appearance. Salespeople often make themselves seem less interpersonally attractive than they desire to be by dressing in a way that violates the dress expectations of the customer. A salesman from Massachusetts, for example, reported to me that he made a serious mistake early in his selling career. He dressed in an expensive, conservative, pin-striped, black suit. This particular salesman was 6'-8" tall and weighed around 240 pounds. His height and size made him physically intimidating and difficult to identify with in the sales interview. Rather than dealing effectively with the problem by choosing less formal and lighter-colored clothing, he accentuated his image problem by inappropriate choice of clothing. He was in a position to sacrifice perceived competence/authoritativeness in order to be perceived as more likeable. Unfortunately, he chose to wear clothing that would have a perceptual effect that was opposite from the one he desired.

Truthfulness, the fifth image dimension that defines the impressions made by salespersons, represents a potentially serious problem for salespeople. This is true because even salespeople working for large organizations with high corporate credibility are tainted to some degree by the "salesperson stereotype." The stertotype nurtures the expectation that the salesperson may be somewhat less than straightforward and honest. "Phony smiles" by the salesperson are particularly likely to trigger the customer's predisposition to view the salesperson as deceptive. The smile may be discernibly "phony" because no crow's-feet appear around the salesperson's eyes, the smile is slightly asymmetrical, the smile appears too quickly, and the long duration of the smile of 15 seconds makes the smile seem less than believable (Ekman & Friesen, 1982).

Finally, a salesperson with a deficit on the *interestingness* image dimension has a very serious impression management problem. The customer's judgment that a salesperson is uninteresting or even dull can be devastating in a vocation where a premium is placed on gregariousness and the ability to involve if not entertain a sales prospect. My own training experience suggests that salespeople judged to be uninteresting frequently *sound* uninvolved with and unenthusiastic about the product/process they are selling; their voice sounds monotone with a narrow pitch and volume range. To correct this problem, the salesperson must emphasize major benefits of the product being sold with detectable variation in vocal emphasis, and must communicate emotional involvement using substantial but appropriate changes in pitch. Voice training may be required.

In many cases the impression management problems illustrated in this section can be solved or at least handled effectively by bringing them to the salesperson's conscious level of awareness. Awareness must precede modification of the specific communicative behaviors/cues that can be shown to have an undesirable impact on an image dimension such as liking or interestingness. Impression management problems such as those just described are not likely to be solved unless the salesperson fully understands the dynamics of impression management in the sales interview. If the impression management problems are severe, they may require the concentrated attention of an impression management trainer.

This conceptualization of the impression management process has proven to be extremely useful in my sales and communication training in impression management. When adapted to the training environment, the stages in the process are converted to steps. This is done so that salespeople can more easily follow the interrelated *sequence* of actions that are associated with successful impression management.

The first part of this training is designed not only to inform the salesperson about the steps in the impression management process but also to give the salesperson hands-on experience in using the four steps in the process. For example, film, videotape, and slides are all used to illustrate the communication that is characteristic of both successful and unsuccessful impression managers. The vocation-specific impression management efforts of salesman Lee Iacocca are featured. Sales trainees actually study and evaluate Iacocca's efforts to sell himself and his corporation in the famous Chrysler television commercials. The efforts of decidedly less successful impression managers such as Gary Hart are also analyzed.

The full set of principles of impression formation and of impression management are distributed to the sales trainees. Mini-lectures and discussion follow where I describe how the principles were derived and the nature of the empirical and theoretical support for the principles. The salespeople then describe specific sales situations where they felt they had problems with a particular image dimension such as credibility or likeability.

The sales trainees do require specific guidance so that they will know how to decide which communicative behaviors/cues must be modified in which way(s) if a particular image dimension is to be affected. This leads to the final part of this impression management program. In trying to project a desired image I stress that three factors may be particularly important for salespeople: (a) the choice of clothing and artifacts, (b) the use of the voice, and (c) the consistent display of behaviors that are appropriately assertive as opposed to being nonassertive or aggressive.

Clothing and artifacts are important because they have been proven to be potentially strong determinants of both perceived competence and likeability. During a separate subsection of the impression management training program, therefore, salespeople are asked to describe *how* they dress (and *why* they dress as they do) when they encounter sales prospects of different ages, gender, socioeconomic background, and nationality. They are asked to indicate which of the appearance guidelines specifically developed for this training program they would use in a given situation. For example, one such appearance guideline stipulates that if you are a large and muscular person, your physical presence may overwhelm the sales prospect—choose softer, lighter shades of blue, gray, or beige to make you seem less powerful and more likeable, friendly, and approachable.

The sound of the voice is also vitally important for the impression manager. For this reason the sales trainees are put through a series of voice training exercises designed to develop the capacity to use the voice in such a way as to enhance one or more of the image dimensions known to be strongly affected by the voice; this subsegment of the program includes a brief audiotaped demonstration by the noted trainer Zig Ziglar on how to use the voice expressively. Finally, the sales trainees are asked to demonstrate how they can use the specific vocal guidelines that are provided to enhance one of the dimensions of the image they project. For example, one vocal guideline stipulates that salespeople should seek to minimize flatness, nasality, and tenseness in their speaking voices because these vocal qualities are associated with an individual who is nondynamic, uninteresting, and withdrawn.

The last set of training exercises is designed to help the salesperson behave in the sales interview in a way that is appropriately assertive. In order to establish the importance of assertiveness in the sales interview, behaviors of the nonassertive and aggressive salesperson are illustrated (Leathers, 1986). The participating salespeople are put through a series of roleplaying situations and their behavior is measured by their peers in terms of *degree* of nonassertiveness, aggressiveness, and assertiveness.

Finally, the culmination of the impression management program for salespeople is a 15-minute sales interview that is videotaped. The salesperson attempts to sell her or his major product to a professional buyer. The salesperson attempts to utilize relevant and appropriate principles of impression management to make the desired impression. Subsequent evaluation by the trainer, professional buyer, and the salesperson's peers focuses on how skillfully the salesperson used relevant impression management principles in order to achieve specific goals.

SUMMARY

This chapter emphasizes the central importance of communication in the sales interview. The communication phenomenon of overriding importance in the sales interview in turn is identified as impression management. Unfortunately, our knowledge of the dynamics of impression management in personal selling has remained quite limited. This chapter is designed to correct that information deficit by spelling out the steps in the impression management process that salespeople must use if they are to be successful impression managers.

In one sense the image dimensions over which an impression manager can exercise control may be situation specific. For example, some of my graduate students are currently studying the impression management efforts of particularly successful realtors. Preliminary reports indicate that the "truthful" and "assertive" image dimensions are most important to realtors. In the job interview the image dimension of interpersonal attractiveness may be particularly important. Finally, attorneys and physicians still probably both attach the highest priority to judgments clients/patients make about their credibility in general and the competence dimension of credibility in particular.

Although this chapter is designed to be useful to the corporate salesperson who is actively engaged in persuasion, the reader should remember that the key ideas and concepts are derived from and based upon theory and research. The relationships between impression theory and research, and application, is a reciprocal one, however. There can be little doubt that researchers and theorists can refine and sharpen their models of impression management by what they learn from assessing the effectiveness of impression management activities in a real-world context such as the sales interview.

REFERENCES

Alessandra, A., Cathcart, J., & Wexler, P. (1988). *Selling by objectives*. Englewood Cliffs, NJ: Prentice-Hall.

Almaney, A. J., & Alwan, A. J. (1982). *Communicating with the Arabs*. Prospect Heights, IL: Waveland Press.

Atkinson, M. (1984). *Our master's voices: The language and body language of politics*. London: Methuen.

Baumeister, R. F. (1982). A self-presentational view of social phenomena. *Psychological Bulletin, 92,* 3–26.

Bixler, S. (1984). *The professional image*. New York: Perigee.

Burgoon, J. K., & Saine, T. (1978). *The unspoken dialogue*. Boston: Houghton-Mifflin.

Caldwell, D. K., & O'Reilly, C. A., III. (1982). Responses to failure: The effects of choice and responsibility on impression management. *Academy of Management Journal, 25,* 121–136.

Cody, M. J. & O'Hair, H. D. (1983). Nonverbal communication and deception due to gender and communicator dominance. *Communication Monographs, 50,* 175–192.

Ehrlichman, J. (1982). *Witness to power: The Nixon years*. New York: Simon & Schuster.

Ekman, P. (1985). *Telling lies: Clues to deceit in the marketplace, politics, and marriage*. New York: Norton.

Ekman, P., & Friesen, W. V. (1982). Felt, false, and miserable smiles. *Journal of Nonverbal Behavior, 6,* 238–252.

Friedlander, M. L., & Schwartz, G. S. (1985). Toward a theory of strategic self-presentation in counseling and psychotherapy. *Journal of Counseling Psychology, 32,* 483–501.

Fry, P. S., & Grover, S. C. (1983). An exploration of the child's perspective: Children's perceptions of parental treatment, personal anxiety, and attributions of blame in single-parent families. *Journal of Psychiatric Treatment and Evaluation, 5,* 353–362.

Galinat, W. H., & Muller, G. F. (1988). Verbal responses of different bargaining strategies: A content analysis of real-life buyer–seller interaction. *Journal of Applied Social Psychology, 18,* 160–178.

Gardner, W. L., & Martinko, M. J. (1988). Impression management in organizations. *Journal of Management, 14,* 321–338.

Gschwandtner, G. (1985). *Nonverbal selling power.* Englewood Cliffs, NJ: Prentice-Hall.

Gifford, R., Ng, C. F., & Wilkinson, J. (1985). Nonverbal cues in the employment interview: Links between applicant qualities and interviewer judgments. *Journal of Applied Psychology, 70,* 729–736.

Gorham, J. (1988). The relationship between verbal teacher immediacy behaviors and student learning. *Communication Education, 37,* 40–67.

Gray, J., Jr. (1982). *The winning image.* New York: AMACOM.

Harrigan, J. A., & Rosenthal, R. (1983). Physicians' head and body positions as determinants of perceived rapport. *Journal of Applied Psychology, 13,* 496–509.

Harvey, J. H., & Weary, G. (1984). Current issues in attribution theory and research. *Annual Review of Psychology, 35,* 427–459.

Heath, C. C. (1984). Participation in the medical consultation: The coordination of verbal and nonverbal behavior between the doctor and patient. *Sociology of Health & Illness, 6,* 311–338.

Kern, J. M. (1982). Predicting the impact of assertive, empathetic-assertive, and nonassertive behavior: The assertiveness of the assertee. *Behavior Therapy, 13,* 486–498.

King, R. H., & Booze, M. B. (1986). Sales training and impression management. *Journal of Personal Selling and Sales Management, 6,* 51–60.

Kleinke, C. L. (1986). Gaze and eye contact: A research review. *Psychological Bulletin, 100,* 78–100.

LaFrance, M., & Mayo, C. (1978). Cultural aspects of nonverbal communication. *International Journal of Intercultural Relations, 2,* 71–89.

Lange, A. J., & Jakubowski, P. (1976). *Responsible assertive behavior.* Champaign, IL: Research Press.

Leathers, D. G. (1986). *Successful nonverbal communication.* New York: Macmillan.

Leathers, D. G. (1988, November). *Impression management training: Conceptualization and application.* Paper presented on a program of Applied Communication Section, convention of Speech Communication Association, New Orleans, LA.

Marks, R. B. (1988). *Personal selling: An interactive approach* (3rd ed.). Boston: Allyn & Bacon.

Muehlenhard, C. L., & Scardino, R. J. (1985). What will he think? Men's impressions of women who initiate dates and achieve academically. *Journal of Counseling Psychology, 32,* 560–569.

Onkvisit, S., & Shaw, J. (1987). Self-concept and image congruence: Some research and managerial implications. *The Journal of Consumer Marketing, 4,* 13–23.

O'Sullivan, M., Ekman, P., Friesen, W., & Scherer, K. (1985). What you say and how you say it: The contributions of speech content and voice quality to judgments of others. *Journal of Personality and Social Psychology, 48,* 54–62.

Plax, T. G., Kearney, P., McCroskey, J. C., & Richmond, V. P. (1986). Power in the classroom VI: Verbal control strategies, nonverbal immediacy and effectively learning. *Communication Education, 35,* 43–55.

Plotkin, H. M. (1987). What makes a successful salesperson. *Training and Development Journal, 41,* 54–56.

Rasicot, J. (1986). *Silent sales.* Edina, MN: AB Publications.

Richmond, V. P., Gorham, J. S., & McCroskey, J. C. (1987). The relationship between selected immediacy behaviors and cognitive learning. In M. L. McLaughlin (Ed.), *Communication yearbook 10* (pp. 574–590). Beverly Hills: Sage.

Richmond, V. P., McCroskey, J. C., & Payne, S. K. (1987). *Nonverbal behavior in interpersonal relations.* Englewood Cliffs, NJ: Prentice-Hall.

Riggio, R. E., & Friedman, H. S. (1986). Impression formation: The role of expressive behavior. *Journal of Personality and Social Psychology, 30,* 421–427.

Schlenker, B. R. (1980). *Impression management.* Monterey, CA: Brooks/Cole.

Schlenker, B. R. (1985). Identity and self-identification. In B. R. Schlenker (Ed.), *The self and social life* (pp. 65–99). New York: McGraw-Hill.

Stewart, D. W., Hecker, S., & Graham, J. L. (1987). It's more than what you say: Assessing the influence of nonverbal communication in marketing. *Psychology & Marketing, 4,* 303–322.

Street, R. L., Jr., & Brady, R. M. (1982). Speech rate acceptance ranges as a function of evaluative domain, listener speech rate, communication context. *Communication Monographs, 49,* 290–308.

Tedeschi, J. T., & Riess, J. (1981). Identities, the phenomenal self, and laboratory research. In J. T. Tedeschi (Ed.), *Impression management theory and social psychological research* (pp. 3–22). New York: Academic Press.

Wendel, R. F., & Gorman, W. (1988). *Selling: Personal preparation, persuasion, strategy* (3rd ed.). New York: Random.

Wofford, L., Preddy, R., & Gup, B. E. (1982). Mirror, mirror on the wall. *Banker's Management, 165,* 69–73.

FOCUS GROUP RESEARCH: THE COMMUNICATION PRACTITIONER AS MARKETING SPECIALIST

9

CONSTANCE COURTNEY STALEY
University of Colorado at Colorado Springs

Focus groups, or group depth interviews, emerged during the 1950s as a qualitative marketing research technique to get at the "why" behind traditional sample polls. Critics claimed that traditional quantitative research provided "lots of numbers but little insight into what was really going on"; focus groups provided a viable alternative (Bellenger, Bernhardt, & Goldstrucker, 1976, p. 7). Although often dismissed by quantitative researchers as "soft research," the popularity of focus groups has increased to phenomenal proportions today. Thanks largely to Madison Avenue, thousands of focus groups are conducted each year.

In today's marketplace, focus groups represent the most widely used of all qualitative research methodologies (Nelson, 1982). In fact, marketing research rarely "gets beyond qualitative" because focus group results provide adequate data upon which to base marketing decisions ("Profs get primer," 1986). As Van Maanen stated in his preface to *Qualitative Methodology* (1983), "to operate in a qualitative mode is to trade in linguistic symbols and, by so doing, attempt to reduce the distance between indicated and indicator, between theory and data, between context and action" (p. 9). One of the distinct advantages of focus groups is their ability to reduce the distance between manufacturers and product users.

In the marketing arena, focus groups are used to: (a) observe how an advertising idea is understood and determine whether the message is communicated clearly, (b) understand how various target groups interpret advertising messages differently, (c) gain insight about product users and how successfully advertising reaches them, (d) learn the usefulness of specific terminology and language choices used in advertising, and (e) explore possible problems and solutions relating to advertising messages (Hammond, 1986).

Depending on which of these desired objectives is paramount, a focus group may be classified as "exploratory" (generate ideas, develop hypotheses, test constructs), "clinical" (discover consumers' unconscious motives, uncover hidden emotions), or "phenomenological" (view the product from the consumers' vantage point, experience the product as the consumer experiences it) (Calder, 1977; Durgee, 1987).

Because focus groups generally produce immediate practical results, their uses have multiplied. Recently service industries such as health care, real estate, transportation, banking, and telecommunications have adopted the technique to find out what clients or buyers think about new policies, programs, and products. Political candidates use focus groups to learn how they are perceived by the public. Attorneys test case strategies before taking them to a jury. In fact, some experts caution that focus groups, now branded as "sexy" or "glamorous" research, may in some instances preempt other more appropriate methodologies. Certainly, focus groups are more interesting and enjoyable to conduct than traditional survey questionnaires for both sponsor and customer or client (Lydecker, 1986). This growing popularity of the technique may be attributed to the following advantages (Donath, 1986; Krueger, 1988; Wells, 1979):

1. Compared to mail or telephone surveys, focus groups are relatively inexpensive and expedient ($3,000 for an average focus group session).

2. Focus groups are excellent mechanisms for generating hypotheses when little is known about a subject.

3. Group interviews drastically reduce the distance between producer and product user.

4. Focus group interviews are characterized by flexibility, exploration, and the means to probe for further information. Rather than simply rate their opinions on a questionnaire scale of 1 to 7, for example, focus group interviews allow participants an opportunity to explain the reasons behind those opinions.

5. The technique is particularly useful in explaining the contingencies of human behavior ("sometimes I buy 'Product X' . . . but other times, I . . . .")

6. Respondents stimulate each other's thinking and ideas evolve in a snowballing fashion.

7. Findings emerge in a form sponsors readily understand; focus group research has face validity (i.e., makes sense).

8. Participants find focus group research to be both interesting and enjoyable and often feel flattered that the sponsoring organization is interested in their opinions. A secondary benefit of the research lies in the public relations function it performs.

Despite their wide popularity in a plethora of fields, focus groups are rarely used as research tools by the academic community, or more specifically in communication research. A notable exception is found in the pioneering work of Lederman (1983) who used focus group research to explore the attitudes of high communication apprehensives. My purpose in this chapter, however, is not to argue that focus groups are a viable research tool for the communication scholar. Rather, I argue that conducting focus group research is a viable consulting pursuit for the communication practitioner. There is wide agreement that focus group research is only as good as the skills of the focus group moderator (e.g., Axelrod, 1975; Bellenger et al., 1976; Hansler & Cooper, 1986; Sheilds, 1981). Despite little background in the marketing field per se, communication specialists bring the appropriate training, interests, and skills to focus group research.

FOCUS GROUP RESEARCH DEFINED

Participants

Originating from the psychoanalytic tradition, focus groups are typically groups of 8 to 12 people gathered together to *focus* on a topic during a 2-hour discussion. According to some experts, "a focus group is nothing more than an extremely well targeted and designed meeting" (Lydecker, 1986, p. 74). The size of the group is important for two reasons: groups with too few members can cause discomfort by placing an undue burden on each individual participant, and they also run the risk of generating relatively few perceptions. On the other hand, in groups with too many members, each individual participant's allowable contribution time is shortened.

In recent years, however, the trend is toward smaller groups of four or five persons ("Profs get primer," 1986). Members are selected according to various criteria and are typically paid an honorarium ranging from approximately $25 at the low end to hundreds of dollars for highly trained professionals such as physicians or engineers at the high end. Participants are sometimes recruited by the sponsoring organization, sometimes by professional recruiters, and sometimes by the consultant/moderator; however, each group should be homogeneous in nature, and generally participants should be unacquainted prior to the group meeting.

Often the discussion is audiotaped or videotaped and sponsors view the group's interaction from behind a one-way mirror. In some cases observers from the sponsoring organization have contact with the moderator during the meeting in order to request further probing in particular areas. Although the sponsor's identity is usually not revealed during the discussion, its representatives often join participants after the meeting to discuss the subject face-to-face (Rostky, 1986).

Moderator

Preparing for the Discussion.   The focus group discussion is led by a moderator or group leader using a discussion guide prepared in advance. This guide is developed after extensive consultation with sponsors in order to identify the organization's needs. Before the focus group research is conducted, the moderator must fully understand the sponsor's purpose and objectives, translate these objectives into a set of research questions, and develop a discussion outline to ensure that all important points are covered during the discussion (Wells, 1979). Finally, the moderator must prepare emotionally for the task at hand. A moderator who is relaxed, interested, and enthusiastic will generate similar attitudes in focus group participants (Hannah, 1978).

Leading the Discussion.   Moderating the focus group discussion requires considerable sensitivity and skill. Moderators must cultivate an appropriate style, somewhere between highly directive at one end of the continuum and highly nondirective at the other. They must consider the effects of nonverbal communication on the discussion (i.e., arrangement of participants, room decor, etc.). Moderating a focus group requires communication skills in order to:

- build rapport quickly
- set aside personal bias on the topic
- create a relaxed atmosphere
- inspire confidence and trust
- encourage spontaneity and honesty
- listen with a "third ear" and probe for additional information

- know when to feign ignorance or become argumentative as a way to encourage further explanation
- understand group dynamics
- balance contributions
- employ appropriate "pest control" techniques (i.e., discourage over-contributors and those who stray from the subject at hand)
- point out descrepancies between verbal statements and nonverbal expressions
- track and pace the discussion
- process the meaning and implications of participants' remarks as they occur (Bellenger et al., 1976; Caruso, 1976; Kennedy, 1976; Langer, 1978; McQuarrie & McIntyre, 1986; Templeton & Bates, 1976).

According to one expert, "the moderator is like a conductor, orchestrating an improvisation" (Levy, 1979, p. 32).

Synthesizing the Results. Focus group reports range from brief oral summaries of the moderator's impressions, particularly when time and cost are factors, to a full written report after careful analysis of the audiotapes, videotapes, or written transcripts. Moderators often use the "Scissor and Sort" or "Long Couch, Short Hallway" technique by spreading out the transcripts, bracketing important comments, sorting by theme, cutting and stapling, and finally writing the connecting and supporting narrative (Wells, 1979). Reports created in this fashion provide rich detail in the customers' own words as well as an introduction to the problem, discussion of major questions to be answered, summarized results as interpreted by the researcher, and implications of the research for the sponsoring organization. As Krueger (1988) noted, "The analysis process is like detective work. One looks for clues, but, in this case, the clues are trends and patterns that reappear among various focus groups" (p. 109). The researcher's final report consists of one of three levels of information: (a) raw data, (b) summarized data, and (c) interpreted data. Depending on the needs of the sponsoring organization, researchers either merely report participants' comments, provide descriptive summaries of participants' responses, or report, summarize and interpret the meaning of the data.

Each step in conducting focus group research is critical to the success of the research. The moderator must understand group dynamics, prepare adequately, be able to direct the group as well as elicit information, and synthesize from the discussion the client or consumer perceptions sought by the sponsoring organization (Shields, 1981).

THE COMMUNICATION CONSULTANT AS FOCUS GROUP RESEARCHER: A CASE STUDY IN LARGE-SCALE FOCUS GROUP RESEARCH

Project Background

From April to July 1987, I was one of three principal researchers hired to conduct a statewide needs assessment for a large, public charity foundation in Colorado. After exploring a variety of potential models for the process, the organization selected a model that incorporated both quantitative and qualitative research techniques.[1]

Research Design

The model provided for five regional forums (with a town-meeting structure) in which participants separated into small focus groups to discuss women's issues as they affected women in each area of the state. Participants also completed a questionnaire, developed in close coordination with the sponsoring organization, that explored women's and girls' problems, women's group affiliations, and demographic information about forum participants. In each of the five areas, local representatives of the sponsoring organization were responsible for inviting participants, securing a location, and recruiting local women to serve as moderators in the focus group discussions.

The agenda for each 4-hour forum included a half-hour opening session, multiple 2-hour focus groups meeting concurrently, a 30-minute break, and a closing session lasting approximately 1 hour. At the close of each forum, participants were encouraged to voice their comments during an open microphone session.

During the opening portion of each forum, participants were (a) welcomed to the community forum, (b) briefed on the forum schedule, and (c) directed to their appropriate breakout rooms. Participants then engaged in 2-hour focus groups to discuss one of six predetermined topics: health care, child care, education, employment, domestic violence, and housing.

---

[1]This section is adapted from Staley, Beatty, and Kassover (1987). Their unpublished report was later revised and published by The Women's Foundation of Colorado. The information is used here with permission.

Focus groups were led by trained moderators, all of whom had attended a previous 3-hour workshop to familiarize them with the focus group process. Because moderators were volunteers who had little familiarity or experience with focus groups, each moderator was also mailed a 10-page, pretraining packet prior to the training workshop, covering topics such as, "What Are Focus Groups," "Leading the Discussion," "Probing for Further Information," and "Troubleshooting." Group leaders followed a prepared discussion guide (see Appendix), also included in the pretraining packet. Notes were recorded by trained notetakers using specially prepared summary sheets. The discussions centered on three broad areas of inquiry:

Part I: Identification of current problems and needs.

Part II: Assessment of existing programs for women.

Part III: Development of ideas for new programs/solutions/change.

At the conclusion of the focus group discussions, a 30-minute break was scheduled in order to allow moderators and notetakers time to prepare a 10-minute presentation to all participants during the closing session. Court recorders' transcriptions or audiotapes (and later transcription) of the closing session provided a written account of each focus group's report and comments made by forum participants during the open microphone session. Notetakers' summaries provided additional verification of the results of individual focus group discussions.

My role in the project was to design and oversee the qualitative research component. Specifically, I organized the forums, conducted the opening and closing sessions as forum facilitator, oversaw the focus group discussions, trained all moderators and notetakers in each location, and synthesized and interpreted the qualitative research results, which were presented to the sponsoring organization, along with the quantitative survey results, in an 85-page written report.

Results

Demographics.   Questionnaire results indicated that participants in the research were politically active (75% claimed to vote all of the time), well-educated (66% had completed college and/or graduate school), middle aged (most were between 35 and 44 years of age), and Caucasian (73%), with personal incomes of less than $25,000 over the last year (75%). Nearly half were married with an average of 1.7 children.

Quantitative Research Results. When results of the questionnaires were tabulated, the following overall issues emerged:

1. Employment and economics were described as the most important problems facing forum participants.
2. Education, also a key problem, was seen to be intertwined with economics and employment.
3. Health care was described as a particularly critical problem for the poor and the elderly.
4. Child care was ranked low among issues, but open-ended responses underscored its significance.
5. Housing was identified as an important problem only by low-income participants and by the elderly.
6. Violence was an important issue for service providers (safehouse workers and volunteers) and for the lesbian contingent of forum participants.

Qualitative Research Results. Focus group results were summarized by topic and region, and described in terms of overall conclusions such as the following:

1. Forum participants expressed a wide range of both tangible and intangible needs.

2. Participants encouraged the sponsoring organization to move beyond needs assessment toward action to help solve women's problems and meet women's needs.

3. Participants voiced a request that the sponsoring organization use its funds to support existing programs, many of which currently function well but could improve and expand services with increased funding. This alternative was preferable to offering seed money and thereby proliferating new programs to compete for scarce resources.

4. Participants in rural areas expressed feelings of isolation and heightened need due to the inaccessibility of programs in their areas.

5. Participants across the state voiced a need for a statewide information clearinghouse to help women find ways to meet their own needs.

6. Although many of the problems women face relate to concrete issues (pay, child care, etc.), women are also psychologically needy; low self-esteem is viewed as a catalyst precipitating many other problems.

7. Participants saw education as a broad-based solution because it can help alleviate problems in many areas of women's lives.

8. In order to effect change, women need to position themselves in powerful decision-making roles.

9. Women need affordable, available, quality child care.

10. Education and preventative programs must begin with very young children.

11. Women must work to change societal attitudes: education for women is undervalued, violence toward women is tolerated, and discrimination toward women is accepted.

In addition to the desired quantitative and qualitative results, the sponsoring organization received feedback about the focus group experience itself. At the conclusion of each focus group, participants were asked to summarize the group's discussion. Overall, responses were extremely positive. The following testimonies written by forum participants are representative:

"The main point I'd like to make is that I was very impressed by the quality of the leader and participants—a perceptive, sensitive group!"

"I didn't realize that there were so many housing resources available and that all participants would have a piece of information that was relevant to the discussion."

"This forum is INVALUABLE. It allows women the freedom to share concerns and attempt solutions."

"It was good to hear others talk about programs in which they are involved. Ideas were freely given and everyone seemed interested in listening to them all. The group was beautifully led."

"I found talking with other motivated, active women to be helpful since it gave me persons to communicate with and emulate. I benefited from the open discussion. These women are involved and knowledgeable, and they provided both insight and ideas. It was good to exchange information and energies!"

"Our discussion focused on the barriers that exist in education for females, from the need for more financial aid to the pressing problem of child care and juggling day to day problems while attending school. The group was given an opportunity to 'dream' about new programs we would like to see."

"I'm surprised (and gratified) at the spontaneous cohesiveness and the likemindedness of this group in addressing women's mental health, personal growth, and teen pregnancy issues. . . . There was a generally positive, can-do attitude and several possible workable ideas were generated."

The results of the research, presented here in skeletal form, continue to provide guidelines for the sponsoring organization as it directs projects and makes funding decisions concerning the needs of Colorado women.

CONCLUSION

Research applications of the focus group technique are innumerable, both in the marketing field to test consumer reactions, and now throughout the service sector in fields such as education, transportation, banking, real estate, and government. Focus groups generate rich information that might be missed in traditional statistical research: "Unlike paper/pencil questionnaires, focus groups allow respondents to expand on their views. . . . If you ask people why they don't belong [to an organization] and they say the dues are too high, you can go into the reasoning behind that response" (Lydecker, 1986, p. 74). Consider the following examples of research purposes that may employ focus group methodology (Welch, 1985, p. 249):

1. Textbook publishers convene focus groups of professors to identify special promotional incentives to promote book adoptions.
2. A statewide high school vocational education program conducts a needs assessment, querying groups of students, parents, administrators, teachers, and businesspersons to identify new program ideas and areas of needed change.
3. A computer software program company convenes groups of engineers to discuss hypothetical new software packages that would help them do their jobs more successfully.
4. A major food service distributor evaluates reactions of restaurateurs to changes in its pricing formulas.
5. A manufacturing company asks consumers to react to alternative spokespersons for potential television advertising.
6. A motor freight carrier asks distribution managers to react to possible magazine advertisements.
7. A telecommunications company conducts focus groups to request information about customer preferences, economic trends, and new technologies.

8. A movie studio tests audience reactions to alternative endings of a new film.

9. A political candidate tests the effects of advertising messages or political speeches during a national campaign.

10. A bank uses focus groups as a follow-up to a mail-out survey on improved customer services.

11. A city library system conducts focus groups of library users and residents in the local area to determine the image of the public library.

Despite the growing popularity and applicability of focus group research, however, the technique has not escaped criticism. For example, data are voluminous and difficult to analyze, and much depends on the expertise of the moderator (Krueger, 1988). As Wells (1979) put it:

> Group interviewing violates most of the accepted canons of survey research. Samples are invariably small and never selected by probability methods. Questions are not asked the same way each time. Responses are not independent. Some respondents inflict their opinions on others; some contribute little or nothing at all. Results are difficult or impossible to quantify and are not grist for the statistical mill. Conclusions depend on the analyst's interpretative skill. The investigator can easily influence the results. (p. 11)

Validity and generalizability are the most serious concerns voiced by skeptics and newcomers to focus group methodology. To increase validity, the usual suggestion is to continue to conduct groups until the responses of participants become predictable and no new information surfaces—usually after four or five groups are conducted on the same topic. Although focus group research generally sacrifices breadth for depth, focus group researchers agree that results can be cautiously generalized to a similar population. However, "the intent of focus groups is not to infer but to understand, not to generalize but to determine the range, and not to make statements about the population but to provide insights about how people perceive a situation" (Krueger, 1988, p. 96). If research findings will lead to highly visible, important, or expensive decisions, multiple methodologies may be used to increase confidence.

Advocates, on the other hand, counter that all research contains assumptions and biases, and that quantitative research—a survey, for example—is only as reliable as the quality and accuracy of the questions asked. As Krueger (1988) pointed out: "Focus groups are valid if they are used carefully for a problem that is suitable for focus group inquiry. . . . Validity is the degree to which the procedure really measures what it proposes to measure" (p. 41). Furthermore, an item-by-item comparison between the results of a quantitative study and those of a qualitative study attest to the validity of focus group research (Reynolds & Johnson, 1978). A comparison of the results of a large-scale, nationwide mail survey with a 90% return rate and a series of 20 focus groups revealed 97% agreement between the two sets of research findings. In fact, in the one area of disagreement, later sales data verified the accuracy of the focus group results over the survey results.

Beyond such fundamental concerns, however, practical problems also exist. Research companies often do not monitor the recruiting efforts of interviewers (Welch, 1985). The result may be less than reliable information from a new generation of "focus groupies"—those who enjoy the process, not to mention the cash stipend, and participate at every opportunity, even when they lack the appropriate qualifications. In some major cities, focus groups are so prolific that it becomes difficult "to find a 'virgin'—someone who has never participated in one before" (Holcomb, 1985, p. 50).

A further complication exists in the group situation itself that sometimes tends to polarize participants, moving them toward a more emotional or extreme reaction to a product than they might have to the same product in a store ("Profs get primer," 1986). Powerful or charismatic participants may sway the opinions of others. And of course, participants' inherent abilities to conceptualize and to articulate their views, which may in fact be tied to economic level, necessarily influence the outcomes of focus group research. Investigating an issue or product relating to lower economic classes may be more difficult than investigating an upper-middle class issue or product ("Profs get primer," 1986).

A final caveat rests in the centrality of the focus group moderator to the success of the focus group research. Moderators who have difficulty establishing rapport, do not completely understand the sponsor's objectives, bring their own agendas to the discussion, over or undercontrol the participation of group members, follow the discussion guide too closely, or lack well-cultivated communication skills may inadvertently sabotage the research effort (Hollander & Oromaner, 1986).

The glamour of focus group research has attracted many charlatans to the field, often with disastrous results for sponsoring organizations. As one expert put it:

> We desperately need more qualitative researchers but we need good ones, trained ones, truly professional ones. We need to set up demanding college programs, carefully controlled internships, goals, and standards which have to be met if qualitative research is to continue as a viable and dependable tool for the marketer. (Axelrod, 1975, p. 11)

The following suggestions are intended to help you avoid many of the pitfalls outlined in this discussion:

1. First and foremost, obtain specific research objectives from the sponsoring organization. If your queries are met with vague generalizations, persist by ascertaining how the research will be used. This information is essential to the success of the project.

2. Coordinate your activities with the sponsoring organization, particularly in the early stages of the research process. Allow your contact or the committee administering the project to validate the discussion guide, and suggest modifications if necessary, before focus groups are conducted. Often an "insider" can point out oversights or identify a line of questioning in need of elaboration. Besides, this proactive step is good planning and, from a pragmatic point of view, good business.

3. To the extent possible, supervise the recruitment process and check whether participants have the appropriate qualifications. Holcomb (1985) reported the revelation of a frequent focus group participant who admitted regularly taking extreme positions in focus groups in order to influence others' opinions and skew the findings for the sake of pure enjoyment.

4. Employ the services of an assistant to supervise the audiotaping and take notes during the focus group meeting. This allows you as moderator to give full attention to responses as they are voiced, mentally track where the discussion has been, and plan ahead as the discussion evolves. It also provides you with a means to verify your perceptions of what has transpired.

5. Begin the analysis phase as soon as possible after the groups are conducted, while impressions are fresh in your mind. The urgency and emotion observed in participants' nonverbal messages may tend to fade over time.

6. Follow a verifiable and systematic route during the analysis phase, such that another researcher could legitimately come to the same set of conclusions you have come to. Sit down with the audiotapes, transcripts, and notetaker's summaries, focusing on one issue at a time. Look for emerging themes across groups. Keep a paper trail as you collapse data, summarize findings, search for patterns, and make inferences.

7. As you prepare your final report, oral or written, analyze your audience. Return to the original research objectives identified by the sponsoring organization, reminding yourself of what the organization needs from you and how your findings will be used. Write (or speak) pragmatically from your client's perspective, including all the information you believe will be useful and eliminating extraneous sidelines.

Those of us in the communication field have well-developed interest and training in such academic areas as group processes, nonverbal communication, male–female interaction, and qualitative research techniques. Because of this background knowledge and skill development, communication specialists should market their skills as focus group researchers.

APPENDIX: FOCUS GROUP DISCUSSION GUIDE

(PLEASE BE THOROUGHLY FAMILIAR WITH THE GUIDE *BEFORE* THE FORUM)

(10 minutes)   After group members are seated, have them complete the questionnaire. Remind them to give first impressions and brief answers.

Ask participants to take a piece of blank paper from their packets to begin the discussion. Note that for some questions, participants are asked to write their responses before the group begins discussing them. This will help them organize their thoughts.

(5 minutes)   *Introduction*

Begin with some friendly conversation in order to build rapport. Ask participants to give their names and hometowns (excluding titles or organizational affiliations which may intimidate some members).

Discussion Questions

(40 minutes)   PART I

WRITE   1. Briefly describe what you believe to be the most critical problem facing women in this area of Colorado in terms of (*your topic area*). (write only one)

Ask participants to respond to this question briefly on paper. Collect responses and read anonymously. Begin listing issues on the flip chart—you may write or you may ask an assistant to. (There is something motivating to participants about seeing their ideas displayed before the group.) After listing issues, discuss each one. Then pass papers back in any order; participants need not get their own papers back.

WRITE   2. Rank order these problems (listed on the flip chart) with number one being the most immediate or most critical need and number ___ being the least immediate or least critical.

(Collect papers. Notetakers tally rankings using the ranking sheet provided.)

(15 minutes)   PART II

DISCUSS   3. What existing programs "successfully" address these needs?

4. Why? What makes them work?

5. How could they be improved?

(40 minutes)   PART III

WRITE   6. What new programs could be created to address these needs?

(List ideas on the flip chart again and discuss.)

WRITE   7. Rank order these new programs from 1 to ___, with 1 representing the most needed program.
(Collect papers. Notetakers use the second tally sheet provided.)

DISCUSS   8. What resources are already available in this region of Colorado to help meet the needs identified by the group? What specific steps could women here take to get involved?

(10 minutes)   Summary

WRITE   9. Conclude with a statement like the following:

"You've all been sitting in this room just as I have for the last hour. If you had the assignment of summarizing what this whole group thinks and feels about women and _____, what would say?"

After responses are written, collect them. Give your own brief summary and thank participants.

REFERENCES

Axelrod, M. D. (1975, March 14). 10 essentials for good qualitative research. *Marketing News*, pp. 10–11.

Bellenger, D. N., Bernhardt, K. L., & Goldstrucker, J. L. (1976). *Qualititative research in marketing*. Chicago: American Marketing Association.

Calder, B. J. (1977). Focus groups and the nature of qualitative marketing research. *Journal of Marketing Research, 14*, 353–364.

Caruso, T. E. (1976, September 10). Moderators focus on groups: Session yields 7 hypotheses covering technology trends, professionalism, training, techniques, reports, etc. *Marketing News*, pp. 12–16.

Donath, B. (1986). Straight from the buyer's mouth. *Business Marketing, 71*(10), 69.

Durgee, J. F. (1987). Point of view: Using creative writing techniques in focus groups. *Journal of Advertising Research, 26*(6), 57–65.

Hammond, M. (1986). Creative focus groups: Uses and misuses. *Marketing and Media Decisions, 21*(8), 154, 156.

Hannah, M. (1978). A perspective on focus groups. *Viewpoints, 18,* 4–8.

Hansler, D. F., & Cooper, C. (1986). Focus groups: New dimension in feasibility study. *Fund Raising Management, 17*(5), 78, 80–82.

Holcomb, B. (1985). The focus groupie. *Madison Avenue, 27,* 47–48, 50, 157.

Hollander, S. L., & Oromaner, D. S. (1986, January 3). Seminars fill gap in focus-group training. *Marketing News,* p. 46.

Kennedy, F. (1976). The focus group interview and moderator bias. *Marketing Review, 31,* 19–21.

Krueger, R. A., (1988). *Focus groups: A practical guide for applied research.* Newbury Park, CA: Sage.

Langer, J. (1978, September 8). Clients: Check qualitative researcher's personal traits to get more; Qualitative researchers: Enter marketing process to give more. *Marketing News,* pp. 10–11.

Lederman, L. C. (1983). High communication apprehensives talk about communication apprehension and its effects on their behavior. *Communication Quarterly, 31*(3), 233–237.

Levy, S. J. (1979). Focus group interviewing. In J. B. Higginbotham & K. K. Cox (Eds.), *Focus group interviews: A reader* (pp. 29–37). Chicago: American Marketing Association.

Lydecker, T. L. (1986). Focus group dynamics. *Association Management, 38*(3), 73–78.

McQuarrie, E. F., & McIntyre, S. H. (1986). Focus groups and the development of new products by technologically driven companies: Some guidelines. *Journal of Product Innovation Management, 3*(1), 40–47.

Nelson, J. E. (1982). *The practice of marketing research.* Boston: Kent.

Profs get primer in use, problems of focus groups. (1986, September 12). *Marketing News,* p. 36.

Reynolds, F. D., & Johnson, D. K. (1978). Validity of focus-group findings. *Journal of Advertising Research, 18*(3), 21–24.

Rostky, G. (1986). Unveiling market segments with technical focus research. *Business Marketing, 71*(10), 66, 68.

Shields, D. C. (1981). Dramatistic communication based focus groups interviews. In J. F. Cragen & D. C. Sheilds (Eds.), *Applied communication research: A dramatistic approach* (pp. 313–319). Prospect Heights, IL: Waveland Press.

Staley, C. C., Beatty, K. M., & Kassover, P. O. (1987). *Colorado women: A statewide needs assessment.* Unpublished report, Colorado Springs, CO.

Templeton J., & Bates, T. (1976). Research as giraffe: An identity crisis. *Advances in Consumer Research, IV,* 442–446.

Van Maanen, J. (1983). Reclaiming qualitative methods for organizational research: A preface. In J. Van Maanen (Ed.), *Qualitative methodology* (pp. 9–18). Beverly Hills: Sage.

Welch, J. L. (1985). Researching marketing problems and opportunities with focus groups. *Industrial Marketing Management, 14,* 245–253.

Wells, W. D. (1979). Group interviewing. In J. B. Higginbotham & K. K. Cox (Eds.), *Focus group interviews: A reader* (pp. 2–12). Chicago: American Marketing Association.

Women's Foundation of Colorado. (1988). *An assessment of the needs of Colorado's women and girls.* Denver, CO: Author.

AUDIENCE ANALYSIS SYSTEMS IN ADVERTISING AND MARKETING

10

RALPH R. BEHNKE
Texas Christian University

DAN O'HAIR
Texas Tech University

AUDREY HARDMAN
Las Cruces, New Mexico

Any overview of the history of communication research clearly demonstrates an increasing interest in audience studies beginning with Aristotle's observational methods to the latest interactive electronic systems. Persuasive campaigns are most effective when their appeals are based on sound, relevant information about the publics that they address. Such information has been sought by campaign directors for political figures, corporate image-makers, media product promoters, and many others involved in advertising, marketing, and public relations activities.

Tactics for deriving useful feedback from audiences have varied considerably from simple interviews to sophisticated automated data collecting methods. In some cases, respondents move levers or push buttons to indicate their attitudes about people, concepts, or products. In this way conscious responses are collected, analyzed, and related to the success of various aspects of a marketing campaign. An alternative approach to collecting relevant audience response data is to evaluate nonconscious responses. Researchers have attached sensors to chairs to determine how much movement respondents exhibit during the presentation of stimulus material such as films, slides, or live speeches. Data from such a "wigglemeter" have been related to such relevant variables as audience attention and interest. Some nonconscious responses are more effectively hidden from researchers and require even more sensitive and sophisticated measuring equipment. For example, physiological arousal may be an extremely potent response not overtly visible to observers or interviewers.

Dramatic changes in physiological functioning of audiences, such as pulse rate, blood pressure, and skin responses, may provide useful information in the design of products, media representations of products, or actual marketing campaign strategies.

Computerized response systems have been developed that maximize opportunities for the analysis of direct, immediate, on-line audience responses to selected stimuli. Lazarsfeld and Stanton have been credited with the first systematic attempts at observing and recording on-line audience responses. Since those early efforts a number of techniques have been developed that have improved upon the collection, analysis, and reporting of on-line, immediate audience responses. The latest innovation in the area was a portable computerized response system termed the Computer Audience Response Analysis System (CARAS). In addition to the convenience of portability, CARAS takes full advantage of near-complete automation in the collection and analysis of data. A more complete discussion of CARAS appears later in the chapter.

ANALYSIS OF AUDIENCES

Detailed and comprehensive audience analysis, or analysis of an organization's publics, is often considered to be one of the most critical elements in any communication campaign (Scott & O'Hair, 1989). Recognizing the important elements involved in generating a positive reception to a communication message involves a comprehensive evaluation of diverse components (Wimmer & Dominick, 1987). Public relations, advertising, and marketing scholars and practitioners have identified a number of variables that have shown considerable promise as predictive factors in determining message response. For example, demographic analysis (Newsom & Scott, 1985), psychographic analysis (Alwitt & Mitchell, 1985; Scissors & Surmanek, 1982; Zotti, 1985), values and lifestyle research (Becker & Conner, 1979; Kahle, Beatty, & Homer, 1986; Wells, 1974; Zikmund & d'Amico, 1986), benefits segmentation analysis (Haley, 1971, 1968), and focus group research (Cragan & Shields, 1981) represents a sampling of the methods employed to determine the reaction of public relations messages targeted for specific groups.

Audience analysis techniques were discussed in detail by Scott and O'Hair (1989) that culminated in the Composite Audience Profile (CAP). CAP involves a comprehensive treatment of premessage analysis utilizing three components: demographics, psychographics, and emotional analysis. Demographic analysis is one of the oldest forms of audience analysis and includes gathering information about potential audience members in the areas of gender, age, ethnic origin, religious and political affiliations, and occupational and health status among others.

Psychographic analysis is the second stage of CAP and is comprised of the determination of values and lifestyle characteristics of potential audience members. A number of techniques are available for such an analysis. For instance, some approaches have utilized behavioral tendencies as a basis for predicting individuals' reactions to messages (Bernay, 1971; Wells, 1970; Wells & Tigert, 1971), whereas other methods have employed more specific treatments of behavioral prediction (Haley, 1968; Heller, 1970). Another popular psychographic classification scheme that separates consumers according to lifestyle based segments was described by Zikmund and d'Amico (1986)—the VALS (values and lifestyle) program. This technique was originally developed by Mitchell (1983) who utilized both Maslow's (1954) hierarchy of needs and Riesman, Glazer, and Denny's (1950) concept of social character to formulate nine different lifestyles (Kahle et al., 1986). Each segment describes an essential segment that can be reached through different marketing approaches.

Emotional assessment is the third component of CAP. Undoubtedly, this process is the most complex and difficult of the three and usually is best approached physiologically, although self-report techniques have demonstrated some limited utility in emotional measurement. Brandstatter (1983) developed a system where subjects would list adjectives that best described the emotions they felt when exposed to communication stimuli. Alternatively, Batra and Ray (1986) employed an open-ended response technique where subjects respond according to their felt emotion, and Zeitlin and Westwood (1986) have developed a rating system where subjects are exposed to a stimuli and asked to rate their observations across a battery of items relating to emotional responses. Emotional items such as happy, disgust, exciting, and anxiety are suggested with accompanying evaluations such as "does not describe the stimuli at all" to "very strongly describes the stimuli."

As previously described, premessage analysis is an indispensable method of obtaining information about potential reactions of an audience. Nevertheless, even comprehensive analyses such as CAP stop short of obtaining actual audience feedback about certain messages or stimuli. In response to the limitations generated by pre-message analysis, researchers have created response systems that approach audience analysis by obtaining reactions immediately, almost simultaneously when stimuli are presented. The following sections provide discussion of historical as well as contemporary audience response analysis systems.

AUDIENCE RESPONSE SYSTEMS

Most response instruments involve an input mechanism (typically a button or switch) that is connected to a receiving unit that records responses sent by subjects. Operationally, subjects are exposed to selected stimuli under study (typically broadcasts) and can either respond spontaneously or are cued when to respond. The qualitative assessment generated by response systems can take varied forms. Cognitive, affective, or even behavioral dimensions can be explored by immediate response mechanisms depending upon the research purpose and design. For example, the early Stanton–Lazarsfeld studies employed "like–dislike" response alternatives (Levy, 1982), whereas more recent investigations have utilized "red–green" response modes (Rust, 1985).

Instantaneous on-line feedback generated by response systems could offer advertising and marketing researchers and practitioners a valuable analysis tool in determining audience reaction to messages. Demographic, psychographic, and even values research may not provide enough information to predict a public's reaction to persuasive messages. Consequently, pretesting of a communication campaign's message with a representative audience could be an indispensable technique in determining the appropriate communication strategies. Jensen (1987) made a compelling argument for audience research:

> Critical researchers have seldom taken up audience responses, at least in an empirical sense, but have focused on structural and content data, believing these data could better reveal the production of audience consciousness. Fejes (1984) argues, however, that there is a need for a theory which might be found in earlier empirical audience studies. Researchers who set out to study communication as a social process with ideological ramifications cannot afford to ignore those audiences who are the manifest link between the media and the wider social processes. (p. 22)

Paramount on a list of audience reactions should be what the "consumer" thinks of the product or message. In addition, because some media, such as TV, are "playing" to an active audience, there must be an awareness of the presentational format as well as style. Because of this, advertisers and PR specialists are aware that they are not playing to a passive audience in this case, and audience members become more viable consumers. Levy (1982) suggested that:

> An increasingly competitive and expensive commercial message environment, the growing availability and still uncertain impact of the communication technologies, and mounting pressures on public broadcasting to justify

its very existence have all led communication scholars and policymakers back to Paul Lazarsfeld and Frank Stanton's attempt to measure the 'quality' of the audience experience with a 'machine.' Such qualitative audience measurements are now routinely used by the commercial television networks, the Corporation for Public Broadcasting, and advertisers for companies such as General Mills, DuPont and Polaroid to assess audience flow, to make major programming and time-buying decisions, and for formative research on "pilots." (p. 30)

Since that time, improvements have been made in both methodology and technology in an effort to obtain precise and reliable audience reaction.

According to Lannon (1986), "All consumer research is based on assumptions: about the relationship of attitudes to behavior; about the extent to which a question on a questionnaire even measures an attitude; about how the questions we ask, the mental processes we record, the behavior we report reflect the influence of advertising" (p. RC-6). These attitudes are not only applicable to advertising, however. Conscious of possible negative connotations that the audience members could react to, the research specialist must be even more aware of the content of the messages, and how it is presented and adapted to the target market.

Chaffee and Schleuder (1986) related these reactions to an individual's internal measuring scale in the following manner: "Because attention is a covert mental activity occurring within the 'black box' of a person, its measurement poses a major challenge to methodological inventiveness" (p. 78). It is important to second-guess the internal "black box" of the audience members and determine what they see as important in any type of public relations message. Chaffee and Schleuder (1986) further cited three general approaches that can be found in research literature that are utilized in measuring audience attention: behavioral observation, psychophysiological measurement, and self-reporting.

Behavioral observation is, simply put, monitoring the viewing behavior of the audience. Eye movement, intermittent conversation during the program, and television viewing in an overall natural setting are those characteristics that have been observed. Studies conducted in this setting have concluded that attention paid to programs is low, and at times can be virtually nonexistent.

Psychophysiological measurements, or those indicators of arousal, have measured attention span to television programs by recording the brain waves of a person viewing a program on an encephalogram, or detecting galvanic skin responses. Although these techniques have proven successful in measuring attentional microprocesses, they have not been necessarily strong in measuring attention paid to different types of media (Chaffee & Schleuder, p. 80).

Perhaps the most widely used data gathering is the self-reporting system, a technique dependent on subjects remembering their previous experiences following exposure to stimuli. Self-report techniques enjoy frequent use due to their relatively inexpensive nature and ease of administration. Unfortunately, self-report is perhaps the least effective method of obtaining honest and actual reactions to messages when subjects are asked to recall their feeling and emotions about previous communication message (i.e., experimental subjects may be unable or unwilling to respond in a retrospective manner).

Signiorelli (1986) highlighted an interesting concept when he pointed out that much of the past audience analysis research has dealt with what people say they do when receiving a message, as compared to what they actually do. By saying that viewers will "say one thing and do another," we may come to the conclusion that, indeed, the subjects are providing the researcher with information that they assume the researcher wants to hear. Most of the research done on audience responses has been ex-post-facto. After having viewed a message, the subjects have a time lapse between the actual moment they viewed stimulus material to which they strongly reacted, and the time when they provide answers about that reaction to the researcher. By using an on-line system, which allows audience members to immediately record their reactions to the episode, little time lapse occurs between the event and the analysis, thus reducing the chance for distortion. Not only are the responses from an on-line system immediate, they clearly describe the thoughts of the viewers, which can allow for corrections in messages.

Both conscious and nonconscious response systems have been used for some time in both commercial and academic settings. Although the precise utility of the audience response system is still being debated, its general value as one component of a broader analytic scheme is increasingly accepted. The following discussion centers on some specific cases of successful applications of conscious and nonconscious audience response systems. Although in each case the focus has been on rather specialized applications, the potential for wider generalization of the methods described, to the special concerns of the reader, should become clear.

CONSCIOUS RESPONSE SYSTEMS

Probably the most impressive example of conscious response measurement is found in mass communication research. For over 50 years, "program analyses" have been used to try to determine the qualitative responses of audiences to various forms of distributed mass communications, including radio programs, television programs, and music recordings. Such machines are currently employed by the major commercial networks, the public broadcasting network, major advertisers, and even larger "local" stations to improve their programming decisions. Although the cost of using such methods has been rather high in the past, as the technology is developed and simplified and as the operational and theoretical knowledge is more widely disseminated, it should be expected that implementation of these audience analyses will become more widespread and economically feasible. Such research will no longer be limited to large organizations with even larger budgets but will be affordable to small organizations and even individuals.

The classic example of conscious response measurement is the Lazarsfeld–Stanton Program Analyzer developed over 50 years ago. Many consider it the first serious commercial attempt to evaluate qualitative audience responses to radio programs. The machine proved to have practical value for analyzing patterns of listeners "likes" and "dislikes," moment by moment, over the course of the program. For the first time, (a) highlights and low points in a program could be pinpointed, (b) the effects of sequence on the impact of a program could be ascertained, and (c) varying patterns of response could be compared between and among various audience subtypes, thereby accounting for the effects of such variables as sex, educational level, listening habits, and so on. It can easily be seen, from this discussion, that the program analyzer built a strong bridge between the academic community and the commercial broadcasters—a union that continues today to the benefit of both parties.

According to Levy (1982) the history of the program analyzer shows a growing strength. From its essential beginning with the Lazarsfeld–Stanton device in 1938, its use by major advertising agencies in the 1940s to evaluate commercials, and its continued use in academic settings during that same period by scholars such as Lazarsfeld and Carl Hovland, it proliferated in the 1950s until many complex offspring of that first unit were in use.

Audience Responses to Recorded Stimuli

The Lazarsfeld–Stanton program analyzer was originally used to evaluate recorded material. Respondents, at least on one of the models, pushed a green button when they "liked" the material and a red button to indicate their "dislike." Criticism of these and succeeding response systems has frequently focused on common concerns: (a) Do respondents get too involved in the stimulus material to produce valid button-pushing behavior? (b) Are respondents so engaged by the measurement apparatus that they do not adequately monitor the presentational material? and (c) What is the interaction between the two? The Lazarsfeld–Stanton analyzer produced a graphic representation of the pattern of likes and dislikes of subjects while listening to a recorded program.

The aggregation of subject responses above and below a zero line indicated positive and negative audience reactions, respectively. The real-time graphic display allowed comparison of response levels for various program elements such as dramatization, narration, and commercial messages. Using this system, the extent to which likes or dislikes are sustained over any specified message or time period can easily be estimated. Moreover, listener fatigue or adaptation to a stimulus can be identified when a continuously declining graph pattern is observed.

Historically, audience responses to recorded stimuli have been viewed with some concern by producers and sponsors for a variety of reasons. Among them are: (a) the danger that some of the participants may have been exposed to the material before, and (b) there is a strong general preference for carrying out such research on "live" or at least original auditions. These concerns led to the application of modern versions of audience analysis to live programming.

Audience Responses to Live Stimuli

Because audience responses to live as opposed to "canned" stimuli seem to be generally preferred, a pilot research project was designed that had two key features: (a) It utilized an audience analyzer with five buttons indicating, in successive order, the momentary interest value that audiences placed on presentational stimuli; and (b) the presentational stimuli selected were live television news programs, because of the high but transient impact of current news stories. The general purpose of the study was to investigate viewer reactions to specific content and presentational format of news programs. Responses were taken in real time during the program. Specifically of interest were questions such as: (a) Does interest generally decline during the course of the program? (b) What are the characteristics of stories deemed most interesting by viewers? (c) Can stories sustain interest for longer periods or must they be kept short? (d) What aspects of the program are most interesting? (e) What kind of sports stories are most and least interesting? (f) How interesting are commercials? and (g) What are the comparative interest levels for various program segments (e.g., national news stories, local news stories, happy stories, sad stories, violent stories, sports, weather, poststory comment, on-camera conversation among reporters, and commercial messages)? Even interactions between reporters and program materials can be investigated, as can hair styles, set designs, graphics, and background music.

Response averaging intervals must be carefully selected so that the research design is sensitive to the goal of the study. For example, if a 15-second commercial is under investigation, the sampling rate would be much higher than for a major 5-minute news segment. Figure 10.1 represents the graphic output of the on-line responses of 19 viewers of a television newscast. The graph clearly shows a very responsive audience.

Although some audiences demonstrated strong adaptation to program stimuli, this audience did not. In fact, the highest level of audience interest appears during the last story, the one involving the death of a local police officer.

Although the program segment depicted in Fig. 10.1 does not show it, significant and dramatic differences were found between commercial messages. Even in the "sports" and "weather" segments, it was apparent that audiences differentiated between content elements and expressed a rather wide range of interest even within these rather narrowly defined program segments. Finally, a program analyzer permits researchers to compare interest patterns for various types of consumers. For instance, in general, men were more interested in the sports segment than women and men were far more interested in stories about professional hockey than were women respondents.

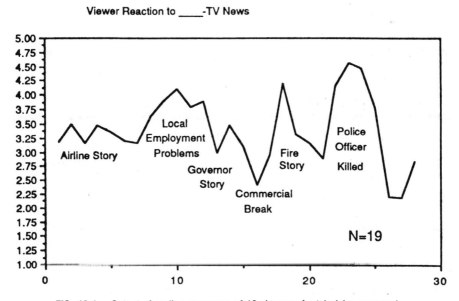

FIG. 10.1. Output of on-line responses of 19 viewers of a television newscast.

Quite often, marketing campaigns are designed to promote individuals. Directors of such campaigns rely heavily on public responses to help design campaign strategies, platforms, and speeches. Such a campaign is ideally suited for the application of an audience analyzer. For example, audiences can be assembled to view current speeches of any particular candidate (this tactic, by the way, is useful when applied to the opposition) and asked to respond, moment by moment, to the speaker's comments. Button pushing behavior can be defined as "agreement" with the speaker, and the cumulative responses of the audience can be traced over the entire speech. Then, specific comments or arguments can be evaluated in terms of the immediate audience responses during the presentation. This technique has certain advantages to postspeaking interviews because no interviewer is interposed in the data collection process and the respondent is not required to remember precisely how he or she may have felt at any given moment in time. The greatest advantage of this form of assessment is that "the ball of string is unwound" and one is able to evaluate segment by segment instead of by lump sum.

NONCONSCIOUS RESPONSE SYSTEMS

The preceding section on conscious response measurement has focused on more or less overt reactions to presentational stimuli. Many recent findings show that covert bodily reactions are correlated with observed behavior (Gale & Edwards, 1983). The fact that micro-momentary exposure to product advertising on the screen of motion-picture theaters caused audiences to buy refreshments is now in the common folklore. Psychophysiologists, studying relationships between mind and body, attempt to interpret covert responses such as changes in heart rate, skin resistance, and the electrical activity of the brain. With the help of modern electronic instrumentation, they detect, analyze, quantify, and interpret the hidden responses of the body to the mind.

In early research, Smith (1922), using skin responses, attempted to determine which words in the lexicon were more arousing. Subjects responded to the emotional content of words, which were read aloud, with varying levels of galvanic skin response. Although there was considerable variability in the responses to words, generalizations could be made about which words produced high emotional response. Exactly which words have the most arousal value varies from time to time (e.g., the words "kiss" and "aviator" were very arousing in the early study cited above) and from individual to individual. Only very simple physiological instrumentation is required to record the skin responses of audience members who are exposed to verbal stimuli. Figure 10.2 is a representation of the responses

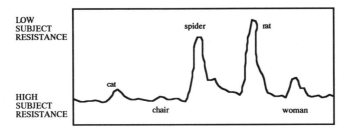

FIG. 10.2.   A representation of the galvanic skin responses of a male university student while listening to stimulus words.

of a male university student to a list of orally presented words. This respondent's chart is reproduced here because it is representative of the actual rank ordering of these concepts, in terms of their arousal value, for the group as a whole.

Covert, physiological response measurement has generated considerable interest outside the research laboratory. Commercial applications of various forms of polygraph testing, outside of law enforcement use, are considerable. Such responses are used to gauge audience reactions to radio and television programs, magazine advertising, recorded music, and films. Major commercial media research films, such as *Preview House* in Hollywood, use measures of physiological arousal to evaluate products. Many feel that arousal information is an excellent confirmation variable for conscious responses. Furthermore, if, as psychologists suggest, behavior has two dimensions (magnitude and direction) then the overt, lever-pushing response can determine direction whereas the level of arousal represents response magnitude.

Although galvanic skin response is one of the most sensitive of the covert response measures, the choice of the most appropriate measure must depend on the information desired. For example, if material is to be evaluated for its humorous impact, an electromyogram can be created. The electromyogram (EMG) is a recording of the electrical signals produced by muscle activity. When the sensing electrodes are placed so as to measure muscle activity during smiling, chuckling, and laughing out loud, the resulting data may be useful in the precise evaluation of humorous material. It is of particular interest here that reactions to such material can be recorded on a moment-by-moment basis. A humorous speech need not simply be judged as a whole, but rather by moments and segments, and then compared for strength and latency of response. Figure 10.3 is a representation of the EMG of a subject listening to a humorous speech. As can be seen, estimates of magnitude and duration are easily attached to specific moments in the speech.

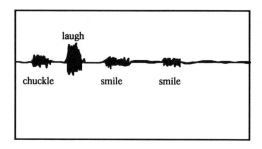

FIG. 10.3. A representation of a subjects' EMG responses while listening to a humorous speech.

Although physiological response assessments are somewhat tedious and expensive to measure, and the interpretation of these responses requires considerable expertise, the *reliability* of measurement is outstanding, usually higher than any other type of audience assessment technique. As the sophistication of such electronic measuring instruments increases, the simplicity of operation will increase as well. Consequently, the expectation is that audience analysis using these measuring instruments will increase substantially in the 21st century.

RECENT DEVELOPMENTS IN AUDIENCE RESPONSE SYSTEMS

One of the better known market research companies is ASI, based in Los Angeles. Although they concentrate specifically on commercials, ASI continues to use a system similar to the Lazarsfeld–Stanton method to conduct their research, and has achieved some of the best results for commercials in the advertising industry. In this case, however, consumers are invited into a theater to respond to various advertisements, television programs, or films. Just as in the studies conducted by CBS, the subjects are asked to respond in a positive or negative manner, according to their likes or dislikes in the program. A computer system monitors their responses, and prints them on a graph. This is only one example of the type of research currently being conducted, but it presents at least two obvious difficulties: (a) The subjects are put into a theater arrangement, which could have an effect upon how they view a program geared for viewing in the home environment, and (b) the system itself, although accurate, is not portable, thereby limiting its use to the theater area.

DEVELOPMENT OF CARAS

The Computerized Audience Response Analysis System (CARAS) was developed as a means of obtaining audience reaction to messages generated in field settings. As mentioned earlier, the inability of previous audience response systems to obtain message reaction in an ecologically valid environment obviated the reliability of responses provided. With a portable system, a targeted audience or public can remain in their natural environment while responding to the message under study.

The system was designed with the ultimate goal being a marketable product that would enable researchers to record and transmit each respondent's evaluations at specific and predetermined times via a hand-held device linked to a computer. Developed by the Communication Resources Center at New Mexico State University, CARAS (O'Hair, Hardman, & Flint, 1987), offered several new aspects: (a) The portability of CARAS allowed for flexible and convenient data collection, (b) CARAS is programmable to allow for a wide range of data type and content, (c) CARAS produces results that can be understood by researchers and practitioners, and (d) CARAS provides the opportunity for on-line real-time data collecting procedures. A diagram of the CARAS system can be found in Fig. 10.4.

Pilot Testing of CARAS

The first test of the system involved graduate students in a Southwestern university communication department utilizing news broadcasts from a local television station. Hardware and software modification were made as a result of the preliminary tests. The first real test of CARAS came as part of a marketing and public relations campaign of a national affiliate television station. The developers were hired to evaluate the programming and news personnel for the local 6 p.m. news program. The following section details the methodology employed in testing the utility of CARAS.

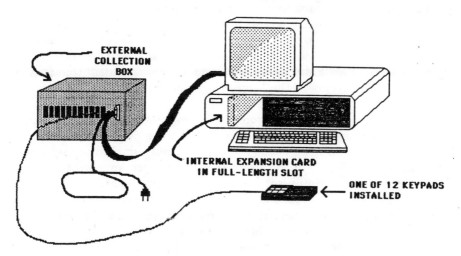

FIG. 10.4. Diagram of computerized audience response analysis system (CARAS).

Selected for the study were 100 females between the ages of 25 and 49. This sample was selected because their "working woman" status was of interest to TV news directors. Subjects included 24 female college students who were employed, 69 females employed on a full-time basis, and 2 females whose occupation was listed as homemaker.

A questionnaire requesting demographic information and normal viewer selections for local newscasts was administered to subjects prior to their viewing the newscast. Subjects were given a brief description of the Audience Response System they were to use while evaluating the newscast, and instructed about the types of questions they would be asked. Content, format, and affective impressions of the stories in the newscast were the main foci of the evaluations. The stimulus utilized in this study involved a live broadcast of a 6 p.m. news program originating from a television station that is a local affiliate of a major network. Questionnaire development, stimulus choice, and targeted response points were derived through a cooperative agreement among the station's general manager and news director, and the principal investigators of this project.

For each session, 10 subjects were assembled in the viewing/experimentation room 30 minutes before the airing of the 6 p.m. newscast. The viewing room was designed to approximate, as closely as possible, a living room environment. Subjects were seated in comfortable chairs arranged in a semicircle in front of a 21-inch color monitor. A set of slides were projected onto a wall near the television screen prompting the subjects when and how to answer the question asked. Subjects were asked to be aware of prompts made by the experimenter on the second screen, and to respond to such prompts by pressing the button on the hand-held device corresponding to their reaction. Subjects were told that depending on the question or prompt being posed, to respond by pressing "1" for a very strong negative reaction, "2," "3," or "4" for a strong positive reaction, and "10" for a very strong positive reaction. For example, if the prompt signaled viewers for an "interesting" reaction, viewers could, at that instant, select how they felt about the interesting characteristics of the newscast according to the scale just described.

Timing and sequencing of prompts for responses were determined by selecting those aspects of the newscast that were designed for analysis. Primarily, each news story was selected for analysis and prompts were given at the conclusion of the story. In addition, prompts were given for the interpersonal communication segments during change-offs between news anchor personnel and weather and sports figures.

Data obtained from this study were analyzed according to several methods. First, CARAS provides both individual sample analysis and accumulated aggregate analysis. For example, each of the sample groups can be separately analyzed for their mean responses to prompt questions.

Furthermore, all 100 subject responses additionally were analyzed for an aggregate response for all questions. Data were reported in both manners. It was the purpose of this research to expand upon the Lazarsfeld–Stanton system and others possessing similar characteristics, and to create an on-line system that would gather time-locked data and immediate responses from audience members to a series of television newscasts. Further, CARAS was designed to create a system unlike those utilized in previous studies—one that is completely portable, and adaptable to different settings as well as different audiences, in order to, as much as possible, create the most realistic viewing situation possible. The system, as designed, can be used in audience analysis, marketing, advertising, employee training, and public relations contexts.

CONCLUSION AND IMPLICATIONS

Audience analysis is an important undertaking in marketing and advertising research efforts for several reasons. Due to the expense of developing, refining, and producing communication campaigns, it is incumbent on researchers to predict and test potential messages prior to their actual dissemination to avoid costly revisions and modifications. Second, audience analysis provides an opportunity to observe firsthand the experiences of respondents as they are exposed to designated messages. Additional insight into the effectiveness and appropriateness of messages can be made that might not be possible without such analysis. Third, audience analysis provides sponsors or clients with the reassurance that marketing and advertising efforts are being produced systematically, scientifically, and professionally. This aspect may be especially important in the event of meager results.

Although audience response analysis systems are prevalent among a small cadre of advertising and marketing specialists, the generalized use of such techniques is not a reality. Given the vast amount of advertising and marketing campaigns that are generated each year, it is surprising how infrequently computerized response systems are utilized. Regardless of the particular methodology employed in media research efforts, instantaneous, on-line response techniques could be integrated into the overall project allowing for a traingulation approach. The following examples constitute only a portion of the potential integration of computerized response systems into overall research schemes.

A number of advertising research groups have relied upon information processing models to better understand how individuals internalize and subsequently respond to media messages (Gardner, Mitchell, & Russo, 1985; Greenwald & Leavitt, 1984; Leigh & Menon, 1987; Petty, Schumann, & Cacioppo, 1983). Information-processing theory seems best suited to the analysis of intermediate memory processes that serves as a basis for understanding the level of attention and depth of process of particular media messages (Leigh & Menon, 1987). Although information-processing studies may employ recall designs as dependent variables in ascertaining message strength, supplemental research utilizing computerized response systems at the time of initial exposure could provide valuable information about encoding and attention processes. Strength of the original sensory input could reveal how and why intermediate memory processes operate as they do in delayed recall designs, and data collection that takes advantage of simultaneous responses to stimuli would facilitate this research.

Although information-processing approaches to marketing and advertising research are useful for understanding the cognitive elements of consumer behavior, studies focusing on the affective dimensions of message analysis have evidenced utility as well (Burke & Edell, 1989; Gardner, 1985; Hill & Ward, 1989; Zajonc, 1980). It would seem that computerized on-line responses systems could generate valuable data in affective or emotional studies. For example, Gardner (1985) conducted experiments to determine the feelings produced by exposure to advertising messages. By manipulating moods, Gardner was better able to understand how affective states affect attitudes toward messages. As with cognitive studies of memory processes, computerized audience responses analysis systems would seem to hold promise as a method of uncovering underlying affective states during exposure to messages, because immediate feedback regarding affective states would yield salient data about attitudes toward advertising messages.

Recent research efforts have focused on the examination of cognitive and affective dimensions present during exposure to coordinated media campaigns (Edell & Keller, 1989; Runyon, 1984; Sternhal & Craig, 1984). Coordinated media campaigns utilize both TV and radio media for the communication of similar or even identical advertising messages. Of concern with these research projects of this type is the initial processing of stimuli and retrieval of stored information about the ad (Edell & Keller, 1989). Researchers of coordinated media use are interested in determining differences in sensory input between TV and radio exposure. Although television messages involve multisensory stimuli (visual and auditory), additional cognitive effort may be necessary to fully process messages, and consumers may not be willing or able to direct full attention to such ads. On-line response systems could provide data that identifies which stimulus is most salient to their attention and retrieval processes. With radio ads, response system data would be valuable in determining the impact of background music or other stimuli during the encoding or decoding process. Finally, response data from both media could be compared to determine the efficacy of coordinated media campaigns.

There is a great deal of potential for the use of computerized audience response systems in marketing and advertising research projects. Identification of appropriate designs and methodology for this type of research technique should be pursued more vigorously by members of media research groups. Although immediate, on-line audience feedback is not a panacea for media research, the advantage of such a methodology should not be ignored.

REFERENCES

Alwitt, L. F., & Mitchell, A. A. (1985). *Psychographical processes and advertising effects: Theory, research, and applications.* Hillsdale, NJ: Lawrence Erlbaum Associates.

Batra, R., & Ray, M. (1986). Affective responses mediating acceptance of advertising. *Journal of Consumer Research, 13,* 234–249.

Becker, B. W., & Conner, P. E. (1979). Personal values of the heavy user of mass media. *Journal of Advertising Research, 21,* 37–43.

Bernay, E. (1971). Creative advertising through life style analysis. In C. King & D. Tigert (Eds.), *Attitude research reaches new heights.* Chicago: American Marketing Association.

Brandstatter, H. (1983). Emotional responses to other persons in everyday life situations. *Journal of Personality and Social Psychology, 45,* 871–883.

Burke, M. C., & Edell, J. A. (1989). The impact of feelings on ad-based affect and cognition. *Journal of Marketing Research, 26,* 69–83.

Chaffee, S., & Schleuder, J. (1986). Measurement and effects of attention to media news. *Human Communication Research, 13,* 76–107.

Cragan, J. F., & Shields, D. C. (1981). *Applied communication research: A dramatistic approach.* Prospect Heights, IL: Waveland Press.

Edell, J. A., & Keller, K. L. (1989). The information processing of coordinated media campaigns. *Journal of Marketing Research, 26,* 149–163.

Gale, A., & Edwards, J. A. (1983). *Physiological correlates of human behavior.* New York: Academic Press.

Gardner, M. (1985). Mood states and consumer behavior: A critical review. *Journal of Consumer Research, 12,* 281–300.

Gardner, M., Mitchell, A. A., & Russo,, J. E. (1985). Low involvement strategies for processing advertisements. *Journal of Advertising, 14,* 4–12, 56.

Greenwald, A. A., & Leavitt, C. (1984). Audience involvement in advertising: Four levels. *Journal of Consumer Research, 11,* 581–582.

Haley, R. (1968). Benefit segmentation: A decision-oriented research tool. *Journal of Marketing, 32,* 30–35.

Haley, R. (1971). Beyond segmentation: *Journal of Advertising Research, 11,* 3–8.

Heller, H. (1970). Defining target markets by their attitude profile. In L. Adler & I. Crespi (Eds.), *Attitude research on the rocks.* Chicago: American Marketing Association.

Hill, R. P., & Ward, J. C. (1989). Mood manipulation in marketing research: An examination of potential confounding effects. *Journal of Marketing Research, 26,* 97–104.

Jensen, K. B. (1987). Qualitative audience research: Toward an integrative approach to reception. *Critical Studies in Mass Communication, 4,* 21–36.

Kahle, L., Beatty, S., & Homer, P. (1986). Alternative measurement approaches to consumer values: The list of values (lov) and values and lifestyle (vals). *Journal of Consumer Research, 13,* 405–409.

Lannon, J. (1986). New technologies for understanding consumer reaction to advertising. *Journal of Advertising Research, 25,* RC6–RC9.

Leigh, J. H., & Menon, A. (1987). Audience involvement effects on the information processing of umbrella print advertisements. *Journal of Advertising, 16,* 3–12.

Levy, M. (1982). The Lazarsfeld–Stanton analyzer: An historical approach. *Journal of Communication, 32,* 30–38.

Maslow, A. (1954). *Motivation and personality.* New York: Harper & Row.

Mitchell, A. (1983). *The nine American lifestyles.* New York: Warner.

Newsom, D. & Scott, A. (1985). *This is pr: The realities of public relations* (3rd ed.). Belmont, CA: Wadsworth.

O'Hair, D., Hardman, A., & Flint, C. (1987). *CARAS: Computerized audience response analysis system* (unpublished technical report). Las Cruces, NM: Communication Resources Center.

Petty, R. E., Schumann D. W., & Cacioppo, J. T. (1983). Central and peripheral routes to advertising effectiveness: The moderating role of involvement. *Journal of Consumer Research, 10,* 135–146.

Runyon, K. E. (1984). *Advertising and the practice of marketing.* Columbus, OH: Merrill.

Rust, L. W. (1985). Using test scores to guide the content analysis of TV materials. *Journal of Advertising Research, 25,* 17–23.

Scissors, J., & Surmanek, J. (1982). *Advertising media planning* (2nd ed.). Chicago, IL: Crain Books.

Scott, J., & O'Hair, D. (1989). Expanding psychographic concepts in public relations: The composite audience profile. In C. Botan & V. Hazelton (Eds.), *Public relations theory.* Hillsdale, NJ: Lawrence Erlbaum Associates.

Signiorelli, N. (1986). Selective television viewing: A limited possibility. *Journal of Communication, 36,* 64–75.

Smith, W. (1922). *The measurement of emotion.* London: Paul Press.

Sternhal, B., & Craig, C. S. (1984). *Consumer behavior: An information processing perspective.* Englewood Cliffs: Prentice-Hall.

Wells, W. (1970). It's a Wyeth, not a Warhol world. *Harvard Business Review, 46,* 26–32.

Wells, W. (1974). *Lifestyle and psychographics.* Chicago: American Marketing Association.

Wells, W., & Tigert, D. (1971). Activities, interests, and opinions. *Journal of Advertising Research, 11*, 27–35.

Wimmer, R. D., & Dominick, J. R. (1987). *Mass media research: An introduction.* Belmont, CA: Wadsworth.

Zajonc, R. B. (1980). Feeling and thinking: Preferences need no inferences. *American Psychologist, 35*, 151–175.

Zeitlin, D., & Westwood, R. (1986). Measuring emotional response. *Journal of Advertising Research, 25*, 34–44.

Zikmund, W., & d'Amico, M. (1986). *Marketing* (2nd ed.). New York: Wiley.

Zotti, E. (1985). Thinking psychographically. *Public Relations Journal, 41*, 26–30.

LEGAL AND POLITICAL CONTEXTS

APPLICATION OF COMMUNICATION RESEARCH TO POLITICAL CONTEXTS

11

KATHLEEN E. KENDALL
University at Albany, State University of New York

Political communication is the process of negotiating the allocation of limited resources (especially money) among groups or masses of people for programmatic reasons, through the exchange of symbols, verbal or nonverbal. The definition alone suggests the relevance of several areas of communication research to political contexts, such as interpersonal communication, mass communication and its effects, and political language. Rigorous and effective research in political communication has direct application or potential for application to problem solving in diplomacy, public administration, electoral politics, media management, reform movements, and public relations.

Once largely the domain of campaign studies, political communication research in recent years has broadened to include more general conceptions. In addition to research directed at theory building, which underlies much of the research done, the main areas are: (a) political news, (b) voter decision making, (c) presidential leadership, (d) political language, (e) the fantasy element in mass-mediated politics, (f) political advertising, and (g) international political communication research. A promising area of research in its infancy is the study of interpersonal communication within politics, and there is serious need for research on communication in state government and for more theory building. Political communication is an interdisciplinary area of study, with important research going on in political science, speech communication, journalism, mass communication, broadcasting, and psychology.

APPLICATIONS AND USES OF POLITICAL COMMUNICATION RESEARCH

Political News

The largest body of research in political communication concerns political news. Key questions are: What sources do people use to get their political information, what role do the media play in setting the agenda for the topics people think about, how and why do the media vary in their treatment of news content (including the question of bias), and what are the effects of political news coverage? An intriguing new topic of research is the role of the new telecommunications technologies in political news.

The question of the sources people use for political information is one that concerns media managers and candidates, officeholders, and citizens at all levels. In a world of limited time and resources, how can you reach your target audience efficiently? Subervi-Velez, Herrara, and Begay (1987) studied the efforts of Democrats and Republicans to reach Latinos through the broadcast media in the 1984 presidential campaign, an important step in understanding the media habits of this fast-growing group. Kebbel (1985) developed a model of news media use, and found that politically active, older, and more educated people are more likely to use multiple sources of political news. Yum and Kendall (1988) studied sources of information in one state's presidential primary campaign, and found that most people use several sources, with newspapers and television about equally relied upon. Atwater and Fico (1986) and Shield and Dunwoody (1986) studied the information-gathering methods used by reporters covering state legislatures: What sources do they use, and what is the role of the reporters' own hierarchy and social network in gaining and sharing information? With the growth in staff size, cost, and influence of state governments, the need to understand communication at that level has increased sharply. Unfortunately, the body of research on this topic is still skimpy.

The influence of the media in setting the news agenda for the general public is a major area of research. What issues dominate the news? Are these the same issues on the minds of the public? Using a panel design and content analysis to trace media coverage of issues, Shaw and McCombs (1977) described public and press agendas across a period of time, and found close convergence. In a longitudinal study of voters in the 1976 presidential election, Weaver, Graber, McCombs, and Eyal (1981) found that factors other than the media influenced the ability of the media to set the agenda, factors such as geographic location and voter demographics, especially education and occupation. Media agenda-setting powers were also influenced by the time period in the campaign, with newspapers and television having a significant impact during the spring primaries, but diminishing during the summer and fall campaign. Considering the agenda-setting powers of the media, the question of who and what influence the media is of obvious interest. Dunwoody and Shields (1986) found that the journalists covering a state government presented the state government world much as it was presented to them in the print materials given them by the state bureaucracy. For people in public relations, for campaign managers, and for media news directors, such independent and careful research findings are of value in understanding their jobs, both the powers and limits.

What can you expect from different media in terms of the quality, quantity, bias, and assumptions of political news coverage? Robinson and Sheehan (1983) compared the differences in news coverage of the 1980 election by CBS-TV and United Press International (UPI), finding major differences but no systematic biases. This intensive empirical comparison provides evidence for several insights into political news: that it is objective but fails to give a valid representation of the larger reality, that it (especially the networks) emphasizes negative coverage to the extent that it serves as "a delegitimizing force in our politics (p. 297), and that although the consequences of media coverage can be clearly demonstrated, these consequences are more often unintended, rather than deliberate efforts to exert power.

Fry and Fry (1986) compared the overall approach in news coverage by media covering the Super Tuesday primaries in 1984, and found television news more descriptive, and newspapers more causal and transactional. Graber (1985) developed a system for analyzing the total message (both verbal and nonverbal) of televised political news through content analysis techniques; there is a real need for this kind of evaluative coding to explore the *interaction* between the verbal and nonverbal elements of the total message. Media biases were disclosed in studies by Moriarty and Garramone (1986) and Sorant (1987). The former analyzed the nonverbal messages (photographs) in three major newsmagazines in the 1984 presidential campaign, finding differences in the presentation of the candidates. Reagan, for example, was the subject of many more photographs than Mondale, and of more favorable photographs early in the campaign; Mondale's photographs were more favorable later in the campaign. The article by Sorant found a systematic bias in the stories of campaign finance in three elite papers, with campaign finance activities usually being portrayed as crafty intrigues attempting to undermine the democratic process. A study by Senter, Reynolds, and Gruenfelder (1986) raised questions about media autonomy. It is a case study examining newspaper responses to criticisms by the Nixon administration, finding that newspapers changed their policies in ways desired by the Nixon administration. There is much of value in such studies for media critics, whether they instruct college-level mass communication courses, evaluate the media for the media, or work for political organizations.

The effects of political news coverage concern a broad range of politicians, campaign managers, media managers, and organizations advocating change, as well as parents and teachers. A fascinating panel survey of 1,200 people by Patterson (1980) chronicled the changes in people's thoughts in a presidential campaign, analyzing the impact of newspapers and television on their thinking. Another excellent long-range study, this time of 21 people studied intensively over a year (Graber, 1988), documented the strong impact of the subjects' prior views as they interacted with media messages during a campaign. She applied the concept of cognitive schema from psychology, and traced the strategies people use to process information by comparing it to the information they already have. Smoller (1986) proposed and tested a theory that television news has a negative influence on the presidency. Using interviews with television news executives, correspondents, and technicians, observation in the White House press room, and an examination of 5,500 news items about the president over a 16-year period, the author found the majority of coverage neutral, but increasingly negative.

Political socialization is an important area of research in political communication, of special significance to those concerned with the education of the young. The nature of political involvement of citizens is much shaped by parents, school, peers, and the mass media in their childhood years. Atkin (1981) provided a valuable survey of research findings on communication and political socialization. School social studies teachers and planners will find specific information here that might influence both curriculum and teaching methods. For example, much research indicates that public affairs news exposure by teenagers leads to more interpersonal discussions of politics. Studies such as that of Drew and Reeves (1980) show that parents and children seldom discuss politics, and although the family environment is an important influence, the evidence for direct transmission of partisan opinions from parents to children is weak (Niemi, Ross, & Alexander, 1978).

The study of "teledemocracy" as a channel of political news and means of participation is only in its infancy. Reports such as Becker and Scarce (1987) chronicle the use of computers, television sets, and telephone lines for town meetings and campaigns involving the initiative, referendum, and recall. Citizens can gain information and give feedback instantly with these new technologies. So far these experiments are not widespread, but the authors argue that they have potential as a complement to the present system. For students of the future of political communication, these accounts are provocative.

Voter Decision Making

A second important area of research examines the process by which voters make their voting decisions. For many years contemporary electoral politics dominated the research in the field. This is not surprising considering the high stakes in jobs, legislation, and public policies resulting from elections, and the public excitement and drama campaigns often engender. How do people cope with the torrent of political information available, relate it to their prior views, and reach a voting decision?

Graber's (1988) ground-breaking study, mentioned previously, examined the patterns in political information processing of 21 people and the content of their major information sources during one presidential election year. Kendall and Yum (1984) studied blue-collar workers and the comparative influence on their voting decisions of issues, images, and homophily (degree of identification with the candidates) in the 1980 presidential campaign. They found that these voters made their presidential choices in much the same way people choose their friends, through identification with their personal qualities and broad world views.

Garramone (1985) developed a conceptual model providing a framework for the study of political information processing, based on the behavior of an active voter who processes information for a variety of motives. In a four-wave survey over a 1-year period, Stamm (1987) studied the presidential choices of college students: When do they decide who to vote for, and who decides first? The author found students making their choices relatively late in the campaign. Rosenberg and McCafferty (1987) devised experiments to study the effect of images on voters. They showed subjects different photographs of the same person to see if they produced different images of key traits (such as integrity and competence), and found that the image perceptions changed markedly depending on the photograph shown. Hellweg, King, and Williams (1988) examined the structures voters use to evaluate political candidates and found that these factors differ significantly depending on election level (from presidential to mayoral). They also found evidence that the incumbent may set the perceptual agenda for the challenger. Zisk (1987) made a comparative study of four state ballot issue campaigns, on topics such as taxes and nuclear power, in the period 1976–1982. The main factors compared were spending, media and grassroots campaigns, and voter rationality.

The question of the voter's cognitive processes has long intrigued political scientists and communication scholars. The aforementioned research also has practical applications for candidates and campaign managers interested in targeting specific voter groups (such as college students and blue-collar workers), in linking campaign topics to long-term voter concerns, and in portraying the candidate image in the most effective

way. Managers of campaigns for state ballot issues will also find direct,
practical information in the Zisk book.

Presidential Leadership

America has no king, but the presidency is the focal point of the modern
American system of national politics and governance. Not surprisingly,
political communication scholars have focused on presidents and how they
lead. In a broad empirical study of almost 10,000 speeches and the speech
contexts of presidents in the period 1945–1985, Hart (1987) discerned
trends and idiosyncracies in presidential behavior never before apparent.
He examined the situations surrounding presidential speeches; for example, where did they speak, before what audiences, and how often. He found
that presidential speaking has tended to be shallow in content; the very
fact that the president has appeared and spoken is important and satisfying to audiences. The media treat the speeches of presidents as actions;
they want a presidential "fix," a statement or statements, every day. The
presidents themselves choose friendly audiences to address, often in their
home states. Hart concluded that presidential speeches have become the
main way presidents lead, the way that they govern. Such a study is of
value to journalists examining the presidency and scholars of individual
presidents.

Denton and Hahn (1986) analyzed interpersonal communication, small
group communication, and mass communication in and from the White
House. In one of their most interesting chapters, they examined President
Ronald Reagan's use of language, finding that his metaphors effectively
identify with contemporary audiences. His metaphors of paths, and of
disease and health, usually everyday, ordinary, traditional metaphors,
sound reasonable, clear, and positive, and they are in the language of
the people. The authors argued that they help to explain the public's
willingness to follow this president. The phenomenon of Reagan's huge
and long-lasting popularity deserves such close scrutiny, and contributes
to the general understanding of the institution of the presidency by citizens, politicians, and campaign consultants alike.

Johnson (1985) studied "lame-duck" presidents and their coverage by
the print media. How do *Newsweek, Time,* the *New York Times,* and the
Washington Post portray the president to the public between Election Day
and the inauguration of the new president? The author found that there
is reason indeed for the expression "lame duck"; the media focus on the
president-elect, treat the incumbent president as old news, and even portray him as a rather pitiable figure. Historians, politicians facing "lame
duck" periods, and journalists would find such information useful. The

president-elect, with this knowledge, can plan to capitalize on the free media spotlight, and the "lame duck" will know that little he or she does will be noticed, making such a period ideal for controversial actions such as executive pardons and last minute appointments. Journalists will be forewarned by the perspective on such a period.

Kellerman (1984) examined the tactics modern presidents have used to get their own way, particularly their skills in defining and articulating their agendas to attract wide support, and engaging in effective interpersonal transactions. Her main focus was on *functional* criteria: Was the president able to accomplish what he wanted to accomplish? She assessed the political skills of six presidents at work in routine, noncrisis conditions: Kennedy and federal aid to education, Johnson and the "War on Poverty," Nixon and the Family Assistance Plan, Ford and the tax cut, Carter and the energy package, and Reagan and the budget cuts. Such a study has practical value not only for students of the presidency, but for political leaders trying to get things accomplished.

Political Discourse

The nature and effect of political discourse or language is another important research topic, including the content, organization, style, and delivery of messages by politicians, and their effects. In this area of political communication perhaps more than any other, the relationship between scholar and practitioner is regularly demonstrated. Sidney Kraus (1962, 1979, 1988), who has been actively engaged in research on presidential debates since 1960, has attended all the general election debates from 1976 to the present, reported on them for television, radio, and the newspapers, and has regularly served as a resource person for the media. His research has directly affected preparation for the debates by presidential candidates. For example, in 1976, a special counsel to President Ford read one of Kraus' books, discussed it with the president, and used its findings in the negotiation and planning of Ford's debates with Jimmy Carter that year (M. Raoul-Davis, personal communication to Kraus, Oct. 27, 1976, in Kraus, 1988, p. 40). Kathleen Hall Jamieson (1984, 1988; Jamieson & Birdsell, 1988), who researches and publishes on the topics of political advertising, political debates, and speechmaking, is interviewed regularly by the media as an "expert on the relationship between television and Presidential campaigns" (Oreskes, 1988).

Other scholar-practitioners in political discourse are Smith (1976, 1977), who has served as a presidential speechwriter, Windt (1980), who has served as a political speechwriter and comments regularly on political communication for Pittsburgh media, Meadow (Bishop, Meadow, & Jackson-Beeck, 1979), who is a partner in a political consulting firm in the Los Angeles area, Chartock (Chartock & Berking, 1970), who is executive director of a National Public Radio station and a regular political analyst for media in the Albany, New York area, and Kendall (Kendall & Yum, 1984; Yum & Kendall, 1988), who has worked as a speechwriter in New York state politics.

Other studies of political discourse such as those by Hart (1984), Corcoran (1979), Trent (1978), and McDevitt (1986) may prove of interest to practitioners as well as scholars. Hart revolutionized the study of political discourse by applying computerized content analysis techniques to the examination of presidential speeches from Truman through Reagan. His computerized dictionary makes it possible to scrutinize speech texts microscopically and quickly. Corcoran's broad and erudite historical and philosophical study compares classical and modern political discourse, finding the impact of modern technology on discourse devastating. Trent examined closely the unique and predictable characteristics of the presidential candidates' "surfacing" stage, when they first launch their candidacy. So regular and set are the rules of this stage that Trent's article could serve as a guidebook for presidential candidates preparing to enter the lists. A very different study is that of McDevitt, who looked at the number of graphic symbols or ideograms used in presidential State of the Union and inaugural addresses, and then examined the extent of media coverage of these symbols. About four out of every seven ideograms used are reported, and the more popular the president, the more ideograms he uses. Such information would prove useful to speechwriters and speechgivers who want good press coverage.

The Fantasy Element in Mass-Mediated Politics

Some researchers view political communication as drama, focusing on the pictures created in the minds of the political audiences. They examine the audience's multiple and subjective views of reality, and the ways in which the media influence those perceptions. For example, Bormann (1982), who has developed a critical approach called fantasy theme analysis, compared the portrayal of the Iranian hostage release by the television networks and by President Reagan in his inaugural address, identifying the nature of the fantasy themes used. Nimmo and Combs (1985) have also been major researchers in this area. In *Nightly Horrors,* Nimmo and Combs used content analysis to compare the coverage of five crises by the three major television networks, finding that the networks adopted distinctly different dramatic themes in each crisis. Savage and Blair (1985) used content analysis and direct observation to compare the gubernatorial transition periods of Governor Clinton of Arkansas in 1978 and 1982. They found that in his words and actions he projected two very different rhetorical visions. These themes presaged the style and substance of his incumbencies quite accurately, the first a term of exuberant activism, the second much more cautious.

These studies, like any good criticism, serve to illuminate the messages and events examined. For students and practitioners of the mysteries of governance and the media, such understanding may have long-term practical value, the value of a good idea.

Political Advertising

Considering that presidential candidates spend the bulk of their funds on advertising, especially television spots, it is not surprising that the persuasive role of political commercials is a major area of research. What is the history of campaign advertising, the structure and content of advertising, the influence of commercials in the formation of political images by voters, and in conveying information? Jamieson (1984) chronicled the history and criticism of presidential advertising from the broadsides of colonial days through 1980. She focused particularly on the years 1952–1980, describing the context, decision-making process, and strategies adopted for advertising in each of these presidential campaigns. One of her important contributions was to counter the view that political advertising is a modern phenomenon, and that negative advertising has escalated in the age of television. With their banners, posters, campaign biographies, songs, and partisan newspapers, 19th-century politicians vilified their opponents and glorified their own images; these often-criticized behaviors are deeply rooted in American politics. This book contains many good ideas for people interested in political advertising.

Devlin (1986) has collected spots, interviewed their creators, and described what spots were shown and why in presidential campaigns since 1972. His articles tell the inside story of the candidates' media teams, the focus of their ads, and the contrasts between the ads. They provide insight through their detail and scope. For example, after studying the Republican and Democratic campaign ads for 12 years, he observed: "I have come to the conclusion that Democrats like to stress issues and constituencies; Republicans like to stress values that are more universal" (p. 53). Students and practitioners of campaign advertising will find much of value here.

Another valuable work to students and practitioners is a book edited by Kaid, Nimmo, and Sanders (1986), containing a series of studies of political advertising representing a variety of research methods. One chapter, by Kolar, focuses on the role of the political parties from 1976 through 1984 in producing television and radio advertisements for presidential, senatorial, and congressional candidates, and in publicizing party strengths and the opposing party's weaknesses. Party coordination and centralizing of resources, production, and candidate advising has brought sophisticated advertising to hundreds of state-level campaigns. In another chapter Kaid and Davidson (1986) reported on a content analysis of 55 commercials from three Senate races in 1982, examining the video styles of the candidates; they also interviewed the producers of the commercials. They found clearly different styles of incumbent and challenger commercials, reported that producers are preoccupied with the viewers' emotional reactions, and observed that the specific state environment in which the campaign ads are shown influences producer decisions. Cundy's (1986) quasi-experimental study in the same book employed magnitude scaling techniques to measure the effect of campaign spots on the general public. One of his major findings was that campaign ads are likely to be most effective early in the campaign when the voters know little about the candidate. Mansfield and Hale (1986) applied Q-methodology in a quasi-experimental study of audience motivations in watching campaign spots. They found two distinctive motivational patterns among the viewers: One group watched the spots for entertainment, social, and nonpolitical reasons, and a second group watched for "surveillance/vote guidance" reasons. In this study with a small student population, the subjects' motivations did not have a significant effect on their perceptions of the commercials. This book is a valuable addition to research on political advertising.

International Political Communication

In the 1980s there has been a steady growth in political communication research in countries other than the United States. Scholars are particularly interested in the interrelationships of politics and the media. Organizations such as the International Political Science Association, which has a Political Communication research group, the International Communication Association, which also has a Political Communication division, and the International Sociological Association foster these developments. This research is potentially valuable to diplomats, journalists, politicians, and scholars in many parts of the world.

Noelle-Neumann's (1980, 1985) Spiral of Silence theory, based on research in Germany, argued that people monitor the climate of political opinion in their environment, and when they find themselves out of step with that opinion, they keep silent. The more out of step they believe they are with the climate of opinion expressed in the media, the more they conform by keeping silent, for fear of social isolation. Her research has provoked a lively discussion and testing of her theory among scholars such as Salmon and Kline (1985), Merten (1985), and Glynn and McLeod (1985). Candidates, political reporters and analysts, and students of public opinion—all those trying to predict and understand the electorate—will find her writings stimulating.

Paletz (1987), editor of a book on political communication research, brought together several international studies focusing on the media in Italy, the Federal Republic of Germany, Brazil, Latin America, and China, as well as the United States. Among them is that of Chen (1987), who examined the changes in American news coverage in two Chinese newspapers. Chen found that the coverage is highly positive to the United States, but reports on the deficiencies of capitalism. The articles give heavy coverage to scientific and technological news from America, and use information about the United States to show the Soviet Union in an unfavorable light. Information about such research would be of potential value to diplomats and journalists dealing with China.

One large international study underway involves 18 French and American researchers collaborating on a comparative study of the 1988 French and American presidential elections (Report on Elections, 1988). They presented their preliminary findings in a report at the International Communication Association in May 1988, and planned to continue the study through the American election. Such research should be of value not only to scholars but also to diplomats and journalists dealing with these two countries.

Manheim (1988) studied the Republic of Korea's public relations preparatory to the 1988 Olympics. He examined the Olympics as a condensation symbol, and found that this powerful symbol had a cathartic and at times uncontrollable effect on the nation. The government was also heavily influenced in its portrayal of the Olympics by the international news media. The story of a magnetic symbol with its own dynamic, overwhelming the people who are trying to control it, may serve as a cautionary tale for other nations dealing with powerful symbols. Policymakers and students of symbol use by governments would learn from such a study.

Charland (1987) contributed to persuasion theory with his study of the issue of independent sovereignty for the province of Quebec, Canada. The party supporting independence in Quebec assumed that the French-speaking audience was already constituted rhetorically, that they already had an identity and ideology, that of the "peuple Quebecois," and developed its arguments from that assumption. Although the referendum on Quebec independence ultimately failed, the party rose to power, won control of the government, and built up substantial support for the referendum based on this adroit assumption about the prepersuasive situation. Charland, building on Kenneth Burke's (1950/1969) concept of identification and McGee's (1975) development of the concept of "the people," took us back to the foundation of rhetorical strength in audience analysis. For anyone concerned with political persuasion, such theory building is important.

NEW DIRECTIONS IN RESEARCH: FUTURE NEEDS

The topic of interpersonal communication in politics is a new area of research promising to have valuable carryover in applied settings. For example, Meadow (1985) called for research on targeted direct mail. Such mailings, he said, are "powerful campaign tools because they create a temporary—very temporary—interpersonal relationship between the candidate (or an endorser of a candidate) and the voter" (p. 149). He also urged that there be more research on the role of telephones in political communication, which, like direct mail, establish a temporary interpersonal tie with the voters. Considering the huge investment of organizational funds on political lobbying at the federal and state level, the interpersonal communication of lobbyists is also a topic deserving of serious research attention.

One excellent recent study in interpersonal-political communication is that of Lasorsa and Wanta (1988). Surveying a population of over 600 members of the general public, they tested the hypothesis that "the more one communicates interpersonally about political issues, the less he or she will conform to the media's agenda of issues" (p. 5). They found some support for this hypothesis, suggesting that the individual cues the voters receive in interpersonal communication may interfere with the messages coming from the media. Another interesting study is that of Husson, Stephen, Harrison, and Fehr (1988), who examined voter perceptions of the interpersonal communication behavior of Ronald Reagan and Walter Mondale, and the relationship of those perceptions to candidate images and voter preferences. Their contribution is to integrate the theory and concepts of interpersonal communication research with the important areas of image perception and voter decision making. They found significant relationships between interpersonal perceptions and voter preferences. Kuo (1985) explored the relationship between media use and interpersonal communication in the area of political learning, examining data from a nationwide survey of 1,700 adolescents. The author found that children learning about politics from the media were more likely to discuss politics with family and friends, and after such discussion were more likely to seek more political information from the media. The media use and interpersonal behaviors were closely linked. Media managers and analysts trying to predict, explain, and influence political behavior may find such studies thought-provoking, and there need to be many more in this area.

Another subject in serious need of more research attention is communication in state government. Most of the studies in political communication focus on the federal level, leaving such topics as state administrative communication, communication within legislative hearings and committees, and legislative speeches virtually untouched. State bureaucracies spend billions of dollars a year, and their managers need assistance in improving organizational communication. As state legislatures continue to raise salaries and lengthen the time spent in session, with a growing professionalization of staff, there is a real need for research findings to guide these communicators.

Some innovative research methods that hold promise for future work in political communication are those used by Graber (1988); Husson, Stephen, Harrison, and Fehr (1988); and Philipsen (1975). After drawing a random sample of subjects, Graber focused on only 21 people, studying them intensively over a 1-year period. She interviewed them repeatedly, and developed detailed profiles of her subjects and their media uses and interpretations. The insights resulting from this methodology are a rich and important source of stimulation for other researchers. Husson et al. (1988) applied an instrument normally used to assess elements of interpersonal communication to a political communication study. They asked subjects to evaluate two presidential candidates with this instrument, and found that the ratings of their interpersonal communication behavior significantly predicted differential preferences for these candidates. The application of concepts and instruments from one area of communication study to another seems a creative and worthwhile venture. Philipsen (1975), a scholar in the area of discourse analysis, used an ethnographic research methodology directly influenced by anthropologists. Through participant observation and interviewing among a group of blue-collar, low-income Whites on the near south side of Chicago, he was able to construct the cultural pattern of speech behavior for that group, the places they talked, the amount they talked, and the strategies and situations for talking, in comparison to other possible responses they made to people. This methodology seems directly applicable to political language research. In addition, it would provide a welcome balance to the usual research on political leadership by focusing on political communication among the general population.

Some of the same suggestions for future research made by Atkin (1980) still hold true today. There continues to be a need for more attention to theory so that political practitioners will be able to go beyond the ad-hoc mode of operation so prevalent in applied situations. Atkins' proposals that there be more utilization of agenda-setting concepts in studies of persuasive situations, more application of the uses and gratifications perspective to reveal why people expose themselves to persuasive messages, and the application of conventional learning and consistency theories to mass media appeals are as sound as they were when he first made them.

Promising new theoretical approaches in the area of political language are those of Edelman (1988), Shapiro (1981), and Corcoran (1990). Edelman stressed the power of political language, first to construct the people who use it, to give them their sense of who they are, and second, to make them symbols to other people. These people and their language have a range of meanings that change with the situation. A recent news story about the changing concepts and strategies of the Italian Communist Party illustrates this point, as the party unveiled a new program emphasizing ecology, feminism, and family issues (Riding, 1989). Edelman's (1988) underlying assumption was that "language is the key creator of the social worlds people experience, not a tool for describing an objective reality" (p. 103). The view is consistent with that of Foucault (1971, 1976), a French poststructuralist scholar whose work he admires.

Shapiro (1981) has a broader and more controversial view than Edelman, finding political meaning in *all* our speech practices. Politics, in effect, is everywhere, in private life as well as public; politics and language are "intimately commingled" (p. 233). Because most people do not realize that the relationship is so close, he said, they therefore are easily used by political language. Like Edelman, he stressed the shaping force of language, but went even further, declaring that "innovative political action . . . *consists in* linguistic action" (p. 233). Both these theorists, in views consistent with Hart (1987), see language as the essence of political action.

Corcoran (1990) provided a valuable survey of theoretical frameworks for analyzing language and politics. Negotiating among the conflicting theoretical positions, he saw danger in expanding the political to include the personal, for "that which incorporates all distinguishes nothing." But he recognized that the individual and society are not completely separate, that society is both outside and inside the individual. Thus, the political is often found in private social and economic relationships. He advocated that the language of politics be examined chiefly in its "narratives of dispute, contestation, and combat," through what he called "the perspective of opposition." As long as political discourse is symbolic, with meaning grounded in conflicting and changing interpretations, the analyst of such discourse—the journalist, political observer, diplomat, scholar, teacher—must approach the job as an opponent, with the goal being to "unpack, undermine, demystify, and expose" the meaning of the contest.

Politics is about power, about the contest over the allocation of scarce resources. Anyone who is working in politics is constantly involved in negotiations to secure, maintain, and strengthen power, and most of that negotiation requires skillful communication. Research by political communication scholars can provide rules, tools, and insights for keeping ahead in this inevitable human game.

REFERENCES

Atkin, C. K. (1981). Communication and political socialization. In D. D. Nimmo & K. R. Sanders (Eds.), *Handbook of political communication* (pp. 299–328). Beverly Hills: Sage.

Atkin, C. K. (1980). Political campaigns: Mass communication and persuasion. In M. E. Roloff & G. R. Miller (Eds.), *Persuasion: New directions in theory and research* (Vol. 8, pp. 285–308). Beverly Hills: Sage.

Atwater, T., & Fico, F. (1986). Source reliance and use in reporting state government: A study of print and broadcast practices. *Newspaper Research Journal, 8,* 53–61.

Becker, T., & Scarce, R. (1987). Teledemocracy emergent: State of the American art and science. In B. Dervin & M. J. Voigt (Eds.), *Progress in communication sciences* (Vol. 8, pp. 263–287). Norwood, NJ: Ablex.

Bishop, G. F., Meadow, R. G., & Jackson-Beeck, M. (Eds.) (1979). *The presidential debates: Media, electoral and policy perspectives.* New York: Praeger.

Bormann, E. G. (1982). A fantasy theme analysis of the television coverage of the hostage release and the Reagan inaugural. *Quarterly Journal of Speech, 68,* 133–45.

Burke, K. (1969). *A rhetoric of motives.* Berkeley: University of California Press. (Original work published 1950)

Charland, M. (1987). Constitutive rhetoric: The case of the people Quebecois. *Quarterly Journal of Speech, 73,* 133–150.

Chartock, A. S., & Berking, M. (1970). *Strengthening the Wisconsin legislature.* New Brunswick, NJ: Rutgers University Press.

Chen, K. H. (1987). Changes of American news coverage in two Chinese newspapers: A comparison. In D. L. Paletz (Ed.), *Political communication research: Approaches, studies, assessments* (pp. 129–147). Norwood, NJ: Ablex.

Corcoran, P. E. (1979). *Political language and rhetoric.* Austin, TX: University of Texas Press.

Corcoran, P. E. (1990). Language and politics. In D. L. Swanson & D. Nimmo (Eds.), *New directions in political communication: A resource book* (pp. 51–85). Beverly Hills: Sage.

Cundy, D. T. (1986). Political commercials and candidate image: The effect can be substantial. In L. L. Kaid, D. Nimmo, & K. R. Sanders (Eds.), *New perspectives on political advertising* (pp. 210–234). Carbondale, IL: Southern Illinois University Press.

Denton, R. E., Jr., & Hahn, D. F. (1986). *Presidential communication*. New York: Praeger.

Devlin, L. P. (1986). An analysis of presidential television commercials, 1952–1984. In L. L. Kaid, D. Nimmo, & K. R. Sanders (Eds.), *New perspectives on political advertising* (pp. 21–54). Carbondale, IL: Southern Illinois University Press.

Drew, D., & Reeves, B. (1980). Children and television news. *Journalism Quarterly, 57,* 45–54.

Dunwoody, S., & Shields, S. (1986). Accounting for patterns of selection of topics in statehouse reporting. *Journalism Quarterly, 63,* 488–496.

Edelman, M. (1988). *Constructing the political spectacle*. Chicago: University of Chicago Press.

Foucault, M. (1971). *The order of things*. New York: Parthenon Books.

Foucault, M. (1976). *The archaeology of knowledge*. New York: Harper & Row.

Fry, D. L., & Fry, V. H. (1986). Language use and political environments in media coverage of "Super Tuesday." *Journalism Quarterly, 63,* 719–727.

Garramone, G. M. (1985). Motivation and political information processing: Extending the gratifications approach. In S. Kraus & R. M. Perloff (Eds.), *Mass media and political thought* (pp. 201–222). Beverly Hills: Sage.

Glynn, C. J., & McLeod, J. M. (1985). Implications of the spiral of silence theory for communication and public opinion research. In K. Sanders, L. L. Kaid, & D. Nimmo (Eds.), *Political communication yearbook 1984* (pp. 43–65). Carbondale, IL: Southern Illinois University Press.

Graber, D. A. (1985). Approaches to content analysis of television news programs. *Communications: The European Journal of Communication, 11*(2), 25–36.

Graber, D. A. (1988). *Processing the news: How people tame the information tide* (2nd ed.). New York: Longman.

Hart, R. P. (1984). *Verbal style and the presidency, a computer-based analysis*. Orlando, FL: Academic Press.

Hart, R. P. (1987). *The sound of leadership: Presidential communication in the modern age*. Chicago: University of Chicago Press.

Hellweg, S. A., King, S. W., & Williams, S. E. (1988). Comparative candidate evaluation as a function of election level and candidate incumbency. *Communication Reports, 1,* 76–85.

Husson, W., Stephen, T., Harrison, T. M., and Fehr, B. J. (1988). An interpersonal communication perspective on images of political candidates. *Human Communication Research, 14,* 397–421.

Jamieson, K. H. (1984). *Packaging the presidency: A history and criticism of presidential campaign advertising*. New York: Oxford University Press.

Jamieson, K. H. (1988). *Eloquence in an electronic age: The transformation of political speechmaking*. New York: Oxford University Press.

Jamieson, K. H., & Birdsell, D. S. (1988). *Presidential debates: The challenge of creating an informed electorate*. New York: Oxford University Press.

Johnson, K. S. (1985). The honeymoon period: Fact or fiction? *Journalism Quarterly, 62,* 869–876.

Kaid, L. L., & Davidson, D. K. (1986). Elements of videostyle: Candidate presentation through television advertising. In L. L. Kaid, D. Nimmo, & K. R. Sanders

(Eds.), *New perspectives on political advertising* (pp. 184–209). Carbondale, IL: Southern Illinois University Press.

Kaid, L. L., Nimmo, D., & Sanders, K. R. (Eds.). (1986). *New perspectives on political advertising*. Carbondale, IL: Southern Illinois University Press.

Kebbel, G. (1985). The importance of political activity in explaining multiple news media use. *Journalism Quarterly, 62,* 559–566.

Kellerman, B. (1984). *The political presidency.* New York: Oxford University Press.

Kendall, K. E., & Yum, J. O. (1984). Persuading the blue-collar voter: Issues, images, and homophily. In R. N. Bostrom (Ed.), *Communication yearbook 8* (pp. 707–722). Beverly Hills: Sage.

Kolar, B. (1986). Fighting back: American political parties take to the airwaves. In L. L. Kaid, D. Nimmo, & K. R. Sanders (Eds.), *New perspectives on political advertising* (pp. 55–81). Carbondale, IL: Southern Illinois University Press.

Kraus, S. (Ed.). (1962). *The great debates: Kennedy vs. Nixon, 1960.* Bloomington, IN: Indiana University Press.

Kraus, S. (Ed.). (1979). *The great debates: Carter vs. Ford, 1976.* Bloomington, IN: Indiana University Press.

Kraus, S. (1988). *Televised presidential debates and public policy.* Hillsdale, NJ: Lawrence Erlbaum Associates.

Kuo, C. (1985). Media use, interpersonal communication, and political socialization: An interactional model analysis using LISREL. In M. L. McLaughlin (Ed.), *Communication yearbook* (pp. 625–641). Beverly Hills: Sage.

Lasorsa, D. L., & Wanta, W. (1988, May). *The effects of personal, interpersonal, and media experience on issue salience.* Paper presented at the International Communication Association Convention, New Orleans, LA.

Manheim, J. B. (1988, August). *Rights of passage: Elections, Olympics, and the external communications of the Republic of Korea.* Paper presented at the Fourteenth World Congress of the International Political Science Association, Washington, DC.

Mansfield, M., & Hale, K. (1986). Uses and perceptions of political television: An application of Q-technique. In L. L. Kaid, D. Nimmo, & K. R. Sanders (Eds.), *New perspectives on political advertising* (pp. 268–292). Carbondale, IL: Southern Illinois University Press.

McDevitt, M. (1986). Ideological language and the press: Coverage of inaugural, state of the union addresses. *Mass Communication Review, 13*(1–3), 18–24.

McGee, M. C. (1975). In search of "the people": A rhetorical alternative. *Quarterly Journal of Speech, 61,* 235–249.

Meadow, R. G. (1985). Political campaigns, new technology, and political communication research. In K. R. Sanders, L. L. Kaid, & D. Nimmo (Eds.), *Political communication yearbook 1984* (pp. 135–152). Carbondale, IL: Southern Illinois University Press.

Merten, K. (1985). Some silence in the spiral of silence. In K. R. Sanders, L. L. Kaid, & D. Nimmo (Eds.), *Political communication yearbook 1984* (pp. 31–42). Carbondale, IL: Southern Illinois University Press.

Moriarty, S. E., & Garramone, G. M. (1986). A study of news magazine photographs of the 1984 presidential campaign. *Journalism Quarterly, 63,* 728–734.

Niemi, R., Ross, R. D., & Alexander, J. (1978). The similarity of political values of parents and college-age youths. *Public Opinion Quarterly, 42,* 503–520.

Nimmo, D., & Combs, J. E. (1985). *Nightly horrors, crisis coverage by television network news.* Knoxville, TN: University of Tennessee Press.

Noelle-Neumann, E. (1980). *Die schweigespirale* [The spiral of silence]. Munich: Peiper.

Noelle-Neumann, E. (1985). The spiral of silence: A response. In K. R. Sanders, L. L. Kaid, & D. Nimmo (Eds.), *Political communication yearbook 1984* (pp. 66–94). Carbondale, IL: Southern Illinois University Press.

Oreskes, M. (1988, October 2). Talking heads, weighing imagery in a campaign made for television. *New York Times,* Sect. 4, p. 1.

Paletz, D. L. (Ed.). (1987). *Political communication research: Approaches, studies, assessments.* Norwood, NJ: Ablex.

Patterson, T. E. (1980). *The mass media election.* New York: Praeger.

Philipsen, G. (1975). Speaking "like a man" in Teamsterville: Culture patterns of role enactment in an urban neighborhood. *Quarterly Journal of Speech, 61,* 13–22.

Report on the French-U.S. Presidential Elections Study, I and II. (1988, May). Papers presented at the International Communication Association Convention, New Orleans.

Riding, A. (1989, March 25). Italy's battered Communists reinvent themselves again. *New York Times,* p. 8.

Robinson, M. J., & Sheehan, M. A. (1983). *Over the wire and on tv.* New York: Russell Sage.

Rosenberg, S. W., & McCafferty, P. (1987). The image and the vote: Manipulating voters' preferences. *Public Opinion Quarterly, 51,* 31–47.

Salmon, C. T., & Kline, G. (1985). The spiral of silence ten years later: An examination and evaluation. In K. R. Sanders, L. L. Kaid, & D. Nimmo (Eds.), *Political communication yearbook 1984* (pp. 3–30). Carbondale, IL: Southern Illinois University Press.

Savage, R. L., & Blair, D. D. (1985). Constructing and reconstructing the image of statecraft: The rhetorical challenges of gubernatorial transitions. In K. R. Sanders, L. L. Kaid, & D. Nimmo (Eds.), *Political communication yearbook 1984* (pp. 242–261). Carbondale, IL: Southern Illinois University Press.

Senter, R., Jr., Reynolds, L. T., & Gruenfelder, D. (1986). The presidency and the print media: Who controls the news? *Sociological Quarterly, 27,* 91–105.

Shapiro, M. J. (1981). *Language and political understanding: The politics of discursive practices.* New Haven, CT: Yale University Press.

Shaw, D. L., & McCombs, M. E. (1977). *The emergence of American political issues.* St. Paul, MN: West.

Shield, S., & Dunwoody, S. (1986). The social world of the statehouse pressroom. *Newspaper Research Journal, 8,* 43–51.

Smith, C. R. (1976). Contemporary political speech writing. *Southern Speech Communication Journal, 42,* 52–67.

Smith, C. R. (1977). Addendum to "contemporary political speech writing." *Southern Speech Communication Journal, 42,* 191–194.

Smoller, F. (1986). The six o'clock presidency: Patterns of network news coverage of the president. *Presidential Studies Quarterly, 16,* 31–49.

Sorant, F. J. (1987). Campaign money and the press: Three soundings. *Political Science Quarterly, 102,* 25–42.

Stamm, K. R. (1987). Cognitive strategies and communication during a presidential campaign. *Communication Research, 14,* 35–57.

Subervi-Velez, F. A., Herrara, R., & Begay, M. (1987). Toward an understanding of the role of the mass media in Latino political life. *Social Science Quarterly, 68,* 185–196.

Trent, J. S. (1978). Presidential surfacing: The ritualistic and crucial first act. *Communication Monographs, 45,* 281–292.

Weaver, D. H., Graber, D. A., McCombs, M. E., & Eyal, C. H. (1981). *Media agenda-setting in a presidential election: Issues, images, and interest.* New York: Praeger.

Windt, T. (1980). *Presidential rhetoric (1961–1980).* Dubuque, IA: Kendall/Hunt.

Yum, J. O., & Kendall, K. E. (1988). Sources of information in a presidential primary campaign. *Journalism Quarterly, 65,* 148–151, 177.

Zisk, B. H. (1987). *Money, media, and the grassroots: State ballot issues and the electoral process* (Sage Library of Social Research, Vol. 164). Newbury Park, CA: Sage.

LEGAL COMMUNICATION: AN INTRODUCTION TO RHETORICAL AND COMMUNICATION THEORY PERSPECTIVES

12

STEVEN R. GOLDZWIG
Marquette University

MICHAEL J. CODY
University of Southern California

In this chapter we face the difficult task of introducing the reader to the rhetorical and communication research on legal communication in a few pages. Because whole books and chapters are written on any *one* aspect of this topic (i.e., language in the courtroom), we have decided to write a chapter that sketches the highlights of research in selected areas, outlines the main findings in each area, and provides ample references to scholarly literature. We first overview how scholars adopting a rhetorical viewpoint study legal discourse, courtroom drama, and storytelling. We then outline several areas pertinent both to the practice of lawyering and to the empirically oriented scholar.

RHETORICAL ANALYSES IN LEGAL SETTINGS

A number of authors have cited the close alliance between the disciplines of speech communication and law (Bunn, 1964; Rice, 1961; Strother, 1961; Weiss, 1959). However, in 1970 Anapol noted a surprising lack of "extensive literature" on the relation between rhetoric and the law. This came as somewhat of a shock because rhetoric can be seen as a source of law and law figures prominently in the rhetoric of Western civilization (Pilotta, Murphy, Wilson, & Jones, 1983).

Both the rhetorical and legal disciplines, argued Anapol (1970), can benefit from a renewal of their classical roots when they enjoy a closer,

rhetoric - persuasion

mutually beneficial association. The lawyer and the law student are encouraged to study rhetoric because the lawyer inevitably practices persuasion (Wiethoff, 1984). Aristotle's ancient treatise, *Rhetoric,* then, is still important to today's attorney because it has been universally acclaimed as a classic in legal theory and philosophy. Lawyers *literally* must develop "the faculty of observing in any given case the available means of persuasion" (McKeon, 1941, p. 1329). As Constans and Dickey (1954) pointed out, lawyers must, among other things, select a jury, do a good bit of convincing expository speaking, handle and cross-examine witnesses, interpret witness testimony in a light favorable to their clients, qualify expert witnesses, state procedural objections, and use opening and closing arguments. All of these functions require rhetoric and a knowledge of rhetorical principles. Thus training in the arts of rhetoric and argumentation is now seen as vital to the prospective lawyer (Koegel, 1951; Matlon, 1982; McBath, 1961; Mills, 1976; Nobles, 1985; Williams, 1955).

Despite calls for studies on the relationship between law and rhetoric and for increased pedagogy on legal communication for the prelaw student, research in legal communication by rhetorical scholars has been a comparatively recent phenomenon. Bartanen (1987), for example, maintained that although forensic (legal) discourse has been an important genre since the days of ancient Greece, rhetorical studies on jury behavior, trial proceedings, and judicial opinions are just now beginning to appear. Part of the neglect in this area may be due to the rhetorical critic's penchant for focusing on "memorable" speeches (Shmukler, 1970). Some of the paucity of rhetorical research probably also can be attributed to the time, expense, and difficulty involved in videotaping and transcribing trial proceedings and in obtaining complete trial transcripts.

A renewed interest in genre studies (Black, 1965; Campbell & Jamieson, 1978; Carlson, 1985; Dicks, 1976; Erlich, 1975) and ardent calls for rhetorical critics to pay more attention to nonidiosyncratic (everyday or normative) discourse (Hart, 1986) as well as recent jurisprudential models of argument drawing upon the works of Perelman and Toulmin (see, e.g., Abbott, 1974; Crable, 1976) all seem to have paved the way for more rhetorical studies in legal discourse. This is not to say that rhetorical scholars have remained idle. In this section of the chapter we briefly outline what has been published, highlight some of the intriguing new research, and, finally, offer our evaluations and suggestions for future legal studies. In the process, we broaden our use of the term *rhetorical* research to include studies in rhetoric, argumentation, and forensics in an effort to outline a number of promising theoretical approaches and qualitative methodologies applicable to the study of the social construction of reality in the courtroom.

Oral Argument

A good number of articles have focused on argument before the Supreme Court, with the case of *Brown v. Board of Education* in 1954 receiving the most case study attention. Strother (1963) outlined the rhetorical uses of social science testimony as evidence in this historic decision. Dickens and Schwartz (1971) compared and evaluated Thurgood Marshall's and John Davis' oral arguments before the Supreme Court in *Brown* to identify rhetorical characteristics common to oral argument. Besides giving practical advice about the rhetorical requirements and problems associated with such argument, they also emphasized that effectiveness is a matter of clarity, adaptability, and judicious selection of rhetorical strategy. Sanbonmatsu (1971) used Burkean analytic techniques to evaluate Darrow's and Rourke's use of identification strategies in the case of *New York v. Gitlow* in 1920. The author featured the importance of focusing on prosecution as well as defense arguments.

Wasby, D'Amato, and Metrailer (1976) are particularly helpful in this area because they discussed the functions of oral argument for both the lawyers and the Supreme Court justices; they featured the pattern and functioning of judicial questioning as key to the process of oral argument. Oral argument reassures the lawyer that the case has been heard and that significant selected arguments gain a fair hearing. This also assists the judges to key in on important issues. In addition, oral arguments legitimate the judges' function, spur communication between colleagues on the bench, and allow the judges opportunity to get information and clarification about disputed arguments in the case. Oral arguments are especially helpful in assisting Supreme Court judges in shaping their strategic approach to the case. Levison (1979) corroborated these findings by concluding that the complexity of a particular ruling is apprehended by the study of oral argument. The question and answer format serves at least three purposes: (a) focusing attention on extralegal concerns that shape legal advocacy efforts, (b) clarifying facts in the case, and (c) shaping judicial strategies for legal decision making. Lawyers who are able to answer judges' questions clearly and more often than their opponents seem to have the advantage.

Legal Reasoning and Judicial Opinion

Law as a specialized form of communication generates its own standards of jurisprudence and employs unique reasoning processes. Wright (1964) claimed that judicial rhetoric was still an open field for research; especially lacking were studies on decisions emanating from the federal bench.

Judicial opinions as rhetorical artifacts supply the grounds for court decisions and display the logic, history, customs, and utilitarian concerns associated with particular cases. Moreover, in communicating judicial decisions, rhetorical strategies following the classical canons of rhetoric are often in evidence. Matters of invention, arrangement, and style are crucial factors in determining legal reasoning processes; even delivery may become a matter for consideration should a decision be appealed. The potential audiences for judicial decisions are wide ranging. They may include the litigants, other judges and lawyers, other governmental branches, law reviews, bar association journals, the news media, and the electorate.

Le Duc (1976) relied on freedom of expression case studies to inquire into how judicial opinions influence the development of legal principles. Both the legal issues selected and legal grounds for opinions as expressed rhetorically determine how legal principle evolves. Rhetorico-legal precedents used today will affect the outcomes of tomorrow. Jones (1976) affirmed Le Duc's position by noting that law as a communication enterprise is often a process of justifying judicial decisions in the *form* of judicial opinions. Jones uncovered a number of practical justificatory categories including: (a) intention of the framers, (b) history, (c) precedents, (d) adaptation to new conditions, (e) current usage, (f) literal meaning constructs, (g) depreciating the original decision, and (h) pragmatic issue proposals. Although such categories cannot be used absolutely to predict judicial decisions, judges also rely on them for their decision making. Interestingly, Jones' study concluded that, in the main, judicial decisions are not based on precedent (*stare decisis*) but rather on other forms of argument according to the categories specified previously.

A number of specific studies take up the task of unraveling judicial justifications and reasoning processes (Makau, 1984; Minnick, 1982; Rabin, 1978). These authors help us to learn a bit more about the court's practical reasoning. Other authors have focused on the opinions of the Supreme Court in an attempt to understand a range of judicial decisions (Bartanen, 1987; Hagan, 1976; Hunsaker, 1978; Rodgers, 1982; Ulrich, 1985).

Reconstructing Reality

Perhaps the most exciting, potentially rewarding, and far-reaching research undertaken to date attempts to describe and interpret the rhetorical construction of reality during the courtroom trial process. Such investigation seems likely to bear fruit because it is being conducted against the backdrop of probative and comprehensive theories of human communication. Moreover, as Dicks (1981) made clear, this new research promises to add to our knowledge of the entire trial process, rather than merely focusing scholarly attention on one aspect of the trial (e.g., opening and closing statements, etc.).

Hample (1979) argued that a dramatistic perspective is useful in understanding the trial process. Trials may be viewed as dramatic morality plays revealing a variety of human motivations. Burke (1969) developed a "grammar" of human motives that has been applied usefully to the analysis and understanding of courtroom interaction. The application of key motivation terms comprising Burke's pentad, *act, agency, agent, scene,* and *purpose,* allows critics to describe courtroom events in ways that explain the complex communication patterns and ratios of decisional structures that inevitably arise (see Ritter, 1985).

The most comprehensive explanation of this perspective developed thus far views trial communication as "storytelling" (Bennett, 1978, 1979). The stories told during the trial will help receivers comprehend complex events to which they were not present physically. The stories created at trial help participants locate the central actions and interpret those actions in order to construct inferences about the people, events, and relationships for accuracy, consistency, plausibility, and adequacy in comparison to other stories surfacing at the trial. Again, Burke (1969) lent a ready framework for analysis with the pentad. The actual "facts" of any particular case may be subservient to the attorney's ability to reconstruct an acceptable story in the present that sheds a favorable light on the past.

Bennett and Feldman (1981) suggested that effective storytelling by trial attorneys is hampered by the fact that any particular case is not presented in a single story; rather, the story must be pieced together from the fragmentary portions of evidence and testimony that could yield several plausible stories and frameworks for interpretation. The job of the prosecution is to construct a case according to a tight story structure that develops a consistent and complete explanation for the criminal act. The defense, on the other hand, must create "reasonable doubt." Three defense case strategies can be identified: challenge (show missing elements in the prosecution's case), redefinition (show how different meanings emerge when changes are made in the interpretation of evidence), and reconstruction (tell a completely different story).

Lawyers will attempt to define stories according to their conceptions of the best strategy. Tactics targeted toward this goal are definition, connection, and establishing credibility. Definitional tactics are used to transform the bits of trial evidence into linguistic terms that fit the developing crime story. The opposition, of course, will try to upset such a symbolic "fit." Connection establishes relationships between described persons, places, and events. Attorneys use innuendo to make or break connections linking evidence to a specific set of elements in the story, which could result in specific inferences. In disestablishing the credibility of evidence, the lawyer's tactics include demonstrating witness testimony as unreliable, exposing a direct lie, showing consistencies and inconsistencies within testimony, revealing poor powers of recall, and/or even using disruptive forms of communication as a means of control (although the latter is generally seen as ineffective). Each of the strategies and the specific tactics illumine the power of the story to structure the social and legal symbolic construction of reality in the courtroom. Dicks (1981) provided an equally valuable and insightful analysis of the rhetorical plans used in the 1972 trial of Angela Davis.

Condit and Selzer (1985) built on the work of both Burke (1969) and Bennett and Feldman (1981) by adapting Burkean pentadic theory and McGee's (1980) concept of the "ideograph" as a tool for comparing a murder trial transcript with the newspaper coverage of the proceedings. They attempted to establish how the text of the actual trial is translated into news—a text for the general public. Interestingly, the analysis revealed that the newspaper "mirrored" the prosecutor's pentadic and ideographic focus, whereas the jury in the courtroom voted for the defendant's acquittal.

Beach (1985) also built on the work of Bennett and Feldman through "naturalistic" observation of a murder trial. Beach's ethnomethodological study focused on conversational "time-traveling" through a communicative process labeled as *storifying*. This method of conversational analysis allows the researcher to investigate narrative structures both spatially and temporally. Thus, stories are seen to organize both time and space in the courtroom setting and allow communicators to discuss past, present, and future events. Relying on a three-dimensional "time-traveling" model developed by Beach and Japp (1983), Beach measured courtroom communicative utterances by temporal duration (a specific segment or an entire court proceeding), chronology (the extent to which the interactants discuss the immediate or distant past, present, and/or future), and levels of time (factual, perceived, and fictitious; probable, improbable, impossible future versus present reality) in an effort to codify reconstruction of reality in the trial setting.

Beach's (1985) review of the trial transcripts revealed that the "turn-taking" activity involved in questions and answers designed to elicit testimony at the murder trial focused mainly on reconstructing the past. The bulk of the interactional work done in the courtroom drama moves across the factual and perceived past. The past can be construed as a temporally "dense" domain where descriptions based on sequential ordering and depth (immediate or distant) make for complex and sometimes conflicting stories that juries must process, organize, and interpret. Tensions can arise between the descriptions of the factual and perceived past; and even when the jury reaches a verdict, some of those tensions may never be fully relieved. Thus, defense trial attorneys must have as their goal the construction of a preferred reality that, when accepted in the present, yields a favorable verdict for clients accused of past criminal action.

Beach (1988) also focused his attention on intercultural communication and courtroom interaction with a view of language as crucial to the social construction of reality and, concomitantly, trial outcomes. Beach (in press-a) reflected on questions related to the researcher's role in the investigation and presentation of the nature of social action in the courtroom. The researcher observes the "naturally occurring [courtroom] interaction" to find the rules and structure of human communication. Rather than "imposing" macro-concepts and theories "onto" the interaction as a template for understanding, the researcher derives theoretical understanding by observing the "moment-by-moment evolution of a conversational involvement" (see also Beach, in press-b).

Evaluation and Suggestions for Future Research

Rhetorical scholars and critics have illuminated our understanding of the processes involved in judicial reasoning and issuing judicial opinions. Often, however, we have learned precious little about the trial process as a whole. The holistic theories of Bennett and Feldman (1981), and Beach (1988, in press-a, in-press b), are new and deserve continued testing and critical scrutiny. By the same token, narrative and conversational models of communication have indeed made a commendable beginning toward an increased qualitative understanding of the legal environment. Yet, we can recommend some needed future directions.

First, as early as 1965, Tucker (1965) called for a pooling of the knowledge gained through quantitative and qualitative research, and, in the main, this has yet to occur. A recent exception to this generalization is the work by Hollihan, Riley, and Freadhoff (1986), which applied structuration theory in an analysis of storytelling in small claims court. Second, the law as a field is not monolithic. A number of authors have pointed to the need for further investigation of civil and tort actions, small claims court, pretrial conferences, discovery procedures and their content, administrative hearings, mediations, and out-of-court settlement processes (among others) (see Dicks, 1981; Hollihan et al., 1986). Third, we should not only place our qualitative research emphasis on a wider variety of legal contexts; we must also continue to press the socio-cultural aspects of the law and rhetoric as key to our contemporary understanding of justice. Studies within the courtroom and without could potentially generate more knowledge about how bias inevitably enters our courtroom and the consequences attached to this invasion. Fourth, the relationships between deliberative and forensic address have yet to be fully disclosed. Comparing and contrasting the discourse of Congress with that of the bench over an issue of joint interest, for example, might yield interesting and provocative results. Such a research program could tell us much more about the courtroom and the cloakroom.

Fifth, there should be more direct contact between the disciplines of communication and law. Each can inform and revivify the other. A recent article by Frug (1988) in the *Stanford Law Review* on "argument as character" is intriguing. It reminds one of the importance of Fisher's (1987) work in advancing narrative (storytelling) as a paradigmatic model for communication. A close reading of Fisher's term "characterological coherence" could probably benefit many authors, as well as interested students. Moreover, Fisher's work has yet to receive substantive attention from the courtroom scholar, an oversight that stands in need of correction. Bennett and Feldman (1981) might be intrigued with Snedaker's (1986) analysis of "storytelling" in opening statements as key frameworks for trial arguments.

COMMUNICATION THEORY, RESEARCH, AND THE LAW

As in the case of rhetorical analyses and the law, interest in conducting empirical research in legal settings has increased dramatically since the early 1970s. Volumes that best prepare a reader to the area include Gunither (1988); Hastie, Penrod, and Pennington (1983); Kassin and Wrightsman (1985, 1988); Kerr and Bray (1982); Matlon (1988); Saks (1977); Simon (1980), and Wrightsman (1987). Considerable attention has also focused on *specific* areas of the law and psychology; for instance, eyewitness testimony (Loftus, 1979; Wells, 1985; Wells & Loftus, 1984; Yarmey, 1979), the use of the polygraph (Ekman, 1985; Lykken, 1985), issues pertaining to special types of victims, such as children and mental patients (Wrightsman, 1987), and the insanity appeal (Blau, 1984; Sales & Hafemeister, 1984; Wrightsman, 1987).

We have focused attention on certain areas relevant to both the communication scholar and the lawyer that deal most directly with communication: interviewing, the defendant's own explanations of crime, evidence, opening and closing statements, and testimony, credibility, and asking questions.

Interviewing

Surprisingly little empirical work has centered on the one communication skill that the lawyer uses daily. However, three perspectives on the issue of legal interviewing exist. The *psychological* perspective dates to the 1950s when interest focused on the requirements of "counselors" (see Wolfe & Cody, 1988). In this perspective, the lawyer is cast in the role of advisor and counselor, and skills relevant to lawyering include: the awareness and insight of a counselor, the ability to identify (objectively) prejudices and to discount the prejudices, and the ability to decode accurately nonverbal communication in order to understand clients' motivations (and "true" motivations). Desirable activities of the lawyer during interviewing include gathering information and judging its legality, understanding and even "uncovering" client motivations, and managing a desired public image. This approach assumes that clients will not necessarily reveal their true feelings or emotions, and assumes that the lawyer-as-psychologist must read nonverbal behaviors accurately and realize that clients will engage in some distortions of facts and/or feelings (clients are assumed to strive to maximize pleasure and minimize emotional threats).

The *dialogic* perspective holds that the lawyer and client should be equal partners in the communication process of interviewing and a significant question becomes how the lawyer can, despite all the trappings of status and power, relinquish power in order to assist client involvement so that a cooperative working relationship is created and maintained. Lawyer activities, then, include avoiding euphemisms, "legal speak," cold "problem-solving" attitudes, and expressions of superiority. In stark contrast to the psychological perspective, the dialogic perspective assumes that clients realize their own feelings, want to participate, and should be provided with every opportunity to participate.

The *utilitarian/functional* perspective simply argues that the main question of legal interviewing deals with how the lawyer can efficiently fulfill client goals, and holds that the lawyer's role is to represent the client. Because time and money are important features of interviewing in the "real" legal world, important skills for lawyers include: skilled listening through which legally germane information can be ascertained, speech skills employable in eliciting the maximum amount of legally relevant information per interview time (given a fixed rate of billing based on the quarter hour), and developing communication skills necessary to take advantage of either cooperative or confrontative interviewing contexts (as would occur during some depositions) in order to best represent the client. Communication is viewed as extremely *strategic* in this perspective, whereas clients' motivations or "true" motivations and the matter of creating rapport are wholly secondary considerations; servicing the needs of clients, especially winning cases or resolving them to clients' satisfaction, is most important.

None of these particular perspectives is associated with any systematic body of empirically oriented research, although each has its advocates who criticize rival perspectives (see Wolfe & Cody, 1988). A more realistic approach to the matter of legal interviewing would be to assume that as lawyers specialize they must develop specific skills for their chosen areas of specialization. There are undoubtedly cases in family law, divorce law, or cases of domestic violence or when clients were victimized that require lawyers to be very comforting, reassuring, and to withhold (possibly) feelings of prejudice. Lawyers who specialize in such areas would find themselves centrally involved in the psychological approach, and will have to contend with the ambivalent feelings experienced by such victims. Lawyers in criminal cases will also have to develop the means of detecting deception and identifying emotional expressions accurately (Ekman, 1985; Leathers, 1986). On the other hand, corporate lawyers on retainer with large firms may be confronted rarely with clients who communicate mixed feelings; rather, they develop long-term relationships with clients that emphasize rapport (the dialogic perspective).

But where do lawyers learn particular skills? As far as we can determine, the typical lawyer "learns" interviewing "skills" by observing others and by accompanying senior level lawyers during the recording of depositions. Although such routine practice may facilitate the socialization of new lawyers in a firm to rules of professional behaviors with particular clients, it probably does little to instill a lawyer's ability to be comforting and/or reassuring, or to decode nonverbal behaviors effectively. Indeed, it would not be wholly surprising to find that the ability to *empathize* with a client's problem *decreases* the longer the would-be lawyer is in law school (a development recorded with medical students; see Wolfe & Cody, 1988). At the moment, we do not know if lawyers are any better or worse than others in comforting skills, decoding skills, deception detection skills, or even efficiency in interviewing. Some survey work (see Wolfe & Cody, 1988) indicates that clients do rate attorneys higher in preference based on relational skills (avoiding interruptions and speaking "legalese"), and rate "being informed of recent developments in my case" high in desirability. The correlates of effectiveness for different areas of specialization is an important area for future research, whereas another line of research would investigate the relative effectiveness of training methods for prelaw majors, law students, or in-house training programs for large law firms.

Explanations for the Crime

One area of communication and the law almost completely ignored by communication scholars deals with how the criminal "accounts" (offers explanations) for why a crime occurred. Certainly, remorse and/or statements of apology to the court or to the victim and/or victim's family may have some impact during sentencing (Savitsky & Sim, 1974). Perhaps an even stronger case can be made for studying the effects of such explanations to parole officers or to the parole board—institutions that have the ability to alter significantly the original sentence. Studies of explanations for serious crimes have been conducted by Carroll and Payne (1977); Felson and Ribner (1981); Henderson and Hewstone (1984); Riordan, Marlin, and Kellogg (1983); and Rothman and Gandossy (1982). Carroll and Payne (1977) provided the more complete assessment, via attribution theory, of communicated causes of crime, perceived responsibility, and determinants of sentencing. Felson and Ribner (1981) interviewed male prisoners and found that criminals who persisted in denying guilt for the offenses of murder and first-degree assault received longer sentences than if they had not denied guilt. Rothman and Gandossy (1982) focused on cases of "white-collar crime," and identified the ideal components judges prefer to hear in accounts—acknowledgement of moral and legal guilt, acceptance of personal responsibility, expressions of remorse, and a justification for why the questionable behavior occurred (i.e., the worker embezzled because he had no money and the children were sick).

Except for a few cases of studying accounts made in traffic court (Cody & McLaughlin, 1988, in press; McLaughlin, Cody, & French, 1989), communication scholars have not studied the important communication process of explaining actions to judges, probation officers, and parole boards. Following Carroll and Payne (1977), a number of psychologists and legal experts have increased efforts at applying attribution theory in this area; however, there are many questions that remain, and the actual communication (credibility, deception, sincerity, etc.) of such explanation should be studied more fully from archival databases of legal transcripts, actual courtroom settings (Cody & McLaughlin, 1988; Hollihan et al., 1986; see work by Beach, 1985, 1988, in press-a, in press-b), or interviews with prisoners (Felson & Ribner, 1981).

Evidence

The study of evidence and its presentation has been a traditional concern of the communication discipline. Works on evidence and its presentation include (to mention a few relevant studies and reviews): Hample (1977, 1978, 1980, 1985); Kassin and Wrightsman (1985, 1988); Kellerman (1980); Loh (1985); Matlon (1988); Miller (1966); Miller, Bender, Florence, and Nicholson (1974); Miller and Boster (1977); Morley (1987); Morley and Walker (1987); Reinard (1988); Reynolds and Burgoon (1983); and Saks and Hastie (1978). Reinard (1988) in particular presented a thorough assessment of the role of evidence in persuasion—types of evidence, effects of evidence, and how receiver characteristics interact with evidence in affecting attitude change.

In legal settings, it is important to note that research indicates that: (a) Jurors do indeed spend a significant amount of time during deliberations discussing evidence and legally relevant issues (compared to nonrelevant ones), but make specific types of errors; (b) presentational formats, and vividly portrayed material, affect the persistence of altered attitude change (an important concern, because trials may last days, or weeks, or even months); and, (c) the quality of, or reliability of, evidence can help to reduce juror bias.

Regarding the first of these issues, research indicates that 82% of issues discussed during jury deliberations are judged as legally relevant (see review by Stasser, Kerr, & Bray, 1982). Statements made by 10 mock juries discussing a burglary case were coded into five categories—references to testimony, opinions on facts of the case, references to instructions, comments on the deliberation procedures, and experience from personal and daily life. Simon (1967; also see Hastie et al., 1983; James, 1959; Stasser et al., 1982) found that 44% of all comments made during deliberation focused on evidence, either references to testimony or opinions on facts, whereas 26% of the statements dealt with comments on the deliberation process and 8% dealt with instructions. Of the statements, 22% dealt with "personal or daily life," however. When statements were coded in terms of relevance to the case, the categories demonstrating the least amount of relevance were ones dealing with "court instructions" (only 62% of the statements were legally relevant) and with "personal experiences" (only 57% of these statements were coded as relevant) (see James, 1959; Stasser et al., 1982).

Hastie et al. (1983) also found that jurors focused on a significant amount of evidence in their analyses, especially on witness credibility. Further, Hastie et al. (1983) concluded that the one category of statements made during deliberations that contained the most errors were responses centering on the judge's instructions. Hastie et al. (p. 97) were also "disturbed" by some jurors' failure to understand and use the "beyond reasonable doubt" standard. Also, Hastie et al. argued that jurors' knowledge of the world and of individuals involved in the facts of the case affect decisions, more so than personality measures, demographics, and attitudes. A juror's personal experiences in urban living, for example, has more to do with interpreting why Mike Tyson travelled to Harlem to pick up a sport coat at 4 a.m. than political party affiliation, age, and so forth.

How evidence is presented is an important aspect that has received years of study by psychologists and communication scholars (see, e.g., Farmer et al., 1977; Matlon, 1988; Miller, Bender et al., 1974; Miller & Fontes, 1979; Petty & Cacioppo, 1981, 1985). Clearly, evidence has to be relevant, and "persuasive" to alter juror's opinions; but it also has to be recalled. One way to make a message memorable is to make its presentation vivid. A vivid message is one that excites the receiver's imagination by making the message either emotionally interesting or concrete or image-provoking. Courtroom evidence is certainly concrete, but may not be particularly interesting. One would like to conclude that vividness is consistently related to persuasion and to increased recall. However, there is insufficient evidence (yet) to warrant such a conclusion (see reviews by Bettinghaus & Cody, 1987; Fiske & Taylor, 1984; Kisielius & Sternthal, 1984, 1986). A Study by Reyes, Thompson, and Bower (1980, cited in Loftus & Goodman, 1985, p. 265–266) demonstrated the importance of vividness. Some jurors read "pallid" versions of testimony, whereas others read "vivid" versions that described (in a drunk driving case) a person knocking over a bowl of guacamole dip, splattering it on the white shag carpet, and later as leaping out of the way of a bright orange Volkswagen—descriptions likely to provoke clear images in the minds of the jurors. Twenty-four hours later, jurors recalled more specific details of the vividly portrayed information than the pallid version. Because many trials may last days or weeks, increased recall of details is an important aspect of communicated evidence. Besides vividness, witnesses are given more credibility if they demonstrate recall of many specific details of the scene of the crime, compared to few specific details (see Bell & Loftus, 1989; Loftus & Goodman, 1985).

Juror biases have been well documented in many studies. Matlon (1988) presented the most thorough discussion of potential biases. A number of studies indicate that biases (i.e., that good looking people are given the benefit of doubt and receive lighter sentences for the same crime as the less attractive criminal) are more pronounced when evidence is weak or lacking in reliability (Kaplan & Miller, 1978; Kaplan & Schersching, 1980; see additional work reviewed in Bettinghaus & Cody, 1987). Quality of evidence, then, is not only related to judgments of guilt or innocence, but also to severity of sentences and the presence of "extralegal" biases.

Opening and Closing Statements

Some of the more recent reviews on opening and closing statements are available in Lind and Ke (1985) and Matlon (1988). The two goals of opening statements are to introduce the juror to the particulars of the case and to create rapport. Matlon (1988) noted that studies have found that 65% to 80% of jurors make decisions early in the trial—during or soon after the opening statements. Pyszczynski and Wrightsman (1981) found that extensive opening statements influenced juror attitudes throughout the trial. Drawing on literature on primacy and recency effects, we can speculate on the kinds of cases to which opening statements are likely to be crucial. Primacy effects are more likely to occur when the subject matter is interesting, the topic is controversial, and the story (or topic) is highly familiar (Rosnow & Robinson, 1967). Lind (1982) also noted that primacy effects are likely when the receivers' task is to make a decision about a person's character. This latter point is compatible with research that indicates we make first impressions within minutes of meeting others. Thus, opening statements (or evidence presented early) may successfully influence jurors if the case centers on the defendant's character (an embezzler, wife abuser, rapist, etc.), or on controversial, interesting, or familiar topics (false or misleading advertising).

However, jurors may not make first impressions or decide guilt early when topics are unfamiliar or uninteresting. For instance, copyright infringement cases involving several companies in different countries may focus on many fine points of the law and require weeks of testimony. Jurors in such cases may attempt to keep an open mind until all the facts are presented. However, this does not mean that the role of the opening statement is in any way diminished. Rather, if the trial does center on complex material, contradictory evidence by experts and weeks of testimony, lawyers are well advised to use the opening statement as a means of presenting the juror with a framework for evaluating testimony. Lawyers can detail what the prosecution and defense lawyers each will attempt to prove, when they hope to prove it, and how they hope to prove it. Thus, as days pass by and contradictory material is presented, jurors are not left in a state of limbo waiting (if not hoping) for some resolution to occur during summation, or closing arguments.

There is no doubt that closing statements are important. Closing arguments focus attention on the important materials, and help to discount the trivial. It is also a time to claim pros and cons concerning various witnesses and attempted strategy, and finalize a theme. That is, a lawyer may claim one of several narrative themes (see Matlon, 1988) during the opening statement, such as the *underdog* theme, the *undefeated* theme, the *victim* theme, or the *contrast* theme. Defense lawyers for DeLorean, for example, elected to use the *victim* theme (DeLorean was a victim of entrapment, they claimed). Once the theme is selected, it is introduced during the opening statements, reintroduced or alluded to during testimony, and capitalized on during the summation. Although summation is important, failures to be effective can stem from the fact that the opposition simply has a better case, the opposition presented a more vivid or memorable case, the delivery of the summation was poorly executed, or the summation statements overstated the case.

Testimony, Credibility, and Asking Questions

Nonverbal, paralinguistic, and verbal indices of speaker credibility are presented in Bettinghaus and Cody (1987), Leathers (1986), Miller and Burgoon (1982), and Matlon (1988). Considerable research has focused, for instance, on speech style. Powerless style of speech (more hedges, hesitations, overtly polite forms of address, etc.) is associated with perceptions of competence, intelligence, credibility, and trustworthiness (as a general rule). Also, witnesses who appear to mimic how lawyers speak, mimic legal terminology, and/or act in a "hypercorrect" manner are rated as less convincing, less competent, less qualified, and less intelligent than speakers who use standard English.

Defendants who are polite and articulate (communicate messages with few grammatical errors) are more likely to be treated leniently than defendants who are impolite and inarticulate (Loftus & Goodman, 1985). As a general rule, jurors seem to be more impressed by relatively high rates of eye contact, fluent speech, thorough answers rich in specific details, relatively fast speech rates, a moderate amount of illustrating, and the avoidance of adaptors; speakers are more persuasive if they demonstrate some level of *dynamism, composure,* and *sociability* (or *affiliation;* jurors are influenced more by speakers they like, rather than dislike) (Bettinghaus & Cody, 1987; Leathers, 1986; Miller & Burgoon, 1982).

Loftus and Goodman (1985) presented one of the better presentations of questioning formats in legal settings. Lawyers can help to reduce the credibility of the opposition's witnesses, for example, by asking many questions that would require the witness to say "I don't know." Also, in using a "narrative" questioning format a lawyer asks few questions in an open-ended manner ("Tell me what happened on the evening of January 6th") that allow the witness to tell his or her own story. In a fragmented questioning format a lawyer may ask a number (100 to 200) of short, closed-ended questions. Jurors (or any observer) exposed to the fragmented format will believe that the lawyer has little confidence, faith, and trust in the witness, and will rate the witness lower in competence, intelligence, and assertiveness (see Conley, O'Barr, & Lind, 1978; Loftus & Goodman, 1985). However, the fragmented questioning format would, as Loftus and Goodman (1985) noted, give the lawyer control over details that were communicated publicly in court, whereas it is possible that the speaker who is given freedom to tell a story may communicate some details detrimental to the case.

EVALUATION AND FUTURE RESEARCH

We did not intend to present a *critical* assessment of the empirical approaches to the study of communication in legal settings. Our intention was to present an overview of major lines of research. However, there are at least two problems with this particular body of literature that must be mentioned. First, the majority of projects cited in this last half of the chapter have utilized mock jurors, usually college students. There is solid evidence that judgments made by students role-playing jurors can be quite different from those of "real" jurors (Miller, Fontes, Boster, & Sunnafrank, 1983). Second, too little attention has focused on whether there are *consistent* relationships between variables. For example, Matlon (1988) presented a thorough and quite detailed analysis of all possible juror biases. Women have been found, in some studies, to be more proconviction in rape cases, to favor young, handsome male lawyers, to favor lower damage awards than men (unless the plaintiff is female), and housewives are characterized as proconviction in cases involving injuries to children, and show more prejudice against plaintiffs who are minors and who are unemployed. Although at least one study in the last 25 years has supported each of these findings, we need meta-analytic research to investigate whether claims of juror bias are consistent and robust.

On one hand, attention to training methods and their relative effectiveness is certainly welcome. Training in lawyer interviewing skills, decoding nonverbal cues, deception detection, and so on, may occur in large law firms, or be offered by some corporations that service lawyers' needs (i.e., Litigation Sciences). However, communication scholars have much to offer in developing such programs. Further, we believe that more and more lawyers will become aware of the fact that witness preparation is not a luxury item that can be billed only to certain clients who can afford it. Rather, preparation of witnesses should be a standard fare. We have heard that only a seven minute preparation of what the procedure of cross-examination is like helped to significantly improve performance and perceptions of credibility. Also, lawyers should become more aware of how the defendant's own explanation or account of the offense can increase or decrease sentences (from the judge or via the parole board). In terms of empirical research, we predict that increased efforts will be made to utilize archival data to assess the robustness or generalizability of experiments, and that more efforts will be made to record or film in courtrooms. We also welcome more research on the problem of vividness and long-term recall of vividly portrayed information.

Communication scholars have a good deal to offer the legal community through either the rhetorical viewpoint or the empirical framework. Jointly, these approaches have informed various aspects and phases of the litigation process. Qualitative studies have significantly contributed to our understanding of such important and diverse topics as the advocacy of individual lawyers, the nature of oral argument, legal reasoning, and judicial opinion, as well as the reconstruction of reality in the courtroom through the focus on narrative accounts. Quantitative research has provided the courtroom answers to key communicative issues like interviewing, defendants' explanation of crime, the opening and closing statements, and the dynamics of courtroom activity. Although the research documented here is open to improvements and refinements through future investigation, we believe it argues powerfully for the interdependent relationship between communication and the law.

REFERENCES

Abbott, D. (1974). The jurisprudential analogy: Argumentation and the new rhetoric. *Central States Speech Journal, 25,* 50–55.

Anapol, M. (1970). Rhetoric and law: An overview. *Today's Speech, 18,* 12–20.

Bartanen, K. M. (1987). The rhetoric of dissent in Justice O'Connor's *Akron* opinion. *Southern Speech Communication Journal, 52,* 240–262.

Beach, W. A. (1985). Temporal density in courtroom interaction: Constraints on the recovery of past events in legal discourse. *Communication Monographs, 52,* 1–18.

Beach, W. A. (1988). Organizing courtroom contexts: Interactional resolutions to intercultural problems. In L. A. Samovar & R. E. Porter (Eds.), *Intercultural communication: A reader* (pp. 200–206). Belmont, CA: Wadsworth.

Beach, W. A. (in press-a). Orienting to the phenomenon. In J. A. Anderson (Ed.), *Communication yearbook 13.* Beverly Hills: Sage.

Beach, W. A. (in press-b). Time and description in courtroom talk. *Social Action and the Law.*

Beach, W. A., & Japp, P. M. (1983). Storifying as time-traveling: The knowledgeable use of temporally structured discourse. In R. N. Bostrom (Ed.), *Communication yearbook 7* (pp. 867–888). Beverly Hills: Sage.

Bell, B. E., & Loftus, E. F. (1989). Trivial persuasion in the courtroom: The power of (a few) minor details. *Journal of Personality and Social Psychology, 56,* 669–679.

Bennett, W. L. (1978). Storytelling in criminal trials: A model of social judgment. *Quarterly Journal of Speech, 64,* 1–22.

Bennett, W. L. (1979). Rhetorical transformation of evidence in criminal trials: Creating grounds for legal judgment. *Quarterly Journal of Speech, 65,* 311–323.

Bennett, W. L., & Feldman, M. S. (1981). *Reconstructing reality in the courtroom: Justice and judgment in American culture.* New Brunswick, NJ: Rutgers University Press.

Bettinghaus, E. P., & Cody, M. J. (1987). *Persuasive communication* (4th ed.). New York: Holt, Rinehart & Winston.

Black, E. (1965). *Rhetorical criticism* (pp. 133–134). New York: Macmillan.

Blau, T. H. (1984). *The psychologist as expert witness.* New York: Wiley.

Bunn, C. (1964). How lawyers use speech. *Speech Teacher, 13,* 6–9.

Burke, K. (1969). *A grammar of motives.* Berkeley: University of California Press.

Campbell, K. K., & Jamieson, J. H. (Eds.). (1978). *Form and genre: Shaping rhetorical action.* Falls Church, VA: Speech Communication Association.

Carlson, A. C. (1985). John Quincy Adams' "Amistad Address": Eloquence in a generic hybrid. *Western Journal of Speech Communication, 49,* 14–26.

Carroll, J. S., & Payne, J. W. (1977). Judgments about crime and the criminal: A model and a method for investigating parole decisions. In B. D. Sales (Ed.), *Perspectives in law and psychology* (pp. 191–239). New York: Plenum Press.

Cody, M. J., & McLaughlin, M. L. (1988). Accounts on trial: Oral arguments in traffic court. In C. Antaki (Ed.), *Analyzing everyday explanation: A casebook of methods* (pp. 113–126). London: Sage.

Cody, M. J., & McLaughlin, M. L. (in press). Interpersonal accounting. In H. Giles & P. Robinson (Eds.), *Handbook of language and social psychology.* London: Wiley.

Condit, C. M., & Selzer, J. A. (1985). The rhetoric of objectivity in the newspaper coverage of a murder trial. *Critical Studies in Mass Communication, 2,* 197–216.

Conley, J. M., O'Barr, W. & Lind, E. A. (1978). The power of language: Presentational style in the courtroom. *Duke Law Review, 6,* 1375–1399.

Constans, H. P., & Dickey, D. C. (1954). The contemporary rhetoric of law. *Southern Speech Communication Journal, 19,* 277–282.

Crable, R. E. (1976). Models of argumentation and judicial judgment. *Journal of the American Forensic Association, 12,* 113–120.

Dickens, M., & Schwartz, R. E. (1971). Oral argument before the Supreme Court: *Marshall v. Davis* in the school segregation cases. *Quarterly Journal of Speech, 57,* 32–42.

Dicks, V. I. (1976). Courtroom controversy: A stasis/stock issues analysis of the Angela Davis trial. *Journal of the American Forensic Association, 13,* 77–83.

Dicks, V. I. (1981). Courtroom rhetorical strategies: Forensic and deliberative perspectives. *Quarterly Journal of Speech, 67,* 178–192.

Ekman, P. (1985). *Telling lies.* New York: Norton.

Erlich, H. S. (1975). ". . . and by opposing, end them.": The genre of moral justification for legal transgressions. *Today's Speech, 23,* 13–16.

Farmer, L. C., Williams, G. R., Cundick, B. P., Howell, R. J., Lee, R. E., & Rooker,

C. K. (1977). The effect of the method of presenting trial testimony on juror decisional processes. In B. D. Sales (Ed.), *Psychology in the legal process* (pp. 59–76). New York: Spectrum.

Felson, R. B., & Ribner, S. A. (1981). An attributional approach to accounts and sanctions for criminal violence. *Social Psychology Quarterly, 44*, 137–142.

Fisher, W. R. (1987). *Human communication as narration: Toward a philosophy of reason, value, and action.* Columbia, SC: University of South Carolina Press.

Fiske, S. T., & Taylor, S. E. (1984). *Social cognition.* New York: Random House.

Frug, J. (1988). Argument as character. *Stanford Law Review, 40*, 869–927.

Gunither, J. (1988). *The jury in America.* New York: Facts on File.

Hagan, M. R. (1976). *Roe v. Wade:* The rhetoric of fetal life. *Central States Speech Journal, 27*, 192–199.

Hample, D. (1977). Testing a model of value argument and evidence. *Communication Monographs, 44*, 106–120.

Hample, D. (1978). Predicting immediate belief change and adherence to argument claims. *Communication Monographs, 45*, 219–228.

Hample, D. (1979). Motives in law: An adaptation of legal realism. *Journal of the American Forensic Association, 15*, 156–168.

Hample, D. (1980). A cognitive view of argument. *Journal of the American Forensic Association, 17*, 151–158.

Hample, D. (1985). Refinements on the cognitive model of argument: Concreteness, involvement, and group scores. *Western Journal of Speech Communication, 49*, 267–285.

Hart, R. P. (1986). Contemporary scholarship in public address: A research editorial. *Western Journal of Speech Communication, 50*, 283–295.

Hastie, R., Penrod, S. D., & Pennington, N. (1983). *Inside the jury.* Cambridge, MA: Harvard University Press.

Henderson, M., & Hewstone, M. (1984). Prison inmates' explanations for interpersonal violence: Accounts and attributions. *Journal of Consulting and Clinical Psychology, 52*, 789–794.

Hollihan, T. A., Riley, P., & Freadhoff, K. (1986). Arguing for justice: An analysis of arguing in small claims court. *Journal of the American Forensic Association, 22*, 187–195.

Hunsaker, D. M. (1978). The rhetoric of *Brown v. Board of Education:* Paradigm for contemporary social protest. *Southern Speech Communication Journal, 43*, 91–109.

James, R. (1959). Status and competence of jurors. *The American Journal of Sociology, 64*, 563–570.

Jones, S. B. (1976). Justification in judicial opinions: A case study. *Journal of the American Forensic Association, 12*, 121–129.

Kaplan, M. F., & Miller, L. E. (1978). Reducing the effects of juror bias. *Journal of Personality and Social Psychology, 36*, 1443–1455.

Kaplan, M. F., & Scherching, C. (1980). Reducing juror bias: An experimental approach. In P. D. Lipsitt & B. D. Sales (Eds.), *New approaches in psycholegal research* (pp. 149–170). New York: Van Nostrand Reinhold.

Kassin, S. M., & Wrightsman, L. S. (Eds.). (1985). *The psychology of evidence and trial procedure.* Beverly Hills: Sage.

Kassin, S. M., & Wrightsman, L. S. (1988). *The American jury on trial: Psychological perspectives.* New York: Hemisphere.

Kellerman, K. (1980). The concept of evidence: A critical review. *Journal of American Forensic Association, 16,* 159–172.

Kerr, N. L., & Bray, R. M. (Eds.). (1982). *The psychology of the courtroom.* New York: Academic Press.

Kisielius, J., & Sternthal, B. (1984). Detecting and explaining the vividness effects in attitudinal judgments. *Journal of Marketing Research, 21,* 54–64.

Kisielius, J., & Sternthal, B. (1986). Examining the vividness controversy: An availability-valence interpretation. *Journal of Consumer Research, 12,* 418–431.

Koegel, O. E. (1951). Speech and the legal profession. *Quarterly Journal of Speech, 37,* 471–472.

Leathers, D. G. (1986). *Successful nonverbal communication.* New York: Macmillan.

LeDuc, D. R. (1976). "Free speech" decisions and the legal process: The judicial opinion in context. *Quarterly Journal of Speech, 62,* 279–287.

Levison, G. L. (1979). The rhetoric of the oral argument in *The Regents of the University of California v. Bakke. Western Journal of Speech Communication, 41,* 271–277.

Lind, E. A. (1982). The psychology of courtroom procedure. In N. L. Kerr & R. M. Bray (Eds.), *The psychology of the courtroom* (pp. 13–38). New York: Academic Press.

Lind, E. A., & Ke, G. (1985). Opening and closing statements. In S. M. Kassin & L. S. Wrightsman (Eds.), *The psychology of evidence and trial procedure* (pp. 229–252). Beverly Hills: Sage.

Loh, W. D. (1985). The evidence and trial procedure: The law, social policy, and psychological research. In S. M. Kassin & L. S. Wrightsman (Eds.), *The psychology of evidence and trial procedure* (pp. 13–39). Beverly Hills: Sage.

Loftus, E. (1979). *Eyewitness testimony.* Cambridge, MA: Harvard University Press.

Loftus, E. F., & Goodman, J. (1985). Questioning witnesses. In S. M. Kassin & L. S. Wrightsman (Eds.), *The psychology of evidence and trial procedure* (pp. 253–279). Beverly Hills: Sage.

Lykken, D. T. (1985). The probity of the polygraph. In S. M. Kassin & L. S. Wrightsman (Eds.), *The psychology of evidence and trial procedure* (pp. 95–123). Beverly Hills: Sage.

Makau, J. M. (1984). The Supreme Court and reasonableness. *Quarterly Journal of Speech, 70,* 379–396.

Matlon, R. J. (1982). Bridging the gap between communication education and legal communication. *Communication Monographs, 31,* 39–53.

Matlon, R. J. (1988). *Communication in the legal process.* New York: Holt, Rinehart & Winston.

McBath, J. H. (1961). Speech and the legal profession. *Speech Teacher, 10,* 44–47.

McGee, M. C. (1980). The "ideograph": A link between rhetoric and ideology. *Quarterly Journal of Speech, 66,* 1–16.

McKeon, R. (Ed.). (1941). *The collected works of Aristotle.* New York: Random House.

McLaughlin, M. L., Cody, M. J., & French, K. (1989). Account-giving and the attribution of responsibility: Impressions of traffic offenders. In M. J. Cody & M. L. McLaughlin (Eds.), *The psychology of tactical communication* (pp. 244–267). Clevedon, England: Multilingual Matters, Ltd.

Miller, G. R. (1966). Evidence and argument. In G. R. Miller & T. R. Nilsen (Eds.), *Perspectives in argument* (pp. 24–49). Chicago: Scott, Foresman.

Miller, G. R., Bender, G., Florence, T., & Nicholson, H. (1974). Real vs. reel: What is the verdict? *Journal of Communication, 24,* 99–111.

Miller, G. R., & Boster, F. J. (1977). Three images of the trial: Their implications for psychological research. In B. D. Sales (Ed.), *Psychology in the legal process* (pp. 19–38). New York: Spectrum.

Miller, G. R., & Burgoon, J. K. (1982). Factors affecting assessments of witness credibility. In N. L. Kerr & R. M. Bray (Eds.), *The psychology of the courtroom* (pp. 169–196). New York: Academic Press.

Miller, G. R., & Fontes, N. E. (1979). *Videotape on trial.* Beverly Hills: Sage.

Miller, G. R., Fontes, N. E., Boster, F. J., & Sunnafrank, M. J. (1983). Methodological issues in legal communication research: What can trial simulations tell us? *Communication Monographs, 50,* 33–46.

Mills, G. E. (1976). Legal argumentation: Research and teaching. *Western Journal of Speech Communication, 40,* 83–90.

Minnick, W. C. (1982). The United States Supreme Court on libel. *Quarterly Journal of Speech, 68,* 384–396.

Morley, D. D. (1987). Subjective message constructs: A theory of persuasion. *Communication Monographs, 54,* 183–203.

Morley, D. D., & Walker, K. B. (1987). The role of importance, novelty, and plausibility in producing belief change. *Communication Monographs, 54,* 436–442.

Nobles, S. (1985). Communication in the education of legal advocates. *Journal of the American Forensic Association, 22,* 20–25.

Petty, R. E., & Cacioppo, J. T. (1981). *Attitudes and persuasion: Classic and contemporary approaches.* Dubuque, IA: Brown.

Petty, R. E., & Cacioppo, J. T. (1985). *Persuasion and communication.* New York: Springer-Verlag.

Pilotta, J., Murphy, J. W., Wilson, E., & Jones, T. (1983). The contemporary rhetoric of the social theories of law. *Central States Speech Journal, 34,* 211–220.

Pyszczynski, T., & Wrightsman, L. S. (1981). Effects of opening statements on mock jurors. *Journal of Applied Social Psychology, 11,* 301–313.

Rabin, D. A. (1978). Gottlieb's model of rule-guided reasoning: An analysis of *Griswold v. Connecticut. Journal of the American Forensic Association, 15,* 77–90.

Reinard, J. C. (1988). The empirical study of the persuasive effects of evidence: The status after fifty years of research. *Human Communication Research, 15,* 3–59.

Reyes, R. M., Thompson, W. C., & Bower, G. H. (1980). Judgmental biases resulting from differing availabilities of arguments. *Journal of Personality and Social Psychology, 39,* 2–12.

Reynolds, R. A., & Burgoon, M. (1983). Belief processing, reasoning, and evidence.

In R. Bostrom (Ed.), *Communication yearbook 7* (pp. 83–104). Beverly Hills: Sage.

Rice, G. P. (1961). The meets and bounds of speech and law. *Central States Speech Journal, 13,* 7–10.

Riordan, C. A., Marlin, N. A., & Kellogg, R. T. (1983). The effectiveness of accounts following transgressions. *Social Psychology Quarterly, 46,* 213–219.

Ritter, K. (1985). Drama and legal rhetoric: The prejury trials of Alger Hiss. *Western Journal of Speech Communication, 49,* 83–102.

Rodgers, R. S. (1982). Generic tendencies in majority and non-majority Supreme Court opinions: The case of Justice Douglas. *Communication Quarterly, 30,* 232–236.

Rosnow, R. L., & Robinson, E. J. (1967). *Experiments in persuasion.* New York: Academic Press.

Rothman, M. L., & Gandossy, R. P. (1982). Sad tales: The accounts of white-collar defendants and the decision to sanction. *Pacific Sociological Review, 25,* 449–473.

Saks, M. J. (1977). *Jury verdicts.* Lexington, MA: Lexington Books.

Saks, M. J., & Hastie, R. (1978). *Social psychology in court.* New York: Van Nostrand Reinhold.

Sales, B. D., & Hafemeister, T. (1984). Empiricism and legal policy on the insanity defense. In L. A. Teplin (Ed.), *Mental health and criminal justice* (pp. 253–278). Beverly Hills: Sage.

Sanbonmatsu, A. (1971). Darrow and Rorke's use of Burkeian identification strategies in *New York v. Gitlow* (1920). *Speech Monographs, 38,* 36–48.

Savitsky, J., & Sim, M. (1974). Trading emotions: Equity theory of reward and punishment. *Journal of Communication, 24,* 140–147.

Shmukler, A. (1970). Some challenges of the student of rhetoric and law. *Today's Speech, 18,* 45–47.

Simon, R. J. (1967). *The jury and the defense of insanity.* Boston: Little, Brown.

Simon, R. J. (1980). *The jury: Its role in American society.* Lexington, MA: Lexington Books.

Snedaker, K. H. (1986). Storytelling in opening statements: Framing the argumentation of the trial. *American Journal of Trial Advocacy, 10,* 15–45.

Stasser, G., Kerr, N. L., & Bray, R. M. (1982). The social psychology of jury deliberations: Structure, process, and product. In N. L. Kerr & R. M. Bray (Eds.), *The psychology of the courtroom* (pp. 221–256). New York: Academic Press.

Strother, D. B. (1961). Persuasion in American legal procedure. *Western Journal of Speech Communication, 25,* 231–236.

Strother, D. B. (1963). Polemics and the reversal of the "separate but equal" doctrine. *Quarterly Journal of Speech, 49,* 50–56.

Tucker, C. O. (1965). Forensics and behavioral science research in the law. *Journal of the American Forensic Association, 2,* 59–65.

Ulrich, W. (1985). The creation of a legacy: Brandeis' concurring opinion in *Whitney v. California. Southern Speech Communication Journal, 50,* 143–155.

Wasby, S. L., D'Amato, A. A., & Metrailer, R. (1976). The functions of oral argument in the U.S. Supreme Court. *Quarterly Journal of Speech, 62,* 410–422.

Weiss, F. R. (1959). How the lawyer uses rhetoric. *Today's Speech, 7,* 6–15.

Wells, G. L. (1985). The eyewitness. In S. M. Kassin & L. S. Wrightsman (Eds.), *The psychology of evidence and trial procedure* (pp. 43–66). Beverly Hills: Sage.

Wells, G. L., & Loftus, E. F. (1984). *Eyewitness testimony: Psychological perspectives*. Cambridge, MA: Cambridge University Press.

Wiethoff, W. E. (1984). The art of persuasion v. social theories of law: A response to Pilotta et al. *Central States Speech Journal, 35,* 187–196.

Williams, D. E. (1955). Group discussion and argumentation in legal education. *Quarterly Journal of Speech, 41,* 396–402.

Wolfe, C. S., & Cody, M. J. (1988). Perspectives on legal interviewing and counseling. *Southern Speech Communication Journal, 53,* 360–384.

Wright, W. E. (1964). Judicial rhetoric: A field for research. *Speech Monographs, 31,* 64–72.

Wrightsman, L. S. (1987). *Psychology and the legal system.* Monterey, CA: Brooks/Cole.

Yarmey, A. D. (1979). *The psychology of eyewitness testimony.* New York: Free Press.

HEALTH CONTEXTS

APPLIED HEALTH COMMUNICATION RESEARCH **13**

GARY L. KREPS
Northern Illinois University

Health communication research has emerged during the 1970s and 1980s as an exciting applied area of communication inquiry concerned with examining the influences of human interaction on the provision of health care and the promotion of health (Arntson, 1985; Kreps, 1988a; Thompson, 1984). It is an inherently applied area of communication inquiry, with many health communication studies designed to either identify, examine, or solve health-care/promotion problems. Health communication is also an extremely broad area of inquiry, examining communication at many different levels and in many different contexts. For example, health communication research has examined such diverse issues as the role of interpersonal communication in developing effective health-care provider/consumer relationships, the role of comforting communication in providing social support, the effects of various media and presentation strategies on the dissemination of health information to people who need such information, the use of communication in coordinating the activities of interdependent health-care providers, and the use of communication strategies for administering complex health-care delivery systems. Four important levels of health communication inquiry are selectively reviewed here: interpersonal, group, organizational, and mediated communication in health care. The chapter also identifies future directions for conducting applied health communication research that can help increase the effectiveness of health-care delivery.

INTERPERSONAL HEALTH COMMUNICATION RESEARCH

A central analytic perspective of many health communication studies has been the role of interpersonal communication in health-care delivery (Kreps, 1988b). Such inquiry has examined the range of communication relationships established between and among health-care providers and consumers, demonstrating how these interpersonal relationships exert powerful influences on health and health-care delivery. Several key topics for interpersonal health communication inquiry have included: therapeutic communication, social support, health-care interviewing strategies, provider–consumer health-care relationships, health education, and the development of interpersonal communication competencies in health care.

Therapeutic Communication

Therapeutic communication is an interpersonally based topic of health communication inquiry that has helped to identify specific interpersonal communication characteristics that lead to individual problem solving, enlightenment, and reorientation. For example, the early work by Ruesch (1957, 1963, 1963), Ruesch and Bateson (1951), Rogers (1951, 1957, 1967), and Carkhuff (1967) examined the interpersonal communication behaviors and characteristics of helpers that enable them to be therapeutic. Later studies by Burleson (1983), Northouse (1977), Pettegrew (1977), Pettegrew and Thomas (1978), and Rossiter (1975) built on the earlier work by examining several specific communication strategies used in therapeutic communication, such as communicating with others empathetically and comfortingly. This body of research strongly supports the contention that establishing and maintaining supportive and caring human relationships increases the potential for therapeutic outcomes in interpersonal communication.

Social Support

Another interesting area of health communication research that is closely related to therapeutic communication is examination of the social support functions of interpersonal communication (Albrecht & Adelman, 1984, 1987; Dickson-Markman & Shern, 1984; Droge, Arntson, & Norton, 1981; Gottlieb, 1981; Query & James, 1989). Social support appears to be a special form of nonclinical therapeutic communication that develops within communication networks, often between family members, friends, and peers. Studies of social support have demonstrated the need for expressive social communication contacts with others to help maintain individual well-being and psychological health (Gottlieb, 1988; Kessler & McLeod, 1985; Query & James, 1989). The social support construct has become increasingly important as the American public has gradually taken more personal responsibility for their own health and health care, depended more on informal relational partners for health information, and begun widespread use of self-help groups for emotional, psychological, and educational health care (Kreps, 1988a).

Health-Care Interviewing Strategies

A great deal of health communication inquiry has centered around planning and directing diagnostic information gathering and patient counseling in provider–patient interviews (see Arntson, Droge, & Fassl, 1978; Carroll & Monroe, 1980; Cassata, Conroe, & Clements, 1977; Cox, 1989; Foley & Shart, 1981; Hawes, 1972a, 1972b; Hawes & Foley, 1973; Levenstein, Brown, Westin, Maguire, Fairbairn, Fletcher, 1989; Schofield & Arntson, 1989; Stewart, McCracken, & McWhinney, 1989). Much of this research has examined interpersonal communication patterns in interviews, identified specific communication characteristics used by health-care providers to control interview communication, developed communication strategies to help health-care providers establish rapport and elicit full and accurate information from health-care consumers, and evaluated strategies to teach health-care providers to develop effective interviewing skills. The research concerning health communication in interviews has tended to be very pragmatic, applied to the realistic concerns of information exchange in health-care interviews.

Provider–Consumer Health-Care Relationships

Recent health communication research has highlighted the important role of interpersonal communication in establishing and maintaining effective and satisfying provider–consumer health-care relationships (Ben-Sira, 1976, 1980; Buller & Buller, 1987; DiMatteo, 1979; DiMatteo, Prince & Taranta, 1979; Street, 1989; Street & Wiemann, 1987; West, 1984). For example, previous research (Greenfield, Kaplan, & Ware, 1985; Kaplan, Greenfield & Ware, 1989) directly relates communication to the physical outcomes of health-care treatment, suggesting that the effectiveness of communication relationships established between health-care providers and consumers significantly influences the success of health care. This research demonstrates that the physical conditions of health-care consumers who interact often with their providers about health-care treatment decisions improve more than the physical conditions of those consumers who are less involved in interaction with providers.

Health Education

Research has also shown that interpersonal communication of accurate and timely information about health and illness (health information) can promote effective health evaluation and maintenance (Feldman, 1976; Maibach & Kreps, 1986; Roter, 1983; Ruben & Bowman, 1986). Health-care providers, especially physicians, have the potential to strongly promote public health and health risk prevention by providing their clients with relevant health information through interpersonal counseling and health education (Center for Health Education, 1984a, 1984b; Maibach & Kreps, 1986; McIntosh, 1974; Pierce, Watson, Knights, Glidden, Williams, & Watson, 1984; Relman, 1982). A national survey of public health beliefs and practices identified primary care physicians as Americans' most preferred source of health information, with 84% of the 1,200 persons surveyed identifying an interpersonal discussion with their personal physicians as their most useful source of health information (Kreps, Ruben, Baker, & Rosenthal, 1988). A growing body of recent research has examined informal health education communication between sexual partners concerning safe sex practices for reducing the risks of sexually transmitted diseases, identifying several social constraints on effective safe sex talk, and developing strategies for helping couples overcome these constraints (Adelman, 1988; Bliss & Stout, 1989; Bowen & Michal-Johnson, 1989; Edgar & Fitzpatrick, 1988; Edgar, Hammond, & Freimuth, in press; Flora & Thoresen, 1988; Freimuth, Edgar, & Hammond, 1987).

Development of Health Communication Competencies

A large body of health communication literature has concluded that the effectiveness of health care depends largely on the communication skills and competencies of health-care providers and consumers, linking interpersonal communication effectiveness to such outcomes as client satisfaction, compliance with treatment regimens, and enhanced recuperation abilities (Arntson, 1985; Ben-Sira, 1976; Cassata, 1980; Cline, 1983; Di-Matteo, 1979; DiMatteo, Prince, & Taranta, 1979; DiSalvo, Larsen & Backus, 1986; Hulka, Cassel, Kupper & Burdett, 1976; Hulka, Kupper, Cassel, & Efird, 1975; Lane, 1982, 1983; Morse & Piland, 1981). Health communication competency is the ability to effectively utilize interpersonal skills to elicit cooperation from, gather information from, and share health information with relevant individuals within the health-care system (Kreps, 1988a, 1988b; Kreps & Query, 1989; Ruben & Bowman, 1986). Communication competencies are equally important both for health-care consumers and for health-care providers, encouraging cooperation between providers and consumers to accomplish health-care goals (Babbie, 1973; Jones & Phillips, 1988; Kreps, 1988a, 1988b; Kreps & Query, 1989). The importance of interpersonal competence in interprofessional relationships between interdependent health-care providers has also been noted in the literature (Hill, 1978; Kreps, 1988a; Kreps & Thornton, 1984).

GROUP COMMUNICATION IN HEALTH AND HEALTH CARE

Groups are a primary unit of health care. Specialized groups of interdependent health-care providers and consumers are used as health-care teams to share expertise and experiences to coordinate health-care delivery and make informed health-care decisions (Schaefer, 1974; Scheff, 1963; Schwartz, 1975; Thornton, 1978). Groups also perform important health communication functions as social support networks (Albrecht & Adelman, 1987; Cobb, 1976; Query & James, 1989).

Health-Care Teams

The ever-increasing specialization of health-care delivery has demanded that a wide range of specialized providers and consumers collaborate on strategies, share relevant health information, and coordinate professional activities to provide effective health-care services (Given & Simmons, 1977; Nagi, 1975). Research has clearly identified the importance of egalitarian versus hierarchical communication structure of health-care teams in eliciting member cooperation and managing group conflict (Baldwin, 1980; Thornton, 1978). The negative effects of physician dominance of teams on open sharing of information and decision making has also been examined (Friedson, 1970; Yanda, 1977). Research has shown that information sharing in hierarchically structured health-care teams is influenced by the relative status of the different health-care specialty areas represented and the articulation of roles in these teams develops primarily as a result of accommodation of lower status team members to those members of higher status (Nagi, 1975; Thornton, 1978).

Support Networks

Research has shown that groups are an important setting for social support for health-care consumers (Droge, Arntson, & Norton, 1981; Froland, Brodsky, Olson, & Stewart, 1979; Wagner, 1966). For example, the family is a primary group that often provides social support to its members (Kitson, Moir, & Mason, 1982). Peer support and counseling groups have been found to provide important support functions for health-care consumers, helping individuals cope with such diverse issues as bereavement (Cluck & Cline, 1986), divorce (Chiraboga, Coho, Stein, & Roberts, 1979), epilepsy (Droge, Arntson, & Norton, 1981), cancer (Morrow, Hoagland, & Carnrike, 1981; Peters-Golden, 1982; Wortman & Dunkel- Schetter, 1979), old age (Campbell & Chenoweth, 1981; Gronning, 1982; Kreps, 1986a; Nussbaum, 1983; Query & James, 1989), and mental illness (Froland, Brodsky, Olson, & Stewart, 1979; Horowitz, 1977; Pattison & Pattison, 1981). Droge, Arntson, and Norton (1981) demonstrated that peer support groups routinely provide their members with information about relevant health-care methods and services, problem-solving interaction, referral services, friendly visits, and assistance in making choices about health-care options available to them, describing how self-help groups for epileptic patients provide members with social support, outlets for expressing feelings, reassurance, and information for problem solving.

ORGANIZATIONAL COMMUNICATION
IN HEALTH AND HEALTH CARE

Organizations, such as hospitals, medical centers, nursing homes, convalescent centers, health maintenance organizations, and clinics, are primary sites for health-care delivery in the modern world (Starr, 1982). Communication has been recognized as a crucial tool for coordinating people and technologies in complex, highly structured, technologically sophisticated health-care delivery systems (Costello & Pettegrew, 1979; Georgopoulos, 1974, 1975; Kreps, 1990; Mechanic, 1972b; Mendelsohn, 1979; Perrow, 1965). Health-care organizations are complex social systems composed of networks of interdependent health-care administrators, providers, consumers, support staff, and others whose activities must be coordinated. Health communication research has been conducted to increase the effectiveness of health-care organizations.

Coordinating Communication Channels to Direct
Organizational Adaptation

Health-care system administrators must direct internal communication between different departments and divisions to coordinate the health preserving activities of the system, while at the same time proactively directing their organizations' interaction with its relevant environment concerning such issues as fund raising, lobbying, personnel recruitment, and media relations (Kreps, 1990a; Perrow, 1965; Pfeffer, 1973; Pfeffer & Salancik, 1977). Feedback about health-care system performance from internal and external information sources has been used in organizational development studies to identify performance gaps and initiate constructive changes in health-care organizations (Kreps, 1986b, 1990b). For example, nurses have been shown to be important information sources within health-care organizations because they are involved with many of the internal activities of the organization and also have daily contact with incoming and outgoing patients, as well as other members of the hospital's relevant environment, that provide them with valuable information (organizational intelligence) about how to get things done in their organization (Kreps, 1986b; Salem & Williams, 1984). Research has shown that failure to recognize and respond to the information resources nurses possess can increase nurse frustration and turnover, whereas involving nurses in organizational decisionmaking can preserve organizational intelligence, enhance organizational effectiveness, and increase nurse retention (Filoramo & Ziff, 1980; Kreps, 1986b; Wolf, 1981).

Communication and Stress in Health-Care
Organizations

Health communication research has examined the influences of role conflict and role strain in increasing stress and burnout in health-care organizations (House, 1970; Pettegrew, Thomas, Costello, Wolf, Lennox, & Thomas, 1980; Ray, 1983). Studies have shown that the many sources of authority in health-care organizations often lead to role conflict, role strain, job-related stress, burnout, and information processing problems for health-care providers (House, 1970; Mullen, 1985; Woodlock, 1983). Patient and provider stress is also influenced by the bureaucracy of communication in health-care organizations (Costello & Pettegrew, 1979; Perrow, 1965; Pettegrew, Thomas, Costello et al., 1980; Starr, 1982). The many rules that govern patient behavior can stifle, frustrate, and limit the social potential of patients (Kreps, 1988a; Mendelsohn, 1979). For example, such institutionalization has been shown to have a dehumanizing influence on patients, especially long-term care patients, such as elderly residents of nursing homes, limiting the effectiveness of health-care treatment (Kreps, 1986a; Mendelson, 1974; U.S. Senate Special Committee on Aging, Subcommittee on Long Term Care, 1974, 1975).

MEDIATED COMMUNICATION IN HEALTH AND HEALTH CARE

Modern societies have become increasingly dependent on media to disseminate health information enabling the sharing of relevant health information among many different people, groups, and organizations within modern societies (Flora, Maibach, & Maccoby, 1989). Media provide forums for information that help societal members recognize and evaluate environmental opportunities and constraints, coordinate their resources and activities in response to their environment, learn about culturally relevant phenomena, and pass on health information to future societies as a form of social inheritance (Flay, 1987b; Kreps, 1988a).

Print Media

Studies of print media, such as newspapers, books, magazines, journals, and pamphlets, have been shown to have great utility as health communication tools to educate consumers about health risks, health maintenance, and health-care services (Feldman, 1976; Freimuth, Greenberg, DeWitt, & Romano, 1984; Kreps & Thornton, 1984). For example, Wright (1975) found, in a survey of the comparative use of newspapers, radio, magazines, and television as sources of health information, that newspapers and magazines were used most often by respondents and printed media were identified as the most useful source of health information. Bishop (1974) found that the more anxious consumers are about a specific health problem, the more likely they are to seek and utilize printed health information. Evidence suggests that journals and textbooks are an important and preferred source of health information for health-care providers (Covell, Uman, & Manning, 1985; Currie, 1976). Yet, Bernier and Yerkey (1979) estimated that approximately two million articles are published in the biomedical literature annually and the publication rate was increasing geometrically, making it virtually impossible for health-care providers to keep abreast of the relevant literature on health-care advances. Evidence suggests that the longer it has been since physicians have graduated from medical school the more outdated their health-care knowledge and practices become (Haynes, McKibbon, Fitzgerald, Guyatt, Walker, & Sackett, 1986).

Telephonic Health Communication

In recent years the telephone has been examined as an interactive health information dissemination medium, with telephone mediated hot-lines and referral services developing as important channels providing support, information, and referral for callers who suffer from assorted health risks such as AIDS, poisoning, domestic violence, alcoholism, drug addiction, and cancer (Freimuth, Stein, & Kean, 1989). Local and national telephone hot-lines provide millions of callers with crisis counseling, helping lonely, depressed, and suicidal callers to work through their emotional problems (Fish, 1986). Data have demonstrated that the Cancer Information Service's toll-free telephone hotline has been an effective tool for disseminating up-to-date information regarding cancer treatment, referral, and clinical research to the public, often used in concert with other media such as print, radio, and television advertisements, commercials, and public service announcements, as well as the Physician Data Query on-line computer database (Freimuth, Stein et al., 1989; Kreps & Naughton, 1986).

Radio and Television as Public Health Communication Media

Radio and television have become increasingly health-oriented in recent years, with increased programming of health education shows (Kreps & Thornton, 1984; Turow & Coe, 1985; Wright, 1975). Evidence suggests that to the extent that the health information presented is correct, health programming trends have helped make television and radio important channels for health promotion (Flay, 1987b). Unfortunately, research also indicates that information presented through mass media does not always promote public health. For example, advertisements for cigarettes and alcoholic beverages have downplayed these products' health risks, aligned their consumption with virility, sophistication, and athletic prowess, and most dangerously are often directed toward high-risk segments of the population, such as youths who may develop hard-to-break negative health habits early in their lives (Jacobson & Amos, 1985; Trauth & Huffman, 1986). Furthermore, dramatic programs on television and popular films often misrepresent health-care problems, their treatment, the health-care system, and health-care professionals (Blackwell, 1967; Kreps & Thornton, 1984; Meyerhoff & Larson, 1985; Turow & Coe, 1985).

Mediated Health Education Campaigns

Mediated communication is often used in public health education campaigns by channelling health information to consumers about health-promoting behaviors (Atkin, 1979, 1981; Flay & Cook, 1981; Flora, Maibach, & Maccoby, 1989). For example, mediated communication has been used, with differing levels of success, to provide consumers with information about the uses and abuses of drugs (Atkyns, McEven, & Hannemann, 1975; Feingold & Knapp, 1977; Fejer, Smart, & Whitehead, 1971; Flay & Sobel, 1983; Goldstein, 1965; Hanneman, 1973), the importance of good nutrition (Kaufman, 1980), how to avoid heart disease (Maccoby & Farquhar, 1975; Solomon, 1984), preventing drunk driving (Atkin, Garramore, & Anderson, 1986), the importance of giving up smoking (Flay, 1987a; O'Keefe, 1971; Puska, Koskela, McAlister, Pallonen, Vartlanian, & Homan, 1979), and reasons and methods for effective contraception (Udry, 1972). Health communication researchers have assessed the use of public service announcements (PSAs) to disseminate health information concerning health risks and health-promoting behaviors, concluding that PSAs have been successful at disseminating health information only when professionally prepared and consistently aired (Atkin, 1979; Freimuth, Hammond, Edgar, & Monahan, 1989; Freimuth, Stein, & Kean, 1989; Freimuth & Van Nevel, 1981; Hammond, Freimuth, & Morrison, 1987). Evidence suggests that the impact of media on health promotion increases when media campaigns are augmented by additional forms of intervention at individual, group, organizational, and societal levels (Flora, Maibach, & Maccoby, 1989).

Communication Technologies as Health-Care Media

Modern health care commonly utilizes a broad range of mediated communication technologies to help handle its complex health information needs (Brenner & Logan, 1980; Day, 1975; Park & Bashshur, 1975). Many health-care organizations regularly use in-house computer and audiovisual information technologies for patient education, information exchange for personnel between shifts, medical procedure documentation, and in-service training (Makris, 1983; Portis & Hunter, 1975; Stoeckle, Lazare, Weingarten, & McGuire, 1971). Computers are used to store and process medical records, information about health-care treatment, referral, and research, as well as analyze laboratory tests, interpret diagnostic data, track physiological monitoring systems, and conduct tomographic scans and noninvasive imaging procedures in nuclear medicine (Anderson & Jay, 1985; Hawkins, Day, Gustafson, Chewning, & Bosworth, 1982;

Hinchcliff-Pelias, 1983; Kreps, Hubbard, & DeVita, 1988; Makris, 1983; Park & Bashshur, 1975; Slack, Hicks, Reed, & VanCura, 1966; Slack, Porter, Witschi, Sullivan, Buxbaum, & Stare, 1974; Zimmerman, 1978). Patient history-taking by computer has also been used effectively to anonymously gather sensitive information, provide consumers with an interactive means of seeking health information, as well as store and process patient health information (Cohen, 1981; Haessler, Holland, & Elshtain, 1974; Slack et al., 1966, 1974). Evaluation research has demonstrated that communication technologies, like MEDLINE and the Physician Data Query, are effective at helping providers and consumers identify relevant health-care literature and quickly access the latest health-care information, although there is serious concern that computer applications in health care have not been well diffused into the health-care system, nor have they been utilized to their fullest potential (Haynes, McKibbon, Walker, Mousseau, Baker, Fitzgerald, Guyatt, & Norman, 1985; Kreps, Hubbard, & DeVita, 1988; Kreps, Maibach, Naughton, Day, & Annett, 1986; Miller, Pople, & Myers, 1982). These information systems have the potential to help bridge the information gap that often exists between the clinical research community that generates state-of-the-art advances in health-care treatment, and practitioners and consumers who need to utilize such health information (Kreps & Naughton, 1986).

DIRECTIONS FOR FUTURE APPLIED HEALTH COMMUNICATION RESEARCH

This selective review of applied health communication research clearly indicates that interpersonal, group, organizational, and mediated communication have important influences on health care/promotion. Yet, health communication research must become far more sophisticated to fully explain the nature of these influences to help providers and consumers use communication most effectively to accomplish their health-care goals. Kreps (1988b) identified several weaknesses in current health communication research, such as a provider bias, a narrow professional focus on medicine and nursing, and failure to focus on the communicative needs and problems of specialized groups of consumers, that must be overcome. The focus of attention in much health communication research has been on the communication needs of health-care providers, often ignoring the needs of health-care consumers (Thompson, 1984). Consumers, as well as providers, of health care have important and challenging interpersonal communication needs in health care. To help consumers achieve their goals future health communication research must focus on how to increase the effectiveness of both consumer and provider communication in health care. Health communication research has favored examination of communication in the fields of medicine or nursing, neglecting other relevant health service areas (Thompson, 1984). Past health communication research has also tended to neglect important groups of underserved consumers, such as women (Corea, 1977; Lennane & Lennane, 1973; Mendelsohn, 1981), the poor (Kosa & Zola, 1975; LaFargue, 1972), minorities (Hoppe & Heller, 1975; Martiney, 1978; Quesada & Heller, 1977; White, 1974), and the aged (Callahan, 1987; Kreps, 1986a, 1988a, Thompson, 1984). Future research should be designed to examine the health communication needs of these underserved groups of health-care consumers.

Thompson (1984) contended that too much health communication research deals oversimplistically with the communication process and, in fact, often does not really focus on communication. This lack of communication focus, she explained, is due to a failure to ground many health communication studies on a well-developed base of communication theory. Kreps (1988a, 1988c) argued that health communication researchers must do a better job of applying their work to improving the health-care system, explaining that far too often health communication researchers have been naively content to report research data without applying these data to help improve health-care delivery. Future health communication research must be extended to help develop and implement relevant policies and programs to resolve serious pragmatic health-care issues.

Seven major pragmatic health-care delivery issues that have been identified in the health communication literature are good examples of fruitful topics for future health communication research that can help increase the effectiveness of health-care delivery (Kreps, 1988a, 1988b; Kreps & Query, 1989):

1. Low levels of *patient compliance* have been linked to the failure to establish effective provider–patient communication relationships (Charney, 1972; DiMatteo, 1979; Lane, 1982, 1983; Stone, 1979). Past research has focused on patient compliance with health-care appointments (Alpert, 1964; Hertz & Stamps, 1977), regimens (Caron, 1968; Davis & Eichorn, 1963; Lane, 1982), and use of prescribed drugs (Blackwell, 1973; Hulka, Cassel et al., 1976; Hulka, Kupper et al., 1975). Most of this literature has emphasized the characteristics of patients that lead to poor compliance, failing to adopt an interactive perspective on the compliance issue that would explore the level of cooperation elicited in the provider–consumer relationship (Kreps, 1988a; Kreps & Thornton, 1984; Lane, 1982, 1983). From a relational perspective the responsibility for health-care cooperation is shared by both the consumer and the provider, and compliance is encouraged by the different interpersonal influence strategies used by communicators (Arntson, 1985; Speedling & Rose, 1985). Research has

demonstrated that the quality of interaction between health-care providers and consumers strongly influences the level of cooperation engendered between these health communicators (Lane, 1982; Stone, 1979).

2. *Miscommunication and misinformation* in health care has been related to inaccurate interpersonal interpretations, ineffective and manipulative message strategies, and failures to seek and utilize interpersonal feedback between health communicators (Golden & Johnson, 1970; Ley, 1972; Ley, Bradshaw, Eaves, & Walker, 1973; Waitzkin & Stoekle, 1972, 1976). Current data suggest that many physicians' communication practices fail to supply clients with satisfactory levels of health information (Hess, Leipman, & Ruane, 1983; Kreps, Ruben et al., 1988; Maibach & Kreps, 1986; Newell & Webber, 1983; Relman, 1982; Ruben & Bowman, 1986). The Center for Health Education (1984a) concluded that inadequate interpersonal communication skills, lack of prevention-oriented training, concerns about patient compliance, perceived lack of support services, and administrative constraints are among the key factors that inhibit the success of physicians' health-care and health education efforts. The role of mediated communication, including new communication technologies, in disseminating relevant and accurate health information is an area of health communication inquiry that is ripe for further exploration.

3. *Insensitivity* in health care has been related to low levels of interpersonal respect, attempts at relational control, and inability to accurately interpret nonverbal messages (Daly & Hulka, 1975; Kane & Deuschle, 1967; Korsch, Gozzi, & Francis, 1968; Korsch & Negrete, 1972; Lane, 1983). Both health-care providers and health-care consumers sometimes communicate insensitively when they are preoccupied with health-care problems. The norm of reciprocity can encourage escalating patterns of insensitivity in response to disrespecting messages in health care, further disrupting the development of satisfying and effective health-care relationships. Applied research that identifies strategies for enhancing the sensitivity of communication in health care can dramatically influence the quality of health-care practice.

4. Unrealistic and unfulfilled consumer and provider *expectations* have been linked to cultural stereotypes, misinterpretations of relational needs, and inflexible relational role performances (Blackwell, 1967; Fuller & Quesada, 1973; Mechanic, 1972a, 1972b; Meyerhoff & Larson, 1965; Walker, 1973). Consumers often expect health-care providers to be all-knowing and all-powerful. These unrealistic expectations can result in significant disappointment when the outcomes of health-care treatments are less than perfect. Provider expectations of dutiful compliance with health-care regimens can be equally unrealistic, leading to anger and resentment when "orders" are not faithfully followed. Unfulfilled expecta-

tions may be related to the growth of malpractice litigation in health care. Research that can help increase the fulfillment of expectations in health care can have an extremely positive influence on the health-care system.

5. Lack of *interprofessional understanding and cooperation* in health care has been linked to ineffective health-care delivery (Boyer, Lee, & Kirschner, 1977; Frank, 1961; Hill, 1978; Kindig, 1975). Competitive and uncooperative interprofessional relationships established between health-care providers have become a major problem in health-care delivery systems. Power and status discrepancies between practitioners often lead to professional domination and conflict between health-care providers (Freidson, 1970). Differences in education, orientation to health care, and evaluations of the value of various health-care roles can lead to ethnocentric provider perspectives about the legitimacy of certain professions in comparison to others. This ethnocentrism may result in conflict over domain consensus and authority due to the overlapping responsibilities and interdependent activities health-care providers often share (Kreps, 1988a; Kreps & Thornton, 1984; Starr, 1982). The broad range of interdependent specialized health-care provider roles and functions in health-care delivery suggests that health-care specialists must elicit cooperation and coordination, collaborate on treatment strategies, share relevant health information, and coordinate professional activities to provide effective health-care services, often as members of health-care "teams" (Given & Simmons, 1977; Nagi, 1975; Thornton, 1978). Future health communication research can be designed to help health-care team members overcome interprofessional status barriers to communication and establish effective interprofessional relationships.

6. *Ethical improprieties* in health communication concerning such issues as informed consent about treatment, equal treatment and access to health care, paternalism, confidentiality, and withholding or misrepresenting health information have been identified in the literature (Kreps, 1988a; Kreps & Thornton, 1984; President's Commission for the Study of Ethical Problems in Medicine and Biomedical and Behavioral Research, 1982a, 1982b). Ethical standards for health behaviors are established through information generated by interaction within a given community, and as such are largely culturally bound (Kreps & Thornton, 1984). Health behaviors, then, are ethical to the extent they are appropriate to the cultural orientations of health communicators. Health communication research is needed that can help mediate cultural differences and help individuals gather and examine intersubjective information about health-care issues to make mutually satisfactory ethical health-care decisions.

7. *Dissatisfaction* with health care by both providers and consumers has been tied to many other health communication problems, such as failure to

express interpersonal empathy, relational dominance, and dehumanization (Ben-Sira, 1976; Kane & Deuschle, 1967; Korsch et al., 1968; Korsch & Negrete, 1972; Lane, 1983; Street & Wiemann, 1987). Dissatisfied health-care providers are more likely than satisfied providers to experience symptoms of job stress and burnout since they are not receiving sufficient psychological benefits from their work. Such burnout can lead to deterioration of professional performance and increased job turnover (Kreps, 1986b). Dissatisfied health-care consumers are less likely to comply with medical advice and more likely to avoid needed treatment because of their negative experiences with the health-care system (Lane, 1982, 1983). Research that can identify the communicative bases of dissatisfaction in health care and suggest strategies for improving the quality of health-care communication can increase the effectiveness of health-care delivery.

CONCLUSION

Health communication is an area of applied communication inquiry with a promising future. Future health communication research has the potential to solve many serious health-care problems, improve the health-care system, and increase the quality of health care. The extent of the pragmatic benefits that can accrue from health communication research is dependent on the ingenuity of health communication researchers in rigorously designing and conducting theoretically and methodologically sound studies that are valid and reliable. Such research can demystify many of the complexities of the health-care system and increase our understanding of the role of communication in preserving and promoting public health.

REFERENCES

Adelman, M. B. (1988, November). *Sustaining passion: Eroticism and safe sex talk*. Paper presented to the Speech Communication Association conference, New Orleans, LA.

Albrecht, T., & Adelman, M. (1984). Social support and life stress: New directions for communication research. *Human Communication Research, 11*, 3–32.

Albrecht, T., & Adelman, M. (1987). *Communicating social support*. Newbury Park, CA: Sage.

Alpert, J. (1964). Broken appointments. *Pediatrics, 34*, 124–132.

Anderson, J., & Jay, S. (1985). Computers and clinical judgment: The role of physician networks. *Social Science and Medicine, 20*, 969–979.

Arntson, P. (1985). Future research in health communication. *Journal of Applied Communication Research, 13*, 118–130.

Arntson, P., Droge, D., & Fassl, H. (1978). Pediatrician–patient communication:

The final report. In B. Ruben (Ed.), *Communication yearbook 2* (pp. 504–522). New Brunswick, NJ: Transaction.

Atkin, C. K. (1979). Research evidence on Mass-mediated health communication campaigns. In D. Nimmo (Ed.), *Communication yearbook 3* (pp. 655–668). New Brunswick, NJ: Transaction.

Atkin, C. (1981). Mass media information campaign effectiveness. In R. Rice & Paisley (Eds.), *Public communication campaigns* (pp. 265–280). Beverly Hills: Sage.

Atkin, C., Garramore, G., & Anderson, R. (1986, May). *Formative evaluation research in health campaign planning: The case of drunk driving prevention.* Paper presented to the International Communication Association conference, Chicago.

Atkyns, R., McEwen, W., & Hanneman, G. (1975). Sources of drug information among adults. *Journal of Drug Education, 5,* 161–169.

Babbie, S. (1973). *Medical communication requirements.* Springfield, VA: U.S. Pacific.

Baldwin, D. (1980). *Interdisciplinary health care teams in teaching and practice.* Reno: University of Nevada/New Health Perspectives, Inc.

Ben-Sira, Z. (1976). The function of the professional's affective behavior in client satisfaction: A revised approach to social interaction theory. *Journal of Health and Social Behavior, 17,* 3–11.

Ben-Sira, Z. (1980). Affective and instrumental components of the physician–patient relationship: An additional dimension of interaction theory. *Journal of Health and Social Behavior, 21,* 170–180.

Bernier, C., & Yerkey, A. (1979). *Cogent communication: Overcoming information overload.* Westport, CT: Greenwood Press.

Bishop, R. (1974). Anxiety and readership of health information. *Journalism Quarterly, 51,* 40–46.

Blackwell, B. (1967). Upper middle class adult expectations about entering the sick role for physical and psychiatric dysfunctions. *Journal of Health and Social Behavior, 8,* 83–95.

Blackwell, B. (1973). Patient compliance. *New England Journal of Medicine, 289,* 249–252.

Bliss, A., & Stout, P. (1989, May). *Evaluating health-related behavior models for AIDS communication.* Paper presented to the International Communication Association conference, San Francisco.

Bowen, S. P., & Michal-Johnson, P. (1989). The crisis of communication in relationships: Confronting the threat of AIDS. *AIDS and Public Policy, 4,* 10–19.

Boyer, L., Lee, D., & Kirschner, C. (1977). A student-run course in interprofessional relations. *Journal of Medical Education, 52,* 183–189.

Brenner, D., & Logan, R. (1980). Some considerations in the diffusion of medical technologies: Medical information systems. In D. Nimmo (Ed.), *Communication yearbook 4* (pp. 609–623). New Brunswick, NJ: Transaction.

Buller, M. K., & Buller, D. B. (1987). Physicians' communication style and patients' satisfaction. *Journal of Health and Social Behavior, 28,* 375–388.

Burleson, B. (1983). Social cognition, empathic motivation, and adults' comforting strategies. *Human Communication Research, 10,* 295–304.

Callahan, D. (1987). *Setting limits: Medical goals in an aging society.* New York: Simon & Schuster.

Campbell, R., & Chenoweth, B. (1981). *Peer support for older adults.* Ann Arbor, MI: University of Michigan Press.

Carkhuff, R. (1967). Toward a comprehensive model of facilitative interpersonal processes. *Journal of Counseling Psychology, 14,* 67–72.

Caron, H. (1968). Patients' cooperation with a medical regimen. *Journal of the American Medical Association, 203,* 922–926.

Carroll, J., & Monroe, J. (1980). Teaching clinical interviewing in the health professions: A review of empirical research. *Evaluation and the Health Professions, 3,* 21–45.

Cassata, D. (1980). Health communication theory and research: A definitional overview. In D. Nimmo (Ed.), *Communication yearbook 4* (pp. 583–589). New Brunswick, NJ: Transaction.

Cassata, D., Conroe, R., & Clements, P. (1977). A program for enhancing medical interviewing using videotape feedback in the family practice residency. *Journal of Family Practice, 4,* 473–677.

Center for Health Education. (1984a). *Physician involvement in cancer risk reduction education.* Baltimore: Author.

Center for Health Education (1984b). *Needs assessment: Physician's role in cancer risk reduction.* Baltimore: Author.

Charney, E. (1972). Patient–doctor communication: Implications for the clinician. *Pediatric Clinics of North America, 19,* 263–279.

Chiraboga, D., Coho, A., Stein, J., & Roberts, J. (1979). Divorce, stress, and social supports: A study in help seeking behavior. *Journal of Divorce, 3,* 121–135.

Cline, R. J. (1983). Interpersonal communication skills for enhancing physician–patient relationships. *Maryland State Medical Journal, 32,* 272–278.

Cluck, G. G., & Cline, R. J. (1986). The circle of others: Self- help groups for the bereaved. *Communication Quarterly, 34,* 306–325.

Cobb, S. (1976). Social support as a moderator of life stress. *Psychosomatic Medicine, 38,* 300–314.

Cohen, S. (1981). Experience with a computerized medical history system in private practice. *Proceedings of 5th Annual Symposium on Computer Applications in Medical Care* (pp. 121–123). Silver Spring, MD: IEEE.

Corea, G. (1977). *The hidden malpractice: How American medicine treats women as patients and professionals.* New York: William Morrow.

Costello, D., & Pettegrew, L. (1979). Health communication theory and research: An overview of health organizations. In D. Nimmo (Ed.), *Communication yearbook 3* (pp. 607–623). New Brunswick, NJ: Transaction.

Covell, D., Uman, G., & Manning, P. (1985). Information needs in office practice: Are they being met? *Annals of Internal Medicine, 103,* 596–599.

Cox, A. (1989). Eliciting patients' feelings. In M. Stewart & D. Roter (Eds.), *Communicating with medical patients* (pp. 99–106). Newbury Park, CA: Sage.

Currie, B. (1976). Continuing education from medical periodicals. *Journal of Medical Education, 51,* 240–244.

Daly, M. B., & Hulka, B. S. (1975). Talking with the doctor, 2. *Journal of Communication, 25,* 148–152.

Davis, M., & Eichorn, R. (1963). Compliance with medical regimens: A panel study. *Journal of Health and Human Behavior, 4,* 240–249.

Day, S. (1975). *Communication of scientific information.* New York: Karger.

Dickson-Markman, F., & Shern, D. (1984, May). *Social support and health: Is quantity as good as quality?* Paper presented to the International Communication Association convention, San Francisco.

DiMatteo, M. (1979). A social psychological analysis of physician–patient rapport: Toward a science of the art of medicine. *Journal of Social Issues, 35,* 12–33.

DiMatteo, M., Prince, L. M., & Taranta, A. (1979). Patients' perceptions of physicians' behaviour: Determinants of patient commitment to the therapeutic relationship. *Journal of Community Health, 4,* 280–290.

DiSalvo, V. S., Larsen, J. K., & Backus, D. K. (1986). The health care communicator: An identification of skills and problems. *Communication Education, 35,* 231–242.

Droge, D., Arntson, P., & Norton, R. (1981, May). *The social support function in epilepsy self-help groups.* Paper presented to the International Communication Association conference, Dallas.

Edgar, T., & Fitzpatrick, M. A. (1988). Compliance-gaining in relational interaction: When your life depends on it. *Southern Speech Communication Journal, 53,* 385–405.

Edgar, T., Hammond, S. L., & Freimuth, V. S. (1989). Mediated and interpersonal strategies for the prevention of AIDS. *AIDS and Public Policy Journal, 4,* 3–9.

Feingold, P., & Knapp, M. (1977). Anti-drug abuse commercials. *Journal of Communication, 27,* 20–28.

Fejer, D., Smart, R., & Whitehead, P. (1971). Sources of information about drugs among high school students. *Public Opinion Quarterly, 35,* 235–241.

Feldman, J. (1976). *The dissemination of health information.* Chicago: Aldine.

Filoramo, T., & Ziff, D. (1980). *Nurse recruitment: Strategies for success.* Rockville, MD: Aspen.

Fish, S. (1986, November). *The crisis "hotline" as mediated therapeutic communication.* Paper presented to the Speech Communication Association conference, Chicago.

Flay, B. R. (1987a). Mass-media and smoking cessation: A critical review. *American Journal of Public Health, 77,* 153–160.

Flay, B. R. (1987b). Evaluation of the development, dissemination, and effectiveness of mass media health programming. *Health Education Research, 2,* 123–129.

Flay, B. R., & Cook, T. (1981). Evaluation of mass media prevention campaigns. In R. Rice & W. Paisley (Eds.), *Public communication campaigns* (pp. 239–264). Beverly Hills: Sage.

Flay, B. R., & Sobel, J. L. (1983). The role of mass media in preventing substance abuse. In T. Glynn, C. Leukefeld, & J. Ludford (Eds.), *Preventing adolescent substance abuse: Intervention strategies* (pp. 4–35). Washington, DC: NIDA Res. Monograph 47.

Flora, J. A., Maibach, E. W., & Maccoby, N. (1989). The role of media across four levels of health promotion intervention. *Annual Review of Public Health, 10,* 181–201.

Flora, J. A., & Thoresen, C. E. (1988). Reducing the risk of AIDS in Adolescents. *American Psychologist, 43,* 965–970.

Foley, R., & Sharf, B. (1981). The five interviewing techniques most frequently overlooked by primary care physicians. *Behavioral Medicine, 11,* 26–31.

Frank, L. (1961). Interprofessional communication. *American Journal of Public Health, 51,* 1798–1804.

Freidson, E. (1970). *Professional dominance: The social structure of medical care.* Chicago: Aldine.

Freimuth, V. S., Edgar, T., & Hammond, S. L. (1987). College students' awareness and interpretation of the AIDS risk. *Science, Technology, and Human Values, 12,* 37–40.

Freimuth, V. S., Greenberg, R. H., DeWitt, J., & Romano, R. M. (1984). Covering cancer: Newspapers and the public interest. *Journal of Communication, 34,* 62–73.

Freimuth, V. S., Hammond, S. L., Edgar, T., & Monahan, J. L. (1989, May). *Reaching those at risk: A content analytic study of AIDS PSAs.* Paper presented to the International Communication Association, San Francisco.

Freimuth, V. S., Stein, J. A., & Kean, T. J. (1989). *Searching for health information.* Philadelphia: University of Pennsylvania Press.

Freimuth, V. S., & Van Nevel, J. (1981). Reaching the public: The asbestos awareness campaign. *Journal of Communication, 31,* 155–167.

Froland, C., Brodsky, G., Olson, M., & Stewart, L. (1979). Social support and social adjustment: Implications for mental health professionals. *Community Mental Health Journal, 15,* 82–93.

Fuller, D., & Quesada, G. (1973). Communication in medical therapeutics. *Journal of Communication, 23,* 361–370.

Georgopoulos, B. (Ed.). (1974). *Organization research on health institutions.* Ann Arbor, MI: Institute for Social Research.

Georgopoulos, B. (1975). *Hospital organization research: Review and source book.* Philadelphia: W.B. Saunders.

Given, B., & Simmons, S. (1977). The interdisciplinary health care team. *Nursing Forum, 16,* 164–184.

Golden, J., & Johnson, G. (1970). Problems of distortion in doctor–patient communication. *Psychiatry in Medicine, 1,* 127–149.

Goldstein, H. (1965). Guidelines for drug education through electronic media. *Journal of Drug Education, 14,* 157–171.

Gottlieb, B. (1981). *Social networks and social support.* Beverly Hills: Sage.

Gottlieb, B. (1988). *Martialing social support: Formats, processes, and effects.* Newbury Park, CA: Sage.

Greenfield, S., Kaplan, S., & Ware, J. (1985). Expanding patient involvement in care: Effects on patient outcomes. *Annals of Internal Medicine, 102,* 520–528.

Gronning, N. (1982, November). *Peer counselor training in gerontology.* Paper presented to the Speech Communication Association conference, Louisville, KY.

Haessler, H., Holland, T., & Elshtain, E. (1974). Evolution of an automated database history. *Archives of Internal Medicine, 134,* 586–591.

Hammond, S. L., Freimuth, V. S., & Morrison, W. (1987). The gatekeeping funnel: Tracking a major PSA campaign from distribution to gatekeepers to target audience. *Health Education Quarterly, 14,* 153–166.

Hanneman, G. (1973). Communicating Drug-Abuse Information Among College Students. *Public Opinion Quarterly, 37*, 171–191.

Hawes, L. (1972a). Development and application of an interview coding system. *Central States Speech Journal, 23*, 92–99.

Hawes, L. (1972b). The effects of interviewer style on patterns of dyadic communication. *Speech Monographs, 39*, 114–123.

Hawes, L., & Foley, J. (1973). A Markov analysis of interview communication. *Speech Monographs, 40*, 208–219.

Hawkins, R., Day, T., Gustafson, D., Chewning, B., & Bosworth, K. (1982, May). *Using computer programs to provide health information to adolescents: BARNY.* Paper presented to the International Communication Association conference, Boston, MA.

Haynes, R., McKibbon, K., Fitzgerald, D., Guyatt, G., Walker, C., & Sackett, D. (1986). How to keep up with the medical literature: 1. Why try to keep up and how to get started. *Annals of Internal Medicine, 105*, 149–153.

Haynes, R., McKibbon, K., Walker, C., Mousseau, J., Baker, L., Fitzgerald, D., Guyatt, G., & Norman, G. (1985). Computer searching of the medical literature: An evaluation of MEDLINE searching systems. *Annals of Internal Medicine, 103*, 812–816.

Hertz, P., & Stamps, P. (1977). Appointment-keeping behavior re-evaluated. *American Journal of Public Health, 67*, 1033–1036.

Hess, J., Liepman, M., & Ruane, T. (1983). *Family practice and preventive medicine: Health promotion in primary care.* New York: Human Sciences Press.

Hill, S. K. (1978). Health communication: Focus on interprofessional communication. *Communication Administration Bulletin, 25*, 31–36.

Hinchcliff-Pelias, M. (1983, November). *The use of computer aided instruction for systematic desensitization in the treatment of communication apprehension.* Paper presented to the Speech Communication Association conference, Washington, DC.

Hoppe, S., & Heller, P. (1975). Alienation, familism, and the utilization of health services by Mexican-Americans. *Journal of Health and Social Behavior, 16*, 304–314.

Horowitz, A. (1977). Social networks and pathways to psychiatric treatment. *Social Forces, 56*, 86–105.

House, R. (1970). Role conflict and multiple authority in organizations. *California Management Review, 12*, 53–60.

Hulka, B. S., Cassel, J. C., Kupper, L. L., & Burdette, J. A. (1976). Communication compliance, and concordance between physicians and patients with prescribed medications. *American Journal of Public Health, 66*, 847–853.

Hulka, B. S., Kupper, L. L., Cassel, J. C., & Efird, R. L. (1975). Medication use and misuse: Physician–patient discrepancies. *Journal of Chronic Diseases, 28*, 7–21.

Jacobson, B., & Amos, A. (1985). *When smoke gets in your eyes: Cigarette advertising policy and coverage of smoking and health in women's magazines.* London: British Medical Association/Health Education Council.

Jones, J. A. & Phillips, G. M. (1988). *Communicating with your doctor.* Carbondale, IL: Southern Illinois University Press.

Kane, R., & Deuschle, K. (1967). Problems in doctor–patient communication. *Medical Care, 5,* 260–271.

Kaplan, S. H., Greenfield, S., & Ware, J. E. (1989). Impact of the doctor–patient relationship on the outcomes of chronic disease. In M. Stewart & D. Roter (Eds.), *Communicating with medical patients* (pp. 228–245). Newbury Park, CA: Sage.

Kaufman, L. (1980). Prime-time nutrition. *Journal of Communication, 30,* 37–46.

Kessler, R., & McLeod, J. (1985). Social support and mental health in community samples. In S. Cohen & S. Syme (Eds.), *Social support and health* (pp. 219–240). New York: Academic Press.

Kindig, D. (1975). Interdisciplinary education for primary health care team delivery, *Journal of Medical Education, 50,* 97–110.

Kitson, G., Moir, R., & Mason, P. (1982). Family social support in crises: The special case of divorce. *American Journal of Orthopsychiatry, 52,* 161–165.

Korsch, B. M., Gozzi, E. K., & Francis, V. (1968). Gaps in doctor–patient communication: Doctor–patient interaction and patient satisfaction. *Pediatrics, 42,* 855–871.

Korsch, B. M. & Negrete, V. F. (1972). Doctor–patient communication. *Scientific American, 227,* 66–74.

Kosa, J., & I. Zola (Eds.) (1975). *Poverty and health—a sociological analysis.* Cambridge, MA: Harvard University Press.

Kreps, G. L. (1986a). Health communication and the elderly. *World Communication, 15,* 55–70.

Kreps, G. L. (1986b). Description and evaluation of a nurse retention organizational development research program. In H. Gueutal & M. Kavanagh (Eds.), *Proceedings of the Eastern Academy of Management* (pp. 18–22), New York: Eastern Academy of Management.

Kreps, G. L. (1988a). The pervasive role of information in health and health care: Implications for health communication policy. In J. Anderson (Ed.), *Communication yearbook 11* (pp. 238–276). Newbury Park, CA: Sage.

Kreps, G. L. (1988b). Relational communication in health care. *Southern Speech Communication Journal, 53,* 344–359.

Kreps, G. L. (1988c). Setting the agenda for health communication research and development: Scholarship that can make a difference. *Health Communication, 1,* 11–15.

Kreps, G. L. (1990a). *Organizational communication: Theory and practice* (2nd ed.). White Plains, NY: Longman.

Kreps, G. L. (1990b). Narrative research and organizational development: Stories as repositories of organizational intelligence. In J. A. Anderson (Ed.), *Communication yearbook 13* (pp. 191–202). Newbury Park, CA: Sage.

Kreps, G. L., Hubbard, S., & DeVita, V. (1988). Overview of the Physician Data Query on-line cancer information system's role in health information dissemination. *Information and Behavior, 2,* 362–374.

Kreps, G. L., Maibach, E., Naughton, M., Day, S., & Annett, D. (1986). PDQ usage trends: Implications for evaluation. In A. Levy & B. Williams (Eds.), *Proceedings of the American Association for Medical Systems and Informatics Congress* (pp. 71–75).

Kreps, G. L., & Naughton, M. D. (1986). The role of PDQ in disseminating cancer information. In R. Salamon, B. Blum, & M. Jorgensen (Eds.), *MEDINFO 86* (pp. 400–404). Amsterdam: Elsevier.

Kreps, G. L., & Query, J. (1989). The applications of communication competence: Assessment and testing in health care. In G. M. Phillips & J. T. Wood (Eds.), *Speech communication: Essays to commemorate the 75th anniversary of the Speech Communication Association* (pp. 293–323). Carbondale, IL: Southern Illinois University Press.

Kreps, G. L., Ruben, B., Baker, M., & Rosenthal, S. (1988). A national survey of public knowledge about digestive health and disease: Implications for health education. *Public Health Reports, 102,* 270–277.

Kreps, G. L., & Thornton, B. C. (1984). *Health communication.* New York: Longman.

LaFargue, J. (1972). Role of prejudice in rejection of health care. *Nursing Research, 21,* 53–58.

Lane, S. (1982). Communication and patient compliance. In L. Pettegrew (Ed.), *Straight talk: Explorations in provider patient interaction* (pp. 59–69). Louisville, KY: Humana.

Lane, S. (1983). Compliance, satisfaction, and physician–patient communication. In R. Bostrom (Ed.), *Communication yearbook 7* (pp. 77–79). Beverly Hills: Sage.

Lennane, K., & Lennane, R. (1973). Alleged psychogenic disorders in women—a possible manifestation of sexual prejudice. *New England Journal of Medicine, 288,* 288–292.

Levenstein, J. H., Brown, J. B., Westin, W. W., Stewart, M., McCracken, E. C., & McWhinney, I. (1989). Patient-centered clinical interviewing. In M. Stewart & D. Roter (Eds.), *Communicating with medical patients* (pp. 107–123). Newbury Park, CA: Sage.

Ley, P. (1972). Comprehension, memory, and the success of communications with the patient. *Journal for Institutional Health Education, 10,* 23–29.

Ley, P., Bradshaw, P., Eaves, D., & Walker, C. (1973). A method of increasing patients' recall of information presented by doctors. *Psychological Medicine, 3,* 217–220.

Maccoby, N., & Farquhar, J. (1975). Communication for health: Unselling heart disease. *Journal of Communication, 25,* 114–126.

Maguire, P., Fairbairn, S., & Fletcher, C. (1989). Consultation skills of young doctors: Benefits of undergraduate feedback training in interviewing. In M. Stewart & D. Roter (Eds.), *Communicating with medical patients* (pp. 124–137). Newbury Park, CA: Sage.

Maibach, E. W., & Kreps, G. L. (1986). *Communicating with patients: Primary care physicians' perspectives on cancer prevention, screening, and education.* Paper presented to the International Conference on Doctor–Patient Communication, Ontario, Canada.

Makris, P. (1983). Informatics in health-care delivery systems. *Information Age, 5,* 205–210.

Martiney, R. (1978). *Hispanic culture and health care—fact, fiction and folklore.* St. Louis: C. V. Mosby.

McIntosh, J. (1974). Process of communication, information seeking control associated with cancer: A selected review of the literature. *Social Science and Medicine, 8,* 167–187.

Mechanic, D. (1972a). Social psychological factors affecting the presentation of bodily complaints. *The New England Journal of Medicine, 286,* 1132–1139.

Mechanic, D. (1972b). *Public expectations and health care: Essays on the changing organization of health services.* New York: Wiley.

Mendelsohn, R. (1979). *Confessions of a medical heretic.* Chicago: Contemporary Books.

Mendelsohn, R. (1981). *Male practice: How doctors manipulate women.* Chicago: Contemporary Books.

Mendelson, M. (1974). *Tender loving greed.* New York: Knopps.

Meyerhoff, B., & Larson, W. (1965). The doctor as cultural hero: The routinization of charisma. *Human Organization, 24,* 188–191.

Miller, R., Pople, M., & Myers, J. (1982). INTERNIST-1, an experimental computer-based diagnostic consultant for general internal medicine. *The New England Journal of Medicine, 307,* 468–475.

Morrow, G., Hoagland, A., & Carnrike, C. (1981). Social support and parental adjustment to pediatric cancer. *Journal of Consulting and Clinical Psychology, 49,* 763–765.

Morse, B., & Piland, R. (1981). An assessment of communication competencies needed by intermediate-level health care providers: A study of nurse–patient, nurse–doctor, nurse–nurse communication relationships. *Journal of Applied Communication Research, 9,* 30–41.

Mullen, W. E. (1985). Identification and ranking of stressors in nursing home administration. *The Gerontologist, 25,* 370–375.

Nagi, S. (1975). Teamwork in health care in the United States: A sociological perspective. *The Milbank Quarterly,* New York: Health & Society Press.

Newell, G., & Webber, C. (1983). The primary care physician in cancer prevention. *Family and Community Health, 5,* 77–84.

Northouse, P. (1977). Predictors of empathic ability in an organizational setting. *Human Communication Research, 3,* 176–178.

Nussbaum, J. (1983). Relational closeness of elderly interaction: Implications for life satisfaction. *Western Journal of Speech Communication, 47,* 229–243.

O'Keefe, M. (1971). The anti-smoking commercials: A study of television's impact on behavior. *Public Opinion Quarterly, 35,* 242–248.

Park, B., & Bashshur, R. (1975). Some implications of telemedicine. *Journal of Communication, 25,* 161–166.

Pattison, E., & Pattison, M. (1981). Analysis of a schizophrenic psychosocial network. *Schizophrenia Bulletin, 7,* 135–143.

Perrow, C. (1965). Hospitals, technology, structure and goals. In J. March (Ed.), *Handbook of organizations* (pp. 136–159). Chicago: Rand McNally.

Peters-Golden, H. (1982). Breast cancer: Varied perceptions of social support in the illness experience. *Social Science and Medicine, 16,* 483–491.

Pettegrew, L. (1977). An investigation of therapeutic communicator style. In B. Ruben (Ed.), *Communication yearbook 1* (pp. 593–604). New Brunswick, NJ: Transaction.

Pettegrew, L., & Thomas, R. C. (1978). Communication style differences in formal vs. informal therapeutic relationships. In B. Ruben (Ed.), *Communication yearbook 2* (pp. 523–538). New Brunswick, NJ: Transaction.

Pettegrew, L., Thomas, R. C., Costello, D., Wolf, G., Lennox, L., & Thomas, S. (1980). Job-related stress in a health care organization: Management/communication issues. In D. Nimmo (Ed.), *Communication yearbook 4* (pp. 626–652). New Brunswick, NJ: Transaction.

Pfeffer, J. (1973). Size, composition and function of hospital boards of directors: A study of organization-environment linkage. *Administrative Science Quarterly, 18*, 449–461.

Pfeffer, J., & Salancik, G. (1977). Organizational context and the characteristics and tenure of hospital administrators. *Academy of Management Journal, 20*, 74–88.

Pierce, J., Watson, D., Knights, S., Glidden, T., Williams, S., & Watson, R. (1984). A controlled trial of health education in the physician's office. *Preventive Medicine, 13*, 185–194.

Portis, B., & Hunter, A. (1975). In-service training by mass media. *Journal of Communication, 25*, 167–170.

President's Commission for the Study of Ethical Problems in Medicine and Biomedical and Behavioral Research (1982). *Making health care decisions: The ethical and legal implications of informed consent in the patient–practitioner relationship* (Vol. 1–3). Washington, DC: U.S. Government Printing Office.

President's Commission for the Study of Ethical Problems in Medicine and Biomedical and Behavioral Research (1982b). *Splicing life: The social and ethical issues of genetic engineering with human beings*. Washington, DC: U.S. Government Printing Office.

Puska, P., Koskela, K., McAlister, A., Pallonen, V., Vartlanian, E., & Homan, K. (1979). A comprehensive television smoking cessation programme in Finland. *Internal Journal of Health Education, 22*, 1–29.

Query, J. L., & James, A. C. (1989). The relationship between interpersonal communication competence and social support among elderly support groups in retirement communities. *Health Communication, 1*, 165–184.

Quesada, G., & Heller, R. (1977). Sociocultural barriers to medical care among Mexican-Americans in Texas. *Medical Care, 15*, 93–101.

Ray, E. B. (1983). Job burnout from a communication perspective. In R. Bostrom (Ed.), *Communication yearbook 7* (pp. 738–755). Beverly Hills: Sage.

Relman, A. (1982). Encouraging the practice of preventive medicine in health promotion. *Public Health Reports, 97*, 216–219.

Rogers, C. (1951). *Client-centered therapy*. Boston: Houghton Mifflin.

Rogers, C. (1957). The necessary and sufficient conditions of therapeutic personality change. *Journal of Consulting Psychology, 21*, 95–103.

Rogers, C. (Ed.). (1967). *The therapeutic relationship and its impact*. Madison WI: University of Wisconsin Press.

Rossiter, C. (1975). Defining therapeutic communication. *Journal of Communication, 25*, 127–130.

Roter, D. (1983). Physician/patient communication: Transmission of information and patient effects. *Maryland State Medical Journal, 32*, 260–265.

Ruben, B., & Bowman, J. (1986). Patient satisfaction (part 1): Critical issues in the theory and design of patient relations training. *Journal of Healthcare Education and Training, 1*, 1–5.

Reusch, J. (1957). *Disturbed communication*. New York: Norton.

Ruesch, J. (1961). *Therapeutic communication*. New York: Norton.

Ruesch, J. (1963). The role of communication in therapeutic transactions. *Journal of Communication, 13*, 132–139.

Ruesch, J., & Bateson, G. (1951). *The social matrix of psychiatry*. New York: Norton.

Salem, P., & Williams, M. L. (1984). Uncertainty and satisfaction: The importance of information in hospital communication. *Journal of Applied Communication Research, 12*, 75–89.

Schaefer, J. (1974). The interrelatedness of decision making and the nursing process. *American Journal of Nursing, 74*, 1852–1855.

Scheff, T. (1963). Decision rules, types of error and their consequences in medical diagnosis. *Behavioral Science, 8*, 97–107.

Schofield, T., & Arntson, P. (1989). A model for teaching doctor–patient communication during residency. In M. Stewart & D. Roter (Eds.), *Communicating with medical patients* (pp. 138–152). Newbury Park, CA: Sage.

Schwartz, W. (1975). Decision analysis: A look at the chief complaints. *New England Journal of Medicine, 300*, 556–559.

Slack, W., Hicks, W., Reed, C., & VanCura, L. (1966). A computer-based medical history. *New England Journal of Medicine, 274*, 194–198.

Slack, W., Porter, D., Witschi, J., Sullivan, M., Buxbaum, R., & Stare, F. (1974). Dietary interviewing by computer. *Journal of the American Diabetics Association, 69*, 514–517.

Smith, R. (1976). *Doctors and patients*. Boise, ID: Syms-York.

Solomon, D. (1984). Social marketing and community health promotion: The Stanford heart disease prevention project. In L. Fredericksen, L. Salomon, & K. Brehony (Eds.), *Marketing health behavior: Principles, techniques, and applications* (pp. 115–135). New York: Plenum Press.

Speedling, E., & Rose, D. (1985). Building an effective doctor–patient relationship: From patient satisfaction to patient participation. *Social Science and Medicine, 21*, 115–120.

Starr, P. (1982). *The social transformation of American medicine*. New York: Basic Books.

Stoeckle, J., Lazare, A., Weingarten, C., & McGuire, M. (1971). Learning medicine by videotaped recordings. *Journal of Medical Education, 46*, 518–524.

Stone, G. (1979). Patient compliance and the role of the expert. *Journal of Social Issues, 35*, 34–59.

Street, R. L. (1989). Patients' satisfaction with dentists' communicative style. *Health Communication, 1*, 137–154.

Street, R. L., & Wiemann, J. (1987). Patients' satisfaction with physicians' interpersonal involvement, expressiveness, and dominance. In M. McLaughlin (Ed.), *Communication yearbook 10* (pp. 591–612). Beverly Hills: Sage.

Thompson, T. (1984). The invisible helping hand: The role of communication in health and social service professions. *Communication Quarterly, 32*, 148–163.

Thornton, B. (1978). Health care teams and multimethodological research. In B. Ruben (Ed.), *Communication yearbook 2* (pp. 538–553). New Brunswick, NJ: Transaction.

Trauth, D., & Huffman, J. (1986, May). *Regulation of alcoholic beverage advertising: Its present state and future directions.* Paper presented at the annual meeting of the International Communication Association, Chicago, IL.

Turow, J., & Coe, L. (1985). Curing television's ills: The portrayal of health care. *Journal of Communication, 35,* 36–51.

Udry, J. (1972). Can mass media advertising increase contraceptive use? *Family Planning Perspectives, 4,* 37–44.

U.S. Senate Special Committee on Aging, Subcommittee on Long Term Care. (1974). *Nursing home care in the United States, failure in public policy: Introductory report.* Washington, DC: U.S. Government Printing Office.

U.S. Senate Special Committee on Aging, Subcommittee on Long Term Care. (1975). *Nursing home care in the United States, failure in public policy: Introductory report and nine supporting papers.* Washington, DC: U.S. Government Printing Office.

Wagner, M. (1966). Reinforcement of the verbal productivity in group therapy. *Psychological Reports, 19,* 1217–1218.

Waitzkin, H., & Stoekle, J. (1972). The communication of information about illness. *Advances in Psychosomatic Medicine, 8,* 180–215.

Waitzkin, H., & Stoeckle, J. (1976). Information control and the micropolitics of health care: Summary of an ongoing research project. *Social Science and Medicine, 10,* 263–276.

Walker, H. (1973). Communication and the American health care problem. *Journal of Communication, 23,* 349–360.

West, C. (1984). *Routine complications: Trouble with the talk between doctors and patients.* Bloomington, IN: Indiana University Press.

White, E. (1974). Health and the Black person: An annotated bibliography. *American Journal of Nursing, 74,* 1839–1841.

Wolf, G. (1981, April). Nursing turnover: Some causes and solutions. *Nursing Outlook,* pp. 233–236.

Woodlock, B. (1983). Levels of exchange and organizational communication. In R. Bostrom (Ed.), *Communication yearbook 7* (pp. 756–771). Beverly Hills: Sage.

Wortman, C., & Dunkel-Schetter, C. (1979). Interpersonal relationships and cancer. *Journal of Social Issues, 35,* 132–155.

Wright, W. (1975). Mass media as sources of medical information. *Journal of Communication, 25,* 171–173.

Yanda, R. (1977). *Doctors as managers of health care teams.* New York: AMACOM.

Zimmerman, J. (1978). Physician utilization of medical records: Preliminary determinations. *Medical Informatics, 3*(1), 27–35.

HEALTH, AGING, AND FAMILY PARADIGMS: A THEORETICAL PERSPECTIVE

14

MARY ANNE FITZPATRICK
University of Wisconsin

Throughout most of human history, the family has been both the primary context of social integration for aged individuals and the principal provider of assistance and economic support to the elderly in need. In our society, a phenomenal growth in the population of aged individuals has occurred within the lifetime of today's individuals. There are more older Americans than ever before (between 25 and 30 million are over 65) and they are living longer. A 65-year-old man can expect to live until 79 and the average 65-year-old woman until 84. Today, we take survival into old age for granted. Such survival, however, brings with it new challenges for the elderly and their families. Although individuals have a much longer life span, they do not necessarily live in complete physical and mental health. In this chapter, I explore the role of family communication as it relates to the health concerns of the aged.

In the first section of this chapter, I discuss health and aging. In particular, I describe various normative and nonnormative decisions that affect families with aging members as well as various communication styles that may be adopted by families. In the second section of this chapter, I propose a typology that categorizes families according to how they process information. Families have distinctive internal working models of family relationships that represent the world of the family and provide guidelines about how to interpret incoming information. These family models, called paradigms, guide the communication that occurs in family decision making.

AGING, HEALTH, AND INTERPERSONAL
COMMUNICATION

Who are the aged? In the United States, persons aged 65 and over are officially identified as old people. Definitions based on the calendar serve to set a floor for government benefits, pension plans, and discounts for goods and services. The aged cover the years from 65 to 100, a span of two generations. Thus, many divide the aged into the young-old, the old, and the very old.

Although a definition of the aged may be straightforward, a definition of health is somewhat problematic. The World Health Organization provides a working definition: *Health* is "a state of complete physical, mental and social well-being and not the absence of disease or infirmity." Accepting cognitive and physical well-being as primitive terms, what is social well-being? At the individual level, social well-being is the ability of an individual to sustain a variety of different types of relationships and a variety of network connections. At the family level, social well-being is the ability of the group to preserve their notion of the family in the face of crisis (Reiss, 1981). Whereas a large body of research considers the aged in terms of physical or mental health outcomes, social well-being is the outcome of concern to me for two reasons. First, although the definition of health gives each of the three concepts equal status, the first two are causally prior to the last. In other words, physical and mental health are likely to affect the social well-being of an individual and of a family. The ultimate endogenous variable in a model of family communication and health should be "social well-being."

Second, interpersonal communication in the family can be tied to social well-being both at the individual and group level. Individuals develop, maintain, and disengage from relationships through their communication. Furthermore, family identity is maintained through the verbal and nonverbal communication that occurs in families. To discuss explicitly the relationships between social well-being and communication does not imply that social well-being is not related to physical and mental health. Rather, the complex relationships between social well-being at both the individual and family level and the other components of a definition of health are beyond the scope of this chapter.

Admittedly, although communication can be linked to each level of social well-being, these two outcomes can be conflicting ones in a given family. In certain families, the health of the individual is maintained in the face of the breakdown of the family, whereas in others, the family takes precedence over the individual's social well-being. In this chapter, I focus on linking particular patterns of decision-making communication to family well-being.

Family Transitions

How is social well-being accomplished at the family level? Social well-being is accomplished through the successful negotiation of family transitions with predictable patterns of interpersonal communication.

Individual and family well-being may be severely challenged during times of change and transition. Such transitions may be normative (i.e., expected) or nonnormative (i.e., unexpected) developmental stages in family life. Normative developmental stages are those that can be predicted to occur within a given time period. For the most part, changes in family roles, membership, and structure take place over an extended period of time and allow the individuals involved some preliminary socialization. Such normative decisions are more likely to occur when families have "young-old members." For the young-old, the normative decisions involve the loss of two important roles: the occupational and the parental. With the loss of these two roles, and corresponding changes in sex-role preferences, married couples in this age group may be in line for more conflict, negotiation, and bargaining over what used to be agreed upon issues. As I have demonstrated in the research with married couples in general, bargaining and negotiation come more easily to those with certain marital definitions than to others (Fitzpatrick, 1988). These normative role transitions involve the redefinition of both marital relationships as well as the renegotiation and redefinition of social networks. Married partners lose both direct parental roles as well as occupational ones and many decisions must be made about developing a new set of marital rules. Often couples must define a new set of shared and nonshared activities. And these transitions involve strengthening and building social networks of kin and friends.

Nonnormative transitions are unexpected events. Some of these may be acute and some may be chronic. That is, an elderly person may suffer a stroke on Friday and die within a few days. Alternately, instead of quickly succumbing to cancer, heart attacks, or strokes, elderly people may live much longer albeit in chronically ill health. Because many of the elderly live into the middle years of old age without the comfort and assistance of a spouse (e.g., 70% of women over 75 are widowed and live alone), their families take over much of the direct caregiving, psychological support, and social contact (Treas & Bengston, 1987).

For the elderly, marital role transitions and social network reorganization may be necessary during these nonnormative transitions. The delicate balance of interdependence in a marriage may be substantially shifted due to the failing health of one member of a couple and the same health issues may call for more intense psychological support and assistance from family members and friends.

Anticipatory socialization to these types of transitions is rare for either family members or the elderly person. Many of the particular crises faced by families must be resolved on an ad hoc basis. The sister who has recently lost a job may be the one to take over the care of a parent who has just received a cancer diagnosis. If the cancer emergency had occurred at a different time, other options (for parental care) would have been explored by the family.

These nonnormative transitions may be especially likely to disturb a sense of family identity. The family maintains its identity as a unique group through two primary mechanisms. First, the daily patterns of how a family uses space and time to accomplish its goals gives a family a sense of its identity. Second, family rituals, episodic events that are deeply symbolic, serve also to give a family a sense of its own uniqueness. By definition, a significant crisis arises when either the daily patterns or the central family rituals are disturbed. The gradual weakening of the older family member may affect both daily family patterns as well as disrupt family ceremonials. When the grandmother in a family can no longer leave her bed to participate either in the preparation of the Christmas Eve dinner or take her part at the head of the table in the dinner's ceremonial aspect, the family identity is shaken.

When the central family identity is destabilized and threatened as it is likely to be during a nonnormative health crisis with an aging family member, the family may progress through three identifiable stages (Reiss, 1981):

Stage 1: Emergence of Rules. When operating smoothly, families proceed without any specified rules. During a period of destabilization, rules emerge. These rules may be either explicitly discussed or simply agreed to implicitly. These rules have as their objective both adaptation to the new situation and constraint on family members.

Stage 2: Explicit Family. If the rules do not preserve the family's sense of identity (e.g., they are ineffective, the crisis continues for a long period of time, and so forth), the "family" begins to feel like a burden to all and no one recognizes their own part in the burden. Each starts to partition themselves off from the family.

Stage 3: Rebellion and Action. At this stage, some of the family members reject the family whereas others make themselves responsible for that conservation of the particular sense of family identity.

In the Christmas dinner example, the chair usually held by the grandmother may remain empty and no one may take her role in leading the evening prayers. This Stage 1 rule may not be explicitly expressed but rather may simply emerge as the family members go to the table for the dinner. In Stage 2, if the grandmother's illness continues and she no longer participates in the daily family activities, each family member may begin to feel the family as a burden. Such feelings may take a variety of different forms from the misbehavior of the children to increased emotional distance between a married couple. Finally, at the end stage of this crisis, certain family members may separate themselves either physically or psychologically from the family whereas others will reestablish and conserve the same sense of family identity.

Interpersonal Communication and Family Well-Being

When faced with problems related to aging family members, members have to assess and reassess the meaning of the family. Ideally, families deal with their problems with some form of negotiation or problem-solving strategy. One family member states a position, seeks and obtains validation for that position from other family members, and the family engages in a straightforward problem-solving exchange. In this scenario, family communication is free of distortion, and all members work toward a resolution until some acceptable solution is obtained. Realistically, this scenario occurs more frequently in a certain type of television show popular in the United States in the 1950s than such scenes occur in real families.

Such an unrealistic communication scenario emerges because families have often been compared to small task-oriented groups. The analogy is a poor one, however, because the types of decisions with which families are faced cannot be evaluated along the same dimensions as can those of a small group within an organization. Small group decision making is based on a rationalist model. This model does not assume that small groups always behave rationally but rather that their performance can be assessed relative to a baseline of optimal performance (Steiner, 1972). Decision outcomes in small groups can be compared objectively, for example, in reference to task outcomes (e.g., investment strategies). The decisions of families dealing as they often do with relational outcomes cannot be compared in such a straightforward manner. How does a family handle an increasingly out-of-control aged member with Alzheimer's disease? Many solutions to such a problem exist and one would to hard-pressed to argue that a given solution was the optimal one.

The function of communication in the task-oriented small group is to facilitate the coordination of inputs from all group members in order to foster an organized and collaborative approach to the task. For families, the function of communication is to facilitate the maintenance of the relationship between members or what we have called the families' sense of well-being. Indeed, the function of communication may be to ensure the social well-being of the family rather than that of any given individual member.

Two predominant styles and forms of decision-making communication can be employed to ensure the maintenance of family identity. Decision making within families varies from implicit, nonreflective patterns of interaction to explicit, strategic communication processes. Indeed, contrary to the small group analogy, family decision making may be indirect, implicit, impulsive, and incremental. With this communication style, family members proceed through silent arrangements and a certain amount of stoicism, and tend to avoid any open conflict or discussion of issues or feelings. An alternative pattern of family decision making, at the opposite end of the continuum, is to be direct, explicit, organized, and proactive (Sillars & Kalbflesch, 1989). In this style, family members are explicit in their bargains and agreements, proceed from a sense of mastery, and are open to engaging in conflict and the disclosure of negative feelings.

During family transitions, which of these styles of communication and decision making are families likely to utilize? The style of communication and decision making used during normative and nonnormative transitions depends on the type of family paradigm adopted by a family.

SYSTEMATIC FAMILY VARIATIONS

For over a decade, I have studied communication in marriage, operating from the basic premise that couples can be differentiated by their perspectives on life in general, marriage, and the roles that husbands and wives play. Such different ideologies produce different patterns of communication and different outcomes. Couples in the various marital types I have identified talk about different things, show affection in different ways, approach disagreement differently, undertake persuasion with different strategies, and engage in varying degrees of self-disclosure (Fitzpatrick, 1988).

In this chapter, I argue that families can also be differentiated from one another in systematic and patterned ways. These differences lead to different interaction styles, and subsequently different outcomes for family systems. Family structure and process affects the communication patterns within families, and how families handle the adaptations necessitated by health problems experienced by aging members. Families vary systematically in their values and attitudes about the nature of family life and in their ways of handling information from the surrounding environment. For the past 20 years, Reiss (1981) and his associates (Steinglass, Bennett, Wolin, & Reiss, 1987) have developed a typology of families, comprised of families with different underlying *family paradigms*.

Family Paradigm

A family paradigm is a core set of assumptions, convictions, or beliefs that each family holds about its environment. These assumptions guide the family to sample certain segments of its world and ignore others. The life of each family is organized by an enduring paradigm that emerges in the course of family development. Paradigms are manifest in the fleeting expectations shared by all members of the family and even more importantly in the routine action patterns of their daily lives.

This model (Reiss, 1981) emphasizes the families' construction of reality. The social construction of reality is represented in the families' interaction with its members. Families differ along three dimensions. The first is *configuration* or the sense of mastery in the family as well as their experience of the world as ordered. The second dimension is *coordination* or the view of the family as a unitary, bounded group capable of collaborative approaches to problem solving. The third dimension is *closure*. Here, families can be flexible and open to environmental input or rigid and dependent on tradition.

This approach is similar to the marital typology in that all possible combinations of dimensions are not hypothesized to exist in a sample of families but rather a certain combination of characteristics yields family types. Using these dimensions as typing characteristics, four types of families emerge.

The *consensus-sensitive* family views problem solving as an opportunity to demonstrate family cohesiveness at all costs, ignoring or underutilizing cues from the external environment, and permitting no dissent from family members. The *environment-sensitive* family fully shares perceptions and hypotheses among family members and uses a variety of intra and extrafamilial cues in problem-solving attempts. The *interpersonal-distance sensitive* family neglects to share information and observations among family members because such a practice is constructed as a weakness. This type does, however, effectively use extrafamilial information. The *achievement-sensitive* family shows a mixture of confident engagement in the task and high levels of competition among family members concerning who will achieve the most.

The family paradigm becomes manifest in a particular kind of problem-solving task. The problem-solving task is called the card-sorting procedure (CSP). The CSP focuses on the family's adaptive style, particularly its capacity to explore, understand, and adjust to novel situations. Families come into a laboratory and are seated in separate booths. Each booth has a signal system and a sorting system with seven ruled columns. Family members can talk to one another on a microphone-earphone apparatus. Each member is given a deck of cards with strings of letters on each card. The family is told that they may sort the cards in any way they wish into as many groups as they wish (up to seven). They can use any method for sorting that seems reasonable to them. The family is faced with an ambiguous task and to some extent they must interpret for themselves what the research staff is up to. It is this shared interpretative activity that is of primary interest. Families are asked to perform this task (with slightly different sets of cards) both individually and as a group. Working with these cards, every subject eventually uses either a pattern or a length system for sorting these cards. From a comparison of how the members do on the task individually to how they do as a group, a great deal can be learned about family process.

Configuration measures the family's growth or deterioration in their ability to recognize the underlying patterns (or configurations) in the deck of cards. Thus, are the family solutions subtle, detailed, and highly structured or coarse, simple, and chaotic? Coordination measures how well the members dovetail their work. It is distinctly different than the previous dimension because family members may share solutions that are subtle or coarse. Families are asked to sort the cards one at a time and to press a signal button after each sort. Highly coordinated families press the button at the same time because they are clearly in the task together. Closure refers to the family's proclivity to suspend or apply order to raw sensory experience. Thus, time to completion of each solution can be measured (Reiss, 1980).

This procedure has been utilized for over 20 years to measure family process. It is not linked to the intelligence, abstract information-processing ability, or personality characteristics of individual family members (Reiss, 1981) but measures distinctly different modes through which families gather, interpret, and exchange information. These types of families have been differentially linked to how the family orients to its social environment (Reiss & Oliveri, 1983); to how the families deal with chronic illness and death (Reiss, Gonzalez, & Kramer, 1986) and with alcoholism (Steinglass et al., 1987).

These four family paradigms and their associated conceptual dimensions have direct implications for the types of bonds formed in multigenerational families. Included in these paradigms are a set of expectations regarding the nature of long-term intergenerational family ties and the nature of interdependence and reciprocity across family members.

There are six major relational bonds (Weiss, 1986). The bonds (Cutrona, in press; Henderson et al., 1981) and their specifications follow:

1. *Attachment.* This bond is based on feelings of security linked to the presence of the person to whom there is attachment. In the presence of that person, the individual feels secure and comparatively free from anxiety.

2. *Affiliation.* This bond is based on the recognition of shared interests that may develop through the belief that situations and their challenges are shared. From this sharedness, feelings of mutuality, affection, respect, and loyalty may develop.

3. *Nurturance.* This bond is based on a sense of commitment, investment, responsibility for, or a desire for responsibility for someone perceived as weak and needful. From this can develop investment in the well-being of the other.

4. *Collaboration.* This bond is based on a feeling of shared commitment to the achievement of a goal. The other is seen as a teammate with whom one's own efforts are coordinated. Associated with this bond is a sense of mutual respect from which may derive support for feelings of self-worth.

5. *Persisting Alliance.* This is a bond that appears to be based on feelings of identification of overlapping identities independent of aims or goals. Strongly associated with it are feelings of obligation to help the other and to be helped by the other.

6. *Help Obtaining.* This is a bond to someone perceived as more knowledgeable and wiser, who is looked to for trustworthy support, and who is felt to be a legitimate source of guidance.

Consensus-sensitive families are expected to exhibit strong parent–child attachment even after the children leave home. Within the marital dyad, there is a strong feeling of attachment, given the high levels of interdependence achieved by these couples, as well as a bond of nurturance. In the family relationships, bonds of persisting alliance, nurturance, and help-obtaining predominate. Families of this type have stronger within-in-family network connections and few individual networks.

Distance-sensitive families are expected to exhibit strong persisting alliance bonds among parents and children. Within the marital dyad, there is significantly less attachment than in the other types and a sense of persisting obligation. Because the major relational bond in this family is one of obligation and identification, under stress there may be a negative tone to the interactions. The major network connections will be within the family although these connections are not expected to be as diverse as in the consensus-sensitive family.

Environment-sensitive families are expected to exhibit a greater range and type of both within family relational bonds as well as friendship networks. The attachment bond in the independent marriage is not as intense as in the traditional one. The marital bond in this marriage is also likely to include affiliation and collaboration. The individuals in this family type will have complex networks with closely knit subsections as well as separate networks for each individual.

The achievement-sensitive family may have collaborative relational bonds within the family lasting as long as such bonds are important to the achievement of a goal. The attachment bond is weaker in this marital form than in the others and it tends to be asymmetrical with one spouse more attached than is the partner. Individuals in these family types will have extensive networks not necessarily shared by family members. Although the bonds in these networks will vary, those concerned with affiliation and help-obtaining relational bonds will predominate.

Individuals within various family paradigms employ different communication styles to deal with the process of aging of family members. Families guided by different paradigms will have different interactional styles both within the family and between the family and the external environment.

Family paradigms incorporate both different styles of marital interaction and a different level of social connection. The marital forms suggest different stresses and tensions involved in negotiating these role changes for couples in the various marital types. The loss of the parental and occupational roles should be a significantly more difficult adjustment for those husbands and wives with traditional ideologies. Whereas, those couples with existing high levels of interdependence and the ability to manage conflict should find the negotiation of new activity patterns in the marriage less stressful.

The negotiation of social network connections differs by family paradigm. Because, at the individual level, health is related to the ability to sustain a variety of types of relationships, the elderly in distance-sensitive families experience significantly less social well-being than do the elderly in the other family forms. Even the marital definition supports psychological distance and autonomy. The loss of a marital partner may be less traumatic for the elderly yet other relational bonds will not fill the gap. The normative process of aging will be more stressful in this family type because more pressure may be placed on the parent–child bond as a consequence of the transitions. The family paradigm may be more difficult to maintain in the face of even normative transitions like retirement and the empty-nest phase for this family type although paradigm maintenance is less difficult during normative transitions for other types.

In the other three family paradigms, the normative transitions can be handled more smoothly because of the variety of network connections. For those whose primary connections are family ones, like the consensus-sensitive families, geographical moves away from the family will be problematic, although we hypothesize these moves are less likely to occur. A crisis like the sudden death of a spouse will be experienced differently in the various paradigms depending both on the level of attachment within the marriage and the strength and variety of the network ties external to the marriage (Stroebe & Stroebe, 1986).

What is the process of communication during family decision making?

Consensus-sensitive families utilize the most implicit decision-making communication style of the family paradigms. Because of the shared values in family members and the lack of tolerance of dissent, these members when faced with a crisis related to aging fall back on implicit agreements and silent arrangements, make decisions in an incremental, day-to-day fashion, use pragmatic linguistic codes in which many cohesion devices are lacking as each assumes the understanding of the other, and, in general, engages in conflict avoidance through the use of denial or joking or a variety of other linguistic forms. Although members of this family do not perceive a sense of mastery, stoicism is their virtue.

In reference to conserving the family paradigm, members also follow implicit rules designed to keep the family functioning as a unit. If the father in the consensus-sensitive family has a stroke, and suffers from aphasia, conversations will continue in the family with the same degree of interaction smoothness as before the stroke. No explicit agreement is needed for the son in this family to fill in the gaps in his father's speech and such a process occurs without awareness.

In general, this family may be said to lack communication in that these members do not engage in open discussions. They are able to maintain the family paradigm against strong odds. Difficulties arise when external information can no longer be ignored. This authoritarian father who ran the family business successfully for many years may not be able to relinquish control to his daughter despite his increasing mental and physical frailty. And dissent is not tolerated.

The achievement-sensitive family utilizes the most explicit decision-making style of the family paradigms. The lack of coordination and sense of mastery in this family produce a reliance on explicit decision-making styles with clearly worded agreements and proactive planning and engagement in conflict. Given the competitive nature of this family, such conflict engagement may rely on distributive strategies such as blaming and personal rejection. In reference to conserving the family paradigm, explicit rules will be established and sanctions applied to those who do not follow these rules.

Both the distance-sensitive and the environment-sensitive families use a combination of implicit and explicit decision-making styles, although these family types differ in that distance-sensitives are less likely than environment-sensitives to engage in open conflict. The implicit style used by the distant sensitive families arises less from a sense of agreement than from a sense of preserving tranquility among family members. The combination of implicit and explicit styles may make the conservation of the family paradigm an easier task in these family types.

One major difference does emerge, however, in studies of chronically ill individuals. Contrary to expectations, Reiss et al. (1986) found that in the environment-sensitive families with a chronically ill member, members tended to die significantly more quickly than did the ill members of the other types. And, those who died had been those most compliant with the medical regime. From our perspective, this suggests that under stress, the environment-sensitive family chooses the maintenance of the family paradigm over the well-being of the individual patient. And, the patient may collude in such a decision by becoming strongly associated with the medical establishment by being the "perfect patient." Sometimes the ability to process information from the external environment and to deal with it explicitly in the family setting may be a mixed blessing.

CONCLUSION

I began this chapter with a discussion of health issues associated with the aging family. I argued that family well-being was the major outcome variable that is obviously and directly related to communication processes within families. In the health context, then, it is family well-being that should be explored by communication researchers rather than direct mental or physical health outcomes. Such family well-being is best examined under conditions of family transitions or crises, either expected or unexpected, that families face. Finally, I introduced the notion of "family paradigms" as a theoretical construct that allows direct predictions of the kind of decision-making communication used by different types of families when confronting health crises associated with aging.

Implicit in this discussion of family paradigms are three basic assumptions that must be taken into account when researchers conduct applied communication research. First, families differ from one another in basic organization and worldview. Such differences are, however, systematic and measurable. Further, to say that families are guided by different paradigms and organized by different regimes means that a few, discrete, measurable family patterns may be uncovered in any sample of families. Within variability, distinct primary forms can be identified.

These different family paradigms go beyond sociological descriptions of the family such as female-headed family, single parent, divorced, and so forth to give the researcher more insight into family dynamics. The researcher or practitioner who must design messages to induce change or to present information to families can use the family paradigm as a way to structure the presentation of information. Consensus-sensitive families, for example, have strong family roles based on age and sex hierarchies and would probably find male authority figures more credible. Furthermore, individuals in these families would prefer to be presented with information that stresses how a given course of action stresses already agreed-upon principles of the family life. Environment-sensitive families, on the other hand, are more open to input from children as well as to open conflict and discussion of feelings. A different informational strategy could be effectively applied to these families. Such applications of the theory are speculative, however, and research needs to be conducted to test these concepts.

Second, families guided by different paradigms will have significantly different interactional styles and relational bonds. The basic reason for considering family paradigms is to be able to predict the pattern and structure of the communication transaction within families over specific issues. Different types of families communicate differently. Thus, one style of communication and decision making is not satisfactory to all.

Applied communication researchers must be sensitive to the actual behavioral differences in family communication patterns. In presenting examples of family life, care should be taken to vary communication styles. Families in general are more comfortable with presentations that are similar to their preferred communication style. Indeed, most family members assume that the manner in which they communicate and interact is the way it is in other families.

Third, a variety of organizing family regimes can be said to define successful family functioning. Family functioning is a multidimensional construct that can be approached in three different ways (Fitzpatrick, 1985). First, does the family accomplish major family goals? Such goals are set by the family and can differ by family type. Second, does the organization of the family violate societal principles? The definition of a family has been significantly broadened in the past 20 years. In many ways, the theorists are attempting to follow the changes in family structures in the society. Certain family paradigms may violate the principles of specific theorists. The question becomes: Whose definition of societal principles predominates? Third, does the family contain a "diseased" member? Such diseases may be psychological or even physical. As we have seen, within each family paradigm exists ways to handle both the normal and unexpected changes associated with aging. The ultimate outcome of such coping mechanisms needs to be evaluated against the goals of the family.

Every family has strengths and weaknesses that vary depending on the crisis faced by the family. Researchers must realize this fact and use care in both the design and presentation of their findings on families. One way to ensure such equal treatment is to have members of various types review and discuss research procedures at every stage of the research process. Members of these different family cultures can shed light on family processes.

The central argument of this chapter has been that researchers cannot understand health, communication, and aging without placing the aged in a family context. My approach to this issue has been to argue that there are different family paradigms and these paradigms drive the interaction that occurs between family members and the types of outcomes that can be experienced from those outcomes.

REFERENCES

Cutrona, C. (in press). Social support and stress in transition to parenthood. *Journal of Abnormal Psychology.*

Fitzpatrick, M. A. (1985). Communication in kin relationships. In M. Knapp & G. R. Miller (Eds.), *Handbook of interpersonal communication* (pp. 687–736). Beverly Hills: Sage.

Fitzpatrick, M. A. (1988). *Between husbands and wives: Communication in marriage.* Newbury Park, CA: Sage.

Henderson, S., Byrne, D., & Duncan-Jones, P. (1981). *Neurosis and the social environment.* New York: Academic Press.

Reiss, D. (1980). Pathways to assessing the family: Some choice points and a sample route. In C. Hofling & J. Lewis (Eds.), *The family: Evaluation and treatment* (pp. 86–121). New York: Bruner/Mazel.

Reiss, D. (1981). *The family's construction of reality.* Cambridge, MA: Harvard University Press.

Reiss, D., Gonzalez, S., & Kramer, N. (1986). Family process, chronic illness, and death: The weakness of strong bonds. *Archives of General Psychiatry, 43,* 795–804.

Reiss, D., & Oliveri, M. (1983). The family's construction of reality and its ties to its kin network: An exploration of causal direction. *Journal of Marriage and the Family, 45,* 81–91.

Sillars, A., & Kalbflesch, P. (1989). Implicit and explicit decision-making styles in couples. In D. Brinberg & J. Jaccard (Eds.), *Dyadic decision-making* (pp. 179–215). New York: Springer-Verlag.

Steiner, I. D. (1972). *Group process and productivity.* New York: Academic Press.

Streinglass, P., Bennett, L., Wolin, S., & Reiss, D. (1987). *The alcoholic family.* New York: Basic Books.

Stroebe, W., & Stroebe, M. (1986). *Bereavement and health: Psychological and physical consequences of partner loss.* Cambridge, MA: Cambridge University Press.

Treas, J., & Bengston, V. L. (1987). The family in later years. In M. Sussman & S. Steinmetz (Eds.), *Handbook of marriage and the family* (pp. 626–645). New York: Plenum Press.

Weiss, R. (1986). Continuities and transformations in social relationships. In W. Hartup & Z. Rubin (Eds.), *Relationships and development* (pp. 96–109). Hillsdale, NJ: Lawrence Erlbaum Associates.

SANDRA L. RAGAN
LYNDA DIXON GLENN
The University of Oklahoma

Whereas the health-care literature is replete with studies addressing women's unique health-care problems and the physician–female patient relationship (see, for example, Corea, 1977; Ehrenreich & English, 1978; Emerson, 1970; Fisher & Todd, 1986; Luker, 1976; Ruzek, 1978; Scull, 1980; Stromberg, 1982; Wallen, Waitzken, & Stoeckel, 1979), few studies have dealt specifically with the communication dimensions of such mundane women's health-care issues as contraceptive counseling and prescription, pregnancy testing and prenatal care, and, most importantly, because of its critical role in the early diagnosis of female reproductive cancers, the gynecologic exam. Interestingly, several studies in medical education and women's health journals report that the "interpersonal relationship" or the "communication skills" of the practitioner comprise an important dimension of the patient's and/or the physician's satisfaction with the gynecologic exam (Domar, 1985–1986; Fang, Hillard, Lindsay, & Underwood, 1984; Lesserman & Luke, 1982); yet these studies have neither described specifically the interaction between physician and patient in women's health-care contexts nor have ferreted out the actual interaction patterns that constitute these desired interpersonal/communication skills.

The absence of naturalistic studies of the interpersonal encounter of physician and patient characterizes the state of health communication literature in general. The health communication literature has heightened our awareness of the impact on patients' attitudes of physicians' interpersonal communication (see, for example, DiMatteo & DiNicola, 1982; Geerston, Gray, & Ward, 1973; Kalisch, 1973; Korsch & Negrete, 1972; Kreps, 1988); we realize further that patient dissatisfaction with health-care interactions is positively related to noncompliance (see, for example, Freemon, Negrete, Davis, & Korsch, 1979; Korsch & Negrete, 1972). As Davis (1968) reported, "the doctor must rely on his [*sic*] ability to establish good rapport in order to inculcate in his patient a positive orientation and commitment to the relationship so that ultimately the patient will follow his advice" (p. 284). But we have not sufficiently studied interaction in the context of gynecologic or any other health-care setting to know how this "good rapport" and "positive orientation" are achieved.

In light of the dearth of studies dealing with communication issues in gynecologic caregiving and the virtual absence of descriptions of natural-istic communication in such women's health-care interactions as the an-nual gynecologic exam, this chapter briefly surveys current literature pertaining to gynecologic health-care issues, in particular the pelvic exam; proposes a rationale for conducting research in this area from a discourse analytic perspective; reports on several recent studies that utilize the methodology of discourse analysis to describe actual conversational prac-tices in gynecologic health-care interactions; and suggests directions for subsequent research in this area.

REVIEW OF RELEVANT GYNECOLOGIC HEALTH-CARE LITERATURE

The overriding conclusion that can be drawn from the health-care educa-tion literature about gynecologic health care, in particular the gynecologic examination, is that the exam is perceived negatively by patients and medical practitioners alike. One study (Weiss & Meadow, 1979) showed that 85% of 75 women patient subjects reported negative feelings about their last pelvic exam, including descriptions of anxiety, vulnerability, humiliation, and dehumanization. Other research reports that pelvic ex-ams are abhorred by many women, that such exams are dreaded, post-poned, and traumatizing (Domar, 1985–1986; Leserman & Luke, 1982; Olson, 1981). Such studies also reveal, however, that practitioners, in particular medical students, perceive the pelvic exam to be problematic (Domar, 1985–1986; Fang et al., 1984; Leserman & Luke, 1982; Summey & Hurst, 1986). As Leserman and Luke (1982) attested, "the cultural taboos associated with female genitalia" (p. 31) make the teaching of the routine pelvic examination more problematic than the teaching of other aspects of the physical exam.

Domar (1985–1986) reported that the exam procedure and the lithotomy position "strike directly against traditional values such as modesty and respectability" (p. 75), a view reiterated by Tunnadine (1973) and Alexander and McCullough (1981). Emerson (1970) in her classic ethnographic study of the gynecologic exam also spoke to the problematic nature of this exam as compared with other physical exams. She described the gynecologic exam as a precarious event in the sense that it must simultaneously sustain several contradictory definitions of reality. The medical procedures of the exam itself are, of course, the predominant reality, with the medical definition of the situation justifying both the medical staff's invasion of the patient's privacy and the patient's acquiescence. But the counterdefinitions that must also be maintained in the exam are the acknowledgments of the patient as person and the pelvic area as special, rather than the treating of the patient, in the strictly medical sense, as technical object. Thus, it is well established in the literature that the gynecologic exam is acknowledged by patient *and* practitioner as an invasion of personal space and therefore a procedure that arouses some degree of nervousness and dread among participants, regardless of which end of the examining table they occupy.

The inherent cultural problematics of the exam and the negative affect with which many women patients and, in particular, male health-care providers view it has served to ironically exacerbate women's negative feelings about the exam. Because of the exam's "precarious reality" and the necessity of making it devoid of sexual content, traditional medical school instruction in pelvic examination procedures has consisted of the use of plastic breast and pelvic models rather than live flesh and blood models (Domar, 1985–1986; Fang et al., 1984; Leserman & Luke, 1982). This traditional approach to teaching medical students how to perform a gynecologic exam has focused on technical rather than social, psychological aspects of the exam, according to Leserman and Luke (1982). It is no wonder, then, that the performance of such exams has been widely criticized in women's health-care literature, especially in terms of how physicians treat their patients. Billings and Stoeckle (1977) and Corea (1977) reported such problems as physicians' lack of sensitivity to and respect for women (including ignoring patient education about the exam process, ignoring patient comfort, etc.) as constituting some of women's complaints about the process.

Domar (1985–1986) summarized the findings of four studies that specifically asked women how they felt about pelvic exams and invited suggestions as to how they could be improved. Although the sampling procedures are flawed for these studies (i.e., none of the studies provided information about those potential subjects who refused to participate in the study), they nonetheless shed light on the sources of women's discontent with gynecologic exams. In short, most of the women studied reported that the pelvic exam could be improved by: talking to the doctor prior to the exam, receiving explanations and discussing outcomes of the exam, having the doctor talk about the exam and encourage questions, establishing rapport with the doctor, feeling a sense of caring and concern from the doctor rather than his or her rushing or appearing distracted, and having the doctor give time and instructions on how to relax vaginal muscles prior to the exam (Debrovner & Shubin-Stein, 1975; Haar, Halitsky, & Strickler, 1977; Petravage, Reynolds, Gardner, & Reading, 1979; Weiss & Meadow, 1979). In one study (Weiss & Meadow, 1979), 87% of the subjects recommended changes in the personal interactions between patient and physician.

In light of these patient complaints, recent innovations in the teaching of pelvic exam procedures to medical students have attempted to focus on the social and psychological, the interpersonal aspects of the examination (Domar, 1985–1986; Fang et al., 1984; Leserman & Luke, 1982). Rather than using plastic facsimiles of female reproductive parts and asking students to examine these plastic models, several studies have incorporated the use of gynecologic teaching assistants (GTAs) who have played the role of patient, permitting the student to perform an actual gynecologic exam with patient feedback (see Fang et al., 1984; Leserman & Luke, 1982, for reports of such studies). Whereas the results of these less traditional teaching experiments demonstrate that students who received live model instruction had "significantly better interpersonal skills" than those who received plastic model instruction, such "interpersonal skills" are not clearly delineated in the research design. Rather, Fang et al. (1984) surmised in an overly general summary statement: "the GTAs not only provided instruction through demonstration but also served as ideal role models of interpersonal interactions" (p. 760). In another innovative approach to teaching medical students how to do a pelvic examination, a Women's Health Teaching Group consisting of both women medical students and trained community women was organized to teach routine pelvic exams to health professionals, emphasizing the interpersonal as well as the technical aspects of the exam (Leserman & Luke, 1982). Again, however, the research report does not clarify which "interpersonal" aspects were emphasized. It does report, however, that "communication skills between physicians and patients, patient education, giving patients options, and patient comfort were considered more necessary after the teaching experience" (p. 41).

As Domar (1985–1986) summarized, the education of physicians is changing in that increased emphasis on patients' psychological well-being in the pelvic exam interaction is stressed. Such a "psychosocial orientation" has lead to significant improvements in exam performance, communication skills, patient sense of control and participation, and decreased anxiety and discomfort for patient and medical student alike (Billings & Stoeckle, 1977; Livingston & Ostrow, 1978; Smilkstein, DeWolfe, Erwin, McIntyre, & Shuford, 1980; Vontner et al., 1980).

It appears, then, that medical education is making positive strides in the direction of improving attitudes toward the pelvic exam and, in particular, in incorporating such notions as communication skills, rapport, and other interpersonal aspects of the exam into the training procedures of students. What is disconcerting in this literature is the ambiguity surrounding the discussion of these interpersonal features of a pelvic exam. Which "communication and interpersonal skills" are physicians/medical students being taught that directly contribute to patients' and practitioners' greater satisfaction with the exam procedure? If, as most communication researchers assert, interpersonal communication is a dynamic, transactional process, what is the role of the patient in furthering the "psychosocial orientation" of the exam, in promoting rapport and an increased comfort level for both interactants? At a more basic level yet, what do we know about the actual interaction that occurs between patient and practitioner in the context of a gynecologic exam that might promote interpersonal rapport? It would seem necessary at this point to be able to provide descriptions and analyses of actual exam interactions before we can suggest prescriptions for effective communication and interpersonal skills. The next section of this chapter provides a rationale for investigating the communicative dimensions of gynecologic caregiving by observing and analyzing naturally occurring interaction.

A RATIONALE FOR DISCOURSE ANALYTIC STUDIES OF MEDICAL INTERACTION

"Although there is mounting evidence pointing to the generic importance of communication in defining health and illness in patient–physician encounters, relatively minor attention has been paid to the actual speech organizations within which problems are established, treatments are negotiated, and outcomes are finally realized" (Frankel, 1984a, p. 103).

Frankel (1983, 1984a, 1984b) is undoubtedly the most articulate and prolific proponent of the need to enlist naturally occurring speech activity in the study of the physician–patient relationship. Although several other researchers have conducted discourse analytic studies of doctor–patient interaction (see, e.g., the work of Fisher & Todd, 1986; Todd, 1984; West, 1983, 1984), Frankel's work provides the most complete rationale for the use of "microinteractional analysis" to understand the medical encounter. Frankel (1984a) explained that because much of the work of medicine is accomplished through language in the "mutual participation of social actors in producing orderly exchanges of dialog" (pp. 135–36), we as researchers need to attend to the *production* of health status within communication rather than concentrating only on health status as a *product* of communication:

> If it is the case that knowledge is always bound in its expression to particular social and linguistic contexts, then the properties of action which furnish direction and meaning to medical encounters are interactionally, not individually based . . . for physicians and patients as speakers and hearers this means that neither "end" of the relationship is entirely free to control the substance and flow of a transaction . . . to the extent that the expression of an individual's medical concerns depends upon an order of mutual social participation, the concepts of health, health status, and health and illness have analytic usefulness only insofar as they are enacted, i.e., emerge as operative elements in the stream and structure of communicative events. (p. 136)

In addition to a theoretical concern with the relationship between language and the social interaction of doctors and patients, which has spurred a growing number of discourse analytic studies of medical communication, West and Frankel (in press) pointed to a distinct advantage of discourse-based studies: because such studies depict the actual speaking practices of medical interactants through verbatim transcripts of audio and video recordings, they can in fact display data in a directly observable manner. For example, whereas studies in medical education journals allude to "improved communication and interpersonal skills" when medical students are trained to examine live models, such interaction skills can be actually displayed in the conversational transcripts of discourse analytic studies. Further, as West and Frankel (in press) elaborated, instances of miscommunication between patient and doctor, which have plagued medical discourse and promoted patient dissatisfaction with medical encounters, can be evidenced in the discourse itself.

This need for such discourse analyses becomes more pressing when we survey recent communication studies that unequivocally emphasize the importance of assessing interpersonal dimensions of health-care communication (see, e.g., Burgoon et al., 1987; Kreps, 1988; Street & Wiemann, 1987). Whereas these studies conclude that the relationship between physician and patient is critical to patient satisfaction with the health-care encounter, they do not examine naturally occurring discourse to see how this relationship is mutually negotiated and enacted. Burgoon et al. (1987), for example, found that optimal physician communication behavior exhibited a simultaneous showing of receptivity, involvement, relaxation, and formality: "Physicians' relational messages featuring more perceived receptivity, immediacy, composure, formality, and similarity and less dominance show a substantial relationship to patients' satisfaction (p. 320). Likewise, Wheeless (1987) stated, in summarizing her findings that women patients' perceptions of trust and receptivity correlated with positive feelings toward their gynecologists: "The use of communication that builds trust between patient and doctor and communication that creates a less stressful environment might help in increasing interaction that would build knowledge about one's medical needs, and ultimately, better health care" (p. 208). These findings are based on patients' perceptions, on recall and questionnaire data; there is also a compelling need to examine the actual discourse of health-care provider and patient in order to discover and describe the interaction patterns that mutually create a satisfying interpersonal climate. The remainder of this chapter reports summaries of three discourse analytic studies of women patients' interactions with gynecologic health-care providers (Ragan, 1988, 1989; Ragan & Pagano, 1987) followed by suggestions for further research in women's health-care communication.

ANALYSES OF GYNECOLOGIC HEALTH-CARE INTERACTIONS

Two sets of naturalistic data were collected for the studies described in this section of the chapter: the first consists of approximately eight hours of tape-recorded interaction between a female nurse practitioner and 41 patients who had sought contraception and/or an annual gynecologic exam at a university health center; the second data set is comprised of tape-recorded interactions of 26 female patients who visited an urban public health facility for Native Americans—for pregnancy testing, gynecologic examination, and prenatal care. These 26 patients were treated by a female physician's assistant. Analysis of the verbatim transcriptions produced from the tape recordings of these interactions focuses on several interpersonal aspects of provider–patient encounters, including the display of social (nonmedical) discourse, verbal play, and shared laughter. The next section summarizes results of those analyses and cites examples from the patient–health-care provider interactions.

Sociable Commentary

West (1984) noted that much of medical conversation is devoid of talk that is not specifically devoted to medical goals, that is, talk that is primarily social in function, or as West termed it, "sociable commentary." This absence becomes particularly notable and perplexing when we realize that medical practitioners today are called in to deal with the whole patient, with a myriad complex of that patient's medical and social needs, as Frankel (1984b) attested:

> It is now widely acknowledged that the reasons for seeking health care extend well beyond the boundaries of biological disease, and into the areas of social, emotional, and psychological functioning. Consequently, the recent advances of medical science are in danger of becoming its greatest pitfall, as physicians trained to combat disease encounter increasing numbers of patients whose problems and concerns do not admit to strict biomedical or technological solutions. (p. 103)

West (1984) claimed that most researchers have purposefully excluded the study of "sociable" exchange in their analyses of health-care communication, either because they have not expected to find enough of this phenomenon to study or because they have considered nonmedical talk to be outside the purview of the serious investigation of medical concerns in the health-care interaction. In one of a growing number of empirical analyses of the social exchange patterns in medical discourse, West found that the virtual absence of laughter, greetings, and other features of interpersonal discourse helped to create further relational distance between patient and caregiver. She also found that the production of any existing sociable conversation in medical interactions was under the control of the physician; specific interaction patterns contributing to this control included the physician's ignoring or interrupting any nonmedical talk of the patient and the physician's refusal to join in patient-initiated laughter.

In the data examined for the current studies in gynecologic health-care interactions, the transcripts were replete with instances of "sociable commentary," with conversational asides that only peripherally related to the expressed medical agendas of patient or caregiver or that were devoid of medical content altogether. Further, laughter was a prevalent phenomenon in these conversations, shared laughter being a commonplace, as well as joking, teasing, and verbal play, all of which appeared to be mutually enacted rather than controlled by one interactant. At this point, a caveat may need to be inserted to remind the reader that these studies being reported cannot be generalized to gynecologic health-care interactions as a whole; they comprise case studies because data was collected from only one licensed nurse practitioner and one physician's assistant. Further, these caregivers are both female, which may impact the occurrence of social discourse in the medical interactions, and neither is a doctor, which no doubt also affects the interpersonal dynamic of the interactions. Nonetheless, it is useful to investigate in depth medical interactions that have occurred and could occur in the context of women's health care, particularly when existing literature reports the absence of social discourse in women's health-care interactions and prevalent patient dissatisfaction with these interactions (Kallen & Stephenson, 1981; Todd, 1984; West, 1983, 1984). Especially because women's health-care contexts have been undervalued and largely unexplored in the literature, it is imperative that we be able to describe such environments before we can prescribe effective interpersonal behavior on the part of the patient or the caregiver.

Role-Taking: Treating the Patient With Empathy

In the data analyzed for both the university health center and the public health-care facility, the caregiver continually acknowledges awareness and appreciation for the anxiety, discomfort, occasional pain, and frequent embarrassment that are inherent to some women in a pelvic examination. *Role-taking,* or a direct expression of empathy, frequently occurs, particularly when the provider is giving a woman her first pelvic exam, as in the following extract:

Provider: Well if you can remember to keep your tummy muscles relaxed and your thigh muscles as relaxed as possible it's real hard to do when especially when you're (hhh) uptight=

Patient: Well, isn't everybody? huh huh huh huh=

Provider: =heh heh heh uh yeah (.hhh) but you know if you tighten those up it tightens up your vaginal muscles okay?

Patient: Um hm.

Provider: And if you can remember that the speculum is smaller than a guy (1.0) that sometimes helps too okay? So it's nothing *huge* we're gonna put in there.

Especially when one considers the medical jargon that frequently obscures clarity and produces miscommunication and patient dissatisfaction in health-care interactions (see West & Frankel, in press), the nurse's use of the vernacular in this instance is notable. Many women can recall a physician's advising that they "relax" during the course of a pelvic exam, but this health-care practitioner's verbal techniques are expansive. Following her indirect request that the patient relax her muscles, the nurse expresses empathy for the patient's probable anxiety—"it's real hard to do especially when you're uptight." She addresses a range of physical and psychological needs of this patient by not only giving advice that will enhance the patient's physical comfort, but in addition by using the analogy that the "speculum is smaller than a guy," a comforting fact to a woman who has experienced sexual intercourse (as this patient has) but who has not been given a pelvic examination before.

In another instance, when the patient has just nonverbally expressed discomfort with the exam, the nurse is again empathic and sympathetic:

Provider: Doin' okay?

Patient: Yeah: I just tense up.

Provider: Yeah.

Patient: I don't *like* this heh heh hehh

Provider: And when you tense up that makes your vaginal muscles more tense.

Patient: (hhh) umm: deep breaths right?

Provider: Yep heh heh heh heh=

Patient: =heh heh heh

Provider: Relax (2.5) try to make those muscles as loose as possible

Patient: hah hah hah

Provider: That is real *real* hard to do.

Patient: Yeah heh heh heh heh
          [ ]

Provider: heh heh it's easy for *me* to say I'm on *this* end of the examining table right?

Patient: um right.

The examination conversations contain many instances of this provider's attempts to relax the patient physically as well as psychologically. She carefully explicates the exam procedures and constantly monitors the patient's state, skillfully interweaving instructing, relaxing, empathizing, and examining in her talk.

Much of the patients' dissatisfaction reported in the health communication literature centers around beliefs that they are treated as presenting symptoms rather than as whole persons. In the data for the studies reported, the health-care provider monitors patients' emotional and physical status, continually expressing interest in their overall well-being. In the data set from the university health center, for example, the licensed nurse practitioner (LNP) asks 200 questions of the patients (comprising 55% of the 366 questions asked overall) that are nonmedical in nature. She inquires of patients' family lives, their classes and school problems, their vacation plans, and so forth. Further, this LNP offers information about herself, even to the point of self-disclosing her own health habits, as for example, in the following excerpt:

Provider: I can always tell when I drink too much coffee. I get irritated and I have to eliminate more frequently=

Patient: =Do ya? Hm

Provider: So it definitely does have an effect.

In the talk immediately preceding the excerpt just given, the LNP has asked the patient whether she has to urinate frequently. In providing information about her own urinary habits, she is informing the patient about a possible reason for frequent urination if the patient is concerned about this. The LNP's personalization of this discussion with an admission of her own health practices possibly creates rapport while also giving information.

Shared Laughter/Verbal Play

Our studies of gynecologic health-care interaction also analyze shared laughter and verbal play as interpersonal dimensions of patient–caregiver communication. Whereas West (1984) reported from her analyses that "doctor–patient talk contains few 'laughing matters' " (p. 126), we did not find this true of examining-room conversations. In the 41 interaction transcriptions analyzed in the university health center study (Ragan, 1988; Ragan & Pagano, 1987), 149 instances of shared laughter were coded; that is, both patient and caregiver joined in laughter initiated by the other. (By contrast, West found that doctors joined in patient-initiated laughter only 6% of the time, whereas patients joined in doctor-initiated laughter only 22% of the time.)

Laughter was frequently interspersed with information giving, information eliciting, and role-taking, as shown in the following excerpt:

Provider: Have have you noticed after you've been on the pills that your periods are don't last as long or are they shorter or=

Patient: =Yes they're shorter
         (8.5)

Provider: It's a lot nicer havin' em for a shorter length of time isn't it heh heh heh
         [ ]

Patient: heh heh yes it is

Provider: (Bet) you can tell just like clockwork too when you have your
           periods can't ya?
Patient: Um hm
Provider: Plan holidays around them heh heh heh
                                        [ ]
Patient: heh heh heh=
Provider: =(vacations) no abnormal tenderness in here is there?
Patient: No.

This example is interesting also in that the LNP achieves several agendas
during the course of this examination talk: She gives and gets information,
she expresses empathy, she initiates laughter, and she examines the
patient. This instance is possibly an exemplar for creating rapport with a
patient, for treating the patient as person rather than as symptom or
technical object, while also conducting the exam procedure. This conversational instance displays that caregivers *can* manage to attend to the
interpersonal/relational process without sacrificing the need to efficiently
examine the patient.

In further analyses of instances of joking, teasing, and verbal play in
a gynecologic exam interaction (Ragan, 1988, 1989), findings indicate that
patient and female health-care practitioner cooperate to mutually produce
moments of playfulness in the exam. In the following example the practitioner has just completed the pelvic exam:

Provider: All done: (2.4) that's *it:*
           (3.5)
Patient: (hhh) Gee *that* was fun.
                             [   ]
Provider: heh heh heh heh heh
                            [   ]
Patient: heh heh heh heh heh heh
           (1.2)
Provider: Oh you wanna do it *again?* heh heh heh heh=
Patient: =heh heh heh
Provider: Okay so I'll run all this stuff to the lab.

The occurrences of shared laughter, amplified by the facetious tones with
which the patient offers, "gee that was fun," and the practitioner later
responds, "Oh you wanna do it again?", achieve a playfulness in the exam
that must be jointly produced by interactants. Here, and in many instances

from these exam transcripts, we see a patient and a health-care practitioner mutually enacting an "interpersonal encounter," which, no doubt, adds to the satisfaction of each in the exam interaction. Whereas the literature has emphasized the need for interpersonal and communication skills in the physician, it is highly probable that such "skills" are interactively achieved; that is, it is equally necessary for the patient to demonstrate interpersonal competence in the exam. Such transcripts as the ones just presented might be useful heuristically to display how such interactive competence, and resulting communication satisfaction for both participants, could be enacted.

IMPLICATIONS AND DIRECTIONS FOR ADDITIONAL RESEARCH

In addition to displaying and describing patient–provider interpersonal interaction through naturalistic discourse, as in the examples cited in the preceding section, it would be useful to enlist both women patients and their gynecologic health-caregivers to assess their communication satisfaction with gynecologic encounters. Transcripts, used in conjunction with audio and video recordings, could be evaluated by both interactants for their effectiveness in achieving desired interpersonal outcomes. In addition, both interactants could be interviewed in order to assess which communication and interpersonal skills were seen as desirable in the gynecologic health-care encounter; in this way, any disparities between the two perspectives could surface. The education of both practitioner and patient could benefit from an approach that incorporated both perspectives.

Whereas studies are beginning to address the need for patient as well as physician education in promoting effective health-care encounters, there is as yet too little emphasis on the interactive dimension of health-care communication, which is as dependent on the patient's interpersonal competence as the caregiver's. As Domar (1985–1986) asserted, the educational pelvic exam, in which the patient receives extensive explanation about the exam both before and during it, has met with mixed success in terms of improving patients' positive responses. Studies have not been conducted, however, that attempt to teach women patients about their contributions to potentially satisfying interpersonal/communication aspects of the exam. As with traditional teaching methods for medical students that incorporated the use of plastic models, the emphasis on patients' education has been in teaching them the technical aspects of the exam (e.g., holding a hand mirror while the physician explains the anatomy seen) rather than the interpersonal. Thus, the education for the patient as well as the medical caregiver must focus on instruction that encompasses the entirety of the encounter, not merely the technical procedure of the exam. Although we are well aware that it is the nonmedical aspects of the exam which create psychological discomfort for both parties, we continue to permit the medical model of health care to largely inform our teaching of both caregiver and patient. The interpersonal process of gynecologic health care deserves equal focus and attention if the pelvic exam is to lessen the mortality rate of women's reproductive cancers.

At this point, it might be useful also to reiterate that this interpersonal process is unique in that it involves female patients whose female parts are being examined. In the discourse analytic studies of gynecologic interaction reported (Ragan, 1988, 1989; Ragan & Pagano, 1987), the health-care providers were also female. Is there an inherent advantage to a female health-care provider examining the female parts of female patients? It is certainly probable that the interpersonal dynamic of the exam in the excerpts cited—in particular, role-taking, empathy, shared laughter, and verbal play—are mediated by the gender of the provider as well as by her status. Thus, we need to know more about what roles both gender and status play in gynecologic health care. Ragan and Pagano (1987) collected questionnaire data of their subjects after the exam interaction and discovered that 98% of them would recommend the practitioner they had just seen to a friend. Whereas the study does not ascribe a causal relationship between verbal interaction (as displayed in the verbatim transcripts from the exam interactions) and patients' overwhelming satisfaction with the nurse practitioner, it raises interesting questions about both whether the interactions directly contribute to satisfaction and, if so, whether they would be seen as effective if the health-care provider were male and/or a doctor. Some studies indicate that female health professionals are preferred by a majority of women gynecological patients (Haar et al., 1975; Engleman, 1974); an additional study found that women patients prefer a female practitioner regardless of her professional level (i.e., the distinction between physician and nurse practitioner was a much less important factor than gender for many women, especially low-income and Mexican-American subjects; Alexander & McCullough, 1981). Thus, future studies assessing the role of communication and interpersonal dynamics in gynecologic health care will need to test for the effects of the health-care provider's gender and status. Alexander and McCullough (1981) asserted that much of the improvement in satisfaction with the use of female physicians and nurse practitioners appears due to reduced embarrassment and improved communication; if these are inherent features of female patient–female practitioner gynecologic interaction that, due to cultural mores, cannot be as effectively achieved by male practitioners, then our medical practices need to reflect that insofar as possible.

In addition to taking into account women patients' preferences for the sex and role of their gynecologic examiners, we also need to realize patients' individual differences and unique coping styles before we can adequately assess the role of communication in the gynecologic exam. Domar (1985–1986) stressed the need for tailoring the exam to the individual in terms of educational and psychological preparation for it; in her study, individual differences in coping styles had a strong impact on the efficacy of preparation. She also asserted that coping styles and anxiety levels may be very different for adolescents prior to their first pelvic exams than for women with more gynecologic experience. Intuitively, one would surmise that the history of gynecologic experience would affect the caregiver as well: medical students' anxieties about performing the exam probably differ from veteran ob-gyns'. Thus, in addition to weighing the effects of gender, role, and individual coping styles and anxiety levels in assessing communication in the gynecologic exam, it would make sense to approach future research from a developmental or life-span perspective, taking into account the history and experience of participants vis-a-vis gynecologic health care.

To summarize, future study in communication and gynecologic health care calls for research that takes an interpersonal perspective, beginning with the analysis of naturalistic discourse but later incorporating a pluralistic methodology, including survey, questionnaire, and experimental data, in order to test for patient and health-care provider satisfaction with specific interpersonal dynamics. Provider *and* patient education need to be taken into account in assessing communication effectiveness in the gynecologic encounter, as well as individual preferences for examiner's sex and status, different patient coping styles, and the life-span experiences of both interactants.

It is difficult to suggest future research in health-care communication in the gynecologic context without also advocating a feminist and a phenomenological perspective to guide it. The feminist paradigm—one that regards gender roles as having direct impact on the phenomenon under investigation, one that considers women's experiences not only as different from men's but as appropriate (and heretofore undervalued) data for analysis, and one that seeks both to understand and to change social life (Foss & Foss, 1989)—is appropriate for this context because of its inherent female and culturally problematic nature. Further, Husserl's (1952) insistence on suspending presuppositions about the nature of reality and systematically describing the phenomenon itself gets realized in the investigation of everyday social interaction—in this case, the gynecologic exam interaction itself. McBride and McBride (1981) incorporated this phenomenological perspective in advocating women's "lived experience" as the beginning point and the theoretical underpinning for women's health care: "To take seriously the lived experience of women as one's starting-point, is to reject, whatever the details of one's subsequent methodology may be, a long-standing alternative tradition of preferring the standpoint of the external, supposedly 'scientific' and 'objective' observer to that of the actual subjects of one's study in their real-life situations" (p. 46). Thus, to study communication and women's health care is to also study women's "lived experience," both as it is told in interview and as it occurs in natural interaction. Without these descriptive-explanatory stages in theory building, we will not be able to prescribe effective health-care communication in the gynecologic context.

REFERENCES

Alexander, K., & McCullough, J. (1981). Women's preferences for gynecological examiners: Sex versus role. *Women and Health, 6*(3/4), 123–134.

Billings, J. A., & Stoeckle, J. D. (1977). Pelvic examination instruction and the doctor–patient relationship. *Journal of Medical Education, 52,* 834–839.

Burgoon, J. K., Pfau, Parrott, R., Birk, T., Coker, R., & Burgoon, M. (1987). Relational communication, satisfaction, compliance-gaining strategies, and compliance in communication between physicians and patients. *Communication Monographs, 54,* 307–324.

Corea, G. (1977). *The hidden malpractice: How American medicine treats women as patients and professionals.* New York: William Morrow.

Davis, M. S. (1968). Variations in patients' compliance with doctors' advice: An empirical analysis of patterns of communication. *American Journal of Public Health, 58*(2), 274–288.

Debrovner, C., & Shubin-Stein, R. (1975). Psychological aspects of vaginal examinations. *Medical Aspects of Human Sexuality, 9,* 163–164.

DiMatteo, M. R., & DiNicola, D. D. (1982). *Achieving patient compliance: The psychology of the medical practitioner's role.* New York: Pergamon.

Domar, A. D. (1985–1986). Psychological aspects of the pelvic exam: Individual needs and physician involvement. *Women and Health, 10*(4), 75–90.

Ehrenreich, B., & English, E. (1978). *For her own good.* Garden City, NY: Anchor Press/Doubleday.

Emerson, J. (1970). Behavior in private places: Sustaining definitions of reality in gynecological examinations. In H. P. Dreitzel (Ed.), *Recent sociology, No. 2: Patterns of communicative behavior* (pp. 73–79). New York: Macmillan.

Engleman, E. G. (1974). Attitudes toward women physicians. *Western Journal of Medicine, 120,* 95–100.

Fang, W. L., Hillard, P. J., Lindsay, R. L., & Underwood, P. B. (1984). Evaluation of students' clinical and communication skills in performing a gynecologic examination. *Journal of Medical Education, 59,* 758–760.

Fisher, S., & Todd, A. D. (Eds.). (1986). *Discourse and institutional authority: Medicine, education, and the law.* Norwood, NJ: Ablex.

Foss, K., & Foss, S. (1989). Incorporating the feminist perspective in communication scholarship: A research commentary. In K. Carter & C. Spitzack (Eds.), *Doing research on women's communication: Alternative perspectives in theory and method* (pp. 65–91). Norwood, NJ: Ablex.

Frankel, R. M. (1983). The laying on of hands: Aspects of the organization of gaze, touch, and talk in a medical encounter. In S. Fisher & A. Todd (Eds.), *The social organization of doctor–patient communication* (pp. 19–51). Washington, DC: Center for Applied Linguistics Press.

Frankel, R. M. (1984a). From sentence to sequence: Understanding the medical encounter through microinteractional analysis. *Discourse Processes, 7,* 135–170.

Frankel, R. M. (1984b). Physicians and patients in social interaction: Medical encounters as a discourse process. *Discourse Processes, 7,* 103–105.

Freemon, B., Negrete V. F., Davis, M., & Korsch, B. M. (1979). Gaps in doctor–patient communication: Doctor–patient interaction analysis. *Pediatric Research, 5,* 298–311.

Geerston, H. R., Gray, R. M., & Ward, R. (1973). Patient non-compliance within the context of seeking medical care for arthritis. *Journal of Chronic Disorders, 26,* 689–698.

Haar, E., Halitsky, V., & Stricker, G. (1977). Factors related to the preference for a female gynecologist. *Medical Care, 13,* 782–790.

Husserl, E. (1952). *Ideas* (Gibson WRB, Trans.). New York: Macmillan.

Kalisch, B. J. (1973). What is empathy? *American Journal of Nursing, 73,* 1548–1552.

Kallen, D. J., & Stephenson, J. J. (1981). Perceived physician humaneness, patient attitude, and satisfaction with the pill as a contraceptive. *Journal of Health and Social Behavior, 22,* 256–267.

Korsch, B. M., & Negrete, V. F. (1972). Doctor–patient communication. *Scientific America, 227,* 66–74.

Kreps, G. L. (1988). The pervasive role of information in health and health care: Implications for health communication policy. In J. Anderson, (Ed.), *Communication yearbook 11* (pp. 238–275). Beverly Hills: Sage.

Leserman, L., & Luke, C. S. (1982). An evaluation of an innovative approach to teaching the pelvic examination to medical students. *Women and Health, 7*(2), 31–42.

Livingston, R., & Ostrow, D. (1978). Professional patient- instructors in the teaching of the pelvic examination. *American Journal of Obstetrics and Gynecology, 132*(1), 64–67.

Luker, D. (1976). *Taking chances: Abortion and the decision not to contracept.* Berkeley: University of California Press.

McBride, G. B., & McBride, W. L. (1981). Theoretical underpinnings for women's health. *Women and Health, 6*(1/2), 37–55.

Olson, B. (1981). Patient comfort during pelvic examinations. *Obstetrics Gynecology, 301,* 146 151.

Petravage, J., Reynolds, L., Gardner, H., & Reading, J. (1979). Attitudes of women toward the gynecologic examination. *Journal of Family Practice, 9*(6), 1039–1045.

Ragan, S. L. (1988). *Nurse practitioner/patient goals displayed in verbal play in the gynecologic exam interaction.* Paper presented at the Ninth Annual Temple University Discourse Analysis Conference, Philadelphia.

Ragan, L. A. (1989, May). *When it is not a laughing matter: Unshared laughter in gynecologic health care interactions.* Paper presented at the annual meeting of the International Communication Association, San Francisco.

Ragan, S. L., & Pagano, M. (1987). Communicating with female patients: Affective interaction during contraceptive counseling and gynecologic exams. *Women's Studies in Communication, 10,* 45–57.

Ruzek, S. B. (1978). *The women's health movement.* New York: Praeger.

Scull, D. (1980). *Men who control women's health: The miseducation of obstetrician-gynecologists.* Boston: Houghton-Mifflin.

Smilkstein, G., DeWolfe, D., Erwin, M., McIntyre, M., & Shuford, D. (1980). A biomedical-psychosocial format for an educational pelvic examination. *Journal of Medical Education, 55,* 630–663.

Street, R. L., & Wiemann, J. M. (1987). Patients' satisfaction with physicians' interpersonal involvement, expressiveness, and dominance. In M. L. McLaughlin (Ed.), *Communication yearbook 10* (pp. 591–612). Beverly Hills: Sage.

Stromberg, A. (1982). *Women, health and medicine.* Palo Alto: Mayfield.

Summey, P. S., & Hurst, M. (1986). Ob/gyn on the rise: The evolution of professional ideology in the twentieth century—part 2. *Women and Health, 11*(2), 103–122.

Todd, A. D. (1984). The prescription of contraception: Negotiations between doctors and patients. *Discourse Processes, 7,* 171–200.

Tunnadine, P. (1973). Psychological aspects of the vaginal examination. *Human Sexuality, 7,* 116–138.

Vontner, L., Irby, E., Rakestraw, P., Haddock, M., Prince, E., & Stenchever, M. (1980). The effects of two methods of pelvic examination instruction on student performance and anxiety. *Journal of Medical Education, 55,* 778–785.

Wallen, J., Waitzken, H., & Stoeckle, J. D. (1979). Physician stereotypes about female health and illness: A study of patient's sex and the informative process during medical interviews. *Women and Health, 4*(2), 135–146.

Weiss, L., & Meadow, R. (1979). Women's attitudes toward gynecologic practices. *Obstetrics and Gynecology, 54*(1), 110–114.

West, C. (1983). "Ask me no questions . . ."—an analysis of queries and replies in physician–patient dialogues. In S. Fisher & A. Todd (Eds.), *The social organization of doctor–patient communication* (pp. 75–105). Washington, DC: Center for Applied Linguistics Press.

West, C. (1984). *Routine complications: Troubles with talk between doctors and patients.* Bloomington: IN: Indiana University Press.

West, C. & Frankel, R. M. (in press). Miscommunication in medicine. In N. Coupland, H. Giles, & J. Wiemann (Eds.), *The handbook of miscommunication and problematic talk.* Avon, England: Multilingual Matters.

Wheeless, V. E. (1987). Female patient and physician communication and discussion of gynecological health care issues. *Southern Speech Communication Journal, 52,* 198–211.

DENTIST–PATIENT COMMUNICATION: A REVIEW AND COMMENTARY

16

RICHARD L. STREET, JR.
Texas A&M University

In recent years, the role of interpersonal communication in the delivery of health care has been a focus of study among practitioners, educators, and researchers. We have recognized that, in spite of sophisticated technologies for diagnosis and treatment, talk between the patient and health-care provider remains the primary means by which information is exchanged and understanding achieved (Shuy, 1976). In addition, qualities of the provider–patient relationship such as trust, cooperation, and commitment to the patient's well-being, strongly impinge on outcomes of medical care such as patients' satisfaction, adherence to prescribed regimens, recovery rate, and utilization of health-care services (Becker, 1985; Ben-Sira, 1980; Speedling & Rose, 1985). These features of relationships emerge interactively as the communicators assign meaning to one another's verbal and nonverbal behaviors over the course of the encounter (DiMatteo, 1979; Pendleton, 1983).

There are, of course, various health professional–patient relationships. However, researchers primarily have limited their study to physician–patient interaction (Pendleton, 1983; Street, in press) although nurse–patient (e.g., Salyer & Stuart, 1985) and therapist–client encounters (e.g., LaCrosse, 1975) have received substantial attention. In spite of its ubiquity and importance as a health-care service, dentist–patient interaction has been largely overlooked by scholars (Zimmerman, 1988). In this chapter, I argue that the study of the dentist–patient communication should benefit practitioners in their efforts to understand and improve dental care delivery as well as provide a naturalistic context for examining communication theory. Specifically, topics discussed in this chapter unfold as follows: (a) the practical and theoretical significance of explicating dentist–patient interaction, (b) a review of research on dental outcomes related to dentists' communication with patients, and (c) a "communicative-function" perspective for examining dentist–patient interaction.

WHY STUDY DENTIST–PATIENT INTERACTIONS?

As a graduate student, I recall that the most popular rationale for a thesis or dissertation topic was "Nothing's been done on it," to which one faculty member usually responded, "Perhaps for good reason." The significance of studying dentist–patient communication should not be presumed because it has received limited empirical attention. Rather, as a communicative phenomenon, the dentist–patient encounter has both practical and theoretical import.

Research within other health-care contexts (e.g., teaching hospitals, outpatient clinics, psychotherapy sessions, pediatric clinics) has revealed that the manner in which practitioners and patients interact with one another has a significant impact upon medical outcomes such as patients' satisfaction, compliance, and understanding of medical information (Heszen-Klemens & Lapinska, 1984; Pendleton, 1983; Street, in press). Given that communicative processes within physician–patient encounters significantly influence medical outcomes, practitioners and educators of dental care should be interested in the extent to which features of dentist–patient communication similarly impinge upon dental outcomes.

For the interpersonal communication theorist, the dental consultation is an interesting context for examining theoretical issues related to communicative processes. Specifically, dentist–patient communication has important implications for advocates of "relational" (Burgoon & Hale, 1984) and "functional" (Cappella & Street, 1985; Patterson, 1983) approaches to social interaction. For example, dentist–patient pairs may vary greatly in terms of the longevity of their relationships (e.g., some have interacted with one another previously; others are meeting for the first time), emotional states (dentists may experience little anxiety about the dental visit; patients may be highly anxious), and the diversity of their personal characteristics (collectively, dentists and patients represent a broad spectrum of ages, education levels, and social classes) (Weinstein, Milgrom, Ratener, Read, & Morrison, 1978). Research in other social contexts (e.g., social conversations and interviews) has demonstrated that such individual and relational differences impinge upon the communicative structure of interactions as well as the participants' perceptual and evaluative judgments of interlocutors and of the interaction (Giles & Street, 1985; Patterson, 1983). Thus, the study of dentist–patient communication should be of interest to researchers and teachers of communication and dental care.

RESEARCH ON DENTIST–PATIENT COMMUNICATION

Patients' Preferences for Dentists' Communicative Style

Practically all of the research relating to dentist–patient communication focuses on relationships between patients' perceptions of dentists' behaviors and patients' satisfaction with dental care, utilization of dental services and/or experience of dental anxiety. Three dimensions of dentists' communication with patients typically emerge as having powerful effects on patients' responses to dental care. These include perceptions of the dentist's affiliativeness, dominance, and informativeness.

Affiliation. A substantial amount of the research on personal and professional qualities of the dentist–patient relationship has been conducted by Norman Corah and his associates. In three surveys, Corah and his colleagues (Corah, O'Shea, & Bissell, 1986; Corah, O'Shea, Bissell, Thines, & Mendola, 1988; O'Shea, Corah, & Thines, 1986) have found that patients express greater satisfaction with dentists and experience a reduction in their dental anxiety when their dentists are perceived to encourage questions, to pay attention when the patient is talking, to take the patient seriously, to be calm, and to reassure the patient. Gale, Carlsson, Eriksson, and Jontell (1984) similarly reported that patients interacting with a "communicatively oriented" dentist (i.e., one who explained procedures, engaged in small talk, and solicited feedback on how the patient was feeling) rated their dentists more positively than did patients seeing a dentist who did not have this orientation. It is important to note that in the Gale et al. (1984) study, patients considered both groups of dentists as professionally competent but, nonetheless, preferred the more personable provider.

Taken collectively, these studies reveal that attributes of dentists' behaviors related to the notion of *affiliativeness* significantly affect dental outcomes. In a general sense, affiliation refers to the degree of involvement, behavioral and cognitive (Cappella, 1983; Cegala, Savage, Brunner, & Conrad, 1982), immediacy (i.e., psychological closeness to another; Mehrabian, 1972), and affective orientation (e.g., friendly vs. hostile) one interactant displays toward another (Patterson, 1983). Highly affiliative interactants tend to listen attentively, like one another, show care and concern, display enthusiasm toward and interest in a topic or partner, solicit one another's views, and produce empathic and supportive utterances (Patterson, 1983; Street & Cappella, 1985). Similar to findings in physician–patient interaction (Buller & Buller, 1987; Pendleton, 1983; Street & Buller, 1987; Street & Wiemann, 1987), one could hypothesize that a direct relationship exists between a patient's perception of a dentist's affiliativeness and patient's satisfaction, utilization of dental services, and reduction of dental anxiety. As a test of this proposition, Street (1989) surveyed 490 patients immediately after their visit with practitioners of general dentistry. A strong correlation was observed between patients' satisfaction with dental care and perceptions of the dentists' communicative involvement as measured by the perceptiveness, attentiveness, and responsiveness subscales of Cegala's (Cegala et al., 1982) Interaction Involvement Measure.

Informativeness. Because of their concern for dental health and (in many cases) anxiety and uncertainty about dental treatment, patients typically have a strong need for information about dental health and procedures. Thus, it is not surprising that dental outcomes have been related to the extent to which dentists were believed to be informative about dental hygiene and treatment. Dworkin (1984) reported that dentists who provided information and expectations regarding the use of nitrous oxide observed a corresponding increase in the effectiveness of the drug and a decrease in the patients' experience of pain and aversion of treatment. Rankin and Harris (1985) found that patients preferred providers who explained about equipment, procedure, and techniques and disliked dentists who rarely offered explanations. Finally, O'Shea et al. (1986) solicited *patients'* recommendations regarding what dentists could do to help alleviate the patients' fear of dental treatment. Nearly one half of the patients' suggestions advised dentists to be more informative: explain about procedures to be performed, provide specific information during treatment, warn about pain, coach the patient about coping with pain, and help the patient de-emphasize the perceived threat of treatment. Finally, Zimmerman (1988) reported that, among patients' preferences for dentists' behavior, the three most important related to information giving: explaining the patient's dental condition, instructing the patient on how to improve dental health, and explaining the treatment procedure.

Dominance. Communicative dominance represents the extent to which an interactant dominates the interaction or controls the behavior and opinions of interlocutors. Communicative dominance is typically accomplished through such behaviors as holding the conversational floor for extended periods, interruptions, criticism, touch, directives (e.g., "be sure to floss at night"), close-ended questioning, and control of conversational topics (Norton, 1983; Patterson, 1983).

One of the more difficult communicative objectives for the dentist is to establish an acceptable level of communicative control during interactions with patients. On one hand, patients' satisfaction has diminished when dentists were perceived as domineering (Street, 1989) or critical of the patient's behavior (Corah, O'Shea, & Bissell, 1985; Rankin & Harris, 1985). On the other hand, because of the dentist's expertise and status, patients typically allow dentist substantial control over the interaction (Coleman & Burton, 1985). For the dentist, the delicate balance between being sufficiently but not overtly dominant is exemplified in the findings of two studies. O'Shea et al. (1986) discovered that patients *expect* dentists to command or instruct the patient regarding desirable behaviors (e.g., to be calm) *but* to allow the patient some control over the procedure and experience of pain (e.g., ask what the patient wants done, let the patient stop the dental treatment when feeling pain). Patients also vary in their acceptance of the dentist's authority. Rankin and Harris (1985) reported that, of the patients surveyed in their investigation, 44% "disliked," 28% were "not sure," and 28% "liked" dentists who scolded them for poor oral hygiene and not taking proper care of teeth.

Patients appear to prefer dentists who are in control of the interaction but not overly domineering. If dentists are too domineering, patients may be too intimidated or lack the opportunity to share information and concerns with the dentist. On the other hand, patients expect to benefit from the dentist's expertise, knowledge, and skills. Thus, if dentists are too passive patients may perceive them as not fulfilling their responsibilities as a *provider* of dental care.

Summary. Dental outcomes such as patients' satisfaction, reduction of anxiety, and utilization of dental services appear to be promoted when dentists are perceived to interact with patients in an affiliative, informative, and active but nondomineering fashion. These preferences for the dentist's communicative style are quite similar to those reported by patients for physicians' behavior (Ben-Sira, 1980; Buller & Buller, 1987; O'Hair, 1986; Street & Wiemann, 1987) and could be attributed to several factors. First, many patients (albeit not all) are concerned about their health and dental well-being. Thus, these patients are serious, active, and highly involved in their interactions with health-care providers *and* expect the same from doctors and dentists. Secondly, the patients' anxiety about dental care, uncertainty about their health status, and lack of medical knowledge create a need for the health-care provider to be concerned, competent, and committed to the patient's well-being. Hence, patients seek dentists who communicate receptiveness, responsiveness, and commitment to the patient's health as well as dentists who provide expert dental care and advice (Corah, O'Shea, & Bissell, 1985; Hornung & Massagli, 1979). Finally, many patients have information and concerns to share with their dentists. If dentists dominate the interaction by frequently interrupting, criticizing, and allowing the patient little opportunity to talk, the patient may be unwilling or unable to share his or her concerns.

Although these relationships may emerge generally, there is some indication that different types of patients may vary, perhaps dramatically, in their preferences for a dentist's communicative style. Although not specifying a particular group of patients, Rankin and Harris (1985) observed that a noticeable percentage of patients are comfortable with authoritarian dentists. Likewise, some patients may need more affiliative dentists than do others. Differences among patients potentially mediate relationships between dentists' communication and dental outcomes. These include dental anxiety, gender, age, education/socioeconomic status (SES), and previous visits to a particular dentist.

Patients' Characteristics and Preferences For Dentists' Communication

Dental Anxiety. The fear of dental treatment is a major factor influencing patients' attitudes toward dentists and decisions to seek dental care (Corrah, O'Shea, & Ayer, 1985; Liddell & May, 1984; Milgrom, Fiset, Melnick, & Weinstein, 1988). Patients experiencing dental anxiety tend to report less satisfaction with dental care in general (Milgrom et al., 1988) and to perceive dentists as less informative and friendly (Rankin & Harris, 1985). Dentists understand that alleviating the patients' anxiety significantly enhances satisfaction with dental care. Thus, to reduce anxiety, most dentists claim they use the strategy of "talking to the patients" (Corah et al., 1985).

Given these differences related to the patients' anxiety, more fearful patients also may vary in their reactions to and preferences for dentists' communicative styles. Street (1989) hypothesized that, relative to less anxious clients, worried patients may prefer more substantial communicative involvement from dental care providers in order to alleviate their anxiety and to gain adequate information about the condition or treatment. Also, anxious patients tend to be less assertive (Milgrom et al., 1988) and may be more tolerant of the dentist's efforts to dominate or "take charge" of the interaction because of their fear, perceived helplessness, and/or uncertainty about the dental condition or procedures. However, Street's (1989) findings failed to support these claims. Patients, regardless of their level of anxiety, preferred responsive, attentive, and nondomineering dentists. Although these findings suggest that dental anxiety may not be related to patients' preferences for the dentist's manner of communicating, Street's measure of anxiety had only marginal reliability and may not have tapped into the totality of the patient's apprehensions about dental treatment.

Repeat Versus Initial Visit Patients.   When first interacting with another, conversants tend to base their impressions of partners on the partner's communicative behavior, or how the partner talks and acts. However, after developing a relationship, interactants' impressions are grounded less in the surface features of the other's communicative style and more in their shared past experiences (Giles & Street, 1985; Patterson, 1983). Applying these notions to the provider–patient relationship, "new" patients are likely "hyperattentive" to the manner in which the health-care provider communicates with them (Friedman, 1979) and, because of limited (if any) information about the provider, will assess the quality of health care delivered in relation to ostensible features of the provider's behavior toward them. Repeat patients, on the other hand, can recall previous experiences with a particular provider to gauge the quality of care received. Thus, repeat patients may be less concerned about the provider's communicative style per se. In medical settings, two studies have reported that repeat patients indeed were more tolerant of physicians' communicative dominance than were new patients (Buller & Buller, 1987; Street & Wiemann, 1987). DiMatteo and Hays (1980) also discovered that the longer the patient had been with a particular physician, the less important were perceptions of the physicians' personal style as determinants of patients' satisfaction. A similar finding has been reported in dental contexts. In Street's (1989) investigation, new patients were not as satisfied with less communicatively involved dentists as were repeat patients.

Patients' Sex.   Relative to men, women typically have more frequent dental visits (Biro & Hewson, 1976), have expressed greater satisfaction with dental care (Street, 1989), and have expressed higher levels of dental anxiety (Biro & Hewson, 1976; Liddell & May, 1984; Milgrom et al., 1988). Given that women generally exhibit more affiliative expressiveness than do men (Patterson, 1983) and given their experience of higher levels of dental anxiety, one could hypothesize that men and women differ in their preferences for a dentist's communicative style. However, research in medical (Buller & Buller, 1987; DiMatteo & Hays, 1980; but see Street & Wiemann, 1987) and dental (Street, 1989) settings has revealed few differences in satisfaction with a provider's interpersonal style as a function of the patient's sex. These null results are somewhat surprising given that there is considerable evidence that indicates that dentists and physicians communicate differently to male and female patients. For example, in medical (Waitzkin, 1985) and dental (Rankin & Harris, 1985) contexts, women have received more explanations and information about treatment and diagnosis than have men. One possibility worthy of future research is that health-care providers are interacting differently to male and female patients because they are being influenced by differences in the communicative styles of these patients or are adapting their behavior toward what the providers perceive as the communicative preferences of each.

Patients' Age.   Relative to younger clients, older patients (35 and over) have expressed greater satisfaction with dental care (Street, 1989) but also have reported less satisfaction with dentists who did not explain treatment fully and who did not notice the patients' cooperative behavior (Rankin & Harris, 1985). Speculatively, middle-age and older patients may be more concerned about their medical and dental conditions than are younger patients (perhaps because health concerns become more salient with age). Thus, these patients prefer substantial communicative involvement and information from health-care providers, and are highly satisfied with health and dental services when providers satisfy these expectations (see DiMatteo & Hays, 1980). Health-care providers may also recognize that the patient's needs and concerns vary with age and thus adapt their communicative manner accordingly. In support of this notion, Waitzkin (1985) reported that physicians provided more information, explanations, and time to patients over 50 years of age than to younger patients. Street and Buller (1988) also noted that physicians nonverbally interacted with patients over 30 years of age in a more responsive (maintained closer interpersonal distances and used more vocal acknowledgers such as "I see," "uh-huh") and less domineering (shared conversational floortime more equally) than they did when conversing with patients under 30. Whether similar phenomena characterize dental contexts is unclear and worthy of future research.

Patients' Education and SES.   Extant research indicates that there are at least two problematic issues pertaining to the manner in which the patient's education and the related notion of social class impact provider–patient communicative processes. The first concerns whether patients differing in their education or SES levels vary in the manner in which they evaluate a provider's communicative style. Ben-Sira (1980) proposed that, because their medical knowledge and health information is less than that of more educated patients, less educated patients rely more on their perceptions of the provider's "affective" behavior (e.g., care, concern, and interest in the patient) than on the provider's "instrumental" behavior (e.g., diagnosis and treatment skills) to evaluate the quality of health care received than do more educated patients. Street (1989) found evidence supporting this proposition in dental contexts. In his study, the correlation between patients' satisfaction and perceptions of the dentist's communicative involvement was stronger for patients having a high school education or less than it was for college educated patients. Relatedly, Jenny, Frazier, Bagramian, and Proshek (1973) reported that, when citing a reason why they were satisfied with their child's dental care, high SES parents were more likely to mention the dentist's technical competence, whereas low SES parents were more likely to cite the quality of the dentist–patient relationship. These findings are consistent with some (Ben-Sira, 1980; DiMatteo & Hays, 1980) but not all (Street & Wiemann, 1987) research in medical contexts.

A second problematic issue concerns the discrepancy between how providers *actually* communicate with patients of varying education levels and SES classes and how these patients *perceive* the provider's communicative response. For example, physicians generally provide fewer explanations and less information to less educated and poorer patients than to their more educated and wealthier counterparts (Pendleton & Bochner, 1980; Waitzkin, 1985). However, at least in dental settings, patients with high school educations or less have considered dentists more informative than have more educated patients (Rankin & Harris, 1985). This would suggest that less-educated, working-class, and blue-collar patients receive less desirable communicative responses from providers but perceive them more positively. This contention was partially supported in a study by Street and Wiemann (1988). Although actual communication behaviors were not recorded and analyzed, less-educated patients *perceived* their physicians as less domineering than did college-educated patients.

Two factors may account for these phenomena. First, relative to their counterparts, less-educated and working-class patients may prefer less information about medical and dental care. This seems unlikely, however, given research verifying that these patients desire substantial medical and dental information from providers who in turn generally underestimate their informational needs (Cartwright, 1967; Frazier, Jenny, Bagramian, Robinson, & Proshek, 1977). A more likely explanation is that, given the social and power differences between the two (Bochner, 1983), less-educated and lower SES patients may be more tolerant and accepting of providers' behaviors (i.e., a "halo" effect; Street & Wiemann, 1988) and are less likely to exhibit assertive and challenging responses (cf. Haug & Lavin, 1981). These accounts are, of course, speculative and point to the need for studying the impact of patients' education and social standing on dental care delivery.

Dentists' Responses to Patients' Characteristics

Not only do patients differ in their preferences and tolerances for dentists' communicative styles, but dentists in turn interact differently with patients as a function of their perception of the patient's attitudes and personal characteristics. For example, Weinstein, et al. (1978) reported that dentists provided a higher level of restorative services to patients considered "appreciative" of dental care than to patients considered "unappreciative." Corah, O'Shea, and Bissell (1986) recently found that patients unknowingly perceived as "sophisticated" by dentists in turn perceived their dentists as more understanding, taking the patient more seriously, and less critical than did patients considered less sophisticated. Patients deemed more "likeable" perceived their dentists as more understandable, reassuring, calm, patient, and curious about the patient's health than did patients viewed less likeable by dentists. In summary, dentists' attitudes toward patients influence the manner in which dentists interact with patients and, by implication, may influence the quality of dental care delivered to patients.

A CRITIQUE OF PREVIOUS RESEARCH

Although making important contributions toward understanding the role and impact of communication within dentist–patient encounters, previous research on this topic suffers from several limitations. I offer the following critique not to attenuate the value and significance of previous work; rather, I hope this analysis provides insight and serves as a useful heuristic for future scholarship in this area.

The major limitation of previous research is that it has focused almost exclusively on patients' *perceptions* of dentists' behavior. Only a couple of investigations have studied the *actual* communicative responses of dentists and patients (e.g., Coleman & Burton, 1985). There are at least two problems stemming from research programs that examine only the patients' perceptual judgments. First, although investigations have repeatedly demonstrated that patients' satisfaction, reduction of dental anxiety, and utilization of dental services are correlated with the extent to which patients perceive the dentist's style as attentive, concerned, nondomineering, informative, involved, and supportive (Corah, O'Shea, & Ayer, 1985; Corah, O'Shea, & Bissell, 1985; Corah, O'Shea, Bissell et al., 1988; Harris & Rankin, 1985; Street, 1989), there is uncertainty regarding what *specific* communicative acts produce these judgments.

The complex nature of the relationships between perceived and actual communicative characteristics of the provider's behavior has been revealed in research in medical contexts. Although patients respond favorably to health-care providers perceived as "affiliative" and "nondomineering," there is little consistency regarding what behaviors produce these perceptions. For example, some have found that patients' satisfaction has been enhanced by the physician's use of forward leans and direct body orientation when interacting with the patient (Harrigan, Oxman, & Rosenthal, 1985; Larsen & Smith, 1981), whereas others have not supported these relationships (Comstock, Hooper, Goodwin, & Goodwin, 1982; Street & Buller, 1987). The extent to which the physician is authoritative (e.g., giving orders, opinions, and directives) has positively related (Davis, 1971; Lane, 1983) and has negatively related (Carter, Inui, Kukull, & Haigh, 1982; Heszen-Klemens & Lapinska, 1984) to patients' compliance with prescribed regimens. In fact, of the plethora of verbal and nonverbal behavior responses, only the act of information giving, consistently discriminates among medical outcomes related to patient's satisfaction, recall, and adherence to prescribed regimens (Hall, Roter, & Katz, 1988).

A second limitation concerns the possibility that perceptions of another's behavior are distorted because these judgments may be formulated in a selective and biased manner. Perceptual judgments are produced when raw sensory inputs are given meaning in relation to the interactant's goals, affective experience, and situational expectancies. In social settings, perceivers are motivated to attend to those stimulus features deemed salient to the situation at hand and then rely on their conceptions of reality (e.g., in the form of stereotypes, situational knowledge, understanding of others, etc.) to "create" a judgment or attribution of another. By their very nature, many interpersonal judgments contain information that is incomplete and inferred. For example, Stafford and Daly (1984) discovered that conversationalists tend to differentially interpret a previous interaction depending on whether their perceptual goal was to form impressions of their partner or to recall the content of their interaction.

Thus, there may be at least two forms of perceptual distortions: (a) How one perceives an interlocutor's behavior may not correspond with the actual characteristics of the person's behavior, and (b) different perceivers may assign different interpretations to the same behavior (Street & Hopper, 1982; Thakerar & Giles, 1981). An example of both phenomena has been documented in medical contexts. Street and Wiemann (1988) compared patients' perceptions of physicians' communicative styles with the physicians' self-assessments of their "typical" behavior when conversing with patients. Not only was there little correspondence between the physicians' and patients' perceptions, there was also a consistent tendency for less-educated and older patients to perceive the provider's communication more positively than did more educated and younger patients. In summary, one cannot presume a veridical relationship between perceptions of a health-care provider's behavior (e.g., caring, attentive, nondomineering, etc.) and specific behaviors (e.g., gaze, interruptions, empathic utterances, etc.). Substantial research is needed on the interface between actual and perceived dimensions of dentists' and patients' communicative behavior.

A third limitation of previous research is its focus on the dentist's communicative acts without considering *how the patient is communicating*. Research in other contexts, such as interviews and social conversation, frequently has demonstrated that a conversant's satisfaction with partners and with the interaction as a whole are less the result of what interlocutors do or say per se and more a function of these responses relative to the interactant's own communicative responses (Giles, Mulac, Bradac, & Johnson, 1987; Street, Mulac, & Wiemann, 1988). For example, a dentist who provides advice and recommendations for dental care may be perceived as informative and responsive by a patient asking for and discussing information on these topics, or this dentist may be considered domineering and intimidating by a diffident patient.

A patient's postinterview response (e.g., satisfaction or compliance) may in large part depend on how the patient chooses or is able to communicate (Anderson, DeVellis, & DeVellis, 1987). Was the patient able to ask questions? Was she able to give opinions on treatment procedures? Did he feel comfortable to look at the doctor and interrupt if he felt inclined? The fact that research traditionally has ignored the patient's responses may account for the inconsistent findings regarding relationships between health-care outcomes and specific communicative acts exhibited by physicians (Comstock et al., 1982; Hall et al., 1988; Street & Buller, 1987).

Finally, much of the research on dentist–patient communication has been conducted atheoretically. The absence of a comprehensive conceptual framework guiding these investigations has hindered researchers' efforts to remedy the problems stated earlier. The usefulness of relevant theoretical frameworks applied to physician–patient interaction are limited because they tend to downplay the role of the communication process. For example, Ben-Sira's (1980) social interaction theory of the physician–patient relationship does not examine communication per se but rather distinguishes between "affective" and "technical" features of the physician's behavior. The physician's technical abilities relate to medical skills such as giving treatment and diagnosing. Affective behavior represents the physicians's time for, interest in, and devotion to the patient and the patient's health. These global perceptions of a physician's style are accomplished communicatively yet the model does not address this issue.

A popular approach of discourse analysts represents applying critical theory to verbal exchanges between provider and patient. These scholars describe how the interface between providers' and patients' utterances functions to maintain the physicians' (Fisher, 1984; Long, 1985; West, 1984) and dentists' (Coleman & Burton, 1985) authority and control over the patient, regulate information exchange and understanding (Waitzkin, 1985), and negotiate the social and communicative roles performed by the interactants (Byrne & Long, 1976; Stiles, Orth, Scherwitz, Hennrikus, & Vallbona, 1984). Although providing insight into the provider–patient relationship, these works are insufficient for generalizing relationships between communicative processes (e.g., the communicative structure of provider–patient interactions and factors mediating these patterns) and medical care outcomes (e.g., patients' satisfaction, adherence, understanding, and utilization of health-care services). For explicating these issues, a "communicative-function" framework should be useful.

A COMMUNICATIVE FUNCTION PERSPECTIVE

As mentioned earlier, conversants formulate attributions and evaluations of their interlocutors and interactions less in terms of their individual communicative responses and more with respect to the interface between their own and partners' behavior. Thus, when explicating communicative processes, researchers should examine the functional significance of "patterns" of verbal and nonverbal behavior exchange, that is, conversants' responses vis-à-vis those of their partners. Rather than focusing on individual communicative channels (e.g., speech acts, dialect, kinesics, etc.), a functional approach to communication examines the collectivity of behaviors that perform certain communicative functions such as maintaining coherent dialogue and topic development, signaling affiliation and rapport, regulating communicative control and dominance, and managing interpersonal impressions (Cappella & Street, 1985; Patterson, 1983). A functional perspective embraces the assumption that communicative functions emerge from the conversants' goals and motivations during the interaction, from the behaviors produced to accomplish these goals, and from the conversants' interpretations of the pattern of communicative exchange.

Communicative Functions of Dentist–Patient Interaction

Typically, dentists and patients have mutual goals for the medical visit (i.e., information sharing and helping the patient) yet differ in terms of their knowledge of dental health and of their communicative roles in the interaction (i.e., expert provider-educator vs. client-learner). The similarities between the interactants' desired outcomes for the interaction and the differences between their social roles and knowledge should be reflected in the structure of communicative responses (Stiles et al., 1984). As revealed earlier in this chapter, three different "functions" of interpersonal communication are particularly salient within dentist–patient encounters: affiliation, dominance, and information exchange.

Communicative Dominance–Submissiveness. In most out-patient visits, dentists are the dental experts and patients have voluntarily solicited their help (Coleman & Burton, 1985). Both parties typically approach the encounter with the expectation that the dentist is the primary problem solver. Thus, the dentist will presume to exercise (and the patient will allow) considerable influence regarding the content and structure of the interaction (cf. Applegate, 1986). Hence, although dentists may be more or less dominant with certain kinds of patients, in most interactions dentists and patients will create complementary patterns of communicative exchange reflecting relatively greater dominance and control by the dentist and relatively less by the patient. In one of the few studies of actual dentist–patient interaction, Coleman and Burton (1985) indeed reported that dentists control interactions by talking more, controlling topics, and dictating the tempo of the interaction (e.g., through speech rate and pause behavior). In turn, patients assume submissive roles by allowing dentists these communicative options and displaying deference. Coleman and Burton's (1985) findings are quite comparable to similar results observed in medical contexts (Byrne & Long, 1976; Shapiro, Najman, & Chang, 1983; Smith & Larsen, 1984; Street & Buller, 1987, 1988; West, 1984).

Affiliation. Given that both providers and patients *typically* desire to communicate effectively and to establish rapport (DiMatteo, 1979; Speedling & Rose, 1985), we also expect dentists and patients to establish mutually acceptable levels of behaviors indicative of affiliation. For the patient, an acceptable degree of affiliativeness displayed in the encounter implies the health-care provider is responsive, involved in the encounter, and understands the patients' condition (cf. DiMatteo, 1979; Friedman, 1979). For the provider, such perceptions by the patient tend to be associated with patients' satisfaction, involvement in health-care regimens, and utilization of services (Corah, O'Shea, & Ayer, 1985; Corah, O'Shea, & Bissell, 1985; Corah, O'Shea, Bissell et al., 1988; Street, 1989).

The degree of expressed affiliativeness (e.g., constancy of gaze, frequency of gestures, directness of body lean and orientation toward a partner, and facial expressiveness; Cappella, 1983; Mehrabian, 1972) may vary from interaction to interaction and is contingent upon such factors as personal predilections, nature of the task, relational history between the participants, and communicative roles (Giles & Street, 1985; Patterson, 1983). However, mutually acceptable expressions of affiliation typically are characterized by reciprocal response patterns as interactants coordinate and match their behaviors around personal, partner, and situational constraints (Cappella, 1983; Patterson, 1983).

For example, in a situation in which the patient is highly anxious about the dental condition or treatment, both dentist and patient may display high levels of involvement through directness of body orientation, forward body leans, gaze toward partners, verbal responsiveness, facial expressiveness, and touch to comfort or reassure. In a routine dental exam in which the patient has no complications or fear, there is likely little need for personal involvement between the interactants. Thus, there may be lower levels of affiliative intensity such as less social touch, more gazes away from partners, more indirect body orientations, less facial expressiveness, less intimate talk, more task activity (e.g., conducting the dental treatment), and more abrupt topic changes (cf. Street & Buller, 1987; Street & Wiemann, 1987). Nevertheless, in both situations the participants conceivably will achieve an acceptable degree of nonverbal expressiveness that is indexed by the relative similarity among affiliative behaviors. In medical settings, two studies of family practitioner–patient interactions indeed reported that physicians and patients tended to converge behaviors related to affiliation and involvement including forward lean, body orientation, gaze, gestures, and response latencies (Smith & Larsen, 1984; Street & Buller, 1987).

Information Exchange. An objective highly valued by the doctor and patient is the efficient, accurate exchange of information. Information, conveyed through the content of speech acts, is a resource valuable to both individuals. For the dentist, information is crucial for diagnosis, selection of treatment, and assessment of the patient's comfort; for the patient, information fosters understanding, uncertainty reduction, cooperativeness, and recovery (Corah, O'Shea, & Ayer, 1985; Corah, O'Shea & Bissell, 1986; Corah, O'Shea, Bissell et al., 1988; Zimmerman, 1988). Research is almost nonexistent regarding information exchange in dentist–patient encounters. However, given related research in the medical domain, one could hypothesize that the informing process in dental consultations is accomplished through verbal exchanges characterized by both reciprocity and complementarity.

As mentioned earlier, the roles of dentist as expert-educator and patient as client-learner result in patterns of communicative exchange characterized by complementarity. This pattern is evident not only in terms of the "control" of the interaction, but also in terms of the manner in which information is exchanged. For example, Stiles et al. (1984) described how the provider's and patient's roles are manifest in various speech act pairs. When directing the "informational flow" of the consultation, the provider's questions, explanations, and instructions are coupled with the patient's answers, acknowledgments, and agreements, respectively; when the patient assumes a more direct role in the informing process, the patient's explanations and descriptions of medical condition are complemented by the provider's responses of confirmation and acknowledgment.

Although the "structure" of information exchange typically emerges through complementary speech act pairs (i.e., as provider and patient exchange positions as being the primary information giver), the kind and amount of information exchange may reflect reciprocal qualities. As a resource, information exchange may be subject to the reciprocity norm (cf. Roloff, 1985). Thus, the dentist and patient may converse with the expectation that the quantity and specificity of information revealed in the message of one partner (e.g., in describing a problem) should elicit a similarly informative response from the other (e.g., explanation of the cause of the problem). As indirect support of this contention, there appears to be a direct relationship between how much the patient talks during the consultation (and presumably the more information they convey) and the amount of information provided by doctors (Bochner, 1983; Greenfield, Kaplan, & Ware, 1985).

Summary.   Because they have similar communicative goals and desired outcomes, dentists and patients likely will demonstrate convergence among behaviors indicative of affiliation and informativeness; that is, they will reciprocate or produce these behaviors at relatively similar levels. On the other hand, the role and power differences between dentists and patients should be manifested in complementary patterns of verbal and nonverbal behaviors related to their communicative roles and for control of the interaction. These functions can emerge concurrently because the behaviors signalling affiliation (i.e., verbal responsiveness, reassurances, empathic comments, gaze, body position, gestures, vocal backchannels, response latencies) are often different from behaviors accomplishing dominance and control (i.e., topic initiation, criticism, directiveness, standard accent, unilateral touch, long turn durations, interruptions, and pauses within speaking turns) that in turn may be different from behaviors serving the informative function (e.g., explanations and descriptions).

The evidence reviewed in this chapter would suggest that when interactants achieve an appropriate balance of the aforementioned communicative functions, positive dental outcomes will result. However, I do not want to underestimate the potential difficulties inherent in these interactions.

Dentist–patient consultations are quite susceptible to communicative misperceptions and misunderstandings. Not only do they vary in their communicative roles and medical knowledge, but doctors and patients also differ in how each understands disease in terms of its aetilogy and social effects (Helman, 1985). Under such circumstances, empathic understanding may be difficult to achieve. Thus, it is not surprising that doctors and patients often misperceive one another's characteristics, intentions, and behaviors. For example, dentists may underestimate the patient's desire for information about dental procedures and dental health (Zimmerman, 1988). Also, in medical contexts, doctors generally perceive patients to be more ignorant, dissatisfied, and fearful than in actuality (Bochner, 1983), and often think they are conversing in lay language when patients do not perceive them as doing so (Bourhis, Roth, & MacQueen, 1989). In turn, the patient's reverence of doctors may lead to perceptions of the doctor's communicative style that are overly positive and incongruous with what doctors perceive as characteristic of themselves (Street & Wiemann, 1988). In summary, it is certainly important for researchers to ascertain relationships between the communicative structure of dentist–patient interactions and various dental outcomes such as satisfaction and the reduction of dental anxiety. However, insight into these relationships may be limited unless efforts are also taken to discover dentists' and patients' perceptions and expectations for the event.

CONCLUDING NOTE

In this chapter, I have attempted to review and critique extant research related to dentist–patient communication and to offer a communicative perspective that should serve as a useful conceptual guide for future research on this topic. Because of the paucity of research on dentist–patient interaction, most of the generalizations forwarded here are more suggestive than conclusive. Although to some extent relying on research on physician–patient interaction to garner insight into the dentist–patient relationship, I am well aware that the two are not isomorphic by any means. Because of the constraints imposed by dental treatment, communicative exchanges between dentists and patients likely resemble physician–patient interaction only at the beginning and termination of the dental visit. Hopefully, research on dentist–patient interaction will blossom in its own right so that more sophisticated theory and pedagogy may evolve.

REFERENCES

Anderson, L. A., DeVellis, B. M., & DeVellis, R. F. (1987). Effects of modeling on patients' communication, satisfaction, and knowledge. *Medical Care, 25*, 1044–1056.

Applegate, W. H. (1986). Physician management of patients with adverse outcomes. *Archives of Internal Medicine, 146*, 2249–2252.

Becker, M. H. (1985). Patient adherence to prescribed therapies. *Medical Care, 23*, 539–555.

Ben-Sira, Z. (1980). Affective and instrumental components on the physician–patient relationship: An additional dimension of interaction theory. *Journal of Health and Social Behavior, 21*, 170–180.

Biro, P. A., & Hewson, N. D. (1976). A survey of patients' attitudes to their dentist. *Australian Dental Journal, 21*, 388–394.

Bochner, S. (1983). Doctors, patients, and their cultures. In D. Pendleton & J. Hasler (Eds.), *Doctor–patient communication* (pp. 127–138). London: Academic Press.

Bourhis, R. Y., Roth, S., & MacQueen, G. (1989). Communication in a hospital setting: A survey of medical and everyday language use amongst patients, nurses and doctors. *Social Science and Medicine, 28*, 339–346.

Buller, M. K., & Buller, D. B. (1987). Physicians' communication style and patients' satisfaction. *Journal of Health and Social Behavior, 28*, 375–388.

Burgoon, J. K., & Hale, J. (1984). The fundamental topoi of relational communication. *Communication Monographs, 51*, 193–214.

Byrne, P. S., & Long, B. (1976). *Doctors talking to patients: A study of the verbal behavior of general practitioners consulting in their surgeries.* London: Her Majesty's Stationery Office.

Cappella, J. N. (1983). Conversational involvement: Approaching and avoiding others. In J. Wiemann & R. Harrison (Eds.), *Nonverbal interaction* (pp. 113–148). Beverly Hills: Sage.

Cappella, J. N., & Street, R. L., Jr. (1985). A functional approach to the structure of communicative behavior. In R. L. Street, Jr. & J. N. Cappella (Eds.), *Sequence and pattern in communicative behavior* (pp. 1–29). London: Edward Arnold.

Carter, W. B., Inui, T. S., Kukull, W. A., & Haigh, V. H. (1982). Outcome-based doctor–patient interaction analysis: Identifying effective provider and patient behavior. *Medical Care, 20*, 550–568.

Cartwright, A. (1967). *Patients and their doctors.* London: Routledge & Kegan-Paul.

Cegala, D. J., Savage, G. T., Brunner, C. C., & Conrad, A. B. (1982). An elaboration of the meaning of interaction involvement: Toward the development of a theoretical concept. *Communication Monographs, 49*, 229–248.

Coleman, H., & Burton, J. (1985). Aspects of control in the dentist–patient relationship. *International Journal of the Sociology of Language, 51*, 75–104.

Comstock, L. M., Hooper, E. M., Goodwin, J. M., & Goodwin, J. S. (1982). Physician behaviors that correlate with patient satisfaction. *Journal of Medical Education, 57*, 105–112.

Corah, N. L., O'Shea, R. M., & Ayer, W. A. (1985). Dentists' management of patients' fear and anxiety. *Journal of the American Dental Association, 110,* 734–736.

Corah, N. L., O'Shea, R. M., & Bissell, G. D. (1986). The dentist–patient relationship: Perceptions by patients of dentist behavior in relation to satisfaction and anxiety. *Journal of the American Dental Association, 111,* 443–446.

Corah, N. L., O'Shea, R. M., & Bissell, G. D. Thines, T. J., & Mendola, P. (1988). The dentist–patient relationship: Perceived dentist behaviors that reduce patient anxiety and increase satisfaction. *Journal of the American Dental Association, 116,* 73–76.

Davis, M. (1971). Variations in patients' compliance with doctors' orders: Medical practice and doctor–patient interaction. *Psychiatry in Medicine, 2,* 31–54.

DiMatteo, M. R. (1979). A social psychological analysis of physician–patient rapport: Toward a science of the art of medicine. *Journal of Social Issues, 35,* 12–33.

DiMatteo, M. R., & Hays, R. (1980). The significance of patients' perception of physician conduct. *Journal of Community Health, 6,* 18–34.

Dworkin, S. F. (1984). Cognitive modification of pain: Information in combination with N₂O. *Pain, 19,* 339–351.

Fisher, S. (1984). Institutional authority and the structure of discourse. *Discourse Processes, 7,* 201–224.

Frazier, P., Jenny, J., Bagramian, R., Robinson, E., & Proshek, J. (1977). Provider expectations and consumer perceptions of the importance and value of dental care. *American Journal of Public Health, 67,* 37–43.

Friedman, H. S. (1979). Nonverbal communication between patients and medical practitioners. *Journal of Social Issues, 35,* 82–99.

Gale, E. N., Carlsson, S. G., Eriksson, A., & Jontell, M. (1984). Effects of dentists' behavior on patients' attitudes. *Journal of the American Dental Association, 109,* 444–446.

Giles, H., Mulac, A., Bradac, J., & Johnson, P. (1987). Speech accommodation theory: The next decade and beyond. *Communication Yearbook, 10,* 13–48.

Giles, H., & Street, R. L., Jr. 1985. Communicator characteristics and behavior. In M. Knapp & G. Miller (Eds.), *Handbook of interpersonal communication* (pp. 205–262). Beverly Hills: Sage.

Greenfield, S., Kaplan, S., & Ware, J. (1985). Expanding patient involvement in care. *Annals of Internal Medicine, 102,* 520–528.

Hall, J. A., Roter, D. L., & Katz, N. R. (1988). Meta-analysis of correlates of provider behavior in medical encounters. *Medical Care, 26,* 657–675.

Harrigan, J. A., Oxman, T. E., & Rosenthal, R. (1985). Rapport expressed through nonverbal behavior. *Journal of Nonverbal Behavior, 9,* 95–110.

Haug, M. R., & Lavin, B. (1981). Practitioner or patient: Who's in charge? *Journal of Health and Social Behavior, 22,* 212–229.

Helman, C. G. (1985). Communication in primary care: The role of patient and practitioner explanatory models. *Social Science and Medicine, 20,* 923–931.

Heszen-Klemens, I., & Lapinska, E. (1984). Doctor–patient interaction, patients' health behavior, and effects of treatment. *Social Science and Medicine, 19,* 9–18.

Hornung, C. A., & Massagli, M. (1979). Primary care physicians' affective orientation toward their patients. *Journal of Health and Social Behavior, 20,* 61–76.

Jenny, J., Frazier, P. J., Bagramian, R. A., & Proshek, J. (1973). Parents' satisfaction and dissatisfaction with their dentists. *Journal of Public Health Dentistry, 33,* 211–221.

LaCrosse, M. B. (1975). Nonverbal behavior and perceived counselor attractiveness and persuasiveness. *Journal of Counseling Psychology, 22,* 563–566.

Lane, S. D. (1983). Compliance, satisfaction, and physician–patient communication. *Communication Yearbook, 7,* 772–798.

Larsen, K. M., & Smith, C. K. (1981). Assessment of nonverbal communication in the patient–physician interview. *Journal of Family Practice, 12,* 481–488.

Liddell, A., & May, B. (1984). Some characteristics of regular and irregular attendance for dental check-ups. *British Journal of Clinical Psychology, 23,* 19–26.

Long, B. L. (1985). A study of the verbal behavior of family doctors. *International Journal of the Sociology of Language, 51,* 5–25.

Mehrabian, A. (1972). *Nonverbal communication.* Chicago: Aldine.

Milgram, P., Fiset, L., Melnick, S., & Weinstein, P. (1988). The prevalence and practice management consequences of dental fear in a major US city. *Journal of the American Dental Association, 116,* 641–647.

Norton, R. (1983). *Communicator style.* Beverly Hills: Sage.

O'Hair, H. D. (1986). Patient preferences for physician persuasion strategies. *Theoretical Medicine, 7,* 147–164.

O'Shea, R. M., Corah, N. L., & Thines, T. J. (1986). Dental patients' advice on how to reduce anxiety. *General Dentistry, 34,* 44–47.

Patterson, M. L. (1983). *Nonverbal behavior: A functional perspective.* New York: Springer-Verlag.

Pendleton, D. (1983). Doctor–patient communication. In D. Pendleton & J. Hasler (Eds.), *Doctor–patient communication* (pp. 5–56). New York: Academic Press.

Pendleton, D., & Bochner, S. (1980). The communication of medical information in general practice consultations as a function of the patients' social class. *Social Science and Medicine, 14A,* 669–673.

Rankin, J. A., & Harris, M. B. (1985). Patients' preferences for dentists' behaviors. *Journal of the American Dental Association, 110,* 323–326.

Roloff, M. E. (1985). Conversational profit-sharing: Interaction as social-exchange. In R. L. Street, Jr. & J. N. Cappella (Eds.), *Sequence and pattern in communicative behavior* (pp. 161–189). London: Edward Arnold.

Salyer, J., & Stuart, B. J. (1985). Nurse–patient interaction in the intensive care unit. *Heart and Lung, 14,* 20–24.

Shapiro, M. C., Najman, J. M., & Chang, A. (1983). Information control and the exercise of power in the obstetrical encounter. *Social Science and Medicine, 17,* 139–146.

Smith, C. K., & Larsen, K. M. (1984). Sequential nonverbal behavior in the physician–patient interview. *The Journal of Family Practice, 18,* 257–261.

Speedling, E. J., & Rose, D. N. (1985). Building an effective doctor–patient relationship: From patient satisfaction to patient participation. *Social Science and Medicine, 21,* 115–120.

Stafford, L., & Daly, J. A. (1984). Conversational memory: The effects of recall mode and memory expectancies on remembrances of natural conversations. *Human Communication Research, 10,* 379–403.

Stiles, W. B., Orth, J. E., Scherwitz, L., Hennrikus, D., & Vallbona, C. (1984). *Social Psychology Quarterly, 47,* 244–254.

Street, R. L., Jr. (1989). Patients' satisfaction with dentists' communicative styles. *Health Communication, 1,* 137–154.

Street, R. L., Jr. (in press). Accommodation in medical consultations. In H. Giles, N. Coupland, & J. Coupland (Eds.), *Contexts of accommodation: Developments in applied sociolinguistics.* Cambridge, England: Cambridge University Press.

Street, R. L., Jr., & Buller, D. B. (1987). Nonverbal response patterns in physician–patient interactions: A functional analysis. *Journal of Nonverbal Behavior, 11,* 234–253.

Street, R. L., Jr., & Buller, D. B. (1988). Patients' characteristics facing physician–patient nonverbal communication. *Human Communication Research, 15,* 60–90.

Street, R. L., Jr., & Cappella, J. N. (1985). Sequence and pattern in communicative behavior: A model and commentary. In R. L. Street, Jr. & J. N. Cappella (Eds.), *Sequence and pattern in communicative behavior* (pp. 243–276). London: Edward Arnold.

Street, R. L., Jr., & Hopper, R. (1982). A model of speech style evaluation. In E. B. Ryan & H. Giles (Eds.), *Attitudes toward language variation: Social and applied contexts* (pp. 175–188). London: Edward Arnold.

Street, R. L., Jr., Mulac, A., & Wiemann, J. M. (1988). Speech evaluation differences as a function of perspective (participant versus observer) and presentation medium. *Human Communication Research, 14,* 333–364.

Street, R. L., Jr., & Wiemann, J. (1987). Patients' satisfaction with physicians' interpersonal involvement, expressiveness, and dominance. *Communication Yearbook, 10,* 591–612.

Street, R. L., Jr., & Wiemann, J. (1988). Differences in how physicians and patients perceive physicians' relational communication. *Southern Speech Communication Journal, 53,* 420–440.

Thakerar, J. N., & Giles, H. (1981). They are—so they spoke: Noncontent speech stereotypes. *Language and Communication, 1,* 255–262.

Waitzkin, H. (1985). Information giving in medical care. *Journal of Health and Social Behavior, 26,* 81–101.

Weinstein, P., Milgrom, P., Ratener, P., Read, W., & Morrison, K. (1978). Dentists' perceptions of their patients: Relation to quality of care. *Journal of Public Health Dentistry, 38,* 10–19.

West, C. (1984). *Routine complications: Trouble with the talk between doctors and patients.* Bloomington, IN: University of Indiana Press.

Zimmerman, R. S. (1988). The dental appointment and patient behavior. *Medical Care, 26,* 403–414.

COMMUNICATION WITHIN THE NURSING HOME   17

JON F. NUSSBAUM
University of Oklahoma

JAMES D. ROBINSON
University of Dayton

Communication is always bound by the context within which the interaction transpires. The context frames the communicative event and often can be the single best explanation of the communication. This chapter concentrates upon a truly unique environment rich in communicative phenomena: the nursing home. Our purpose is to describe the nursing home environment and to discuss what we know about the communication that transpires within the context of the nursing home. Specifically, we concentrate on the communication and the effects of that communication within three types of relationships occurring within the nursing home: the resident–resident relationship, the resident–family relationship, and the resident–staff relationship. The chapter concludes with possible implications that can be drawn from the existing literature and offers suggestions to communication scholars who wish to research the nursing home environment.

The Nursing Home Environment

As just mentioned, one cannot attempt to understand the communication that transpires within an environment without first having some knowledge of that environment. This is especially true with nursing homes that exert so much dominance over those who live, work, and visit within the walls of the facility.

Prior to describing just what a nursing home is, one needs to discuss the notion of long-term care. Koff (1982) wrote that "long term care is intended to provide the individual user with choices among a variety of services, used singly or in combination, that will minimize the disabilities of chronic illness, support as independent a lifestyle as is practical, and prevent further complications of chronic health conditions" (p. 1). Kane and Kane (1982) were a bit more parsimonious when they defined long-term care as "a range of services that address the health, personal care, and social needs of individuals who lack some capacity for self-care" (p. 4). One important link in the long-term care process is the skilled nursing facility (nursing home). "These facilities provide skilled nursing care for elderly people whose overall physical and/or mental condition has declined to a point where they require 24-hour care not available through other community or family resources" (Remnet, 1981, p. 175). Brody (1977) and Nussbaum, Robinson, and Grew (1985) stressed that nursing home facilities serve the dual purpose of maximizing health status as well as maintaining psychosocial well-being.

Nursing homes, at least in this country, are in no small measure a creation of our government. The Social Security Act of 1935 created the unique for-profit system of nursing homes now operating across this country. The Medicare and Medicaid legislation of the middle 1960s changed the nursing home industry from a family enterprise to a big business (Moss & Halamandaris, 1977). Koff (1982) reported that as we began the decade of the 1980s, there were approximately 20,000 nursing homes with close to 1.5 million beds. Nursing homes employ close to 1 million people with the country spending about $28 billion per year on nursing home care (Estes & Lee, 1985). These facts point to the "normality" of nursing homes in our society, yet tell us very little as to what actually happens within the nursing home environment.

At their core, nursing homes are medical institutions. From admission procedures, to meals, to activities, nursing homes are run to be efficient, money-making institutions. Schedules are closely followed and any departure from the schedule is a unique occurrence. Most nursing homes are organized much like hospitals with an administrator overseeing all activity. A medical doctor typically directs the medical staff whose daily activities are coordinated by a head nurse. Other professional staff beyond licensed nurses typically include a dietician, an activities coordinator, an assistant administrator who handles admissions and bookkeeping, physical and occupational therapists, and an individual to supervise the laundry. Obviously, the exact makeup of the nursing home is dependent on such regional factors as state and local regulations. In general, however, with the numerous federal regulations and the preponderance of large corporations dominating the industry, nursing homes across the country have more similarities in procedures than dissimilarities.

These similarities extend not only to the operational procedures of nursing homes but also to the architecture. The typical nursing home is built utilizing some form of the hub and spoke design. A nursing station is the hub and resident rooms make up the spoke. Often, at the end of the spoke is an activities room. A well-furnished lobby usually is located very near the main entrance of the facility with administrative offices nearby. The dining facility is typically near the middle of the nursing home. The size of the nursing home is obviously dependent on the number of rooms and the "plushness" of the facility is directly related to the number of private pay residents versus Medicare and Medicaid residents.

Two excellent descriptions of nursing homes exist in the literature for those who wish more information (Gubrium, 1975; Howsden, 1981). Gubrium and Howsden both performed an ethnographic study of nursing homes and their descriptions of the environment are "thick" and quite informative.

Nursing Home Residents

At any one time, close to 5% of the elderly population reside inside nursing homes (Kastenbaum & Candy, 1981; Van Nostrand, 1981). Using the most recent census data from the Administration on Aging (1985), over 1.5 million elderly individuals are currently living in a nursing home. Rice (1985) estimated that by the year 2000 over 2.3 million elderly individuals will reside in nursing homes. Of this number, 91% will be 75 years of age or older. These numbers are quite conservative because, as Kastenbaum and Candy (1981) wrote, as many as one in four elderly individuals will spend some time in an extended care facility.

Individuals normally do not choose to reside in nursing homes unless they need special care. An elderly individual who finds him or herself living in a nursing home is "someone who has reached, either suddenly or gradually, a state of collapse or deterioration in human behavioral functioning which requires prolonged service from at least one other human being" (Koff, 1982, p. 2). The typical nursing home resident is "a person who is female, widowed, white, age 81, who has a disease of the circulatory system as a primary diagnosis, and who depends on assistance to bathe, dress, use the bathroom, and get about" (Van Nostrand, 1981, p. 403). Although it is true that a majority of nursing home residents are experiencing physical difficulties, it is not true that these physical problems adversely effect the psycho-social needs of the elderly residents.

In other words, the communicative desires of these elderly individuals within nursing homes are very similar to the communicative desires of elderly individuals living outside of the nursing home (Nussbaum, 1983a, 1983b).

RESIDENT–RESIDENT COMMUNICATION

The popular image of a nursing home is an institution where physically impaired elderly individuals are waiting to die. We fear being "admitted" to a nursing home because that admission represents the final stage of life (Moss & Halamandaris, 1977). Rarely are nursing homes considered to be an environment rich in interactive opportunities. Recent research, however, has indicated that many residents of nursing homes lead quite active social lives. Koger (1980); Parmelee (1982); Ward, Sherman, and LaGory (1984); Nussbaum (1983a, 1983b), and others have found a direct relationship between nursing home resident participation in social activities and psychological well-being. Here, we review the literature that addresses friendship within nursing homes.

Friendship Within Nursing Homes

Feelings of Closeness.   Lowenthal and Haven (1968) were among the first social gerontologists to investigate the importance of maintaining at least one, stable intimate relationship throughout life. The closeness felt within an intimate relationship has been shown to be a much more important predictor of psychological well-being in old age rather than counts of interaction (e.g., Nussbaum, 1985). A growing body of literature has concentrated on the closeness felt in friendship relationships and suggests that the special nature of friendship is especially significant to happiness for the elderly (Arling, 1976; Baldassare, Rosenfeld, & Rook, 1984; Hass-Hawkins, 1978; Nussbaum, 1983a; Nussbaum, Holladay, Robinson, & Ragan, 1985; Philbad & Adams, 1972; Restinas & Garrity, 1985; Strain & Chappell, 1982; Wood & Robertson, 1978).

Restinas and Garrity (1985) studied the nursing home resident characteristics most conducive to sociability and the bonds underlying nursing home friendships. Several major conclusions can be drawn from their data analysis. First, residents with frequent visitors from outside the nursing home were no less sociable than residents who received far less visits. Before this study, it was commonly thought that the residents who entertained frequent outside visitors would spend little energy making and maintaining friendships within the nursing home. Residents who receive frequent visits from family and friends do have friends within the nursing home and remain socially active after the visits.

A second conclusion that flows from the Restinas and Garrity (1985) investigation is the importance of physical proximity for friendship formation. Outside of nursing homes it is a common belief that those who live and work near each other are more likely to interact and to form friendships (e.g., Gans, 1967). Lawton and Simon (1968); McClannahan (1973); and Fireston, Lichtman, and Evans (1980) suggested that room location within a nursing home would be a major predictor of whom the residents interact with. Indeed, the results of the Restinas and Garrity (1985) study support the proximity-friendship relationship. Those elderly individuals who were neighbors within the nursing home and therefore met in the hallways and in the dining area interacted more often with one another and formed friendships.

The age of the elderly residents of a nursing home was also found to be a predictor of communication and friendship formation. Many individuals in our society feel that elderly individuals would like very much to interact with people of all ages. Research, however, suggests that individuals of the same age prefer to interact with each other (Philbad & Adams, 1972; Nussbaum, 1985). Within the nursing home, residents who were the same age tended to cluster together. It appears to be much easier for contemporaries to interact and to form friendships.

Downs, Javidi, and Nussbaum (1988) investigated loneliness within the nursing home environment and found self-reported feelings of loneliness to be lower in nursing homes than feelings of loneliness reported by elderly individuals living outside the nursing home. This evidence supports the earlier findings by Nussbaum (1983a) who found remarkably high levels of life satisfaction for nursing home residents who were able to maintain close friendships within a nursing home. The explanation offered for the low levels of loneliness reported by nursing home residents is the homogeneous environment of the institution. The elderly residents are placed into an environment with individuals with similar problems and of similar ages. In addition, these elderly individuals are placed next to each other and made to eat in a common dining hall. The homogeneous environment is so overpowering that factors salient in the outside world such as social class and ethnicity were not predictors of friendship within the nursing home (Restinas & Garrity, 1985).

The implication of the foregoing discussion is quite profound. When individuals enter into a nursing home, they do not necessarily have to become a social isolate. "For residents who are able to communicate, the nursing home may offer new friendships. Indeed, withdrawing from the larger world may enable residents to enter a new social world" (Restinas & Garrity, 1985, p. 380).

Conversational Content. One area of research that communication scholars have become interested in are those communicative behaviors that signal friendship within an interaction. One such behavior is the content of the conversation. Nussbaum (1983b) reported that conversational content can signal a withdrawal from society. He reasoned that as an elderly individual's communicative world diminishes, the topics of conversation entered into by that individual will become less activity oriented and more self-oriented. The placing of a person within a nursing home that removes that individual from the "active" world might hasten this disengagement by forcing conversation on such self-oriented topics as health and personal discomfort.

Nussbaum (1983b) investigated the reported conversational content of elderly interaction as it related to the ability of the aged to adapt successfully to life. Subjects participating within the study lived in these distinct environments: their own home; a retirement community; and a nursing home. Sixteen separate topics of conversation were investigated ranging from hobbies and community events to death, health, and problems of old age. Results from the study indicate that elderly individuals living in their own home or in a retirement community enter into conversation on the topics of their own health, community events, and world and national events more than elderly individuals living in a nursing home. Nussbaum (1983b) concluded that the lack of conversation on community and world events represented a disengagement from the outside world for individuals residing in a nursing home. Although the lack of conversation on one's own health may be a denial mechanism or an adaptive response it remains troublesome given the preconceived notion that the institution would "force" self-oriented conversations. This appears to be far from the truth because topics of one's family, religion, personal discomforts, and old times are discussed just as much across all environments.

RESIDENT–FAMILY COMMUNICATION

Neglect?

One of the more common myths of our society is that families neglect their elderly members. "If only the family would take care of their aged members, there would be no need for institutions like nursing homes." Nothing could be further from the truth than the notion that older individuals are neglected and alienated by their families (Morgan, 1981; Shanas, 1979a, 1979b). Much evidence exists to refute the idea of family alienation (Morgan, 1981). Sussman and Burchinal (1962a, 1962b), Troll (1971), Johnson and Bursk (1977), Johnson (1978), Cicirelli (1981), and others have shown the importance of the family as a social, interactive stronghold for the elderly. To this day, the family remains the primary caregiver and service provider for elderly individuals.

York and Calsyn (1986) studied the factors that affect family involvement in nursing home care. Their results shatter the myth that family members (mostly adult children) are uninvolved in the lives of elderly nursing home residents. From preadmission to visiting after admission, the family is involved. For this chapter, the most important information reported by York and Calsyn (1986) concerns family visits to nursing homes. Their sample of 76 patients and their families reported an average of 12 visits per month. Perhaps more important is the consistency of visits before and after admission. Families tend to maintain patterns of involvement established prior to admission. Thus, if family members visited their elderly kin prior to admission within the nursing home twice a week, this pattern of visitation would continue after placement within the nursing home.

Effects of Family Involvement

The evidence of family involvement with institutionalized kin is overwhelming. However, the total picture of family involvement is not all good news. Wood and Robertson (1978), Nussbaum (1983a, 1985), Aizenberg and Treas (1985), and York and Calsyn (1986) each discussed problems that occur because of family involvement into the lives of the elderly. Although these difficulties can be seen in the general population, the problems associated with family involvement into the lives of nursing home residents may be magnified because of the institutional setting.

Several theories have been advanced by social gerontologists to explain the consistency of family involvement throughout the life span (see Bengston, Olander, & Haddad, 1976; Cicirelli, 1983a, 1983b). A common variable in each of the theories is the notion of "filial obligation." Filial obligation is a sense of duty felt by adult-children to give help to their elderly parents. Cicirelli (1981) pointed out that this duty or obligation felt by adult-children should in normal circumstances not interfere with the closeness felt by family members toward their elderly kin. However, admission to a nursing home is far from a normal occurrence. The sense of duty on the part of the adult-children can become a feeling of guilt that may impact resident–family interaction.

Nussbaum (1983a, 1985) reported evidence that closeness toward family may be detrimental toward overall feelings of well-being for nursing home residents. This conclusion is supported by York and Calsyn (1986) who reported data that suggest that families "expressed frustration, resentment, and guilt concerning their visits; very few actually said that they look forward to visiting" (p. 187). It is not hard to imagine that these feelings of guilt and resentment can be detected by the nursing home residents that in turn can effect any feelings of well-being by the elderly residents.

Elderly individuals consistently report a great need to remain independent from their family (e.g., Cicirelli, 1981). Once an elderly individual is admitted into a nursing home, the feeling of independence quickly disappears. Visits by family members to the nursing home can reinforce the loss of independence (Nussbaum, 1985). One of the great paradoxes of life is the relationship between family caring and feelings of well-being. It appears that we all need our family for psycho-social support, but too much of the family can, at times, remind us of problems and be harmful to our overall well-being.

RESIDENT–STAFF COMMUNICATION

The staff of any long-term health-care facility is an important source of interpersonal contact for the residents who live within that nursing home. Nurses, and in particular nurse aids, spend a great deal of time interacting with the elderly residents of nursing homes. Because nurse aides provide as much as 70% of the nursing care a resident receives (Wallace & Brubaker, 1981), the aides are in an excellent position to create and maintain interpersonal relationships with the elderly residents of nursing homes.

Resident–Staff Relationships

Resident–staff relationships are important to residents for many reasons. In addition to making life more pleasant and satisfying, Noelker and Harel (1978) provided evidence that suggests that resident–staff relations impact the longevity of the elderly resident. Their data imply that the residents of nursing homes actually live longer and prefer to remain in the nursing home longer when the residents perceive close relationships with the staff.

Miller and Lelieuvre (1982) found that the quality of life for the elderly residents of a nursing home is significantly improved when those residents have close relationships with staff members. This research demonstrates that elderly residents who receive attention and verbal praise from the staff experience less pain than residents with less satisfying relationships with staff members. The resident–staff relationships appear to play a very important role in the life satisfaction and longevity of the institutionalized elderly.

The findings are remarkable because they suggest that quality of life, well-being, and longevity of the institutionalized elderly can be increased on a psycho-social level that may be quite separate from the "pure-medical care" provided by the nursing home. The question becomes, then, what is it about satisfying resident–staff relationships that differs from resident–staff relationships that are not satisfying. Thus far, a paucity of empirical research exists that has attempted to answer this question.

Resident–Staff Conversation

Recently Nussbaum, Robinson, and Grew (1985); Nussbaum and Robinson (1984); Nussbaum, Holladay, Robinson, and Ragan (1985); and Robinson and Nussbaum (1986) began a program of research investigating the interpersonal relationships of the nursing home staff and the elderly residents. This research documents the interactive behavior of the nursing home staff in an attempt to understand the resident–staff relationship and the impact of this relationship on the quality of life within a nursing home. A summary of this exploratory research program is in order.

For the most part, conversations between the nursing staff and the elderly resident of long-term health-care facilities are patient oriented. Nussbaum, Robinson, and Grew (1985) researched resident–staff conversations and found the most common topics of their conversation to be: "the patient's family," "old times," "problems with old age," "hobbies of the patient," "death," and "the patient's health." The nursing staff reported very little conversation concerning "community events" and "world or national events" with the residents. In addition, the nursing staff disclosed very little personal information about themselves. The staff reported little conversation to the elderly residents about their "own families," "plans after work," "their job," "personal problems," and "their own health."

Because nurses and nurse aides provide different services within the nursing home and have such different educational experiences and social skills training, nurse–resident and nurse aide–resident interactions were examined to see how they differed. Although there were some similarities, there were also a great many differences. Consequently, the following review of research results is presented in terms of nurse–resident and nurse aide–resident interactions.

Nurses and nurse aides enter into conversations with the elderly residents of nursing homes on different topics. Nurses talk to the residents about "their health" more often than aides. Both nurses and aides report that they intentionally modify their communicator style when talking with the elderly residents. Norton (1978) conceptualized an individual's style of communication as the way the individual verbally or paraverbally interacts to signal how literal meaning should be taken, interpreted, filtered, or understood. How a message is communicated is often more important than the actual message (e.g., in the case of sarcasm) because the way a message is communicated defines the relationship between communicants and provides the context for interpreting the message. Research suggests that nurses and aides try to be more open, dramatic, dominant, relaxed, friendly, and attentive in conversations with the residents than they are with conversational partners who reside outside of the nursing home.

Nurses who feel high levels of affinity toward the residents discuss different topics with the residents (e.g., old times, religion, problems of old age, and community events). Nurses who feel high levels of affinity also communicate in a more friendly style than nurses who feel less affinity toward the residents.

Nurse aides who feel very close to the residents report talking in a more friendly, open, and relaxed manner in conversation with the residents than nurse aides who feel more distant to the residents. In addition, aides who feel high levels of affinity toward the residents discuss different topics (e.g., religion, hobbies of the patient, the aide's personal problems, and the aide's family) more often than nurse aides who feel less affinity towards the residents.

Satisfaction With Work

It is not surprising that resident–staff interaction is related to job satisfaction (Nussbaum & Robinson, 1984). Staff members who are satisfied with their jobs talk with the residents on different topics of conversation than staff members who are less satisfied with their jobs. Satisfied nurses talk about "religion," "problems of old age," and "community events" with the residents. Satisfied nurse aides talk about "patient's hobbies" and "religion," whereas dissatisfied nurse aides talk about their "own health" with the residents more than nurse aides who are satisfied with their jobs.

Resident–staff interaction also impacts the life quality of the staff member. In fact, a small direct relationship between affinity and job satisfaction has been observed. Nurses and nurse aides who felt high levels of affinity with the residents also report more satisfaction with their jobs than the staff members who felt more distant to the residents.

In a recent investigation of the friendship networks in nursing homes, Nussbaum, Holladay et al. (1985) concluded that residents would indeed benefit from friendships with staff members. It was found that such relationships are related to satisfaction with life and with living in the health-care facility.

In short, the evidence suggests that resident–staff relationships impact the quality of life for the resident and the staff person alike. Recognizing the importance of resident–staff relationships, many authors have begun calling for skills training to improve resident–staff relationships (cf. Bridge & Speight, 1981; Cohn, 1979; Paulan & Rapp, 1981). Unfortunately few scholars have offered empirical support that would indicate the specific kinds of skills that should be taught.

Robinson and Nussbaum (1986) suggested one effective way of providing staff members with insight into the importance of their relationships with the residents. By exposing nursing staff personnel to Hoffman and Reif's (1978) simulated aging experience, some indices of care quality and job satisfaction improved. Job satisfaction for nurse aides (but not for nurses) was increased and anecdotal evidence of improved resident–staff interactions and quality of care were observed.

IMPLICATIONS FOR COMMUNICATION RESEARCH

What We Know About the Social World of the Nursing Home

The nursing home environment provides social scientists with a most unique context for the purpose of studying human behavior. Since the Social Security Act of 1935 and bolstered by the Medicare and Medicaid legislation of the 1960s, the nursing home industry continues to grow and to affect the lives of an ever increasing population of elderly individuals. Living within the nearly 25,000 nursing homes spread across this country are close to 2 million individuals who lead quite active social lives. Describing and understanding the social lives of the elderly residents of nursing homes is a new research endeavor.

To date, social scientists have learned that direct participation in social activities can lead to higher levels of psychological well-being for the elderly residents of nursing homes. A quite common social activity for most of us, friendship formation, does flourish within a nursing home. Indeed, nursing homes provide a unique environment that can aid with the formation of friendships for an elderly individual. On the other hand, the institutional regiment of the nursing home combined with the societal attitude of the nursing home as a "place to die" can lead to a social withdrawal on the part of the elderly resident that results in a decline of communicative activity.

A major myth within our society has been proven false by researchers who have studied family involvement within nursing homes. Families remain extremely important throughout the life span. This is especially true for nursing home residents. Families continue to visit their kin within nursing homes and play a major role within their lives. As a matter of fact, families can become too involved, which, at times, can insult the independence of the elderly individual. Research done within nursing homes points to the differing functions served by friendship versus family relationships in old age. At this time, friendship within the nursing home is more closely linked to the psychological well-being of the elderly resident than family relationships.

Nursing home residents also communicate and form relationships with individuals who work for the institution. Social scientists have uncovered information that points to a direct link between a satisfying, close resident–staff relationship and quality of life within a nursing home. Nurses and nurse-aides who work within a nursing home do interact differently with the residents, yet, both nurses and nurse-aids who report closeness with the residents also report more satisfaction with their work.

What We Want to Know About Nursing Homes

Obviously, much work needs to be done before we can come to a minimal understanding of the nursing home environment and its impact upon the lives of those who live and work within the walls of the institution. Much of this work to be done can be of interest to the social scientists within the field of communication.

First and foremost, rich descriptions of the nursing home environment must be performed. Quite frankly, too little is known concerning the day-to-day lives of individuals who live within the nursing home. Although research to date has shown that interaction and relationship development are keys to quality of life, what transpires within the various communicative interactions and how relationships develop between residents and between residents and the staff remains speculative. Thick descriptions similar to those performed by Gubrium (1975) can serve as a good baseline for communication researchers who wish to understand the basic interactional features of the nursing home environment.

Beyond simple description of what transpires within a nursing home are questions of why certain communicative events lead to improvement in the quality of nursing home life. The existing research suggests that friendship formation is not only a social reality within nursing homes but appears to be an important ingredient of an elderly resident's ability to lead a successful life within the nursing home. The friendship relationship appears to be more closely linked to psychological well-being than the family relationship. The question is why does friendship function in a more positive way than does the various family relationships. Part of the answer to this question might be the communicative differences that exist between friendship and family relationships. In addition, researchers need to address the optimal requirements for successful relationship development among residents within the nursing home. Questions remain as to exactly how the "institution" and the strict schedules and rules within that institution inhibit relationship development.

A final item that falls within the "what we want to know" section of this chapter deals with the ability of communication researchers to discover the behaviors of the nursing home staff that can improve resident–staff relationships. Once the communicative behaviors are known, communication trainers need to develop in-service programs to educate the nursing home staff in appropriate relational skills.

Suggestions for Communication Research Within the Nursing Home

To answer all of the questions posited in the foregoing section of this chapter, communication researchers must venture into the nursing home. For whatever reason, communication researchers have shied away from entering actual environments where interactions transpire to study communication. Nursing homes are not easy institutions to gain access for the purpose of social scientific research. However, if sound research is to address communication within nursing homes, the obvious first step is to venture from the campus to the institution.

Two sound methods of research are currently employed by social scientists who study human behavior within nursing homes. Communication scholars have utilized survey methods to interview residents as well as staff concerning their interactive behavior (e.g., Nussbaum, 1983a; Nussbaum, Robinson, & Grew, 1985). A second method utilized to gather information about the social world of the nursing home is the ethnographic method employed by both Gubrium (1975) and Howsden (1981). Both methods are descriptive and are quite useful for uncovering many of the unknown aspects of life within a nursing home.

As mentioned at the beginning of this chapter, it is essential to completely understand the nursing home environment before moving on to explanations of "why" certain behaviors transpire within the institution. Both the survey method and ethnography can provide thick description of the environment that will enable social scientists to build predictive models of social behavior within the nursing home. The authors of this chapter firmly believe that the environment, to a very large extent, dictates and controls much of the interaction that transpires within the nursing home. Therefore, a description of the nursing home environment would be an excellent start to an understanding of the communication within nursing homes.

Baltes, Kinderman, Reisenzein, and Schmid (1987) conducted a study that can serve as an additional excellent model for communication researchers interested in the communicative world of the nursing home environment. Baltes et al. (1987) directly observed naturally occurring behavioral sequences within a nursing home. They discovered a microecology within the institution that was characterized by overcare. Stated simply, dependency on the part of the residents was rewarded. Baltes et al. (1987) asked of social scientists, "How can we get staff or social partners to provide social contact in a continuous and immediate fashion following behavior other than dependent self-care?" (p. 402). This question is one our field should address. We as communication scholars need to study and understand the environments where communication transpires for the ultimate purpose of changing those environmental contingencies that inhibit quality communication. Through this effort, communication researchers can impact quality of life within nursing homes.

REFERENCES

Aizenberg, R., & Treas, J. (1985). The family in late life: Psychosocial and demographic considerations. In J. Birren & K. Schate (Eds.), *Handbook of the psychology of aging* (pp. 169–189). New York: Van Nostrand Reinhold.

Arling, G. (1976, November). The elderly widow and her family, neighbors and friends. *Journal of Marriage and Family*, 757–768.

Baldassare, M., Rosenfeld, S., & Rook, K. (1984). The types of social relations predicting elderly well-being. *Research on Aging, 6,* 549–559.

Baltes, M. M., Kinderman, T., Reisenzein, R., & Schmid, U. (1987). Further observational data on the behavioral and social world of institutions for the aged. *Psychology and Aging, 2,* 390–403.

Bengston, V., Olander, G., & Haddad, A. A. (1976). The generation gap and aging family members: Toward a conceptual model. In J. Gubrium (Ed.), *Time, roles and self in old age* (pp. 237–263). New York: Human Sciences Press.

Bridge, W., & Speight, I. (1981, November). Teaching the skills of nursing communication. *Nursing Times*, pp. 125–127.

Brody, E. (1977). *Long-term care of older people.* New York: Human Science Press.

Cicirelli, V. G. (1981). *Helping elderly parents: The role of adult children.* Boston: Auburn House.

Cicirelli, V. G. (1983a). Adult children and their elderly parents. In T. Brubaker (Ed.), *Family relationships in later life* (pp. 31–46). Beverly Hills: Sage.

Cicirelli, V. G. (1983b). Adult children's attachment and helping behavior to elderly parents: A path model. *Journal of Marriage and the Family, 45,* 815–823.

Cohn, L. (1979). Coping with anxiety: A step-by-step guide. *Nursing 79, 9,* 34–37.

Downs, V. C., Javidi, M., & Nussbaum, J. F. (1988). A comparative analysis of the relationship between communication apprehension and loneliness for elderly nursing home and nonnursing home residents. *Western Journal of Speech Communication, 52,* 308–320.

Estes, C. L., & Lee, P. R. (1985). Social, political and economic background of long term care policy. In C. Harrington, R. Newcomer, C. Estes, & Associates (Eds.), *Long term care of the elderly* (pp. 17–39). Beverly Hills: Sage.

Fireston, I. J., Lichtman, C. M., & Evans, J. R. (1980). Privacy and solidarity: Effects of nursing home accommodation on environmental perception and sociability preferences. *International Journal of Aging and Human Development, 11,* 229–241.

Gans, H. (1967). *Levittowners.* New York: Pantheon Books.

Gubrium, J. F. (1975). *Living and dying at Murray Manor.* New York: St. Martin's Press.

Hass-Hawkins, G. (1978). Intimacy as a moderating influence on the stress of loneliness in widowhood. *Essence, 2,* 244–258.

Hoffman, T., & Reif, S. (1978) *Into aging.* Thorofare, NJ: Slack.

Howsden, J. L. (1981). *Work and the helpless self: The social organization of a nursing home.* Lanham, MD: University Press of America.

Johnson, E. S. (1978). Good relations between older mothers and their daughters: A causal model. *The Gerontologist, 18,* 301–306.

Johnson, E. S., & Bursk, B. J. (1977). Relationships between the elderly and their adult children. *The Gerontologist, 17,* 90–96.

Kane, R. A., & Kane, R. L. (1982). Long term care: A field in search of values. *Values and long-term care.* Lexington, MA: Heath.

Kastenbaum, R., & Candy, S. E. (1981). The 4% fallacy: Many die where few have lived. In R. Kastenbaum (Ed.), *Old age on the new scene* (pp. 262–268). New York: Springer-Verlag.

Koff, T. H. (1982). *Long-term care: An approach to serving the frail elderly.* Boston: Little, Brown.

Koger, L. J. (1980). Nursing home life satisfaction and activity participation: Effect of a resident-written magazine. *Research on Aging, 2,* 61–73.

Lawton, M. P., & Simon, B. (1968). The ecology of social relationships in housing for the elderly. *The Gerontologist, 8,* 108–115.

Lowenthal, M., & Haven, C. (1968). Interaction and adaptation: Intimacy as a critical variable. *American Sociological Review, 33*(1), 20–30.

McClannahan, L. (1973). Therapeutic and prosthetic living environments for nursing home residents. *The Gerontologist, 13,* 424–429.

Miller, C., & Lelieuvre, R. (1982). A method to reduce chronic pain in elderly nursing home residents. *The Gerontologist, 22,* 314–323.

Morgan, L. A. (1981). Aging in a family context. In R. Davis (Ed.), *Aging: Prospects and issues* (pp. 98–112). Los Angeles: University of Southern California Press.

Moss, F. E., & Halamandaris, V. J. (1977). *Too old, too sick, too bad: Nursing Homes in America.* Germantown, MD: Aspen Systems.

Noelker, L., & Harel, Z. (1978). Predictors of well-being and survival among institutionalized aged. *The Gerontologist, 18,* 562–567.

Norton, R. (1978). Foundation of a communicator style construct. *Human Communication Research, 4,* 99–112.

Nussbaum, J. F. (1983a). Relational closeness of elderly interaction: Implications for life satisfaction. *The Western Journal of Speech Communication, 47,* 229–243.

Nussbaum, J. F. (1983b). Perceptions of communication content and life satisfaction among the elderly. *Communication Quarterly, 31,* 313–319.

Nussbaum, J. F. (1985). Successful aging: A communication model. *Communication Quarterly, 33,* 262–269.

Nussbaum, J., Holladay, S., Robinson, J., & Ragan, S. (1985, November). *The communicative world of the nursing home resident: A preliminary analysis of in-depth interviews concentrating upon friendship.* A paper presented at the annual meeting of the Speech Communication Association, Denver.

Nussbaum, J., & Robinson, J. (1984, November). *Nursing staff communication as a predictor of affinity with nursing home residents and satisfaction with work.* A paper presented at the annual meeting of the Speech Communication Association, Chicago.

Nussbaum, J. F., Robinson, J. D., & Grew, D. J. (1985). Communication behavior of the long-term health care employee: Implications for the elderly resident. *Communication Research Reports, 2,* 16–22.

Parmelee, P. A. (1982). Social contacts, social instrumentality, and adjustment of the institutionalized aged. *Research on Aging, 4,* 269–280.

Paulan, A., & Rapp, C. (1981). Person-centered caring. *Nursing Management. 12*(9), 17–21.

Philbad, C., & Adams, D. L. (1972). Widowhood, social participation, and life-satisfaction. *International Journal of Aging and Human Development, 3,* 323–330.

Remnet, Y. L. (1981). The elderly in long term care facilities. In R. H. Davis (Ed.), *Aging: Prospects and issues* (pp. 175–187). Los Angeles: University of Southern California Press.

Restinas, J., & Garrity, P. (1985). Nursing home friendships. *The Gerontologist, 25,* 376–381.

Rice, D. P. (1985). Health care needs of the elderly. In C. Harrington, R. Newcomer, C. Estes, & Associates (Eds.), *Long term care of the elderly* (pp. 41–68). Beverly Hills: Sage.

Robinson, J., & Nussbaum, J. (1986, November). *The impact of simulated aging on nursing staff self reports of job satisfaction and performance.* A paper presented at the annual meeting of the Speech Communication Association, Chicago.

Shanas, E. (1979a). Social myth as hypothesis: The case of the family relations of old people. *The Gerontologist, 19,* 3–9.

Shanas, E. (1979b). The family as a social support system in old age. *The Gerontologist, 19,* 169–174.

Strain, L. A., & Chappell, J. L. (1982). Confidants: Do they make a difference in quality of life? *Research on Aging, 4,* 479–502.

Sussman, M. B., & Burchinal, L. (1962a). Kin family network: Unheralded structure in current conceptualizations of family functioning. *Marriage and Family Living, 24,* 231–240.

Sussman, M. B., & Burchinal, L. (1962b). Parental aid to married children: Implications for family functioning. *Marriage and Family Living, 24,* 320–332.

Troll, L. E. (1971). The family of later life: A decade review. *Journal of Marriage and the Family, 33,* 263–290.

Van Nostrand, I. F. (1981). The aged in nursing homes: Baseline data. *Research on Aging, 3,* 403–416.

Wallace, R., & Brubaker, T. (1981, November). *Biographical correlates of nurse aide employment in nursing homes: Issues for long-term care administration.* A paper presented at the annual meeting of the Gerontological Society of America, Montreal, Canada.

Ward, R. A., Sherman, S. R., & LaGory, M. (1984). Subjective network assessments and subjective well-being. *Journal of Gerontology, 39,* 93–101.

Wood, V., & Robertson, J. F. (1978). Friendship and kinship interaction: Differential effect on the morale of the elderly. *Journal of Marriage and Family, 40,* 367–375.

York, J. L., & Calsyn, R. J. (1986). Family involvement in nursing homes. In L. Troll (Ed.), *Family issue in current gerontology* (pp. 178–188). New York: Springer-Verlag.

AUTHOR INDEX

371

SUBJECT INDEX

A

Advertising. *See also* Marketing
political, 233–234
Aging
  health, family, and aging, 19, 298
  interpersonal communication, 298, 301–302
  family paradigms, 19, 303–308
American Society for Training and Development (ASTD), 134, 138
Applied communication research. *See also* Basic communication research
  definition, 3
  effective, 12–17
  field research, 37–49
  funding, 12, 26
  growth of, 8–10
  linking members of, 11–12
  methodology, 23–56
  need for, 10–11
  process cycle, 24–37
  purpose, 3–4
  researcher-sponsor relationship, 26
  triangulation, 49–53
  versus basic, 4–8
Archival research, 35
Argumentation, 97, 247

Attorney effectiveness/ineffectiveness, 83, 88–89, 90
Attribution theory, 88, 171, 255
Audience analysis systems, 18, 203–221
  behavioral observations, 29–30, 207
  Composite Audience Profile (CAP), 204–205
  Computerized Audience Response Analysis System (CARAS), 214–217
  demographic analysis, 204–205
  emotional assessment, 205
  Lazarsfeld-Stanton Program Analyzer, 209
  phychographic analysis, 205
  psychophysiological measurement, 207, 212–214
  research implications, 217–219
  self-reports, 24, 29, 33, 207, 208
Audience response systems, 206–208
  conscious response systems, 208–212
  nonconscious response systems, 212–214
Authoritarian personality, 144

B

Bargaining. *See* Negotiation
Basic communication research. *See also* Applied communication research

387